The widespread view that 'mystical' activity in the Middle Ages was a rarefied enterprise of a privileged spiritual elite has led to the isolation of the medieval 'mystics' into a separate, narrowly defined category. Taking the opposite view, this book shows how individual mystical experiences, such as those recorded by Julian of Norwich and Margery Kempe, are rooted in, nourished, and framed by the richly distinctive spiritual contexts of their period. Arranged by sections corresponding to historical developments, it explores the primary vernacular texts, their authors, and the contexts that formed the expression and exploration of mystical experiences in medieval England. This is an excellent, comprehensive introduction to medieval English mystical texts, their authors, readers, and communities. Featuring a guide to further reading and a chronology, the *Companion* offers an accessible overview for students of literature, history, and theology.

SAMUEL FANOUS is Head of Publishing at the Bodleian Library, University of Oxford.

VINCENT GILLESPIE is J. R. R. Tolkien Professor of English Literature and Language at the University of Oxford.

A complete list of books in the series is at the back of this book.

THE CAMBRIDGE
COMPANION TO
MEDIEVAL ENGLISH
MYSTICISM

EDITED BY
SAMUEL FANOUS AND VINCENT GILLESPIE

CAMBRIDGE
UNIVERSITY PRESS

CAMBRIDGE UNIVERSITY PRESS

Cambridge, New York, Melbourne, Madrid, Cape Town, Singapore,
São Paulo, Delhi, Dubai, Tokyo, Mexico City

Cambridge University Press
The Edinburgh Building, Cambridge CB2 8RU, UK

Published in the United States of America by Cambridge University Press, New York

www.cambridge.org
Information on this title: www.cambridge.org/9780521618649

First published 2011

Printed in the United Kingdom at the University Press, Cambridge

A catalogue record for this publication is available from the British Library

ISBN 978-0-521-85343-9 Hardback
ISBN 978-0-521-61864-9 Paperback

CONTENTS

v

CONTRIBUTORS

JAMES P. CARLEY York University, Canada

JEREMY CATTO University of Oxford

ROGER ELLIS University of Cardiff

SAMUEL FANOUS University of Oxford

VINCENT GILLESPIE University of Oxford

ANN M. HUTCHISON York University, Canada

HENRIETTA LEYSER University of Oxford

BRIAN PATRICK MCGUIRE Roskilde Universitetscenter, Denmark

ALASTAIR MINNIS Yale University

DENIS RENEVEY University of Lausanne

JAMES SIMPSON Harvard University

NICHOLAS WATSON Harvard University

BARRY WINDEATT University of Cambridge

PREFACE

Mysticism is innately mysterious. As an experience, it claims to have encountered mystery. As a theology, it attempts to analyse that mysterious encounter. As a text, it struggles to articulate mysterious experiences that resist and elude understanding and expression. A Middle English version of Jan van Ruusbroec asserts that mysticism in all its dimensions is always poised on the brink of paradox:

> It maye not be lefte ne ʒit takyn; to wante it is intolerable, to folowe it impossible. It may not be schewed open ne ʒit hid in silence. It excedys alle resoun and witt, and it is abofe alle creatures, and þerfore it may on no wyse be touched. Neuerþelesse, beholdynge ourselfe we feele the spirit of God dryfe vs and put vs into þat inpacient taryngne; bot beholdynge above ourselfe we persayve the spirit of God of oureselfe drawynge vs, and turning vs to nouʒt in hymselfe.[1]

Mystical texts seek to understand or impressionistically describe moments of intense experience (or the transcendence of experience), and do so using an extraordinary array of rhetorical, poetic, and linguistic strategies and subversions. In modern times, the Welsh poet R. S. Thomas has perhaps most memorably expressed the delicate indirections and paradoxical imprecisions fundamental to the symbiosis between the restless yearning of contemplation and the ineffability of mystical experience:

> Godhead
> is the colonisation by mind
> of untenanted space. It is its own
> light, a statement beyond language
> of conceptual truth.[. . .]
>
>   Resting in the intervals
> of my breathing, I pick up the signals
> relayed to me from a periphery I comprehend.[2]

This book seeks to explore the texts and contexts that formed the expression and exploration of such experiences in medieval England. Because the terms *mystic*, *mystical*, and *mysticism* have a very limited currency in medieval religious writing, either in Latin or in the various European vernaculars, most of the essays here distinguish between the alleged experience of some transcendental Other (what is loosely often called a 'mystical' experience) which by its very nature is beyond earthly comprehension or articulation, and the lives, longings, and textual explorations of those seeking after or seeking to understand and articulate such apparent experiences. Whether such 'experiences' were actually products of supernatural intervention, acts of grace from an ineffable Godhead, or the highly encultured outcome of a fertile and visually hyperstimulated subconsciousness (or a mixture of the two) is not necessary for us to assess or appraise. But the spiritual contexts that gave rise to them and the texts that resulted from them are a richly distinctive and challenging part of medieval religious culture. The lives, longings, and textual explorations that were engendered by the perception of such experiences are better described as taking place within the *contemplative life*, their spiritual aspirations yearning towards states of *contemplation* (in which mystical experience might, it was hoped, occur) and their struggles to articulate these complex and interrelated states resulting in *contemplative texts*.

Contemplation might usefully be thought of as a state (perhaps transient, only occasionally achieved, and often fleeting) or a way of life (vowed, professed, or aspired to) of preparing and readying the soul to receive whatever sight, sound, word, or revelation might appear to be offered in a mystical experience. The contemplative usually seeks to place the self in a state of heightened attentiveness and receptiveness (often described as yearning or longing), while at the same time yielding any desire to control, dictate, manage, or generate whatever it is that may (and just as often may not) manifest itself. Hence contemplative writing places great stress on obedience and humility, not (or not just) to generate servile submissiveness but to stress the radical loss of will and control that is a prerequisite of most contemplative states, and is linked to the theological concept of *kenosis* or self-emptying. Much contemplative writing explores these spiritual preparations and their aftermath and consequences. The 'experiences' themselves are often absent presences, traced by their effects and impacts rather than transcribed and analysed through reason and logic.

> His intellect was the clear mirror
> he looked in and saw the machinery of God
> assemble itself? It was one that reflected

the emptiness that was where God
should have been. The mind's tools had
no power convincingly to put him
together. Looking into that mirror was a journey
through hill mist where, the higher
one ascends, the poorer the visibility
becomes. It could have led to despair
but for the consciousness of a presence
behind him, whose breath clouding
that looking-glass proved that it was alive.
To learn to distrust the distrust
Of feeling – this then was the next step
for the seeker? [. . .][3]

The medieval period was no less alert to the paradoxes and tensions of such spiritual longing. The thirteenth-century Franciscan Bonaventure expresses well the fundamentally affective tenor of Christian aspiration to contemplative life, and its counterintuitive need to 'distrust the distrust of feeling':

> If you want to know how these things may come about, ask grace, not learning; desire, not understanding; the groaning of prayer, not diligence in reading; the Bridegroom, not the teacher; God, not man; darkness, not clarity; not light, but the fire that wholly inflames and carries one into God.[4]

Most of the texts discussed in this book are exploring and explaining these thresholds of 'mystical experience' (in preparing for it beforehand and in coming to terms with it afterwards) rather than that experience itself (whatever its cause or nature).

While texts about contemplation and mystical experience certainly circulated in England before the Conquest, the first text produced in England which introduces a radically new form of affective spirituality, Goscelin of St-Bertin's *Liber confortatorius* (*Book of Comfort*), dates from *c.* 1080. From the proliferation of Anselmian spirituality in the twelfth century, contemplative and mystical texts were produced, translated, copied, and circulated in an unbroken continuum until the dissolution of the monasteries and the Henrician reforms of the 1540s. This book explores these texts against the backdrop of changing attitudes to contemplation and mystical experience.

There is a widespread view that 'mystical' activity in the Middle Ages was a rarefied enterprise of a privileged spiritual elite. A consequence of this is that medieval mystical texts have too often been studied in a cultural and even literary vacuum. But the 'religious turn' in medieval studies over the last fifteen years has been dramatic. The study of 'vernacular theology' is a fast expanding area, and as its horizons of expectation have widened, the attractive if previously somewhat remote archipelago known as 'the Middle English mystics' (the works of Richard Rolle, Julian of Norwich, Walter Hilton, the author of the *Cloud of Unknowing*, and, at a push, Margery Kempe) has been revealed to be connected to the mainland of medieval religious writing and culture at multiple points. It is no longer intellectually defensible or culturally desirable to treat this cluster of texts seeking to describe mystical experience aside from the broad sweep of other texts that discuss, describe, and direct catechetic, devotional and contemplative theory and praxis in the period.

While 'the mystics' are widely studied, there is no modern, comprehensive single-volume work which delivers a sustained discussion of medieval English contemplative and mystical texts, authors, readers, and communities across the entire period. The aim of this *Companion*, therefore, is to provide readers who encounter the Middle English mystics with a broad interpretative guide to accompany their reading of primary texts. More importantly and centrally, this book regards mystical texts as a manifestation of contemplative activity practised by individuals or in communities, at particular moments in history, and as part of a wide spectrum of contemporary religious writing and practice. In other words, in this *Companion* medieval accounts of mystical experience and guidance on contemplative activity are firmly rooted in the society, culture, and intellectual environment in which they and their authors and readers were produced, and by which they were inevitably coloured and conditioned.

This *Companion* explores the impact on the medieval social imagination of popular and learned perceptions and preconceptions of the contemplative experience. The love of learning and the desire for God was never confined to the clerical cadres or specialist contemplatives. Mystical and para-mystical activity was far more widespread among every stratum of society and should be perceived as one of a range of experiences in the spectrum of ordinary daily life. An underlying contemplative outlook influenced literary tastes and conditioned social and private behaviour. The growing lay appetite to participate in 'religioun of the herte' is one of the recurrent motifs of this story. Social, political, theological, and linguistic change all contribute to these developments, as do developments in the pragmatic literacy of lay people. The spread (or perhaps simply the fuller articulation and recognition) of contemplative aspiration and mystical experience among lay merchants and gentry is one of the great cultural shifts of the later Middle Ages in England. But its roots lie in the affective spirituality and in the para-monastic practices of hermits and anchorites in the twelfth and thirteenth century.

c. 1405	*Dives and Pauper*
1406/9	*The Vision of William Stranton*
1407	Council of Oxford, to examine heterodox thought and the continuing influence of Wycliffism at Oxford University; first promulgation of Archbishop Thomas Arundel's Provincial Constitutions
1409	Council of Pisa
1409	definitive publication of Provincial Constitutions of Archbishop Thomas Arundel
Before 1410	Nicholas Love's *Mirror of the Blessed Life of Jesus Christ*
After 1410	*The Book of Ghostly Grace*, translation into English of Mechtild of Hackeborn's *Liber specialis graciae*
1413	Death of Henry IV; accession of Henry V
1413	beginning of the events later described in *The Book of Margery Kempe*; meeting between Julian of Norwich and Margery Kempe
1414	death of Archbishop Thomas Arundel; appointment of Archbishop Henry Chichele
1414/15	Foundation of Sheen Charterhouse and Birgittine Syon Abbey by Henry V
1414–18	Council of Constance; resolution of the Schism; confirmation of Birgitta of Sweden's canonization; condemnation of Wyclif's teachings, executions of Jan Hus and Jerome of Prague
1419	latest date for translation of Heinrich Suso's *Hourglass or Clock of Wisdom* as the *Treatise of the Seven Points of Trewe Wisdom*
1421	Death of Henry V; accession of Henry VI
1422	Council of Pavia-Sienna
1427	Thomas Netter, O Carm, *Doctrinale fidei antiquitatum ecclesiae catholicae*
1428	remains of John Wyclif exhumed and burned

1431–49	Council of Basle
?1420–35	*The Mirror for Devout People* composed by anonymous Carthusian of Sheen, probably for a nun of Syon
?1420–35	*The Doctrine of the Heart*, English translation of thirteenth-century guide for nuns, *De doctrina cordis*
1431	execution of Joan of Arc
1425–1430s	composition of *Myroure of Oure Ladye* for the nuns of Syon; translation and reworking of Catherine of Siena's *Dialogo* as *The Orcherd of Syon*, for the nuns of Syon; ?campaign by Syon to produce orthodox vernacular texts
1434	visit of Margery Kempe to Syon Abbey for the Lammastide indulgence
1434–5	translation of Latin Rolle texts into English by Richard Misyn, O Carm
1436	beginning of clerical revision of Margery Kempe's *Book* on feast of Birgitta of Sweden; book 2 begun in 1438
1438	*Gilte legende*, translation of the *Legenda aurea*
1443–7	Osbern Bokenham, OSA, *Legendys of Hooly Wummen*
1451/2–1527/8	Richard Methley, O Carth, author of Latin contemplative diaries and autobiographies
1461	Deposition of Henry VI; accession of Edward IV
1465	*The Vision of Edmund Leversedge*
1469–1535	John Fisher, bishop of Rochester, spiritual adviser to Lady Margaret Beaufort; catholic apologist and martyr under Henry VIII
1470	Restoration of Henry VI, finally deposed 1471; accession of Edward IV
1478–1535	Thomas More, Christian humanist; catholic apologist and martyr under Henry VIII
1482	first foundation of the Observant Franciscans in England

1483	Death of Edward IV; accession, deposition, and death of Edward V; accession of Richard III
1485	Death of Richard III; accession of Henry VII
c. 1485–1540	Thomas Cromwell, administrative genius in service of Thomas Wolsey and then Henry VIII; architect of the dissolution of the monasteries; eventually earl of Essex before his precipitate fall
1489–1556	Thomas Cranmer, protestant-inclined archbishop of Canterbury from 1533; author of the new vernacular liturgies under Henrician reform movement
c. 1491–1556	Ignatius of Loyola, Spanish founder of the Society of Jesus (Jesuits), who were at the forefront of the catholic Counter-Reformation after the Council of Trent
c. 1501	*A shorte treatyse of contemplacyon taught by our lorde Ihesu Cryste, or taken out of the boke of Margerie Kempe of Lynn*, printed by Wynkyn de Worde; reprinted by Henry Pepwell in 1521 as part of a longer anthology of contemplative and para-mystical texts known as the *Cell of Self-Knowledge*
1509	Death of Henry VII; death of Lady Margaret Beaufort; accession of Henry VIII
d. 1521	John Norton, O Carth, prior of Mountgrace from 1509, author of Latin contemplative texts
1521	Henry VIII, *A Declaration of the Seven Sacraments, against Martin Luther*; Henry rewarded with Papal title of *defensor fidei* (*Defender of the Faith*)
1520s–1541	printed works of devotion, contemplation and orthodox catechesis published by brethren of Syon such as Richard Whitford, William Bonde, and John Fewterer in attempt to address Lutheran teachings
1529	Thomas More, *Dialogue Concerning Heresies*
c. 1530s	*Myroure of Oure Ladye* printed (composed c. 1430)
1533/4	John Fewterer, *The myrrour or glasse of Christes passion*

1534	Act of Succession; Act of Supremacy; execution of Elizabeth Barton ('The Holy Maid of Kent'); John Leland commissioned to examine and report on monastic libraries
1535	Thomas Cromwell appointed Vicar-General and 'vicegerent in spirituals'; orders Visitation of monasteries, resulting in *Valor ecclesiasticus*
1535	Thomas More, *Dialogue of Comfort*; execution of Birgittine Richard Reynolds and three Carthusian Priors; execution of Thomas More and John Fisher
1536	Act for the Suppression of Lesser Monasteries; establishment of the Court of Augmentations to administer goods and estates of suppressed houses
1536–7	Pilgrimage of Grace
1539	second Act of Suppression
1540	last monasteries dissolved or surrendered; fall and execution of Thomas Cromwell
1545–63	Council of Trent; beginning of the Counter-Reformation
1547	Death of Henry VIII; accession of Edward VI
1553	Death of Edward VI; accession, deposition, and death of Jane Grey; accession of Mary I
1553–8	Marian restoration; refounding of some austere contemplative and monastic communities; Cardinal Reginald Pole as archbishop of Canterbury
1555	refounding of Carthusian community at Sheen
1558	Death of Mary Tudor; accession of Elizabeth I
1558	death of Cardinal Reginald Pole; end of Marian restoration of Catholic hierarchy and institutions
d. 1569	Robert Parkyn, reader of medieval contemplative books

1575–1641	Augustine Baker, Benedictine and spiritual guide to women religious, preserver and re-worker of medieval contemplative texts; prolific spiritual author
d. 1582	Teresa of Avila, O Carm, Spanish Carmelite contemplative; author of contemplative and spiritual works; Doctor of the Church; influential (with Ignatius of Loyola and John of the Cross) in the codification of contemplative experience as part of the Counter-Reformation
1585–1645	Mary Ward, founder of the Institute of the Blessed Virgin Mary
d. 1591	John of the Cross, O Carm, Spanish Carmelite contemplative; author of many contemplative and spiritual works such as *The Ascent of Mount Carmel* and *The Dark Night of the Soul*; Doctor of the Church
1596–1665	foundation of recusant Benedictine convents for English catholic women: Brussels (1596), Cambrai (1623), Ghent (1624), Paris (1651), Boulogne (1652), Dunkirk (1662), and Ypres (1665).
1603	Death of Elizabeth I; accession of James I/VI
1606–15	foundation of Benedictine priories for recusant English men: Douai (1606), Dieulouard (1608), St Malo (1611), and Paris (1615)
1609	Benet of Canfield, *Rule of Perfection*
1625	Death of James I/VI; accession of Charles I
1670	Serenus Cressy's printed edition of Julian of Norwich's *Showings.*

ABBREVIATIONS

ANTS	Anglo Norman Text Society
EETS	Early English Text Society
SS	Supplementary Series
OS	Original Series
ES	Extra Series
EHR	*English Historical Review*
EMTS	*Exeter Medieval Texts and Studies*
JEH	*Journal of Ecclesiastical History*
MMTE I–VII	*Medieval Mystical Tradition in England*, 7 vols., 1980– (vols. 1–6 ed. Marion Glasscoe, vol. 7 ed. Eddie Jones; vols. 1–2: (Exeter: Exeter University Press), vols. 3– (Woodbridge: Boydell and Brewer))
O Carm	Carmelite
O Carth	Carthusian
O Cist	Cistercian
ODNB	*Oxford Dictionary of National Biography*
OED	*Oxford English Dictionary*
OESA	Augustinian Hermit
OFM	Franciscan
OP	Dominican
OSA	Augustinian Canon
OSB	Benedictine
PBA	*Proceedings of the British Academy*
PL	*Patrologiae cursus completus, series Latina*, ed. J. P. Migne *et al.* 221 vols. (Paris 1844–64)
RSTC	A. W. Pollard and G. R. Redgrave (eds.), *A Short-Title Catalogue of Books Printed in England, Scotland and Ireland, and of English Books Printed Abroad 1475–1640*; second edition, revised and enlarged, begun by W. A. Jackson and F. S. Ferguson, completed by K. F. Pantzer (London: The Bibliographical Society), vol. 1 (A–H) (1986), pp. 620; vol. 2 (I–Z) (1976), pp. 504; vol. 3 (indexes, addenda, corrigenda).
TRHS	*Transactions of the Royal Historical Society*

I

NICHOLAS WATSON

Introduction

Transcendent experience in history

This book is about an important body of writings, written or read in England between the Norman Conquest and the Reformation, which theorize, teach, or perform a personal address to, experience of, or relationship with God. The book's title refers to these works as *mysticism*, but this word defines only part of the book's scope. A fuller account requires several other keywords: *devotional, affective, visionary*, and most notably *contemplative*, used as the book's defining generic term, for reasons that will become clear. How we think of these keywords influences both the approach we take to the field and the writings we assume to define it.

Used together, *mysticism* and its companions draw attention to two features of the writings they describe. First, these writings are phenomenological, concerning individual felt experience in addition to systems of knowledge or belief. Second, they represent this experience as transcendent, involving an encounter – whether direct or mediated, transformatively powerful or paradoxically everyday – with God. The terms thus affirm a cosmology in which the idea of 'transcendent experience' is neither meaningless nor contradictory. In this cosmology, even though God is taken to exist beyond the order of creation, he is also accessible to it, even immanent within it, interacting with it directly and communicating with it, not only in formal and predictable ways – such as through religious rituals and the institutions that undergird them – but with apparent spontaneity and by way, at least on occasion, of mysteriously selected individuals.

In a sense, such a cosmology is necessary to all forms of Christian belief. Even Christian cultures in which religious experience has been a source of anxiety – such as eighteenth-century Anglicanism, with its rationalist fear of Nonconformist 'enthusiasm', born of the previous century's record of violent religious conflict – have recognized the necessity of an experiential relationship with God. This is partly because the experience of God is understood as a proof of God's existence, the source of the event called *conversion*. But it is also because the Christian forms of such experience assert two of the doctrines by means of which the religion defines itself against its rivals, from polytheism to Neoplatonism, to Judaism and Islam, to Deism. The first doctrine is that each individual human soul is made in the Trinitarian image of God, mirroring the divine likeness; and the belief that God has, in turn, chosen to be made in the image of the human, entering the order of creation in the incarnate Christ, that 'scandal to the Jews and folly to the Gentiles' (1 Corinthians 1:23).

Yet the medieval culture that produced this corpus of writings not only had a distinctive account of such experience, understanding the relationship between the soul and God available through contemplation in a newly bodily and emotionally laden way. This culture also took such experience with special seriousness, making it increasingly central to religious life as the period wore on, devoting considerable literary, visual, and human resources to it, reposing extraordinary trust in its validity, and in the process permanently shaping the sensibilities, and (to a considerable extent) even the content, of western Christianity.

This last truth has not been widely recognized. Modern Protestant and Catholic Christians are much influenced by the emphasis on a personal relationship with God first promoted by an evangelical movement that traces its revivalist roots to the very 'enthusiasm' abhorred by eighteenth-century Anglicans. Even Catholics, however, tend to be unaware that the ultimate source of evangelical pietism is the affective reworking of the Christian faith in medieval contemplative thought and practice. From its devotional focus on the objects and people connected with the birth of Jesus – the stable, crib, ox, ass, shepherds, angels, and wise men featured on Christmas cards – to its theological emphasis on the human person of Jesus, to its soteriological insistence that salvation begins with personal acceptance of Christ as saviour: modern Christian language, practice, and even theology, before it is Lutheran or Wesleyan, is massively and unsuspectingly medieval. Indeed, its very ignorance of this fact is an effect of the epochal events that brought the medieval period to a violent close. The beginnings of the late-medieval tradition of affective contemplative thought in the eleventh century are mysterious. But there is nothing mysterious about the sixteenth-century end of the tradition, as English religious reformers determinedly destroyed or turned their backs on most of the texts and artefacts which had nurtured what remained a strong strain of its piety, while Catholics read only medieval texts that seemed least 'Protestant', most different from the heresies that had sprung up around them, or at least most in tune with their own, suddenly more anxious, doctrinal orthodoxies.

Despite its antiquity and stance of worldly disengagement, medieval contemplative writing is thus an often unconsciously politicized field, which readers with even a residually Christian background approach with more latent knowledge than they may realize, and which scholarship – its attitudes to the field even now inflected by categories inherited from the sixteenth century – has difficulty analysing without prejudice (that most telling indicator of our collective acts of intellectual repression). In the body of this book, the most important solution to the problem of prejudice is historicization. After this chapter, subsequent chapters move, period by period, from the first phases of post-Conquest contemplative thought to the end of the Middle Ages and beyond, into the early history of the reception of this thought in the sixteenth and early seventeenth centuries. The scope of these chapters – like their generic breadth, their attention to writings in all three of medieval England's main languages, and their alternating focus on texts and on contexts – indeed itself constitutes an attack on prejudice. They seek to decenter a field too often narrowly understood as focused around a smallish group of Middle English works of the mid-fourteenth to early fifteenth centuries whose characteristic themes are taken to have been distinctive to that seventy-five year period and rendered abruptly irrelevant by the Reformation. This introductory chapter is also concerned with history, especially that of the field and its terminology. But its principal interests are methodological. Its job is to ask questions such as: what, from the perspective of the English Middle Ages, is mystical or contemplative writing? What, if anything, makes it into a coherent area of enquiry? And what, if any, is its claim upon our attention?

One set of answers to these questions, well-established in the scholarship, is phenomenological and theological. Mystical writing is a record of individual religious experience, which is coherent in as much as the direct apprehension of God has distinctive features (at least, within a given theological tradition), and merits interest simply by dint of being real (whether in a psychological or a theological sense). The long history of this approach to contemplative writing is our concern in the next section of this chapter. Reports of individual experiences feel immediate, even when they are centuries in the past – an historically contingent cultural fact about ourselves whose own past includes the very contemplative traditions under scrutiny here, which helped create the category of experience whose interest we now take for granted. The phenomenological approach still has a hold, even over those whose thinking is not explicitly theological. Despite the theoretical problems associated with using texts as windows that open onto experience, especially individual experience, not to mention the problems involved in discussing religious experience in particular, elements of this approach remains indispensable to any study of contemplative writing, and are in evidence throughout this book.

The present chapter, however, offers another, carefully secular, approach to the field of contemplative writing, one partly inflected by general intellectual history but more importantly concerned with the history of thought about a specific cultural practice: the practice of *otium*, or private leisure, a term anciently associated with contemplation. It prefers this approach for two reasons. First, the idea of practice can act as a useful bridge between texts and experiences (or texts and their historical functions). Second, such an approach can view even a private experience like contemplation – an experience which, in its own account of itself, reaches beyond this world towards eternity – as part of a wider cultural field: as profoundly imbricated, despite its declared status as otherworldly and private, in the political, the social, and the ethical. *Otium*, for example, had further associations with pleasure, as well as with choice, privilege, reward, and the gratuitous: all terms relevant to the history of contemplation which also have functions in different cultural discourses. For reasons to be explored now, the scholarly field of medieval contemplative writing has had prolonged difficulty deciding on either its terminology or its canon. Besides serving as an appropriate point of entry into the historically oriented studies that follow, this chapter's concern with contemplative writing as an expression of *otium* thus also makes a proposal about how this field might frame itself more clearly.

Mystical theology and spirituality studies

Why should such a proposal be necessary? As this volume and the professional training of its contributors testify, in the last thirty years the study of medieval English contemplative thought has become, to a marked degree, a subset of literary and historical studies: a standard, secular university discipline within the area of medieval studies. However, the field owes its formation to spirituality studies: an early twentieth-century discipline, which brought insights from the new fields of psychology and sociology to bear on the much older, specifically Catholic, discipline of mystical theology. Both these intimately related religious disciplines add a great deal to the historical study of contemplative writing, not least because they can bring an urgency of informed attention to this writing secular historians cannot easily match. But their terminology and operating assumptions also exert pressures on this study. This is partly for reasons local to medieval England, partly because, despite the historical sophistication of which both are capable, their final concern is with the transcendent: with that which lies beyond, not within, history. The pressures these disciplines exert have had, and continue to have, real effects on the historical study of English contemplative writing, in ways that, perhaps out of mere politeness, are seldom discussed and to an extent that is seldom appreciated. To grasp why these effects might be significant enough to require historians of contemplative writing to exercise special care in framing and naming their subject, a truncated history of the two disciplines and their relation to the field is in order.

Mystical theology analyses writings from the Early Church to the present and draws on a number of medieval contemplative theologians for its basic categories. Its tripartite division of the ascent to God into purgative, illuminative, and unitive phases, for example, is indebted to Bonaventure's *De triplici via* (*On the Triple Way*) (1260s).[1] Indeed, mystical theology's canon of orthodox mystics and its counter-canon of mystical heretics is so heavy with medieval names – Bernard and the Victorines through to Ruusbroec in the first category; Marguerite Porete, often Eckhart, and the so-called Brethren of the Free Spirit in the second – that it would be proper to describe the discipline as an outgrowth of medieval contemplative theology. Yet mystical theology began to take its modern shape as a discipline only in the early seventeenth century, especially in the commentaries that accrued around the Spanish Carmelite mystics Teresa of Avila and John of the Cross (d. 1582, 1591). These systematized various medieval contemplative theologies in order to harmonize them, so far as possible, with the strict new orthodoxies of the Counter-Reformation. In the process, they necessarily disrupted the continuities and narrowed the range of the theologies on which they built – theologies first developed in France, Germany, the Low Countries, Italy, and Spain, but not, it is important to note, England – transforming what had been a diverse series of arts of contemplation into a single, conceptually powerful science.

It was in this context that the phrase *mystical theology* – originally the title of a fifth-century work of apophatic mysticism, the *De mystica theologia* of pseudo-Dionysius the Areopagite, which delineates the soul's ascent to God as a systematic denial of earthly signs – slowly replaced the earlier *contemplation* and *contemplative theology* as a moniker for the discipline.[2] Unlike *contemplative theology*, a roomy phrase which incorporates an indefinite number of modes of contemplation, *mystical theology* organized the discipline on hierarchic, pseudo-Dionysian principles, focusing fierce attention on union with God as the true goal of the contemplative, now for the first time termed a *mystic*. It was vital to theorize and to experience this *unio mystica* correctly, not least because mystical theology was more likely than earlier contemplative theologies to make esoteric and exceptionalist claims for itself: claims understood as dangerous in rather the sense prophecy was dangerous, constituting a mode of spiritual authority that might challenge the authority of the Church and its Scriptures. After all, outside the pseudo-Dionysian context, *mystic* originally meant *hidden, secret, allegorical*. The first unequivocal use of 'mystic' in the modern sense recorded in *OED* is from as late as 1692 (William Penn): 'Taulerus, Thomas a Kempis, and othere Misticks in that Communion'. In Middle English, *mystik* means 'figurative', generally referring to the spiritual sense of Scripture, and has a close connection with the abstract adjective *misti*, 'obscure'. During most of the Middle Ages theologians did not see a distinction between contemplative theology and experience. From Augustine to Eckhart, the 'I' who ascends to God is at once an individual undergoing an experience and a representative of humanity in general, tracing a predestined trajectory away from the world of appearances back to the Creator. In Richard of St Victor's *Book of the Twelve Patriarchs* (*c.* 1160s), for example – a supple allegorical analysis of the psychology of contemplative ascent – theology and phenomenology are mutually constitutive.[3] From Ruusbroec in the late fourteenth century to the Spanish Carmelites and beyond, late medieval and early modern mystical theology, by contrast, proclaimed the harmony of theology and phenomenology in an atmosphere increasingly fraught with fear of doctrinal and ethical error. The mystic's ascent to God took place, not because the mystic represented all humanity, but because she or he was seen as a member of a vulnerable elite, perilously following a spiritual path whose claim to authenticity depended on its conformity to established dogma.

The place of mystical theology even within Catholic theology was always controversial. England's most prominent seventeenth-century mystic, Augustine Baker, for example, was read with suspicion after his death because of supposed echoes in his writing of Quietism, the condemned view that *unio mystica* (mystical union) involves a renunciation so complete that even the desire for God must be surrendered in order to attain him.[4] It is said to have been the Catholic, John Henry Newman, who quipped that mysticism 'begins in mist and ends in schism'. Despite the eirenic efforts of liberal Catholics such as Baron von Hügel (in *The Mystical Element of Religion*, 1908), mysticism's reputation in official Catholic circles grew only more suspect in the twentieth century, as secular psychologists, such as William James in *The Varieties of Religious Experience* (1902), and Anglican theologians, such as Evelyn Underhill in *Mysticism* (1911), took mystical theology's model of what was now being called 'spirituality' in new, sometimes decidedly non-Catholic, directions.

Initially developed outside Catholicism by intellectuals of various religious and philosophical backgrounds in Britain, the United States, and Germany, spirituality studies began as a pluralistic reaction against what it understood as mystical theology's over-emphasis on dogma, generalizing the term *mysticism* to include non-Christian religious experiences, while often quiet-ly retaining its interest in the evaluation, as well as description, of mystical states. It is through this broad and hard-to-define movement that *mysticism* gained such hold as it has on the modern secular imagination. Between the 1920s and the 1970s – especially in the wake of the Second Vatican Council (1962–5), which opened many doors for Catholic intellectuals wishing to participate in the movement – spirituality studies held out the promise of a purely experiential, non-doctrinal, universal religiosity, in which an East (represented by the Japanese Zen Buddhist D. T. Suzuki) and a West (rep-resented by the American Carmelite Thomas Merton) might, despite two world wars, be one. From the apophatic event described by mystical theo-logy, ineffable in principle and practice but still intensively defined and cir-cumscribed by theological and psychological dogma, *unio mystica* came to denote an experience of God utterly outside rational definition: an escha-tological figure of a longed-for universal resolution of cultural and credal difference – an Omega Point – in the wordless peace of the transcendent.

Long challenged by some, the idea of a pure experience abstracted from language that undergirded this model of spirituality studies was abandoned as untenable in the 1980s, when the search for an unitary and fundamen-tally syncretic account of religious experience was replaced by the more local explorations that (outside the area of consciousness studies) now char-acterize the field, taking a historicist form in the great Classics of Western Spirituality series published since 1977 by Paulist Press. As a contempo-rary discipline, spirituality studies nonetheless retains its antagonism to the dogmatic and its ambition to track the presence of the transcendent in the world, even if the transcendent has now renounced its claim to any discov-erable unity and succumbed to the immanentist and often secular-sounding language of cultural pluralism. Unlike mystical theology, spirituality studies does not now require explicit religious belief. But it still implies it, in as much as it approaches the phenomena that concern it from the viewpoint of belief: an approach that crucially (if sometimes imperceptibly) distinguishes it from other kinds of historical and cultural study.

Mysticism and historicism

How does the study of medieval English contemplative writing fit into this shifting disciplinary landscape? To all intents and purposes, it began awkwardly only in the first half of the twentieth century, after a hiatus extending back three hundred years – all the way to Baker and Serenus Cressy in the seventeenth century – as scholars of disparate background struggled to fit the few well-known Middle English contemplative works into an intellectually comprehensible framework by doing what scholars of continental Europe were also doing: redescribing medieval contemplative theologians as 'mystics'. Early advantage lay with learned Catholics such as David Knowles who, in *The English Mystics* (1927), had little trouble analysing the thought of the Augustinian Walter Hilton or the apophatic author of *The Cloud of Unknowing* – two writers Baker had also admired – using the prestigious template of mystical theology. At once a church historian and a Benedictine monk – anxious to reassert the Catholicity of the English Middle Ages in the face of the powerful historical narratives generated by four centuries of Protestant and nationalist historians – Knowles was aware that his approach to these writers was a blend of the theological and the historical, and no doubt aware that the theology in question was decidedly non-native to medieval England. However, since Hilton and the *Cloud*-author wrote of an ascent to God in language indebted to Augustine, Bernard, Richard of St Victor, and, in the latter case, Pseudo-Dionysius himself, the historical imprecisions involved seemed worth it, if the prize was the reintegration of English contemplative writing within the mystical mainstream.

Not that it proved easy to integrate very much. Faced with writers such as Richard Rolle and Julian of Norwich, whose models of contemplative practice were largely unrelated to those favoured by mystical theology, Catholic scholars floundered. Even the brilliant editor and theological historian Edmund Colledge, writing between the early 1950s and the early 1990s, repeatedly dismisses Rolle's account of union with the blessed in heaven through spiritual song – influential as this was in late-medieval England – as low-grade. Laying an Augustinian theoretical grid across *A Revelation of Love* too coarse to catch anything notable, Paulo Molinari's learned 1958 study, *Julian of Norwich*, demonstrates only the limits of mystical theology as an analytic tool. Most serious, the canon that mystical theology could recognize as 'authentic' English mystical writing remained small: apart from the works of Rolle, Hilton, the *Cloud*-author, Julian, and Margery Kempe, and of a small handful of Latin writers from Edmund of Canterbury in the thirteenth century to Richard Methley, O Carth, in the sixteenth, the only viable candidates for inclusion were a group of meditative effusions like the anonymous *Wooing of Our Lord* and a few continental works (from Catherine of Siena's *Dialogo* to Marguerite Porete's *Mirouer des simples ames*) in Middle English translation. As comparativists have often pointed out – not always with the necessary sensitivity to the historical contingencies involved – mysticism, as defined on the basis of continental texts, had limited relevance to the 'pragmatic and particularist' contemplative traditions of medieval England.

The more pluralistic approaches favoured by spirituality studies from the start encouraged a broader approach to the English contemplative canon. This is clear in the wide-ranging publications of two, early twentieth-century anthologists, Geraldine Hodgson and F. M. Comper – both of them drawing on the huge editorial energies of Carl Horstmann – and the literary historian, Hope Emily Allen, who established the canon of Rolle's writings and identified *The Book of Margery Kempe*, besides doing fundamental work in hunting down versions of *Ancrene Wisse* in all three of its languages.[5] (The initial avoidance of this centrally important text by the majority of religious historians offers a telling example of the blinkering effect of mystical theology as a paradigm for the study of English contemplative writing.) Yet apart from Allen – a remarkable scholar whose public interest in spirituality studies as an academic paradigm was limited to the increasingly explicit feminism of her later work – students of spirituality before the 1970s generally confined their interest in English contemplative writing to the production of further anthologies (often consisting of devout excerpts) and introductory essays, with only timid and occasional ventures into serious analysis.

Paradoxically, it was with the rise of literary scholarship on the 'mystics' in the 1970s and 1980s – mainly through the efforts of Valerie Lagorio and Ritamary Bradley (founders in 1974 of the journal *Mystics Quarterly*) in the United States and of Marion Glasscoe (founder in 1980 of the conference series *The Medieval Mystical Tradition in England*) in Britain – that spirituality studies came into its own in the field. It did so in a distinctive, half-secularized form which blended paradigms drawn from theology, feminism, psychoanalysis, cultural history, and literary theory and criticism with ecumenical inclusiveness. Initially, the canon recognized by these publications was as restricted as that generated by mystical theology: *Mystics Quarterly* (recently reborn as *Journal of Medieval Religious Culture*) began life as *The Fourteenth-Century English Mystics Newsletter*, its aim the study of five writers. But in this heady academic context, *mysticism* was soon a goal to which any serious English contemplative text should aspire, urged on by scholars, few of whom were theologians and many of whom were not religious, but who as a matter of convention wrote as Christians-in-paraphrase, close-reading contemplative works in the empathetic way they were trained to read Langland, the *Gawain*-Poet, and Chaucer. Indeed, it was not long before all three writers were proposed for inclusion in a rapidly swelling canon of English mystics.[6] These particular proposals, which have not on the whole made much headway, may demonstrate little more than spirituality studies's distrust of categories of exclusion. But as scholars of English devotional manuscripts, headed by Ian Doyle, mapped an increasingly coherent field of contemplative writings by examining how and in what company such writings actually circulated, such literary proposals also show the field engaged in rethinking its categories and extending its generic and chronological range.

Some of this important work from the 1970s and 1980s is, no doubt, theologically amateurish, lacking the clarity of purpose mystical theology has retained even in its pluralist contemporary forms, even if feminism did give literary scholars an incisive way of articulating their unease with mystical theology's privileging of the spiritual over the corporeal, and, perhaps, the male over the female. Intriguingly, although much of the impetus for this work came from English departments, some of it is also amateurish from a literary perspective, moving silently between analyses of text and of experience without acknowledging the trickiness of this conflation of the rhetorical and the phenomenological: a sure sign of the influence of early spirituality studies – notably Underhill and her circle – on the field. Even now, when the field has developed, for the present, in a determinedly historicist and secular direction – finally joining the mainstream of medieval English literary and historical scholarship, but distancing itself as never before from theological scholarly paradigms – the danger that crypto-spirituality will leak into its thinking remains, thanks, in part, to the energy of this earlier work and the continuing energy of spirituality studies as a whole. Simply put, it is hard to use words like *spirituality* and *mysticism* without succumbing to their transcendent assumptions.

The term *mysticism* is thus an essential reference-point for the field, standing, as it does, not only for an important complex of theological ideas about the centrality of *unio mystica* to the religious life but for the category of the experiential in general, as seen from the more inclusive perspective of spirituality studies: also standing, at its broadest, for the methodological problem offered by the experiential, and for the history of theological scholarship on that problem. But for those who write (whatever their personal religious beliefs) as professional secular historians of medieval English religiosity, the vexed history of the term, its strong conceptual and emotional pull away from the world of history towards the eternal, and its unhelpful lack of purchase so far as medieval England is concerned, has made it come to seem increasingly problematic: to the extent, indeed, that it must be considered of questionable usefulness, at least for the purposes of local historical analysis.

Perhaps strangely, however, this does not mean that the term should or can be discarded altogether. *Mysticism* is still a vigorous term in religious scholarship, as well as in the historical study of continental contemplative writing – as the substantial German scholarship on *mystik* spearheaded by Ursula Peters, and the Anglo-American scholarship generated by the powerful engine of Bernard McGinn's ongoing, multi-volume *History of Western*

Christian Mysticism, both demonstrate. Moreover, for all its dominance in this book and at this scholarly moment, historicism represents only one set of approaches to medieval contemplative writing (or to any other body of writing); other approaches, including theological ones, have equal legitimacy. At the very least, the survival of the term is crucial if conversations between insular and continental scholars of contemplative writing, and between historians and theologians, are to continue, and it is likely that emergent fields, such as the study of the history of emotions, will also require its use.

But while it may well be profitable to theologians and historians one day to revive the discussion of which medieval English writings are or are not mystical, or to attempt to redefine *mysticism* so that it better fits the medieval English context, for the present an historical field of study cannot readily be sustained using this imported, anachronistic, and, above all, essentially evaluative term. Even though there are good reasons why it cannot turn its back on its traditional terminology, the study of what we must still refer to as *medieval English mysticism* needs, rather, to take place within a differently and more broadly defined set of keywords, principle among which, throughout this book, is the term *contemplation*.

Contemplation and the *vita contemplativa*

Unlike *mysticism*, the term *contemplation* has a real, if complex, historical relationship, both with the activity of contemplation itself, and with the writing that developed, in England and elsewhere, around that activity. In antiquity, *contemplation* referred to a mental act associated with a mode of what Augustine calls 'intellectual vision', the only kind of vision capable of escaping the world of images and attaining knowledge either of the self or of God. *Contemplation* in this context is a rational reflection on incorporeal things which the philosopher, living in retirement from the active life of the world, has a duty to perfect, recognizing and uniting with uncreated truth through the cultivation of inner sight and the exclusion, so far as possible, of distracting bodily or 'corporeal' vision. Neoplatonism held with special clarity that ideas were more real – existed in closer proximity to the One – than material things, just as the soul was more real than the body, ideas more real than their instantiation. Even though contemplation required *otium* (leisure) and encouraged disengagement from career advancement and (often) social activism, it followed that it was at once harder work and more spiritually useful than action, at least for the contemplator. It followed, too, that, as the only means to ascend to the One, contemplation was the ultimate goal of the enlightened individual's earthly life.

From the late fourth century on, Christianity adapted all these ideas, identifying the One with God in Trinity, the soul with the image of God of Genesis 1:27 – Augustine argues that the memory, reason, and will are the 'image', respectively, of Father, Son, and Holy Spirit – and the philosophical life with its own, increasingly organized, cadres of contemplative *religiosi*.[7] It also made fundamental changes: to the spiritual dynamics of the contemplative process, which came to reflect Christianity's distinctive theology of grace by emphasizing the humble receptivity, as well as the self-possession, of the contemplative; and to its ethics, which came to insist more clearly than Neoplatonism on the cosmic and social usefulness of contemplative activity, characterizing the contemplative life as a saintly spiritual warfare. According to Goscelin's *Liber confortatorius* (*Book of Comfort*) (*c.* 1080), contemplatives who withstand temptation assist concretely in the conversion of the world by banishing the vices, and the demons that control them, to hell.[8] By insisting on an ascetic daily regimen that could in theory be embraced by anyone, Christianity also partly modified another feature of many ancient contemplative traditions, their association with economic and educational privilege. While Christian contemplative thought and practice has its own pronouncedly elitist tendencies – tendencies that were only ever partly translated out of their original social register into that of the spiritual – the late-medieval idea that everyone should, in some sense, participate in contemplation has deep roots.

In the early medieval Latin church the *vita contemplativa* was the life lived by members of two, linked professions, hermits and monks – who were said, metaphorically, to have 'left the world' – while the *vita activa* was lived 'in the world' by the laity and those who ministered to them, secular priests and others. (As a result of Gregory the Great's *Pastoral Care* (*c.* 590), theory also recognized a *vita mixta*, lived by abbots and bishops part 'in' the world, part 'out' of it.)[9] Contemplatives were distinguished from actives in various formal ways – they lived by vows, wore distinctive habits, and submitted to physical confinement and other privations – and, like the philosophers from whom they descended, were considered superior to actives in theological theory, now with the help of a host of biblical metaphors. Contemplatives had chosen to follow the counsels as well as the commandments of God, renouncing everything in imitation of the rich young ruler of Mark 10:21, and so earning greater heavenly reward. They had determined to follow Mary sitting at Christ's feet, not Martha busy with practical considerations (Luke 10:38–42). As virgins who had preferred spiritual marriage to the Lamb of God to carnal marriage on earth (Revelation 14:4), contemplatives were the best of the seed scattered by the heavenly sower, bringing forth the fruit of heavenly reward a hundred fold, where the married do so thirty fold (Matthew 13:3–9).[10] As late as *Ego dormio* (*I Sleep, c.* 1345), Rolle conventionally distinguishes between the many who merely follow the

Ten Commandments and the few who 'bicum perfite', who 'forsake al þe world . . . and folow Crist in pouert'. Elsewhere, he echoes scholastic claims that the *perfecti* are so-called because, at the Judgement, they sit in judgement with the apostles, rather than being judged themselves, like the laity.[11] Nobody thought such privileges would be extended to every monk, nun, hermit, or anchoress, both because their educational and social range was so wide and because it was understood that there were always some religious – hypocrites, the 'whited sepulchres' of Matthew 23:27 – who failed to live up to their profession. But the mere possibility that contemplatives might receive a greater heavenly reward than others and escape the Judgement denoted the gap in status that existed between contemplatives and laypeople, even secular priests, in active life.

Originally, the *vita mixta* of bishops and abbots was exceptional. From the twelfth century on, however, some contemplative orders – the canons and, later, the friars – began to engage publicly in active ministries, increasing numbers of laypeople undertook contemplative programmes, and the hierarchic relation between the contemplative and the active was challenged by those who regarded preaching as an activity as important as prayer. In the early Middle Ages, the noun *contemplation* and verb *contemplate* had subtly different frames of reference from the adjective *contemplative*, partly because it was acknowledged that some lived the *vita contemplativa* without real devotion, but mainly because the noun *contemplation* was seldom applied to the activity central to monastic life, the performance of the liturgy. Its ancient roots not in Neoplatonic philosophy but in the communal worship of the synagogue, the liturgy was collective, not individual, associated with the public activities of doxology and intercession, not the private one of contemplation. Despite its emphasis on private spirituality as well as public prayer, the founding work of medieval monasticism, the *Benedictine Rule*, does not refer to contemplation at all.

In the late Middle Ages, however, the adjective *contemplative* slowly followed its noun into renewed identification with an inner state – Rolle's *Ego dormio*, which distinguishes between the institutionally 'perfite' life of the nun and the interiorized 'contemplative' life of the solitary, again witnesses this transition (Rolle, *Ego dormio*, 216–23) – as the association between the term *vita contemplativa* and professional monasticism weakened in parallel with what may have been an ideological weakening of the monastic movement itself. Reviving the long association between contemplation and a mode of seeing that scrutinizes the truth hidden *inside* what is seen, in her *Vision Showed to a Devout Woman* (1380s), Julian sees Christ glorified, and 'in this' experience learns that a 'saule contemplatife' is not necessarily an anchoress, nun, or priest, but anyone 'to whilke es giffen to luke and seke God'.[12] By the time she wrote these words, 'anyone' clearly included devout members of the laity, at least those with the time and education for contemplative activity; equally clearly, this association was still thought controversial. *Fervor amoris* (*Contemplations of the Dread of the Love of God*) (*c.* 1400) is similarly self-conscious about its own modernity when it offers 'lordis and ladies [. . .] housbond-men and wyues' – incapable by dint of their worldly commitments of coming to Rolle's 'hie contemplatif lif' – a restricted contemplative praxis by which they, too, attain 'an hiere degre of love' than normally available to active Christians.[13]

In *On Mixed Life* (1380s), Hilton also makes the argument that the highest forms of contemplation require a commitment only possible for professional contemplatives: an argument whose validity is born out by the fifteenth-century revival of contemplative texts for nuns, especially the Birgittines of Syon Abbey, as well as by the enthusiasm with which Carthusians copied and studied his own works. Yet *On Mixed Life* is famously clear that Hilton, too, considers the laity capable of contemplation. What is more, like the *Cloud*-author, Hilton periodically lets slip his awareness of a view that would have seemed absurd before the twelfth century, but to which the increasing tendency to distinguish sharply between 'inner' and 'outer' states of being had given plausibility: that the laity's very lack of 'outer' signs of contemplative activity – the signs that distinguished professional contemplatives from others – might make them in a perverse (or spiritual) sense better suited to true contemplation than monks and nuns, because they were less susceptible to religious formalism and the hypocrisy that is its inevitable result.[14] In the anti-clerical environment of late fourteenth-century England – in which, for example, the author of *Book to a Mother* (*c.* 1370s) instructs his lay reader to 'make [. . .] professioun' spiritually to Christ as Abbot but at all costs to avoid sinful religious as 'maintainours' of 'Anticristis irreligioun' (123–4) – the inwardness of contemplation could appear impossible except for those living in the very world contemplative practice was designed to leave behind.[15]

Affectivity and thought

What was the practice of contemplation in the Middle Ages, that it could be thus adapted to the lives, not only of educated monks, or of hermits, nuns, and anchoresses with various degrees of learning, but of the laity – even, as with Godric of Finchale in the eleventh century or Margery Kempe in the fifteenth, the uneducated laity? There is more than one answer to this question. But for many medieval witnesses – Rolle, Julian, Hilton, and the author of *Fervor amoris* among them – contemplation is associated in varying proportions with: (1) the private cultivation of a loving *relationship with* God; (2) the humbly receptive *scrutiny of* God – one that can be as profound as the attempt to understand what Julian calls God's 'privy counsailes' and as simple as the passionate gaze at a crucifix; and (3) an implied image of *ascent to* God, which expresses itself through references to 'higher' and 'lower' states. These last echo the hierarchic assumptions made by many forms of mystical theology and have a persistent link with the professional status of the one contemplating.

All these associations are already in place in one of the most influential twelfth-century accounts of contemplation: the *Scala Claustralium* (*The Ladder of Monks*) by the prior, Guigo II, O Carth (*c.* 1150), here quoted in a laicized late Middle English translation of *c.* 1400. Making much of the favoured status of those who, responding to the promptings of grace, give themselves to contemplation, the work describes the private religious practices of reading, meditation, prayer, and contemplation by which 'cloysterers' – and, adds the translation, 'oþere Goddis lovers' – seek to attain a union with God imaged as the fruition of a lover's desire, as 'God is called and prayed as dere spowse to comme to the moornyng sowle that langurith in love'.[16] The erotic imagery here, ubiquitous from Goscelin's *Life of Edith of Wilton* in the late eleventh century to Margaret Gascoigne in the early seventeenth, and especially cultivated by Rolle's fifteenth-century disciples, Margery Kempe and Richard Methley, also links contemplation with the love between the soul and its bridegroom Christ described in the Song of Songs – at least, according to analysis of the Song by Guigo's contemporary, the Cistercian Bernard of Clairvaux. The very titles of the Carthusian Methley's Latin works – *Scola amoris languidi* (*The School of Languid Love*), *Dormitorium dilecti dilecti* (*The Sleeping Place of the Dearly Beloved*, 1484–5) – evoke the Song in its most panting vein (Song 6:8, 5:2). Indeed, the connection between contemplation and love is so strong in the late Middle Ages that the ancient association between the contemplative and the philosophical may seem merely residual to a cultural practice that appears to have rejected the Neoplatonic and Stoic late antique insistence on the rational and the sober in its fervid embrace of the imagistic and the affective. After all, even in the earliest well-known medieval contemplative work, the Benedictine monk Anselm's philosophically intense *Prayers and Meditations*, written fifty years before Bernard and Guido (*c.* 1100), the language of desire is already to the fore, as Anselm sets out a mode of devotional reading primarily intended not to provide information about God but 'to excite the mind of the reader to the love or fear of God, or to pleading [*discussionem*] with him'.[17]

As a dominant feature of late-medieval contemplative writing – one of special significance as contemplative practice came to be adapted to the laity – affectivity is often understood by scholars, not only as a crucial but as a sufficient marker of the late-medieval contemplative mode, which, as a result, comes to be identified entirely with practices and texts that assume the primacy of the will over the reason, feeling over thought, *sapientia* (experiential knowledge) over *scientia* (formal knowledge). (It is no accident that the study of the 'Middle English mystics' in these terms really took off during the anti-intellectual 1970s.) Yet while affective expressions of longing for God are certainly common in the late-medieval contemplative realm, affectivity is also found in non-contemplative genres, including the liturgy, mystery plays, sermons, and other genres. Even if they are closely associated, affectivity and medieval contemplation are not coterminous.

Moreover, even in texts scholars treat as epitomes of anti-rationalism, the intellectual content of contemplative writing is always vitally important – if only in the inverted sense that, in such texts, rationality can represent a powerful mode of apprehension the contemplative must resist, just as the reader of Nicholas Love's *Mirror of the Life of Christ* (c. 1410) is to resist thoughts that lead to doctrinal doubt. When love and affect are elevated – as in the account of how 'luue bindeð' (love binds) near the end of *Ancrene Wisse* (1220s–1230s) or Rolle's astonishing sequence of encomia to love, *Incendium amoris* (*The Fire of Love*), *Melos amoris* (*Song of Love*) and their colleagues (1330s–1340s) – reason is present generally in the form of an apparently fixed divine law or coldly rational human soul, waiting to be burst asunder or set on fire by a love whose influx surprises humankind and God alike.[18] As in Grosseteste's theologically cutting-edge poetic retelling of the redemption as the victory of love over justice in his *Château d'amour* (c. 1220s), such expressions of the power of love are self-consciously modern, aware of themselves as novel. Grosseteste and his colleagues repetitively reenact the dethronement of a rational power of the mind which, in formal theology, is often identified with the immortal soul but which, in this affective account, is seen as a cerebral, academic, and unspiritual absence of fear, wonder, gratitude, and love. Affectivity itself, is, after all, a mode of thought as well as feeling; indeed, it is the very mode of thought that – in deliberate opposition to the logic-building structures favoured by scholasticism – refuses the separation of thought and feeling. When Julian, writing of her occluded vision of the dying Christ, adds 'and thus I saw him and sought him, and I had him and wanted [*lacked*] him', her prose allows no distinction between the knowledge of God and his love; 'and this is and should be our comen working in this life, as to my sight' (Watson and Jenkins (eds.), *Julian of Norwich*, 10.14).

This is how that most explicitly anti-intellectual of contemplative writers, the *Cloud* author – for whom all thoughts must be suppressed before the contemplative can pierce the 'cloude of vnknowyng' with the 'scharp darte of longing loue' – can also, when not himself contemplating, be so directly engaged in the learned critique of contemporary scholasticism. It is how Margery Kempe, through the persistent, probing questions of her narrative persona, can give as much attention to addressing the theological conse-quences of her belief in the mutual desire felt by God and the soul as she does to passionate evocations of such desire. Both *The Cloud of Unknowing* and *The Book of Margery Kempe* use their emphasis on love in the same way they use their choice of the English vernacular: as platforms from which to launch counterattacks on what they see as the arid intellectualism and exclusivity of other modes of religious thought.[19] They are hardly alone in this endeavour. Even contemplative works that seem to exist solely to help the reader generate states of feeling, such as Passion meditations, do so in part by helping the meditator theorize, as well as experience, the difficulty of making supple her hard sinner's heart: placing her, with equal imaginative and theological precision, in the state of abject waiting which precedes and hopes to precipitate the advent of grace.

Perhaps the affective content of contemplative works is more pronounced in the vernacular than in Latin: a reading of the consciously sensual soliloquy *A Talking of the Love of God* against Latin meditations in the Anselmian vein certainly suggests as much. Although there are clear counter-examples, such as the fourteenth-century Italian import, James of Milan's *Stimulus amoris*, even this work was considered an obvious candidate for vernacular-ization (as *The Prickynge of Love*, conceivably the work of Hilton).[20] Even if affectivity began in the cloisters of the Cistercians and the libraries of the Victorines as a spiritually and intellectually aristocratic pursuit, its special appropriateness for those without extensive formal education was rapidly and persistently recognized. Indeed, if as Bernard of Clairvaux and Richard of St Victor both argue, love's chief characteristic is that it overflows rules and boundaries, achieving an 'order without order' (*ordo sine ordine*), the broad late-medieval dispersal of the language of love beyond the religious orders into ever wider institutional and private contexts offers an impor-tant rhetorical parallel to the apparent erosion in the distinctiveness of the monastic life during the later centuries of the period.[21] Nonetheless, for all its growing reach beyond the cloister and the cell into the public rituals and private chambers of the wealthy, and not-so wealthy, laity, affectivity is more than a mode of mindless religiosity suitable for those Rolle calls the *rudi et indocti* (uncultured and uneducated).[22] It is a mode in which the laity, in company with their monastic and eremitic colleagues, learned not only to feel but to think their religious beliefs.

Otium and contemplative practice

Despite the late-medieval affective 'turn' evidenced in contemplative writings, all this suggests that the original, philosophical association of the term *contemplation* is still in play to the end of the Middle Ages – in England as, certainly, on the Continent – and that it is as relevant to the vernacular materials written for or by the laity as it is to the Latin works in the tradition of Anselm, Bernard, Richard, or Guido. Indeed, Middle English contemplative writing needs to be seen as part of a long tradition of works on philosophical retirement: one that might include, for example, Thomas Traherne's *Centuries of Meditation*, William Wordsworth's *The Prelude*, and Henry Thoreau's *Walden*. For if it is affectivity that marks medieval contemplative writings as medieval, it is their enduring association with the philosophical quest for union with the source of truth that distinguishes these writings as distinctively contemplative in orientation.

Such an association is affirmed in very different ways by different genres of contemplative text and modes of practice. But it is most clearly evidenced by the abiding influence of the ancient ideal of *otium* on the contemplative practice both of religious professionals and of the laity: an influence that makes itself felt through two, distinct channels. *Otium* is the state of philosophical detachment and refreshment which those desirous of engaging in reflection seek in order to engender a state of mind in which everyday anxieties gives way to calm but intense thought – and, in its medieval Christian incarnation, reading, meditation, and prayer. Participating in two complementary ancient traditions of thought – a therapeutic tradition, concerned with care of the self; and a philosophical tradition, concerned, rather, with self-knowledge – the language and practices associated with *otium* are widely dispersed throughout the length and breadth of western culture. Its more remote descendants include, on the one hand, the academy, understood as a place of philosophical retirement; and contemporary ideas and practices associated with leisure, which combine the public language of privilege, reward, and holiday with the private language of exercise, discipline, and self-improvement.

In the broadest sense, the eremitic life was a permanent life of leisure, exempting those who enjoyed it from worldly cares and thus anticipating the lasting *otium* of heaven, where all blessed souls join with the angels in eternal contemplation of God. The sustained popularity of three works produced in response to the earliest Christian eremitic movement, in fourth- and fifth-century Egypt – Athanasius's *Life of St. Anthony*, the *Vitae patrum* (*The Lives of the Fathers*), and Cassian's *Conferences* – ensure the continuing power of this account of eremitic identity in late-medieval England; even though all these works, early and late, also share other images of the eremitic life, especially those of work and of spiritual warfare.[23] From the *Life of Christina of Markyate* (c. 1150) to *Ancrene Wisse* and *The Fourfold Exercises of the Cell* of Adam the Carthusian (c. 1200); to the *Remedies Against Temptations* of William Flete (1340s) and *The Cloud of Unknowing*; all the way to Richard Methley's *To Hew Heremyte: A Pystyl of Solytary Lyfe Nowadayes* (c. 1500) and Simon Anker's *Fruit of Redemption* (printed in 1514): all these eremitic works subscribe to the view that hermits (as Rolle puts it in *Incendium amoris*, ch. 14) sit to contemplate, rather than kneel to pray, focusing not on the liturgy but on interior exercises which keep the soul in as intimate as possible a relationship with the divine (see ch. 5 below; Rolle, *Incendium amoris*, ch. 14).

Although its tropes have a distinct history, running through Ambrose and Jerome rather than the *Vitae patrum*, the discourse of virginity in works inflected by eremiticism – from the *Liber confortatorius* and Aelred of Rievaulx's *De institutione inclusarum* (*Instructions for Enclosed Women*) (1160s) down to laicized works such as *Pore Caitiff* and *The Book of Margery Kempe* in the late fourteenth and early fifteenth centuries – has the same intention, working as it does with the ascetic assumption that the link between the soul's purity and the history of the body it inhabits is unbreakable. Retirement from the world is prudent for those who protect their treasure in a fragile vessel (2 Corinthians 4:7). But it also gives the virgin (or her counterpart, the devout widow) the leisure she would otherwise lack to meet with Christ her bridegroom in the secret recesses of her heart. The more dramatic ascetic exercises that are a prominent feature of contemplative writings up to the thirteenth century and are only partially displaced by affective or penitential exercises thereafter – the vigils, fasting, confinement, and flagellations that constitute the medieval version of ancient gymnastic discipline and, perhaps, of modern athleticism – belong within the category of the leisured, in so far as they assist the soul to detach itself from the body and its humdrum routines and are impossible to sustain for those whose energies are needed for the practice of the active life.[24] Christina of Markyate's cramped spell in the cupboard of a hermit friend did not only protect her from the wiles of parents and would-be lovers. It also acted as a stage in an inner detachment from the world she later furthered by way of more ordinary ascetic rigours. At the end of the period, Thomas More's celebrated hairshirt, proudly preserved to this day by the Birgittine nuns of

Syon, was a token both of the spiritual heroism of this advocate of the *vita mixta* and of his regret at his inability, as a public official, to indulge in the disciplines of the body as he would have liked. (It is faintly visible in Thomas Holbein's famous portrait of More.)

Eremitic *otium* was a full-time job. Hermits were vital to the late-medieval theorizing of individual contemplative practice as an indispensable supplement to liturgical performance, while the informality of their lives – the fact that they did not live under the obedience of an abbot – gave them something in common with the laity that monks and even secular priests did not share. As living symbols of interiority, hermits and anchoresses asserted by their existence the separation of contemplative practice from the professional contexts of monastery and institutional church. Yet hermits – at least, the more educated hermits who, after Rolle in the fourteenth century, often joined one of two eremitic orders, the Carthusians and the Carmelites – were also specialists, whose contemplative expertise continued to put them in a class of their own to the end of the Middle Ages. Hence both the semi-monopoly they may have enjoyed over the circulation of texts like *The Cloud of Unknowing*; and the persistence with which fifteenth-century laypeople contrived to be buried in Carthusian graveyards, identifying with hermits in will as they could not in deed.

There was also, however, a more limited idea of *otium* than the eremitic, initially associated with monasticism. In partial contrast with eremitism, monasticism was communal in impulse, with ancient links both to philosophical sects such as Stoicism that practised collective living and to early Christian ideals of lay community, expressed through the endlessly elaborated doxological rituals that became the liturgy. The relationship the *Benedictine Rule* imagines between a monk and his abbot (a word derived from the Hebrew word *abba*, father) has much in common with the intimately domestic relationships early bishops were meant to cultivate with their flocks. But monks and nuns practised their own version of solitary *otium* within the convent, in a protected part of the monastic day, given to leisure pursuits such as contemplative reading, understood as a break from the liturgy and a continuation of the manual labour which was also part of their afternoon responsibilities. 'Idleness (*otiositas*) is the enemy of the soul', begins the famous chapter of the *Rule* which discusses this part of the monastic day, immediately making explicit the dangerous but necessary relationship between *otium* and its shadow and antonym: *otiositas*, the state of torpor which leads to the quintessentially monastic sin of *acidia*, sloth or despair, as the enervated soul, worn out by the repetitive strain of ritual, slides under the influence of the 'noonday demon' (Psalm 90:6).[25] Anselm's *Prayers and Meditations* were written to combat just such a state, as they invite their users, in the words of Matthew 6:6, to 'enter into thy chamber (*in cubiculum tuum*), and having shut the door' – excluding all external cares, even those of the monastic *opus Dei* – 'pray to thy father' (Meditation 3, *Meditation on Human Redemption*). The rich Latin and vernacular meditative tradition that links his book with a work like the early fifteenth-century *Orcherd of Syon* – which offers the nuns who read in it a mottled selection of garden walks through the text it translates, Catherine of Siena's *Dialogo* – can be understood as a sustained effort on the part of those who contributed to it to encourage successive generations of monks, nuns, and the devout to use the pleasurable, if potentially dangerous, 'ease' of afternoon time for personal spiritual benefit.[26] The superbly sensual imagery associated with works in this tradition – where Jesus is liable to be called 'honey-sweet' and the blood that pours forth from his wounds may evoke grief but is equally likely to arouse in the meditator an erotic desire to lick or to drink – is a direct result of the twin demands this genre needs to meet: to edify, but also to entertain, to fill the mind of the meditator with beautiful and improving images that drive away boredom in much the same way medieval medical practice prescribed blood-letting to drive away depression. Jesus, here, really is the soul's 'leche', her doctor.

Otium in this narrower and less demanding sense was easily adapted to busy lay routines, and the 'mixed' life Hilton and the author of *Fervor amoris* imagine for devout lay readers was possible in part because of the initially improbable association made in the monastic tradition of the contemplative, not with rigour, but with relaxation. The entertainment value of Love's *Mirror* or other evocations of Christ's life and death, such as *The Privity of the Passion*, is as obvious as that of poetic meditations like *A Talking of the Love of God*.[27] Here contemplation – understood as a mode of prayerful private reading which may or may not, on a given day, lead to the intense, visionary meditations on Christ's life found in *The Book of Margery Kempe* and described in Hilton's *Scale of Perfection*[28] – is similar to other devout practices associated with *otium*. These include the reading of saints' lives and penitential treatises; the study of the creation and its history through reflection on *mappaemundi*, encyclopaedias, chronicles, and travel narratives; or the plying of a needle in pious embroidery. Indeed, in so far as they lead to knowledge of God via knowledge of his creatures or his creation, all such practices could be thought of as, in an extended sense, contemplative exercises.[29]

More anxiously, especially in the context of lay religiosity, texts and practices designed to induce contemplation of this kind share many strategies with secular literature, as it ministers, not to pious *otium* but to the morally lax pastimes of deliberately indulged *otiositas*. Indeed, this association of the secular with the sinful is made explicit at the opening of the founding text of the courtly secular tradition, Guillaume de Lorris's *Roman de la rose* (*c.* 1225). Here, *Amant*, a figure not of the affective desire for Christ but rather of sexual passion, is welcomed into the walled Garden of Delight – through a small door ironically evocative of both the 'strait gate that leads to life' of Matthew 7:14 and entry into a monastery – by the damsel *Oiseuse* (*otiositas*): initiating a poem, and a literary mode, whose ruminative eroticism has its contemplative side, but in which the object of contemplation has been decisively secularized. Characteristic of secular literature as a whole, the *Roman* does not concede its sinfulness and, in its continuation by Jean de Meun (*c.* 1260), even purports to lead the reader to knowledge of God, as he can be known through his creation. But as with its most famous English descendant, Chaucer's *Canterbury Tales*, and as it makes clear through its virulent attack on the ideology of virginity, the *Roman* has no truck with the perfectionist ideals that underlie even the most generalized works in the contemplative tradition.[30] As Will acknowledges in talking to Imaginatif in Langland's *Piers Plowman* (B.12, 1–228), a more distant English relation of the *Roman de la rose*, once the self-consciously literary is allowed into the protected garden of *otium*, it is impossible fully to distinguish the 'play' even of the virtuous from the time-wasting, and potentially damnable, vanity of secular entertainment.[31]

Anglo-Norman and Middle English religious works often contrast their own purity of purpose with the frivolity of secular courtly writing. In a late-medieval culture in which monastic leisure was routinely attacked as idleness by polemicists, it is not surprising that the ideal of contemplative ease was sometimes displaced, at least temporarily, by an opposing ideal appropriate to the active life, one of labour.[32] Reformist works written in the ambit of the Lollard movement are especially likely to advocate a diligent pious reading whose end is fiercely ethical, rather than philosophical, concerned, not with the love or knowledge of God, but the study of his 'law'. Yet for all their distrust of the language of leisure, choice, and privilege associated with *otium*, even implacably earnest lay 'rules' such as *Book to a Mother* and the *Holy Boke Gratia Dei* (*c.* 1370, *c.* 1400) understand reading, meditation, and prayer as comfort, as well as work.[33]

Despite identifying the contemplative life with God's commandments, not his counsels, and claiming that 'bot a man chese þe best part while he is in þis world' – the life of Mary, not Martha – 'he schal neuer come in heuene', *Book to a Mother* offers the 'bodiliche mete' of Christ the Book to its reader in narrative form: a form explicitly designed to help her experience 'þe liuinge of Crist', not merely as a subject of earnest enquiry but with 'hot brennynge loue' (McCarthy, *Book to a Mother*, 20.12–14, 32.12–14).

When the devout layperson saying matins in the *Holy Boke* imagines Christ and the angels descending holding baskets full of the 'relefe' of heaven (see John 6:12), where 'likyng and fest is euer at þe full', the 'mete' the angels distribute is both salvation, necessary to all, and a source of 'comfort' for those who would be perfect and in whom this imaginative vision is vouchsafed.[34] For all that they conceive of contemplative reading as necessary to their readers, not voluntary – as ministering to their salvation, not as increasing a certain heavenly reward – such works still rely on the ideal of philosophical retirement. They cast their lay readers as hermits of the soul, working out their salvation not only through the active works of mercy but also through a process of self-distancing from the world that is clearly related to the contemplative ideal. If late-medieval secular literature offers one vision of the future of contemplative *otium* in the delicious ambiguities of the literary, these fiercely reformist works offer another in the attempts by puritanical laypeople, before and after the Reformation, to conceive of the whole of their lives as lived 'in the world but not of it' (see John 17:11–16), in a state of cultivated inner detachment to which many Christians, evangelical and other, aspire even today.

Conclusion: historicism and transcendence

By sidelining the very texts and topics focused on by mystical theology and spirituality studies – the themes of spiritual ascent and visionary experience, neither of which has received real attention here – this chapter perhaps testifies by its silence to another general need even the historian still has of the term *mysticism*: to provide a counterbalance to the full secularization of contemplative experience that might follow from treating it solely as a cultural practice. After all, while the sudden, irruptive experiences of divine love that are the goal of the exercise described in *The Cloud of Unknowing* are readily categorized as products of *otium*, the same is less obviously true of visions such as those of Julian of Norwich; of the continental women visionaries so eagerly read in twelfth- to fifteenth-century England, from Hildegard of Bingen to Birgitta of Sweden; or of the otherworld visions associated with the ritual penance of the Patrick's Purgatory pilgrimage. Visionary writings – not to mention the late-medieval discourse of *discretio spirituum* (*discernment of spirits*) whose aim was the verification of visionary experience – reference a tradition whose roots are in Old Testament prophecy and the apocalyptic literature of the intertestamental period, and to this extent appear to need a somewhat different set of tools from those developed here, as well as a less scrupulously neutral approach to the awkward question it is particularly hard to prevent visionary texts from raising: did it happen?[35]

Visions, too, are a cultural practice – just as visionary writing is an ethical and political practice – one whose links to the contemplative exercise of meditation, recently explored by Barbara Newman, are also links to the discourse of philosophical *otium* with which this chapter has been concerned.[36] Nonetheless, the especially stark simultaneity of earth and heaven, the realms of history and of the transcendent, characteristic of works in the visionary mode, still speak especially clearly to the continuing challenge all contemplative writing presents for the secular historian. Secular historiography and literary scholarship have a bad record in their dealings with the religious, because they tend to understand the sacred, not merely through secular categories, as does this chapter, but as a part of a dead belief system whose sole source of life was always only the world and the world's interests. That the transcendent had power in and of itself for an intellectual culture centred around it – that, despite the looming presence in all contemplative discourse of the world, the visionary ascent to God might in part be means to understanding the transcendent in its own, sacred terms – is hard for the models developed in these disciplines to admit; simply because the sacred, as ineffable, demands recognition precisely as that which lies outside secular models. Yet to make this admission is essential if the secular is not to reveal itself as another belief system, a reactive modernist system constructed around a deliberately blinkered – and, in a world in which religious belief and prejudice are still powerful, dangerous – exclusion of the transcendent as a category in its own right, at play in history even as it points beyond it. In constant and difficult dialogue both with theological paradigms that presuppose the transcendent and with other historical disciplines that presuppose its absence, the secular study of medieval contemplative writing is thus engaged in thinking through an important contemporary problematic.

NOTES

1 In José de Vinck (trans.), *The Works of Bonaventure, Cardinal, Seraphic Doctor, and Saint* (Paterson, NJ: St Anthony Guild, 1960).
2 Michel de Certeau, *The Mystic Fable*, trans. Michel B. Smith (Chicago, IL: Chicago University Press, 1992), 94–7 traces the shift from *contemplative* or *spiritual* to *mystic* and *mystical* during the seventeenth century; the whole of ch. 3, 'The New Science' (79–112), is relevant.
3 Grover A. Zinn (trans.), Richard of St Victor, *The Book of the Patriarchs, The Mystical Ark, Book Three of the Trinity*, Classics of Western Spirituality (New York: Paulist Press, 1979).
4 James Gaffney, *Augustine Baker's Inner Light: A Study In English Recusant Spirituality* (Scranton, PA: University of Scranton Press, 1989).
5 Geraldine Hodgson (ed.), *Some Minor Works of Richard Rolle With the Privity of the Passion* (London: J. M. Watkins, 1923); F. M. M. Comper, *The Life of*

Richard Rolle Together With an Edition of His Lyrics (London: J. M. Dent, 1928); Carl Horstmann (ed.), *Yorkshire Writers: Richard Rolle of Hampole and His Followers*, 2 vols. (London: Swann Sonnenschein, 1895–6); Hope Emily Allen, *Writings Ascribed to Richard Rolle Hermit of Hampole* (New York: MLA and London: Oxford University Press, 1927); John Hirsch, *Hope Emily Allen: Medieval Scholarship and Feminism* (Norman, OK: Pilgrim Books, 1988).

6 Edward Vasta proposed *Piers Plowman* as a mystical work in *The Spiritual Basis of* Piers Plowman (The Hague: Mouton, 1965). The claim was made for *Pearl* as early as 1925, by Sister Mary Madaleva in *Pearl: A Study in Spiritual Dryness* (New York: Appleton, 1925), and has recently been made again by Annika Sylén Lagerholm, *Pearl and Contemplative Writing* (Lund: Lund University, Department of English, 2005). Chaucer's possible use of contemplative discourse is explored by Thomas H. Bestul in 'Chaucer's *Parson's Tale* and the Late-Medieval Tradition of Religious Meditation', *Speculum* 64 (1989), 600–19.

7 John Hammond Taylor (trans.), Augustine, *The Literal Meaning of Genesis*, 2 vols., Ancient Christian Writers 41–2 (New York: Newman Press, 1982), Book 12. Gareth B. Matthews and Stephen McKenna (trans.), Augustine, *On the Trinity Books 8–15* (Cambridge: Cambridge University Press, 2002).

8 Monika Otter (trans.), Goscelin of St Bertin, *The Book of Encouragment and Consolation (Liber Confortatorius)* (Woodbridge: D. S. Brewer, 2004), bk II (63–7).

9 Henry Davis (trans.), Gregory the Great, *Pastoral Care*, Ancient Christian Writers 11 (Westminster, MD: Newman Press, 1950); F. J. Steele, *Towards a Spirituality for Lay-Folk: The Active Life in Middle English Religious Literature From the Thirteenth Century to the Fifteenth* (Salzburg: Institut für Anglistik und Amerikanistik, 1995).

10 On Martha and Mary, see Giles Constable, *Three Studies in Medieval Religious and Social Thought* (Cambridge: Cambridge University Press, 1995). For examples of the other topoi, see Bella Millett and Jocelyn Wogan-Browne (eds.), *Holy Maidenhood* in *Medieval English Prose for Women: Selections from the Katherine Group and* Ancrene Wisse (Oxford: Clarendon Press, 1990).

11 S. J. Ogilvie-Thomson (ed.), *Richard Rolle, Prose and Verse*, EETS OS 293 (1988), *Ego Dormio* 95–7; Nicholas Watson, *Richard Rolle and the Invention of Authority* (Cambridge: Cambridge University Press, 1991), ch. 2.

12 Nicholas Watson and Jacqueline Jenkins (eds.), *The Writings of Julian of Norwich: A Vision Showed to a Devout Woman and A Revelation of Love* (University Park, PA: Penn State Press, 2006), 13.23–4.

13 Margaret Connolly (ed.), *Contemplations of the Dread and Love of God*, EETS OS 303 (1993), A83–92. *Fervor amoris* is likely the original title of this work.

14 See especially *De imagine peccati*, in John P. H. Clark and Cheryl Taylor (eds.), *Walter Hilton's Latin Writings*, 2 vols., Analecta Cartusiana 124 (Salzburg: Institut für Anglistik und Amerikanistik, 1987); Phyllis Hodgson (ed.), *The Book of Privy Counsel* in *The Cloud of Unknowing and Related Treatises*, Analecta Cartusiana 3 (Salzburg: Institut für Anglistik und Amerikanistik, 1982); also Nicholas Watson, 'The Middle English Mystics', in David Wallace (ed.), *The Cambridge History of Medieval English Literature* (Cambridge: Cambridge University Press, 1999), pp. 539–65.

15 Adrian James McCarthy (ed.), *Book to a Mother: An Edition with Commentary* (Salzburg: Institut für Anglistik und Amerikanistik, 1981).

16 Phyllis Hodgson (ed.), *Denis Hid Divinite*, EETS OS 231 (1955), *A Ladder of Foure Ronges*, pp. 100.6–7, 111.12–15.

17 F. S. Schmidt (ed.), Anselm, *Orationes sive meditationes* in *S. Anselmi Opera Omnia* (Edinburgh: Nelson, 1946), vol. III. Translation my own.

18 Bella Millett (ed.), *Ancrene Wisse*, EETS OS 325 (2005), 7.346–66.

19 Phyllis Hodgson (ed.), *The Cloud of Unknowing and the Book of Privy Counselling*, EETS OS 218 (1944; repr. 1981), 14.29–30; Nicholas Watson, 'The Making of *The Book of Margery Kempe*', in Linda Olson and Kathryn Kerby-Fulton (eds.), *Voices in Dialogue: Reading Women in the Middle Ages* (South Bend, IN: University of Notre Dame Press, 2005), pp. 395–434.

20 M. Salvina Westra (ed.), *A Talking of the Love of God* (The Hague: Nijhoff, 1950); Harold Kane (ed.), *The Prickynge of Love*, 2 vols. (Salzburg: Institut für Anglistik und Amerikanistik, 1983).

21 The phrase 'ordo sine ordine' is from Bernard: J. Leclercq, C. H. Talbot, H. M. Rochais (eds.), *De diligendo deo*, in *Sancti Bernardi Opera Omnia* (Rome: Editiones Cisterciences, 1957–), III, 119–54. Equally important is Richard of St Victor, *De quattuor gradibus violentae charitatis*, in Richard of St Victor, *Épître à Séverin sur la charité/Les quatre degrés de la violente charité*, ed. Gervais Dumeige (Paris, J. Vrin, 1955).

22 Margaret Deanesley (ed.), *The 'Incendium amoris' of Richard Rolle of Hampole* (Manchester: Manchester University Press, 1915), Prologue.

23 Tim Vivian and Apostolos N. Athanassakis (trans.), Athanasius, *The Life of Antony* (Kalamazoo, MI: Cistercian Publications, 2003); Henri d'Arci, *Vitas patrum;* Basilides Andrew O'Connor (ed.), *A Thirteenth-Century Anglo-Norman Rimed Translation of the Verba Seniorum* (Washington, DC: Catholic University of America Press, 1949/1950); Colm Lubheid (trans.), Cassian, *Conferences* (New York: Paulist Press, 1985).

24 See Nicholas Watson, 'With the Heat of the Hungry Heart: Empowerment and *Ancrene Wisse*', in Mary C. Erler and Maryanne Kowaleski (ed.), *Gendering the Master Narrative: Women and Power in the Middle Ages* (Ithaca, NY: Cornell University Press, 2003), pp. 52–70.

25 Leonard Doyle (trans.), *The Rule of Saint Benedict* (Collegeville, MN: Liturgical Press, 2001), ch. 48; Marilyn Dunn, *The Emergence of Monasticism: From the Desert Fathers to the Early Middle Ages* (Oxford: Blackwell, 2000). On the noonday demon, see Giorgio Agamben, *Stanzas: Word and Phantasm in Western Culture*, trans. Ronald L. Martinez, Theory and History of Literature 69 (Minneapolis, MN: University of Minnesota Press, 1993), to which the rest of this section is further indebted.

26 Phyllis Hodgson and Gabriel Liegey (ed.), *The Orcherd of Syon*, EETS OS 258 (Oxford, 1966), Prologue.

27 *The Privity of the Passion*, in Horstmann, *Yorkshire Writers*, I, pp. 198–218.

28 See Naoë Kukita Yoshikawa, *Margery Kempe's Meditations: The Context of Medieval Devotional Literatures, Liturgy and Iconography*, Religion and Culture in the Middle Ages (Aberystwyth: University of Wales Press, 2007).

29 Knowledge of God through his creatures is the first mode of contemplation in Edmund of Abingdon's *Speculum ecclesie*. See, e.g., A. D. Wilshere (ed.), *Mirour*

de seinte eglyse, ANTS 40 (1982), ch. 6: 'Coment homme deit contempler Dieu en cheque creature' (How one should contemplate God in every creature) (B-Text 6.1–25).

30 Félix Lecoy (ed.), Guillaume de Lorris and Jean de Meun, *Roman de la Rose* (Paris: H. Champion, 1965), pp. 532–662. On the poem's ethical ambiguities, see Alastair Minnis, *Magister Amoris: The* Roman de la Rose *and Vernacular Hermeneutics* (Oxford: Oxford University Press, 2002). Hugh White, *Nature, Sex, and Goodness in a Medieval Literary Tradition* (Oxford: Oxford University Press, 2000), pp. 110–38. Spiritual perfectionism is one of the main targets at which the second half of the poem (involving La Vieille, Nature, and Genius in particular) is aimed. For Chaucer's relation to this specifically secular thematics, see Nicholas Watson, 'Chaucer's Public Christianity', *Religion and Literature* 37 (2005), 1–18.

31 A. V. C. Schmidt (ed.), William Langland, *The Vision of Piers Plowman: A Critical Edition of the B-Text* (London: J. M. Dent, 1998), B. 12.1–28.

32 For attacks on secular writing, see, e.g., Thomas G. Duncan and Margaret Connolly (eds.), *Anglo-Norman Miroir of Robert of Greetham*, in *The Middle English Mirror: Sermons from Advent to Sexagesima*, Middle English Texts (Heidelberg: Universitätsverlag Winter), pp. 1–36. On the ideology of labour, see Kellie Robertson, *The Laborer's Two Bodies: Literary and Legal Productions in England, 1350–1500*, The New Middle Ages (New York: Palgrave Macmillan, 2006).

33 For the possible Lollard affinities of *Book to a Mother*, see Alan J. Fletcher, 'A Hive of Industry or a Hornets' Nest?: MS Sidney Sussex College 74 and its Scribes', in A. J. Minnis (ed.), *Middle English Religious Texts and their Transmission* (Woodbridge: D. S. Brewer, 1994), pp. 131–55.

34 Mary Luke Arntz (ed.), *þe Holy Boke Gratia Dei* in *Richard Rolle and þe Holy Boke Gratia Dei: An Edition with Commentary*, Elizabethan and Renaissance Studies 92:2 (Salzburg: Institut für Anglistik und Amerikanistik, 1981), pp. 73.15–74.16.

35 Rosalynn Voaden, *God's Words, Women's Voices: The Discernment of Spirits In the Writing of Late-Medieval Women Visionaries* (Woodbridge: D. S. Brewer, 1999); Nancy Caciola, *Discerning Spirits: Divine and Demonic Possession in the Middle Ages* (Ithaca, NY: Cornell University Press, 2003).

36 Barbara Newman, 'What Did It Mean to Say "I Saw"? The Clash between Theory and Practice in Medieval Visionary Culture', *Speculum* 80 (2005), 1–43.

2

BRIAN PATRICK MCGUIRE

c. 1080–1215: culture and history

In a collection of Latin moralizing tales or *exempla* compiled at Clairvaux in the 1170s, the following story is found:

> A certain monk of Clairvaux was obliged because of a legal case and with the permission of his superior to go to England, where he had a distinguished family. He was a nephew of Walter Espech, who was the founder of the monastery of Rievaulx. When the monk was on his journey, he left the road for a certain church so that he could celebrate mass, for he was a priest. When he had finished, a certain religious woman called on one of the companions of the monk. She had her own cell adjoining the church, so that through its window she could see whatever was happening at the altar. She asked who might be the monk who had celebrated mass and from where he came. When she was told, she said to her respondent: 'From the time when I began to live here, no one has gone to this altar to celebrate the holy mysteries, whose movements amid the holy rites I have failed to see. Whatever was going on, I have been able to see clearly. But today this was not the case, for there was such a collection of heavenly dwellers around the priest while he offered the sacrifice that because of the multitude of holy angels I could not at all see what was taking place in the manner that I am used to seeing it all.'[1]

A second story is part of the Canterbury monk Eadmer's account of the life of St Anselm (d. 1109) and describes a vision Anselm had as a result of his desire to perceive something of what he had read in the Bible:

> And so he applied his mind with the greatest effort to this purpose, so that he might deserve to receive according to his faith through the reasoning of his mind those matters which he knew were hidden behind a cover of darkness. Then it happened one night that he was caught up in such thoughts and lay awake on his bed before vigils. In his meditation he tried to understand how the prophets could perceive things past and future as if they belonged to the present, and how they could present them with no hesitation in their speech and writings. And now while he was completely caught up in such wondering

and desired so powerfully to understand, he saw by means of the rays from his own eyes directly through the midst of the masonry of the church and dormitory how the monks were going about whose task it was to prepare the altar and other places in the church for matins. They were lighting candles, and finally he saw how one of them took a rope in his hands and rang the bell in order to wake up the brothers. When it sounded the community of brothers got up from their beds. He was amazed at what had happened. He realized that for God it was an insignificant matter to show to the prophets in the spirit what would happen, since he had granted to him to be able to see with his own eyes what was happening in spite of so many obstacles.[2]

These two visions are an indication of interest in the mystical life in England in the twelfth century. In the one we meet a female anchorite who discovered the spiritual presences engendered by the saying of mass by a devout Clairvaux monk, who was a member of the Norman aristocracy. In the other we encounter a prior of the Norman monastery of Bec who later became archbishop of Canterbury and whose search for intellectual insight brought him to the threshold of mystical experience.

Descriptions of visions and other intense spiritual experiences easily lead the historian into the question of whether the vision really took place. I cannot deal with the supernatural, but I can look at mysticism in terms of people and what they perceived as lived experience. I will be considering how a few individuals in English society from shortly after the Conquest and until the Fourth Lateran Council in 1215 tried to describe a spiritual ascent towards the presence of God. Thus I am dealing with an *affective search for union*, the merging of the individual with the foundation of its being, a return to the source of all being. This search for God is often expressed in the language of love and in our period it is often conveyed in terms of friendship. For as the Cistercian abbot of Rievaulx, Aelred (d. 1167), wrote, if God is love, then he is also friendship.[3]

The fact of human friendship is implicit in both our stories of visions. The first could not have been told at Clairvaux without there having been a bond of closeness between the monk who was the object of the vision and the compiler of the *exemplum* collection in the 1170s, Prior John. The two monks had to be able to trust each other in order for the one to reveal such a deeply personal experience to the other. In the second story it must have been Anselm himself who told his biographer Eadmer about how he attained the same type of spiritual insight as the prophets of the Bible. Contemplative experience as it is conveyed to us in historical sources is often found together with or conveyed through the affective medium of friendship or at least of deep trust between human beings. At times it is impossible to distinguish between the search for affective closeness to God and the pursuit of friendship or love between human beings: in seeking closeness to God, monks describe how they find each other's friendship. In the affective writings of the twelfth century there are at times no absolute distinctions between loving God intensely and loving other human beings. In the words of Aelred of Rievaulx: '. . . when this friendship, to which we admit only a few, is poured out over all and by all is poured upon God, and when God will be all things in all'.[4]

The literature of mysticism is one of human affectivity seeking a divine embrace. On the surface of both visions we find an historical context. In the first it is a village, perhaps in Yorkshire, with a parish church to which was attached an anchorite's cell. The woman had both a window to the church and one to the outside world, from which she asked about the monk priest who had celebrated the mass. He had been given a special privilege to leave his monastery of Clairvaux and to travel back to his home country on business. The revelation of his holiness by the presence of angels opens to us a rare moment when the anchoritic world coalesces with the monastic one.

The other vision is purely monastic. It is the story of how Anselm, apparently soon after he was made prior at Bec, sought to understand how it had been possible for the prophets to see present and future events. In gaining a similar insight Anselm was united all the more firmly with the monastic world that he had chosen. This story is told in connection with Eadmer's description of how Anselm's attachment to the community of Bec grew. In his vision of the monks' daily routine, Anselm became more closely bound to their way of life.

Anselm's vision could have taken place at any time between 1060 and 1078, when he was prior at Bec, but would not have been written down by his biographer Eadmer until after about 1100. Our Cistercian vision can be dated to after the foundation of Rievaulx in 1131 and before the Clairvaux collection was drawn up in the 1170s.

Reformation, renaissance and renewal: perceptions of individuality

The village and monastic worlds described in these two stories reflect the growth of religious devotion that characterized the century from about 1070 to 1170. Various names have been given for this period: two of them are 'renaissance of the twelfth century' and first medieval reformation of the Church. The term 'renaissance' was taken up by the American medievalist Charles Homer Haskins in his landmark 1927 book, *The Renaissance of the Twelfth Century* (remarkably, still in print). Haskins was mainly concerned with a revival of interest in classical Latin learning, but he ended his landmark study with a chapter on the rise of the university in western Europe, an institution that had not existed in Antiquity and so a birth and not a rebirth. But Haskins saw the foundation of universities at Paris, Bologna, and Oxford as the result of a great interest in studying and commenting on texts that went back to Antiquity. At the same time he was concerned with the flowering of Latin poetry and rhetoric, again influenced by classical models.

In the tradition of Haskins, a more recent study, *Renaissance and Renewal in the Twelfth Century* (1982), has considered the renewal of learning in terms of education. Today, more than thirty years later, these papers still make up the best summary we have of what it was that makes the twelfth century in western Europe so special, and here what is said about the Continent also applies to England. Already in 1970, however, R. W. Southern had published a study of 'England's First Entry into Europe'. Here he showed England as 'a colony of the intellectual empire of France' in academic and aristocratic terms. Thus we find schools at Oxford, but many more in Paris, and English scholars flocked to Paris, while no French scholars apparently came to England.

The development of learning in the twelfth century has thus been well mapped out, but a corresponding growth of what we might call spirituality and the pursuit of the contemplative life has not received the same attention. The Benedictine monk and scholar Jean Leclercq, however, in his contribution to the *Renaissance and Renewal* volume made theology into more than an academic business. He repeated the classic distinction he had already provided in his study *The Love of Learning and the Desire for God* between scholastic theology, based on intellectual categories, and a monastic, affective theology, seeking experience and union. In following Leclercq's pursuit of interior knowledge of God, we have to supplement the concept of renaissance with the phenomenon of what Colin Morris aptly has called the papal reform movement, 'which aimed at the cultic purity of the church, at freedom from simony, clerical concubinage and lay control'.[5] It is here that we find an institutional foundation which supported a growing interest in the contemplative life. A purified church provided an environment in which anchorites and monks and nuns could pursue the love of God.

A central figure of the papal reform movement is Peter Damian (1007–72), whose writings are on fire with zeal for transforming the life of the Church, as in removing simony, forbidding same-sex bonds among clerics, and ending clerical marriage. Peter Damian's letters are for the most part small or large treatises on various subjects connected to the reform, and at times he would write to lay persons with such concerns, as in describing to a nobleman of Ravenna how he daily was to recite the canonical hours and how he was to understand their mystical meaning. Peter spoke of 'the

Middle Ages, as today, hardly anyone has made use of John of Forde. The work exists in but a single medieval manuscript and its modern translation has been among the least-sold books of Cistercian publications. While Gilbert's sermons were often transmitted together with Bernard's (and soon were attributed to the abbot of Clairvaux himself), John of Forde's *magnum opus* was all but forgotten.

John of Forde's obscurity may be due to the general disappearance of monastic theology from the intellectual map of Europe by the end of the twelfth century. Certainly the eighty-six sermons by Bernard plus the contribution of Gilbert of Hoyland provided more than enough material for meditation for any monk or scholar who was fascinated with the idea of using the Song of Songs as a text to be used as a foundation for contemplation.

Whatever the reason for the neglect of John of Forde, it is worth noticing that both he and Gilbert were at English Cistercian monasteries. Together with Aelred of Rievaulx they signal the fact that the Cistercian monks of England, as their Carthusian contemporaries, were concerned with the contemplative life and created a literature to convey their experience of its content. Even though it should be noted that Bernard's secretary, Geoffrey of Auxerre, also tried his hand at a commentary on the Song of Songs, we can justly speak of an English monastic devotion to the Song as an entry to the contemplative life.

The saga of the anchorite: searching for spiritual experience

John of Forde is perhaps much better known today for his *Life of Wulfric of Haselbury*, thanks to the partial translation by Pauline Matarasso contained in her outstanding collection of twelfth-century Cistercian writings.[26] John never knew Wulfric but was encouraged to write about this man who had chosen to live for almost thirty years in separation from the world but with access to it through a window, just as our anchorite who is described above in the *exemplum* from a Clairvaux collection.

An anchorite is distinguished from a hermit, who had more freedom of movement but who also dedicated himself to a life of prayer and meditation. Godric of Finchale (d. 1170), who lived on the River Wear in Co. Durham, was a hermit, and he was a favourite of Aelred of Rievaulx.[27] Thus a monk could become attached to a hermit or anchorite, whether alive or dead, as we also can see in the much better known story of Christina of Markyate and her spiritual bond with the abbot of St Albans, Geoffrey.[28]

Wulfric's life in John of Forde's description is full of practical sense and what we today would call community service. But at the heart of it was ascetic discipline. Thus he would not let himself get distracted by his visitors but would keep to the business at hand: 'as soon as he felt his interlocutor sliding to other matters he would shut the window and retire to the inner cell'.[29] John used Wulfric's discretion and love of solitude to 'remind certain members of our Order not to go out so often and when they do, to conduct themselves with greater discretion and reverence' (pp. 240–1). Because of his concentration on interior life, Wulfric was a model for John, who confessed that he had seldom been able to concentrate his attention with no interruptions for a single 'or even half a psalm' (ch. 19, p. 245). For John, Wulfric's attentiveness to the office was a greater wonder than the fact that at least on one occasion he seems to have had what we would call a mystical experience:

> That a good man and a friend of God who habitually sang the Psalter right through with unwavering attention should be granted an hour's ecstasy will astound no one. For my part it is the concentration of that exceptional soul that I truly admire and venerate. (ch. 19, p. 245)

At the end of this chapter John of Forde used the term used by St Paul about himself 'I knew a man' (2 Cor. 12:2). This formulation became a standard way for medieval spiritual writers to speak about themselves without using the first person. John thus remained anonymous about his own experience or that of someone known to him in his monastery. This man was in doubt about Wulfric, especially because he was a 'simple man' who by definition would have had 'fewer powers of concentration'. But then this doubter himself had an experience of being able to concentrate completely on the contents of the office, so that each single verse he sang took on new meaning for him. In this way he came to understand and believe in the grace that had been given to Wulfric.

Such a story brings us to the very centre of twelfth-century contemplative spirituality as perceived in a monastic English text. It was a question of listening to and speaking the words of the Psalms and the Gospels in order to receive God's grace. There is nothing apophatic about this approach. It is based on words that are sung and said and whose meaning and significance become of vital importance for the individual. And here there is no difference between the choir of the monastery or the cell of the hermitage. As in our initial Clairvaux story, monastic and eremitical spirituality meet in shared spiritual experience.

In his meditation on the language of the Bible, Wulfric is described in the language of the Song of Songs as 'one of the watchmen who go about the city' (Song 3:3) (ch. 31, p. 248). In so doing he kept watch over the earthly Jerusalem, until dawn when he would go about his work, which involved copying manuscripts. At night, then, John of Forde saw Christ speaking to his soul with the words, 'My beloved is mine and I am his' (Song 2:16).

Wulfric was seen on one occasion by the son of the local priest, Brichtric, at prayer in his cell. He stood before a great light over the altar. It then moved and disappeared through the north window of the church (ch. 35, p. 249). Such intimations of mystical experience are relatively rare in twelfth-century texts. In Christina of Markyate (*c.* 1096–*c.* 1160), we find many miraculous events, especially in terms of her prophetic knowledge, but the main purpose of the story seems to be to tell how this determined young woman gained her anchorhold and escaped an unwanted betrothal. Her biography reveals a landscape of Anglo-Saxon hermits and anchorites settling in villages and the countryside. Thanks to the careful study of Ann K. Warren, we can see how these people received support from royal and aristocratic patrons.[30] The evidence for aristocrats only appears in the thirteenth century, but from Henry II onwards, we can see how English kings provided a financial foundation for recognized anchorites. The Pipe Roll accounts allow us to follow individuals almost year by year. In 1171 and 1172, for example, Henry 'added four new anchorites to his alms lists, more than doubling his ongoing commitment' (Warren, *Anchorites*, p. 139). Warren sees this increase in connection with the Becket controversy and Henry's desire to express 'piety and orthodoxy'. Similarly Christopher Holdsworth considers the young John's conversion to the Cistercian life at Forde at this same time as possibly connected with the Becket crisis.[31] The controversy about secular and religious power and the ensuing murder of the archbishop seem to have unleashed a wave of religious feeling which benefited both anchorites and monasteries.

How fair is it to speak of an ethnic English flavour to the anchoritic life a century after the Conquest? Many of the names on Ann Warren's lists for the reign of Henry are definitely not Anglo-Saxon (see, for example, in *Anchorites*, Table 5, p. 141). The reign of Henry may indeed have brought the disappearance of an earlier Anglo-Saxon dominance in the eremitical movement. Certainly we can contrast the world of Christina and Wulfric in the first half of the twelfth century with that of the men and women on Henry II's lists. We are witnessing here the silent merging of the old English population with the Norman conquerors, the same phenomenon we indirectly perceive in the life of Aelred of Rievaulx, the English boy who learned how to engage in diplomatic relations with Norman lords such as Walter Espech. The same Walter whose nephew went to Clairvaux to become a monk and then returned for a business trip to England, during which his sanctity was revealed to a female anchorite.

In the lives of anchorites such as Christina, Wulfric and the less well-known people mentioned on the Pipe Rolls of Henry II, contemplative communities in twelfth-century England make their appearance. They were made up of practical people who knew how to deal with village gossip or else themselves became the object of such gossip, as Aelred warned his sister not to be (*De institutione inclusarum* (*Instructions for Enclosed Women*), 2, p. 638). Their days were spent in contact with the cares and concern of their communities; their nights were often devoted to prayer and perhaps sometimes ended in contemplation. It is here that parish life met the presence of eternity, with the anchorite hidden behind the windows that at one end gave access to the liturgy and at the other to the street.

It is difficult to combine our fragments of knowledge about the anchorite with much more detailed information about the spread of reformed monasticism in this period. But there is no doubt that both in the village and in the monastery, there were excitement and real spiritual ferment. The description of the attractiveness of Rievaulx to the young Aelred in the 1130s harmonizes perfectly with William of St Thierry's enthusiastic words about the Clairvaux that he at about the same time found under Bernard.[32] Aelred could not pull himself away from Rievaulx, while William wanted to convert to Clairvaux. Aelred remained at Rievaulx, and here he shared his biographer Walter Daniel's love of the place and its surroundings.[33]

We get only passing glimpses of the ways that twelfth-century men and women perceived their physical surroundings. But there is no doubt that for anchorites and monks trained in the language of the Psalms and the Gospels, everything they saw came to reflect the glory of God. In the midst of a tough, brutal society, with class differences and a warrior aristocracy, men and women from the conquered race as well as representatives of the conquerors could convert to the cloister or the cell. A few there sought a life of contemplation. Sometimes these people became so attractive that the ruling class sought them out and insisted that they take on important functions, as when Hugh was called from La Grande Chartreuse to become bishop of Lincoln.

It is impossible to provide a chronological overview of this period from about 1080 to 1215 in terms of *progressive development* of contemplative activity. But it would be appropriate to contrast the relatively rare mentions of mystical insight from the second half of the eleventh century with the abundant indications from the second half of the twelfth century. Anselm's moment of insight, which may have taken place in the 1060s, is a lonely experience, while Cistercian and Carthusian contemplative experience, as seen in the sermons on the Song of Songs by Bernard, was transmitted to all the brethren. Hermits and recluses seem to have been present through the entire period, but they became more visible and more widely appreciated in the second half of the twelfth century. As always for the historian there is the question of sources: does an increase in them indicate the development of a phenomenon or simply accidental survival? In my mind there did take place a greater interest in contemplative experience. The appearance and spread of contemplative monasticism in England, especially with the Cistercians and Carthusians, in England helped propagate knowledge of the mystical life.

We can end this review of the historical and cultural background for the growth of the contemplative life in twelfth-century England with a final story from the Clairvaux collection with which I began. An English clerk who had lived in sin was saved at his death by the prayer that he had learned from a Cistercian monk. The monk had told him to offer himself each day to Mary and to St John. When the demons took hold of his soul, Mary sent John to save him. Then the dead man appeared to his father, who was still alive, and revealed to him how he had been saved. He explained that he would find a copy of the prayer he had used at the foot of his bed. The text of the prayer is as follows:

> God, who hanging on the holy cross for our salvation commended for our salvation the virgin mother to the virgin disciple, grant graciously of your goodness that they may care for me in this pilgrimage, free me from all evil, seek your mercy for me, and come to me at my death and bring me into eternal life, through you, Jesus Christ, saviour of the world, who with God the Father and the Holy Spirit lives and reigns, God for ever and ever. Amen[34]

A simple prayer and a naïve story that have no place in the literature of mysticism? I am not so sure. Such prayers and stories were circulating through England and all of western Europe in the twelfth century and were part of the spiritual transformation of the culture. Such tales were told by monks to each other in order to provide hope and courage, and they also went from monks to secular clerks and from there out to the laity. Anyone who was devout in his prayers, especially to Mary, could have hope. The saints, who provided a way to Christ, united this world and the next. Mysticism as the hidden knowledge of the divine emerges from the context of such prayers and devotions.

NOTES

1 My translation, from Olivier Legendre (ed.), *Collectaneum exemplorum et visionum clarevallense*, Corpus Christianorum. Continuatio Mediaevalis 208 (Turnhout: Brepols, 2005), p. 144. Note that this collection of *exempla* has previously been called the *Liber visionum et miraculorum*, as in Brian McGuire, *Friendship and Faith: Cistercian Men, Women, and their Stories, 1100–1250*, Variorum Collected Studies Series (Aldershot: Ashgate, 2002).

2 R. W. Southern (ed.), *The Life of St Anselm by Eadmer* (Oxford: Clarendon Press, 1972), pp. 12–13 (my translation).

3 *De spiritali amicitia* I.69–70, p. 301 in A. Hoste and C. H. Talbot (eds.), *Aelredi Rievallensis Opera Omnia*, Corpus Christianorum. Continuatio Mediaevalis 1 (Turnhout: Brepols, 1971).

4 From the closing lines of *De spiritali amicitia* III.134, p. 350 (cf. 1 Cor. 15:28). See Brian McGuire, *Friendship and Community: The Monastic Experience* (2nd edn, Ithaca, NY: Cornell University Press, 2010).

5 *The Papal Monarchy: The Western Church from 1050 to 1250* (Oxford: Clarendon Press, 1991), pp. 489–90.

6 Owen J. Blum (trans.), *Peter Damian Letters 1–30*, The Fathers of the Church, Mediaeval Continuation I (Washington, DC: Catholic University of America, 1989), Letter 17.17, p. 154.

7 *The Making of the Middle Ages* (New York: Hutchinson, 1953), pp. 250–1.

8 Jan Ziolkowski (ed.), *Nigel of Canterbury: Miracles of the Virgin Mary, in verse*, Toronto Medieval Latin Texts (Toronto: Pontifical Institute of Mediaeval Studies, 1986).

9 Robert L. Benson and Giles Constable (eds.), *Renaissance and Renewal in the Twelfth Century* (Cambridge, MA: Harvard University Press, 1982), p. 294.

10 See Margaret Gibson, *Lanfranc of Bec* (Oxford: Clarendon Press, 1978). R. W. Southern, *Saint Anselm. A Portrait in a Landscape* (Cambridge: Cambridge University Press, 1990), esp. chs. 11, 'A New Archbishop's Problems of Obedience', and 12, 'The Liberty of the Church'.

11 Southern (ed.), *The Life of St Anselm*, xiv, pp. 23–4: 'How he cured a sick youth simply by looking at him'. Paul J. Archambault (trans.), *A Monk's Confession: The Memoirs of Guibert of Nogent* (University Park, PA: Pennsylvania State University Press, 1996), bk I, ch. 17, pp. 61–2.

12 Southern (ed.), *The Life of St Anselm*, v, p. 9.

13 Maurice Powicke (ed.), *The Life of Ailred of Rievaulx by Walter Daniel* (Oxford: Oxford University Press, 1978), pp. 14–16.

14 Edmund Colledge and James Walsh (trans.), *The Ladder of Monks and Twelve Meditations by Guigo II* (Kalamazoo, MI: Cistercian Publications, 1981), p. 68.

15 Decima L. Douie and Hugh Farmer (eds. and trans.), *The Life of St Hugh of Lincoln* (London: Nelson, 1961), I, chs. 3–4, pp. 53–60. *The Life of St Hugh of Lincoln*, 2 vols. (Oxford: Clarendon Press, 1985), II, ch. 9, p. 44.

16 Theodore Berkeley (trans.), *The Golden Epistle: A Letter to the Brethren at Mont Dieu* (Kalamazoo: Cistercian Publications, 1976), V.16, p. 14.

17 Hoste and Talbot (eds.), *De institutione inclusarum*, in *Aelredi Rievallensis Opera Omnia*, trans. as 'A Rule of Life for a Recluse' by Mary Paul Macpherson, in *Aelred of Rievaulx: Treatises and Pastoral Prayer* (Kalamazoo, MI: Cistercian Publications, 1982).

18 Jerome Taylor (trans.), *The Didascalicon of Hugh of St. Victor*, Records of Western Civilization (New York: Columbia University Press, 1991), p. 225, n. 53.

19 Grover A. Zinn (trans.), *The Mystical Ark*, in *Richard of St Victor* (New York: Paulist, 1979), ch. 4, p. 157.

20 Robert Lechat, 'Les Fragmenta de Vita et Miraculis S. Bernardi par Geoffroy d'Auxerre', *Analecta Bollandiana* 50 (1932), pp. 83–122, esp. ch. 49, pp. 115–16.

21 Legendre (ed.), *Collectaneum exemplorum et visionum clarevallense*, xliii [137], p. 339. The link from l'Aumône to England might be explained by the fact that it had founded the first English Cistercian houses at Waverley and Tintern.

22 'Bernard and the Embrace of Christ', in Brian Patrick McGuire, *The Difficult Saint: Bernard of Clairvaux and his Tradition* (Kalamazoo, MI: Cistercian Publications, 1991), pp. 227–49, esp. p. 244. Kilian Walsh (trans.), *On the Song of Songs I* (Kalamazoo, MI: Cistercian, 1977), III.5, p. 3. J. Leclercq, C. H. Talbot and H. M. Rochais (eds.), *Sancti Bernardi opera* I, (Rome: Editiones Cistercienses, 1957).

23 Irene Edmonds (trans.), *On the Song of Songs IV* (Kalamazoo, MI: Cistercian Publications, 1980), IV.14, p. 210; *Sancti Bernardi Opera* II, p. 316.

24 The sermons are published together with Bernard's own in *PL* 184, and are translated by Lawrence C. Braceland: *Gilbert of Hoyland: Sermons on the Song of Songs* (Kalamazoo, MI: Cistercian, 1988–9), I–III.

25 Wendy Mary Beckett (trans.), *John of Forde: Sermons on the Final Verses of the Song of Songs* (Kalamazoo: Cistercian, 1977–84), vols. 1–6, based on Edmund Mikkers and Hilary Costello (eds.), *Ioannis de Fordea. Super extremam partem cantici canticorum sermones cxx*, Corpus Christianorum. Continuatio Mediaevalis 17 and 18 (Turnhout: Brepols, 1970).

26 Pauline Matarasso, *The Cistercian World* (Harmondsworth: Penguin, 1993), pp. 235–73.

27 J. Stevenson (ed.), Reginald of Durham, *Libellus de vita et miraculis S. Godrici heremitae de Finchale*, Surtees Society (London, 1847), pp. 176–7.

28 C. H. Talbot (ed.), *The Life of Christina of Markyate*, (Oxford: Clarendon Press, 1987). See Talbot's revised translation with an Introduction and Notes by Samuel Fanous and Henrietta Leyser, Oxford World Classics (Oxford: Oxford University Press, 2008).

29 Matarasso (trans.), *The Cistercian World, Life of Wulfric*, ch. 3, p. 240.

30 *Anchorites and their Patrons in Medieval England* (Berkeley: University of California Press, 1985), esp. pp. 128–54.

31 See p. 29 in Hilary Costello and Christopher Holdsworth (eds.), *A Gathering of Friends: The Learning and Spirituality of John of Forde* (Kalamazoo, MI: Cistercian Publications, 1996), esp. Holdsworth's 'Two Commentators on the Song of Songs: John of Forde and Alexander Nequam', pp. 153–74.

32 *S. Bernardi Vita Prima* I.35, in *PL* 185, col. 247D.

33 Powicke (ed.), *The Life of Ailred*, pp. 12–13.

34 Legendre (ed.), *Collectaneum exemplorum*, [1], p. 3.

3

HENRIETTA LEYSER

c. 1080–1215: texts

The Nun of Barking in her Anglo-Norman *Life of Edward the Confessor* (*c.* 1165) tells the story of how one day when the king was at mass at Westminster he had a vision of Christ; the priest was saying the words of consecration when 'the good, the pious, the sweet Jesus appeared'.[1] With his right hand he blessed the king; in response Edward bowed – 'he bowed his head and bowed with his whole body to that divine presence that never grows old, to the joy that never ceases, to the beauty that never grows old, to the goodness that does all good things and to that very sweetness did he bow with great love' (p. 205). According to the Nun of Barking, Edward's companion, Earl Leofric likewise saw Jesus and thus was able both to bear witness to the vision and to share in the king's joy. Both king and earl were moved to tears. They wept 'tenderly'; 'with sweet tears they were sustained, and with sweet tears fed' (p. 205). When mass was over they continued to describe to the other what each had seen: as they spoke 'with the words were mingled sighs and tears with sweet desire' (p. 206; for the full story see pp. 203–6).

The lyricism of this vision is all the more marked when we compare it with its source. The story derives from an Anglo-Saxon text of the second half of the eleventh century.[2] Here, the focus is not on King Edward but rather on Leofric who has accompanied the king to mass. We are given a detailed description of the church – of a curtain 'triple-threaded . . . woven very thick' (p. 281) behind the altar and of the cross beyond. Above the cross Leofric sees a hand; at first he thinks it is someone crossing himself but when he looks more closely he sees (through the curtain and despite its thickness) that 'the blessing hand was stirring and moving upwards. Then he was afraid, and doubted whether it were as it seemed to him' (p. 281). But the hand then appeared 'as clearly as he could see his own; the fingers were fair, narrow and long, and the outlines of the nails and the large fleshy part below the thumb – all was visible – and from the little finger to the arm, and some part of the sleeve. Then he dared not look at it any longer, but hung his head down, and it then ceased its blessing' (pp. 281–2).

Leofric's vision in its original form is a remarkable testimony to the religious sensibilities of an eleventh-century layman; no less remarkable is the way the story was transformed over the next one hundred years. In place of the concern with concrete details – the thickness of the curtain, the shape of the fingers – we have in the Nun of Barking's account, sighs, tears, and sweet desire. The fear and awe felt by the eleventh-century Leofric has been replaced by feelings of joy, beauty and goodness, in other words with precisely those emotions generally associated with a mystical experience. It is the purpose of this chapter to attempt to trace through other texts how and why the twelfth century developed this new language for its encounters with God.

Any study of change in the eleventh and twelfth centuries in England is bedeviled by the controversies surrounding the Norman Conquest and its impact. For Leofric's heirs and their peers the Conquest was an undoubted tragedy; what is much less certain is the extent to which it eradicated Old English culture, supplanting it with new ideas imported from the Continent. Over thirty years ago Richard Southern made a strong case for the argument that 1066 ushered in 'England's first entry into Europe', so that England became in the twelfth century little more than 'a colony of the intellectual empire'.[3] More recent work now stresses the vitality and diversity of Anglo-Saxon culture and the ways in which its influence continued to be felt across the divide of 1066.

A figure who straddles the Norman Conquest is Goscelin of St. Bertin (c. 1035–c. 1107). Goscelin came to England c. 1060 to join the household of Bishop Herman, bishop of Ramsey and Sherborne. (Goscelin's arrival may be taken as a reminder, pace Southern, that Anglo-Saxon culture was never simply insular.) After the Conquest – which initially at least he saw as a victory for a barbarous people and an unmitigated disaster – Goscelin made a career for himself as the hagiographer of choice for Anglo-Saxon saints who either had no Lives or whose Lives needed refurbishing. He thus became, according to William of Malmesbury (1095–1143), second only to Bede (d. 735) as an advocate of native saints. Despite his prolific output his best-known works remain his two earliest: his Life of Edith and the Liber confortatorius (Book of Comfort) both associated with Wilton.[4] Wilton was a house Goscelin knew well from his first days in England where he may have acted as chaplain and tutor to Eve (c. 1058–c. 1125), for whom the Liber confortatorius was written after Eve's abrupt departure, as Goscelin saw it, from Wilton to become a recluse at Angers.

Wilton was a tenth-century foundation, strongly linked with the house of Wessex. Edith herself (c. 961–84) was the daughter of King Edgar and owed her canonization to King Aethelred. Eve was possibly a niece of Bishop

Herman. Both Edith and Eve were brought up at Wilton, Edith from the age of two, and Eve it would seem from seven. Wilton in other words was an important part of the court establishment, not at first sight an obvious place for radical spirituality. Edith herself was renowned for the splendour of her purple clothing and the extent of her menagerie. But Wilton also took seriously its role as a school. Eve was an exceptionally learned young woman and Edith too had been well educated, taught by the Lotharingian priests Benna and Radbod whom her father had invited to England. How far the sentiments Goscelin ascribed to either woman reflect this education, or how far they tell us about Goscelin rather than about either Edith or Eve is of course impossible to fathom but we should not ignore the circumstantial detail he gives us, and we can allow for the possibility that the devotional climate he depicts reflects the spiritual life of Wilton as well as his own literary imagination.

Edith was a child blessed from the very moment of her birth: 'a ray of sunlight shone out continuously from the crown of her head, and rose high, and clearly lit up the royal bedchamber'.[5] As a young girl at Wilton she progressed from strength to strength until she reached the exalted point where more important than even her studies were her mystical experiences:

> ... from now on, as if the heavens were open and she had the eyes of Stephen bestowed upon her (Acts 7:55), she was taken up in rapture to the festivals of the saints, the joys of the angels, to Christ himself, the glorious spouse illuminating everything; clinging to him with her whole mind and struck with the holy wound of his love, from the midst of her studies she hastened towards him with her entire affection and, taking to herself the wings of a dove, she ardently desired to fly to his sanctifying embraces and to be at rest there (Ps. 54:7), crying out with the longings of the bride: 'Your name is as perfume poured forth and your sweet smell is above all aromatical spices. Draw me after you, we will run to the odour of your ointments.'
>
> (Song: 1:2, 4:10, 1:3) (p. 33)

The language of the Song of Songs runs throughout the *Life of Edith* in ways more commonly associated with mystical writings of the twelfth century; how important the Song really was to Edith we cannot tell but Goscelin does suggest that she fashioned for herself a rich spiritual life. In her 'manual of devotions' she wrote out chosen prayers and she commissioned the building of a chapel to be decorated for her by her teacher Benno with paintings of the Passion: 'as she had fashioned them in her heart, he brought forth the pictures' (p. 53).

Goscelin's *Liber confortatorius* is written in a very different register from his *Life of Edith*. It is both a work of lamentation in which Goscelin grieves for his loss of Eve's company and a book of instructions to Eve on how to deepen her spiritual life. What is revealing is not only the list of books Goscelin recommends – they include Augustine's *Confessions*, a work that was only just then beginning to be re-read in England[6] – but also the way in which he urges Eve to develop an intensely emotional and personal Christocentric piety:

> ...with all the sighs of desire pour out your heart to God your salvation, desire him in your very marrow, take hold of him, embrace him...conceive him, carry him, give birth to him, feed him...See therefore how he stretches out loving arms on the cross, inviting us to himself with that kindness by which he redeemed us, prepared as we come to take us up of his own will, to gather, embrace, cherish us.[7]

The notion that the crucified Christ might embrace us appears much later in England in the vision of the hermit Bartholomew of Farne (d. 1193) who, as he was meditating on the Cross saw Christ 'greet him in return and with arms outstretched, take him up into his embrace as a new bearer of the Cross'.[8] While this particular conceit can be traced to Cistercian stories dating from the 1170s we can see a precursor already in Goscelin's letter to Eve.

Goscelin's evident attachment to Eve has in the past struck historians as both embarrassing and distasteful. Thanks to the work of Stephen Jaeger[9] and of Brian McGuire, it is possible now to place Goscelin's affection in an appropriate context, to understand it as an example of what Jaeger calls 'ennobling love' and McGuire simply as the kind of friendship about which we should not ask too many questions, not because we suspect impropriety but because of the impossibility of being able 'to distinguish between the search for affective closeness to God and the pursuit of friendship or love between human beings' (see above, pp. 30–1).

Friendship as a theme takes us straight to the writings of Anselm, archbishop of Canterbury (*c.* 1033–1109) and to Aelred, abbot of Rievaulx (1110–67). Anselm and Aelred are both characters with whom it is easy – possibly deceptively so – to feel bonds of empathy. Each laid stress on the compassion of God, each valued the spiritual dimension afforded by the company and conversation of their fellow men but the comparison should not be stretched too far since in temperament they were very different. For Anselm one of the great moments of his life was when he clarified in his own mind his proof of the existence of God; for Aelred the turning point came when he first saw Rievaulx and fell in love with it. The lessons they gave as spiritual directors reflect the contrast between these two experiences.

Anselm's prayers and the lessons he gave on how to pray have been hailed as 'creat[ing] a new kind of poetry – the poetry of intimate personal devotion', a judgement that remains valid even though it is important to note the extent to which Anselm was building on native traditions.[10] The prayers are to be prayed with the heart: 'the purpose of the prayers and meditations' is, Anselm explains, 'to stir up the mind of the reader to the love or fear of God, or to self-examination. They are not to be read in a turmoil but quietly, not skimmed or hurried through, but taken a little at a time, with deep and thoughtful meditation' (*The Prayers and Meditations of St Anselm*, p. 89). The overall effect is to portray a God of mercy but yet one who is beyond man's reach and whom ultimately the individual sinner seems doomed to fail. Thus in the second of the prayers Anselm sends to the Countess Matilda he laments his absence at the crucifixion:

> So much as I can, though not as much as I ought,
> I am mindful of your passion....
> Alas for me, that I was not able to see
> the Lord of Angels humbled to converse with men...
>
> Alas for me that I did not deserve to be amazed
> in the presence of a love marvellous and beyond our grasp.
> Why, O my soul, were you not there
> to be pierced by a sword of bitter sorrow
> when you could not bear
> the piercing of the side of your Saviour with a lance?
>
> (p. 95)

In Anselm's *Proslogion* the sense of the immensity of God and the limitations of man come across with even greater force:

> O my soul,
> have you found what you were looking for?
> I was seeking God,
> And I have found that he is above all things,
> and that than which nothing greater can be thought.
> I have found him to be
> life and light, wisdom and goodness,
> eternal blessedness and the bliss of eternity,
> existing everywhere and at all times.
> If I have not found my God
> what is it that I have found and understood
> so truly and certainly?
> But if I have found him,
> why do I not experience what I have found?
> Lord God,
> if my soul has found you,
> why has it no experience of you? (p. 255)

When we turn to Aelred we find a striking contrast; Aelred has a much less anguished sensibility. Aelred's God can indeed be found and his sweetness experienced: 'he who has been sought so long, so often implored, so ardently desired, comely of aspect beyond the sons of men, looking out as it were through the lattice-work, invites to kisses: "Rise up, hasten, my friend, and come."'[11] For Aelred, in contrast to Anselm, Gospel events may indeed be re-lived, re-captured and appropriated and Christ in this way will be made present. Thus Aelred's reader is urged to enter the house of Simon the Pharisee, and to kiss Christ's feet: 'Kiss, I say, those feet, press your fortunate lips to them, so that after you no sinner may be afraid of them, no one, whatever crimes he has committed may flee from them, no one may be overcome by the consciousness of his own unworthiness' (p. 34). Likewise, Aelred urges his sister, a recluse, to share imaginatively in every aspect of Christ's life, from the moment of the annunciation through to the crucifixion. She must stand with the Virgin and John at the foot of the cross. She must kiss Christ's wounds so that her lips 'stained with his blood, will become like a scarlet ribbon' (p. 91). She must help to carry the body to the tomb, stay with Mary Magdalen and with her witness the Resurrection. With this sense of the immediacy of God's presence comes the possibility of mystical experience:

> How often [Christ] came to your side to bring you loving consolation when you were dried up by fear, how often he infused himself into your innermost being when you were on fire with love, how often he shed upon you the light of spiritual understanding when you were singing psalms or reading, how often he carried you away with a certain unspeakable longing for himself when you were at prayer, how often he lifted up your mind from things of earth and introduced it into the delights of heaven and the joys of Paradise.   (p. 96)

Aelred is full of admiration for his sister's way of life; but community life, quite as much as the eremitical, may prepare the soul for mystical joy. Cistercian humanism, the belief in the transformative power of human love, in the ability of man to rise from self love to the love of friends and hence to the love – and to the vision – of Christ suffuses all of Aelred's writings. 'Who is there', asks Aelred, 'that can love another, if he does not love himself since, from a comparison with that love by which he is dear to himself, a man ought to regulate his love for his neighbour.'[12] Friends can and do sustain each other's social and spiritual lives and it is through this mutual love that they may come to develop intimacy also with God:

> . . . thus a friend praying to Christ on behalf of his friend, and for his friend's sake desiring to be heard by Christ, directs his attention with love and longing

to Christ; then it sometimes happens that quickly and imperceptibly the one love passes over into the other, and coming, as it were, into close contact with the sweetness of Christ himself, the friend begins to taste his sweetness and experience his charm. Thus ascending from that holy love with which he embraces a friend to that with which he embraces Christ, he will joyfully partake in the abundance of the spiritual fruit of friendship, awaiting the fullness of all things in the life to come.   (p. 131)

True friendship is sealed by a 'spiritual kiss', so called since it is made not 'by a meeting of lips but by a mingling of spirit, by the purification of all things in the Spirit of God' (p. 76). This, says Aelred:

> I would call...the kiss of Christ, yet he himself does not offer it from his own mouth, but from the mouth of another, breathing upon his lovers that most sacred affection so that there seems to be, as it were, one spirit in many bodies...The soul, therefore, accustomed to this kiss and not doubting that all this sweetness comes from Christ...sighs for the kiss of grace and with the greatest desire exclaims: 'Let him kiss me with the kiss of his mouth.' So that now, after all earthly affections have been tempered, and all thoughts and desires which savor of the world have been quieted, the soul takes delight in the kiss of Christ alone and rests in his embrace, exulting and exclaiming; 'His left hand is under my head and his right hand shall embrace me.'
>
> (pp. 76–7)

Aelred has sometimes been described as the 'Bernard of the north'. The bonds between Aelred and St Bernard (1090–1153) were undoubtedly strong – Aelred's first work, *The Mirror of Charity*, was written specifically at Bernard's request and prefaced by him. Aelred had evidently claimed that his lack of formal education made him unsuitable for the task. On the contrary, Bernard had replied, such a lack is an advantage: 'cliffs and mountains' will have served Aelred better than 'the bookshelves of the schoolmasters.'[13] The Holy Spirit, not some grammarian, is to be Aelred's teacher. Underlined here is that culture clash to which McGuire (following Jean Leclercq) has drawn attention, the clash between on the one hand 'scholastic theology, based on intellectual categories' and on the other 'a monastic, affective theology seeking experience and union' (see above, p. 32). For the new theology The Song of Songs was the key text and in its use St Bernard's influence on Aelred in particular, and on the English Cistercian community as a whole, was very marked. When Bernard died in 1153 he had still only reached the beginning of ch. 3 of his *Commentary on the Song of Songs*. The monks who completed it were Englishmen. Gilbert of Hoyland, abbot of Swineshead (d. 1172), picked up from where Bernard had stopped and continued to ch. 5, verse 9. John, abbot of Forde (*c.* 1150–1214), started at ch. 5 verse 8 and continued until the task was done. This *Commentary on The Song of Songs* (to which we will return) was however much less widely known than John's *Life of Wulfric of Haselbury*, a text itself suffused with the language of The Song.

According to John, Wulfric of Haselbury (*c.* 1090–1154/5) had been ordained priest at a young age, though it was not clear that he had at first any sense of vocation. But Wulfric experienced a moment of conversion and became a changed man. God 'breathed into his nostrils the breath of life',[14] and before long Wulfric had had himself enclosed in a hermit's cell adjoining the church of Haselbury Plucknett. From the window of his cell Wulfric would in turn console the afflicted and rebuke the great. (King Stephen, for one, experienced the sharpness of his tongue.) Wulfric had had little formal education but his teacher was the Holy Spirit and his words 'like loaves fresh from the oven ... gave off to those who heard them a delicious scent of purity and simplicity of heart' (*Cistercian World*, p. 239). But Wulfric was not available at all times. Sometimes quite abruptly, he would shut his window and retire into his inner cell. 'Anyone gifted with spiritual understanding will excuse him wholly', explains John (in language taken straight from the Song of Songs), for such a man will know 'the inner fragrance that recalled him, the sacred and secret rapture that dragged him irresistibly – and yet how happy – back. Least of all will it surprise those who have merited to be brought into the king's chambers and who have heard the zealous concern, the pressing entreaties of the Bridegroom for the quiet of the Bride' (p. 240). But it was especially at night-time that Wulfric would 'work out his own salvation' and replenish himself ready for the demands made upon him in the day: 'Surely that was the time, when blessed Wulfric was released from the cares of men and Christ himself was at leisure, after a fashion, since all the world was fast asleep or nodding off, the time when in the joy of his love he would speak to Wulfric's holy soul, saying: "My beloved is mine and I am his"' (p. 248).

Wulfric's powers of concentration as he sang his psalter were as astounding as they were enviable. And they were rewarded: John of Forde commented 'that a good man and a friend of God who habitually sang the Psalter right through with unwavering attention should be granted an hour's ecstasy will astound no one' (p. 245). But was it possible that a man of Wulfric's limited educational means could really meditate so deeply? Yes – replies John, for it is not intellectual powers but the cultivation of virtue and of the love of God that open the doors to heaven. In evidence, John recounts a vision granted to the son of the priest of Wulfric's parish. The boy (Osbern) needs to borrow an aspersorium for his father. He decides to use Wulfric's and goes to his cell to tell him:

> On opening the door of the cell he saw a light of dazzling brightness over the centre of the altar. The saint was standing motionless before the steps, gazing at the light. The boy, lost in wonder, handed the aspersiorum to someone else to give to the priest and returned to what he had seen. Having silently closed the door until he could just peep through with one eye, he watched the light move gradually towards the left-hand corner of the altar and thence, crossing a chest that stood beside it, go out through the north window. When Osbern asked what the beautiful light was that he had seen above the altar, the holy man said: 'Did you see it then, boy?' 'I saw it, master.' 'Ah! If you were here around midnight you might often see the like and, what's more, have your nostrils filled with so sweet a fragrance that all the world's delights would count for little in comparison' (Matarasso (ed.), *Cistercian World*, p. 249).

> On another occasion when Wulfric was praying 'suddenly there stood before him an angel. Snatching, as it seemed to Wulfric, his spirit from his body, he whisked him aloft to the heavens and showed him God's glory and all that was the hope of the saints... and ever afterwards he guarded the memory of those blissful moments.'   (*Wulfric of Haselbury*, pp. 35–6)

John of Forde's *Life of Wulfric* was an immediate success: three of four extant manuscripts were written within his own lifetime. By contrast John's *Commentary on the Song of Songs* did not achieve a wide circulation in England though its distinctive character is well worth noting. John followed the customary Cistercian interpretation of The Song, with Christ as Bridegroom and the individual soul as the Bride, but he also considered reading the text with the Virgin as the Bride. John was not in this respect a pioneer – a mariological interpretation had been suggested in the early twelfth century not only by Rupert of Deutz (*d.* 1129) but more importantly for England (where there is not much evidence that Rupert's work was known), by Honorius of Autun (d. *c.* 1140). Five twelfth-century manuscripts of Honorius's treatise are extant – three from Worcester, one from Evesham, and another from Malmesbury. The distribution is significant since the West Country was the home to Old English traditions and of a very pronounced cult of the Virgin. Worcester, Evesham, and Malmesbury were all dedicated to the Virgin with Evesham and Malmesbury producing two of the first collections of the Miracles of the Virgin. Such collections bear witness to the strength of devotion in the twelfth century to Mary and of the development of an affective piety focused on her and her son. Mary, Bride of the Church and Queen of Heaven, was seen now as having brought into the world a God who could be adored, approached, and cherished. Nowhere is this illustrated more vividly than in the *Life of Christina of Markyate.*

Christina of Markyate (*c.* 1096–*c.* 1156) had fled from an arranged marriage to become a hermit in a cell near St Albans; later she became the head of the small community which had gathered around her. Christina was never canonized and her *Life*, written by a monk of St Albans, remained unfinished. Nevertheless it is clear from its pages that Christina was regarded as a mystic – 'often whilst she was speaking she was rapt in ecstasy and saw things that the Holy Spirit showed her. At such times she felt and knew nothing of what was going on about her.'[15] Her story, right from the start is intimately linked with devotion to the Virgin and to the humanity of Christ. Before she was born, on a Saturday, 'a day specially set aside by the faithful for the devotion to the Mother of God . . . [sometime] between the Feasts of the Assumption and the Nativity of our Lady' her mother had had a sign that her child would be 'taught by the example and strengthened by the protection of Blessed Mary, ever a virgin' (p. 35). When she was a girl Christina's parents took her on a pilgrimage to St Albans. As a result of this visit Christina vowed herself to God and henceforth considered herself as married to Christ. Her sense of vocation ran counter to her parents' plans for her and in consequence they treated her very badly; on one occasion when her mother had been particularly brutal to her over her refusal to consummate her marriage, Christina had a vision of Mary, granted her by Christ 'who amidst all these trials wished to comfort his spouse, and gave her consolation through His Holy Mother' (p. 75). At last – and because Mary had given Christina's husband terrible nightmares – Christina was released from her marriage vows and given the opportunity of inheriting the hermitage where she had up to now been living in hiding. At this juncture, Christina had the first of two experiences which both merit quoting in full – the first for its sheer luminosity and the dazzling affirmation Christina receives:

> . . . a wonderful thing, more wonderful than any wonder, happened. For once when Christina was at prayer and was shedding tears through her longing for heaven, she was suddenly rapt above the clouds even to heaven, where she saw the queen of heaven sitting on a throne and angels in brightness seated about her. Their brightness exceeded that of the sun by as much as the radiance of the sun exceeds that of the stars. Yet the light of the angels could not be compared to the light which surrounded her who was the mother of the Most High. What think you then was the brightness of her countenance which outshone all the rest? Yet as she gazed first at the angels and then at the mistress of the angels, by some marvelous power she was better able to see through the splendour that encompassed the mistress than through that which shone about the angels, though the weakness of human sight finds brighter things harder to bear. She saw her countenance therefore more clearly than that of the angels;

and as she gazed upon her beauty the more fixedly and was the more filled
with delight as she gazed, the queen turned to one of the angels standing by
and said: 'Ask Christina what she wants, because I will give her whatever she
asks.'

(p. 111)

The second passage relates to a period when Christina had again been forced
into hiding and this time had been severely assailed by sexual temptations.
Finally, a vision sets her free:

> Then the Son of the Virgin looked kindly down upon the low estate of his
> handmaid and granted her the consolation of an unheard-of grace. For in
> the guise of a small child he came to the arms of his sorely tried spouse and
> remained with her a whole day, not only being felt but also seen. So the
> maiden took him in her hands, gave thanks, and pressed Him to her bosom.
> And with immeasurable delight she held him at one moment to her virginal
> breast, at another she felt his presence within her, even through the barrier
> of her flesh. Who shall describe the abounding sweetness with which the
> servant was filled by this condescension of her creator? From that moment
> the fire of lust was so completely extinguished that never afterwards could it
> be revived. (p. 119)

Throughout Christina's *Life* her love for God is described, as in this passage, in human terms. Christina had been encouraged as a child to imagine
God as 'good, beautiful and everywhere present' and in consequence had
talked to him 'on her bed at night, just as if she were speaking to a man
she could see' (p. 37). Near the end of the *Life* Christina and her nuns are
entranced by the appearance of a pilgrim with 'well-shaped features [and
a] handsome beard' (p. 185). This is Christ himself whom, unawares, they
entertain. Likewise, friendships with actual men bring Christina closer to
God. Thus the hermit Roger, with whom for a time she lived in hiding in
a spirit of 'holy affection' is said to have trained her in 'prayer and contemplative meditation...first by word, then by example...he taught her
things about heavenly secrets which are hardly credible, and acted as if
he were on earth only in body, whilst his whole mind was fixed on heaven'
(p. 105). Later, when she has herself become a spiritual mentor to her patron
Abbot Geoffrey of St Albans, Christina becomes anxious about the extent
of her love for Geoffrey, asking 'whether anyone can love another more
than himself at least in matters that pertain to the love of God' (p. 181).
In a vision she learns, and is then able to tell Geoffrey himself, 'among the
many edifying topics which they discussed together...that there was only
one thing in which a person should not place another before self, God's
love' (p. 183). It is hard to resist the conclusion that such 'edifying topics' included The Song of Songs. Although Christina's *Life* seems to have

only one verbal borrowing from The Song – it occurs in a passage describing the relationship between Geoffrey and Christina: 'He withdrew under the shadow of him whom lovers find, and when he grew cold in divine love, he was glad to realize that after speaking with her, he grew fervent' (p. 139) – this is nonetheless a telling reference. St Albans possessed a copy of Bede's *Commentary on the Song of Songs*, dated *c.* 1100–30, containing an illumination of the bride and groom that breaks new ground by portraying them as lovers about to kiss, rather than as stiffly regal. The conclusion is inescapable: in twelfth-century England the Cistercians held no monopoly on spiritual friendships and the paths they opened to the knowledge and love of God.[16]

Christina of Markyate together with Wulfric of Haselbury have at times been seen as examples of a 'native' tradition, an underclass, as C. H. Talbot saw it, anxious to preserve its own traditions in the face of the 'organised and disciplined forms of religious asceticism' introduced by the Normans (Talbot (ed.), *The Life of Christina of Markyate*, p. 12). The number of hermits with Anglo-Saxon names is indeed striking but closer examination of the spirituality of these hermits and of the patronage they received makes it seem that far from being quaint survivors of earlier traditions these hermits were on the contrary full players in the new religious world of the twelfth century. Certainly hostility between 'natives' and their new masters had existed but by the twelfth century stories abound which suggest that co-option and cooperation were by now recognized as mutually beneficial. Thus both Christina and Wulfric were well connected with influential Anglo-Norman abbeys whose protection they enjoyed and to whom they in turn gave considerable cachet. The same is true of those 'native' hermits and contemplatives from the north of England, Godric of Finchale and Bartholomew of Farne, both of whom were supported by the newly installed Benedictines of Durham. The possibility that the large number of 'native' hermits can be explained by the need for mediators and interpreters between Normans and natives is indeed well borne out in the case of Wulfric,[17] but we must allow also for the much wider context to which these holy men and women belonged. To focus on the particular circumstances of Anglo-Norman England risks overlooking the extent to which men, women and ideas could and did traverse local horizons. Both the spread across England of the new religious orders of Cistercians, Victorines, and Carthusians and the diffusion of particular texts bear witness to the international character of twelfth-century religious life: the immensely popular poem *Jesu dulcis memoria* (*Jesus the Memory is Sweet*), for many centuries attributed to St Bernard, now seems likely to have in fact been composed in England;[18] Christina's Psalter contains the story of St Alexis, the earliest surviving Old French literary text; Roger of

Forde (fl. *c.* 1182) on a trip abroad came across the visions of the German mystic Elizabeth of Schonau (1126–64), had a copy sent back home and asked for another to be made for his mother and her community. Even that most 'vernacular' of saints Godric (credited as he is with the first English song) before he settled at Finchale had been a much-travelled merchant and pilgrim to Jerusalem, Compostella, and Rome. Bearing all this in mind, let us look more closely now at Godric's *Life*, at the timbre of his devotional life and at the part played in it by the vernacular.

Godric's *Life* was written *c.* 1160 by Reginald of Durham. Anxious though Reginald is both to stress Godric's intimate connection with the past through his love for that great Northumbrian saint of the seventh century, Cuthbert, and to recall Godric's struggles with demons there is nonetheless much that is new about his portrayal. It may be worth bearing in mind that Reginald was urged to write the *Life* not only by Prior Thomas of Durham but also by Aelred of Rievaulx. Aelred's own background had points in common with Godric's – both men were of Anglo-Saxon parentage; both had served for a while in secular households and both were devoted to St Cuthbert. Certainly Godric, as Reginald portrays him, displays the kind of Christocentric piety that Aelred had advocated his sister the recluse should develop in her hermitage. When Godric meditates on the cross, as Aelred's sister is urged to do, his visions have a striking immediacy:

> One day when he was singing the Psalms, Godric saw the crucified Christ and the cross in his chapel both move, and after a short time he saw a small child emerge from the mouth of the crucified Christ, the limbs [coming out] little by little: and [this child] descended to the image of the blessed Virgin standing on the same beam of wood and came to rest on her breast. She reached out her hand towards him as he approached and embraced her and held him in her arms for almost three hours. Then the small child returned into the mouth of the crucified Christ, in the same way in which he had come, not walking or moving his feet but smoothly passing through an open space of air. For as long as the boy rested on his mother's breast he acted as if he were alive in the flesh. At his coming and again at his departure, the entire image of the Holy Virgin trembled so that it seemed at any moment about to fall from the beam.[19]

On another occasion:

> The form of the Lord Jesus on the Cross appeared. First it displayed the soles of the feet, marked with the wounds of the nails; next the fullest shape of the whole body, which showed its side with wounded hands, as, soaked in gore and blood, it poured forth streams of saving redemption.　　　(p. 222)

But perhaps most remarkable of all is Godric's vision of the Virgin and of Mary Magdalene. Godric is this time lying before the altar when two women appear whom he either does not or dares not recognize. At last the woman on his right speaks, revealing herself to be the Virgin – the 'Mother of Mercy' – and explaining to Godric that the woman on his left is Mary Magdalene. She promises Godric that together with Mary Magdalene she will be his patron and will succour him in any time of trouble. In response Godric commits himself to her care whereupon both women lay their hands on his head and an extraordinarily sweet smell fills the building. The Virgin then sings to Godric, teaching him the song as if she were instructing a child and telling him that he must sing it at any time he is in need of help. The song is in English:

> Saint Marye Virgine
> Moder Jesu Christes Nazarene,
> Onfo, schild, help thin Godric,
> Onfang, bring helyiclich with thee in Godes Rich

In later years Godric would often sing this song and would recall the visitation, remembering the gossamer-like nature of the women's clothing and how their appearance reminded him of the membrane contained within the shell of an egg.[20]

There is much here that looks forward to the mysticism of the fourteenth century: the song points to Richard Rolle [infra]; the 'membrane of the egg' to Julian of Norwich's comparison of the drops of blood that fell from Christ's crown of thorns with the 'herring scales'.[21] But what is above all noteworthy is that heaven is now speaking in the vernacular, not because Godric understood no Latin for we know that he did but because of God's own gift of tongues. God in twelfth-century England was well versed in the ever-changing vernaculars of his people, whether they were embryonic Middle English or Anglo-Norman. The freedom in turn to speak to God in languages other than Latin has sometimes been seen as particularly advantageous for those women who were to find themselves excluded from the new forms of higher education (in other words universities) that were developing in the late twelfth century but we should not ignore the appeal of the vernacular to men and women of all classes in their search for ways to articulate new forms of devotion. Godric apart, Wulfric of Haselbury, a hermit who frequently rubbed shoulders with the great, nonetheless 'in the intimate exchange of love...called the Lord God his lord in his native tongue' (*The Cistercian World*, p. 237). Aelred of Rievaulx, by any reckoning a figure of international standing, on his death-bed mixed English with Latin. His biographer recalled: 'We heard him say again and again "Hasten, hasten"; and often he drove the word home by calling on the name of Christ in English, a word of one syllable in this tongue and easier to utter and in some ways sweeter to hear. He would say, and I give his own words, "Hasten, *for crist luve*" . . .'[22]

For the use of Anglo-Norman in this new tradition we need look no further than the Barking *Life of Edward the Confessor* with which this chapter began. The Nun of Barking had based her work on Aelred of Rievaulx's *Life of Edward* but while Aelred's work had been written to serve a political purpose – to stress the legitimacy of Henry II's rule through Edward's canonization – the Nun of Barking was chiefly interested in Edward's spirituality. The contrast between the two prologues points up the difference. Whereas Aelred's work is dedicated to King Henry II in honour of Edward reigning now in heaven with God, the Nun of Barking dedicates hers to God himself with whom Edward is living now 'in perfect joy', enjoying as he does 'an abundance of great sweetness in the presence of the Creator'.[23] Contrasts continue in the scene where Edward persuades Edith that theirs is to be a chaste marriage. William MacBain has pointed out how the Nun of Barking has heightened the emotional tension of the scene and has drawn attention to the novelty of her vocabulary, in particular to her use of the concept of *fin' amor* that 'ultimate love' around which medieval romances will revolve.[24] 'Chastity', Edward tells Edith, is 'the Bride of Christ . . . he returns to her all the sweetness of her refined love (fin amur)' (*La Vie d'Édouard Le Confesseur*, p. 152 (ll. 1355–61)). The Nun of Barking deploys the concept of *fin' amor* again in the tale of the Evangelist and the ring Edward had once given him (thinking he was no more than a poor pilgrim). Edward's desire in this episode for spiritual knowledge can be seen as akin to the yearnings of a lover for his lady. '. . . [I]t is possible', concludes MacBain, 'that [the Nun of Barking] was the first northern writer to understand something of the special quality of *fin' amor*. In that event it may perhaps be time to abandon the debate concerning the alleged debt of *fin' amor* to religious mysticism, and investigate instead the debt of religious mysticism to the vocabulary, if not to the ethos, of *fin' amor*' (MacBain, 'Fin'Amour', p. 275).

If, as has sometimes been suggested, The Nun of Barking is to be identified with Clemence of Barking (*fl.* 1163–1200) then she is the author too of a *Life of St Catherine*, a complex text which draws from different discourses – hagiographical, courtly, theological.[25] Catherine from an early age has rejected all earthly lovers, devoting herself rather 'to an immortal lover whose love is chaste and pure and everlasting in its delight' (*Virgin Lives*, p. 5). Enter Maxentius, evil emperor and persecutor of Christians. Catherine attempts to convert him, claiming that his gods are worthless since they cannot 'hear, speak, see, feel or think' (p. 9). Her God, by contrast – and this becomes increasingly apparent as the story unfolds – does all these things. The love she bears Jesus is reciprocated:

...Jesus Christ, my bridegroom, so desires my love that the two of us have already made a covenant that I am his beloved and he is my lover. He is my renown and my honour; he is my glory and my worth. He is my pleasure and my comfort, my sweetness and my delight. I love him so much that I cannot be parted from him; for I love him alone, and him alone do I desire [and] ... he loves me in return. (p. 23)

Some hundred or more years after the writing of the *Life of Catherine* the Dominican John Tauler (*c.* 1300–61) would define mystical experience as being a sense of 'the presence of God in the spirit through the inner joy that is given to us by an entirely personal feeling of that presence'.[26] According to this definition, it would seem that both Barking *Lives* should be numbered among the mystical texts of the twelfth century. But would contemporaries have read them in this way? 'Mysticism' is not a word the twelfth century knew but a case can be made (as with Purgatory) for states to exist before nouns[27] and there can be no doubt that God's request for love rather than propitiation blew open new 'doors to heaven' (*La Vie d'Édouard Le Confesseur*, p. 178, (l. 2181)).

To see the twelfth century as a century of mysticism nonetheless flies against the classic description given by David Knowles in *The English Mystical Tradition* (1961). Here Knowles defines the twelfth century as a 'monastic world' (p. 43), for the most part lacking 'the personal touch, the urgency and the immediacy, that had characterised the instructions of the fathers of the desert' (p. 45), a world that stood in contrast to later centuries 'in which personal, individual problems and values are supreme, a world in which the kinds and degrees of love, divine and human, are matters of earnest debate...' (p. 43). Recent scholarship makes it difficult now to recognize Knowles's twelfth century but there is still much that needs to be done in order to combat the idea that England was somehow different from the Continent and likely therefore to be spared too much 'spiritual enthusiasm'. On the contrary 'spiritual enthusiasm' is precisely what the texts from twelfth-century England are all about. In one of his sermons Aelred tells a story about a nun he knew:

One day it happened that when she was devoting herself with love to private prayer, a sort of wondrous delight came over her, driving out all her mental functions, all her thought processes, and what is more, all the spiritual attachment she had for her friends. Her soul was then rapt up above herself, as if bidding farewell to all the world's burdens. Caught up by some ineffable and incomprehensible light, ... she began to know Christ himself – not as before, according to the flesh – but now not according to the flesh, for the Spirit had led her before the true face of Christ Jesus as he is in himself.[28]

This is just one story of many such, *for crist luve*, that Aelred might have told.

NOTES

I would like to thank Jane Bliss for introducing me to Anglo-Norman; Juliana Dresvina for last-minute help with my references; Brian McGuire for fruitful collaboration, and Timea Szell for her careful reading of my first draft.

1 Östen Södergård (ed.), *La vie d'Édouard le Confesseur: poème anglo-normand du XIIe siècle*, (Uppsala: Almqvist & Wiksells, 1948), pp. 204–5 (ll. 2993–4). I owe all the translations of this text to Jane Bliss.

2 For a recent edition and discussion of the text, see Peter Jackson, 'Osbert of Clare and the *Vision of Leofric*: the transformation of an Old English Narrative', in Katherine O'Brien O'Keefe and Andy Orchard (eds.), *Latin Learning and English Lore: Studies in Anglo-Saxon Literature for Michael Lapidge*, 2 vols. (Toronto and London: University of Toronto Press, 2005), II, pp. 275–92.

3 R. W. Southern, *Medieval Humanism and Other Studies* (Oxford: Blackwell, 1970), pp. 135–57, 158.

4 The translations used here of Goscelin's *Liber confortatorius* and his *Legend of Edith* come from Stephanie Hollis with W. R. Barnes, Rebecca Hayward, Kathleen Loncar, and Michael Wright (eds.), *Writing the Wilton Women: Goscelin's Legend of Edith and Liber Confortatorius* (Turnhout: Brepols, 2004). See also Monika Otter's translation: Goscelin of St Bertin, *The Book of Encouragement and Consolation (Liber Confortatorius), The Letter of Goscelin to the Recluse Eva* (Woodbridge: D. S. Brewer, 2004).

5 'The Vita of St Edith', in *Writing the Wilton Women*, p. 27. Latin original in: A. Wilmart, 'La légende de Ste Édith en prose et vers par le moine Goscelin', *Analecta Bollandiana* 56 (1938), 5–101, 265–307.

6 See Teresa Webber, 'The Diffusion of Augustine's Confessions in England During the Eleventh and Twelfth Centuries' in J. Blair and B. Golding (eds.), *The Cloister and the World: Essays presented to Barbara Harvey* (Oxford: Clarendon Press, 1996), pp. 29–45.

7 'Liber Confortatorius', in *Writing the Wilton Women*, pp. 194–5. C. H. Talbot, 'The Liber confortatorius of Goscelin of Saint Bertin', in M. M. Lebreton, J. Leclercq, and C. H. Talbot (eds.), *Analecta monastica*, ser. 3, *Studia Anselmiana* 37 (Rome: Pontifical Institute of St Anselm, 1955), pp. 106–7.

8 Thomas Arnold (ed.), Simeon of Durham, *Symeonis monachi opera omnia*, Rolls Series 75, vol. 1 (London, 1882), p. 299; quoted and discussed by Peter Dinzelbacher, 'The Beginnings of Mysticism experienced in Twelfth-Century England', in *MMTE* IV, p. 123.

9 C. Stephen Jaeger, *Ennobling Love: In Search of a Lost Sensibility* (Philadelphia: University of Pennsylvania Press, 1999).

10 Benedicta Ward (trans.), *The Prayers and Meditations of St Anselm* (Harmondsworth: Penguin, 1973), p. 9. Latin text: *PL*, 158. See in particular Thomas H. Bestul, 'St Anselm and the Monastic Community at Canterbury and Devotional Writing in Late Anglo-Saxon England', *Anselm Studies* 1 (1983), 185–98, and Anne Savage, 'The Place of Old English Poetry in the English Meditative Tradition', in *MMTE* IV, pp. 91–110.

11 Aelred of Rievaulx, *Treatises; the Pastoral Prayer* (Kalamazoo, MI: Cistercian Publications, 1982), p. 30. For Latin texts of Aelred, see Anselm Hoste and Charles H. Talbot (eds.), *Aelredi Rievallensis Opera Omnia* (Turnhout: Brepols, 1971).

12 Aelred of Rievaulx, *Spiritual Friendship* (Kalamazoo, MI: Cistercian Publications, 1974), p. 130.

13 Aelred of Rievaulx, *The Mirror of Charity* (Kalamazoo, MI: Cistercian Publications, 1990), pp. 70–1.

14 Pauline Matarasso (ed.), *The Cistercian World: Monastic Writings of the Twelfth Century* (Harmondsworth: Penguin, 1993), p. 236. Latin text: John, Abbot of Ford, Dom Maurice Bell (eds.), *Wulfric of Haselbury*, Somerset Record Society 47 (London, 1933).

15 C. H. Talbot (ed. and trans.), *The Life of Christina of Markyate, a Twelfth Century Recluse* (Oxford: Clarendon Press, 1959), p. 171. See now the revised translation of the *Life* by Samuel Fanous and Henrietta Leyser, Oxford World's Classics (Oxford: Oxford University Press, 2008).

16 For the illumination, see Paul Binski and Stella Panayotova (eds.), *The Cambridge Illuminations: Ten Centuries of Book Production* (London: Harvey Miller, 2005), No. 24, pp. 89–90.

17 For Wulfric as a 'hinge-man' between Normans and natives see Henry Mayr-Harting, 'Functions of a Twelfth-Century Recluse', *History* 60 (1975), 357–72.

18 André Wilmart, *Le 'Jubilus' dit de Saint Bernard: étude avec textes* (Roma: Edizioni di storia e letteratura, 1944), pp. 219–43.

19 Reginald of Durham, *Libellus de vita et miraculis sancti Godrici heremitae de Finchale*, ed. J. Stevenson, Surtees Society 20 (London: J. B. Nichols, 1847), p. 100.

20 For the story of the vision, see Reginald of Durham, *Libellus*, pp. 118–120. For the text of the song given here see R. T. Davies (ed.), *Medieval English Lyrics: A Critical Anthology* (London: Faber and Faber, 1963), p. 51. For a discussion of the musical notation of Godric's songs, see Helen Deeming, 'The Songs of Godric: A Neglected Context', *Music and Letters* 86 (2005), 169–85.

21 Julian of Norwich, *Revelations of Divine Love* (Harmondsworth: Penguin, 1998) p. 51 (Long Text, ch. 7).

22 F. M. Powicke (trans.), Walter Daniel, *The Life of Aelred of Rievaulx* (London: Nelson, 1950), pp. 59–60.

23 Aelred of Rievaulx, *Vita S. Edwardi regis*, PL 195, 738b. *La Vie d'Édouard Le Confesseur*, p. 110 (l. 42 and ll. 25–26). For this contrast, see Françoise Laurent, *Plaire et édifier: les récits hagiographiques composés en Angleterre aux XIIe et XIIIe siècles* (Paris: H. Champion, 1998), pp. 263–4.

24 William MacBain, 'Some Religious and Secular Uses of the Vocabulary of Fin'Amor in the Early Decades of the Northern French Narrative Poem', *French Forum* 13 (1988), 261–76.

25 *The Life of St Catherine* has been edited by William MacBain, ANTS 18 (1964). For the translation used here, see Jocelyn Wogan-Browne and Glyn Burgess (trans.), *Virgin Lives and Holy Deaths: Two Exemplary Biographies for Anglo-Norman Women* (London: Dent, 1996).

26 John Tauler, *Sermon XX.1*, quoted in Jean-Yves Lacoste, *Encyclopedia of Christian Theology* (New York; and London: Routledge, 2005), II, p. 1082.

27 For the debate on purgatory, see Jacques Le Goff, *La Naissance du Purgatoire* (Paris: Gallimard, 1981) and for a critique, R. W. Southern 'Between Heaven and Hell', *Times Literary Supplement*, 18 June 1981, pp. 651–2. For a more cautious approach than that adopted here, see John R. Sommerfeldt, 'The Vocabulary of Contemplation in Aelred of Rievaulx's *On Jesus at the Age of Twelve, A Rule of Life for a Recluse* and *On Spiritual Friendship*', in Rozanne Elder (ed.), *Heaven on Earth*, Studies in Medieval Cistercian History 9, Cistercian Studies 68 (Kalamazoo: Cistercian; Mowbray: Oxford, 1983), pp. 72–89.

28 Aelred of Rievaulx, *Sermo de Oneribus* 3, *PL* 195: 371a–b; translation from John R. Sommerfeldt, *Aelred of Rievaulx: Pursuing Perfect Happiness* (Mahwah, NJ: Newman Press, 2005), p. 136.

4

ALASTAIR MINNIS

1215–1349: culture and history

Lights, music, action:

> The greatest Roman noblemen, swathed in silk and purple, preceded [the
> pope] to the accompaniment of drum and chorus, strings and organ, and the
> resounding harmonies of trumpets, and an infinite multitude of clerics and
> people followed. . . . Uncounted lanterns, suspended on ropes throughout the
> streets and alleys, strove to make the brightness of that day succumb to the
> brilliance of their own light. The number of banners and pieces of purple cloth,
> which were unfolded on the houses and the high towers of the Romans, cannot
> be estimated at all.[1]

This vivid scene marked the beginning of the Fourth Lateran Council of
1215, a carefully-orchestrated event which was the crowning glory of Innocent III's pontificate (he died a year later). Unfortunately, the council did
not get off to a good start as far as the English Church was concerned,
since, just as the archbishop of Canterbury, Stephen Langton, was setting
off to attend it, his powers were suspended by Innocent's representatives, as
a punishment for his failure to publish the papal bull censuring England's
barons for forcing their king to assent to Magna Carta. However, Langton was able to return from exile to his See in 1218, when both Innocent
and John were dead.[2] And the zeal with which English clergymen sought
to implement the pope's decrees was undiminished. The bishops and abbots
who had attended the Council apparently brought back with them copies of
the decrees and reiterated those they deemed important in their own constitutions, for the purpose of correcting abuses and promoting reform in the
dioceses.

Here was a moment of hope and optimism, an occasion for reform and
renewal. In England, as in Western Christendom generally, 'a very different
church from that which preceded the council' was created.[3] But in 1349
these notes changed to tragic, as 'The Black Death' moved from mainland
Europe to ravage England.

> In the 23rd year of the reign of King Edward III, a great mortality of men advanced across the globe... Its destruction was so great that scarcely half mankind was left alive. Towns once packed with people were emptied of their inhabitants, and the plague spread so thickly that the living were hardly able to bury the dead. In some religious houses no more than two survived out of twenty. It was calculated by several people that barely a tenth of mankind remained alive... Much wretchedness followed these ills that afterwards the world could never return to its former state.[4]

So, then, a period which began with all the promise of 'the most important single body of disciplinary and reform legislation ever applied to the Medieval Church'[5] ended with the death and devastation brought by plague. The period also saw a shifting of the intellectual centre of gravity from the cathedral schools to the universities, the coming of the friars, the beginnings of a scholastic theological tradition in England, and the establishment of English as the dominant vernacular. There were crucial continuities as well. By 1215 the Cistercian order, an organization of reformed Benedictines which had St Bernard of Clairvaux (1090–1153) as its great father-figure, had united over five hundred abbeys across Europe, thus transforming 'a group of loosely-affiliated monasteries into an international organization';[6] it was upheld as a model of administrative efficiency in the Fourth Lateran Council. The order's distinctive 'affective theology' (whereby God is sought through intensive contemplation of Christ's suffering humanity), to which Aelred of Rievaulx (1109–66, abbot of Rievaulx in Yorkshire) had contributed so much, continued to exert an influence throughout the period under review in this chapter. Its cataphatic thrust and deployment of kinetic imagery are evident in, for example, the English anchoritic texts discussed in the following chapter. It was further stimulated by major trends in the friars' spirituality, particularly that of the Franciscans, and (paradoxically enough) by university study of 'the science of theology'. Here, then, was a highly eventful time, replete with significance for the development of English contemplative theology. After 1349, for good or ill, 'the world could never return to its former state'.

In Innocent III's opening remarks at the Fourth Lateran Council, two world-changing objectives were identified – recapturing Jerusalem and reforming the church. The former policy proved disastrous as the so-called Fifth Crusade ended in failure and ignominy; the latter had far-reaching and long-lasting consequences for medieval Christians in all walks of life. As F. Donald Logan says, the Council's 'decrees were to affect the way Christians lived their Christian lives for centuries to come' (*A History of the Church*, p. 195). However, it must be admitted that, despite the best efforts of reforming bishops, the implementation of the Council's decrees, in England as elsewhere, was patchy and only partially successful. Another major caveat which should be entered is that the element of innovation in the pastoral decrees was not necessarily substantial, as Leonard Boyle has warned: 'By and large the package of constitutions... simply summed up, on the one hand, some local practices which had proven themselves in various parts of Europe and, on the other, some of the theological and legal advances of the renaissance of the twelfth century'.[7] The symptomatic nature of Innocent's great enterprise should therefore be acknowledged; here we may find clear indications of ways in which the Church had been moving for at least a century. It cannot be doubted, however, that the Council lent a major impetus to certain developments – and, according to Boyle's eloquent account, enabled the *cura animarum* (the cure of souls) to 'come into its own for the first time ever'. Parish priests and their parishioners were given 'an identity and a self-awareness, and an honorable, recognized place in the church at large' (p. 31).

Whatever the truth of that claim may be, it is indubitable that by far the largest group of Lateran canons is concerned with reforming the organization of the Church, improving the calibre of its clergymen, and getting layfolk to participate more fully and more comprehendingly in its rites. Innocent was obviously keen on conferences. Reiterating previous legislation, canon 6 asserts that provincial synods should be held once a year. Moreover, every three years, a general chapter of abbots and priors should be convened (canon 12).[8] Given that this inaugurated a new arrangement, the Cistercians ('among whom the celebration of such chapters is of long standing')[9] were to be invited to provide guidance. The founding of new religious orders was forbidden, new monasteries being obliged to use a pre-existing rule (canon 13). Bishops were charged with carefully overseeing prelatical elections, and to satisfy themselves that the best candidate got the job (canon 26). Their responsibility of ensuring that the Word of God is preached sufficiently and properly is also emphasized. If they themselves are unable to do that job, bishops should appoint suitable men to do it for them (canon 10). Furthermore, if in a certain city or diocese there live Christian people who speak different languages, then the local bishop is obliged to provide suitable priests – i.e. with the necessary linguistic skills – to administer to them (canon 9).

The 'office of preacher' is assiduously defended. Those who dare to preach without papal authority or without the approval of their local bishop are to be excommunicated, declares canon 3. This canon encouraged intensive analysis of what exactly the *officium praedicatoris* entailed. A quite extraordinary number of theological 'questions' on the subject were pro-duced throughout the thirteenth century,[10] appearing in quodlibets and in commentaries on Peter Lombard's *Sentences* (established in the 1230s at the University of Paris as the fundamental theological textbook; English universities followed suit, with the practice being established in Oxford in the 1240s). Three major areas of inquiry were defined, all very much in the spirit of the Council's reformist programme. First, there was the necessity of authority; i.e. preachers must be properly authorized and licensed. Secondly, preachers must possess not only the theological knowledge but also the pro-fessional skills necessary for preaching – a recognition which spawned the genre of *ars praedicandi* (the art of preaching). No fewer than seven impres-sive examples were produced by Englishmen in the period covered by this chapter (John of Wales, Alexander of Ashby, Thomas of Chobham, Robert of Basevorn, Ralph Higden, Richard of Thetford, and Thomas Waleys); an eighth was written in the fifteenth century by Simon Alcock. Last, but certainly not least, the preacher's requisite 'conditions' (*conditiones*, i.e. his personal characteristics and moral state) came in for detailed scrutiny. The Lateran fathers were particularly anxious that the priest who performed this high office should practise what he preached. Hence their demand that bishops should promote to sacred orders 'only such as are qualified to dis-charge worthily the duties of the office committed to them' (canon 26). The 'excesses' of deficient clergymen already holding office should be corrected, their morals reformed (canon 7). Clerics are urged 'to live chastely and vir-tuously', so that they 'may perform their duties with a pure heart and chaste body'. Any incontinent priest who, having been suspended from his duties on account of that sin, nevertheless dares to 'celebrate the divine mysteries', is to be deprived of his ecclesiastical benefices forever (canon 14). Decorous dress must be worn; hunting, fowling, watching theatrical performances, and gambling are prohibited. Clerics should neither hold secular offices nor engage in secular pursuits. The frequenting of taverns is particularly frowned upon – an exception being made if one has to lodge there while on a journey. Drunkenness should be eschewed, particularly because it 'banishes reason and incites to lust'; competitions to see who can drink the most are singled out for special censure.

Such anxiety to control the behaviour of clerics extends to another group of individuals, who performed a relatively lowly ecclesiastical function which did not require clerical status – the *quaestores* or seekers after alms, other-wise known as pardoners. It was their task to 'publish' (announce to the public) and dispense indulgences. And Innocent was anxious to ensure that men of the right calibre were recruited. 'Those who are assigned to collect alms must be upright and discreet, must not seek lodging for the night in taverns or in other unbecoming places, nor incur useless and extravagant expenses'; furthermore, they should not wear religious habits to which they have no right (canon 62). Unfortunately, the canon adds, some of their number 'misrepresent themselves', and 'preach abuses' – from other sources we know that *quaestores* sometimes offered absolution from sin in ways that went far beyond their legal remit. These functionaries were not alone in exceeding their powers; their superiors, those responsible for issuing the pardons in the first place, had on occasion granted 'indiscreet and super-fluous indulgences' which offered inappropriately large amounts of remission from purgatorial punishment. Canon 62 chastises those prelates and seeks to impose decorous limits on the amount of remission that may be promised.

It also warns priests against admitting pardoners, or those who claim to be such, to their churches 'unless they exhibit genuine letters either of the Apostolic See or of the diocesan bishop'. Once they pass this security-check, 'they may not preach anything to the people but what is contained in those letters', i.e. confine themselves to announcing the terms of reference of their indulgences and commending them to the public. The emphasis placed on checking the pardoners' credentials indicates an acute awareness of fraud – there were plenty of fake pardoners around, bearing forged documents.[11] Another fraudulent practice addressed in canon 62 is the display of fake relics. Prelates should see to it that people who come to church to venerate relics 'should not be deceived by worthless fabrications or false documents [i.e. documents supposedly authenticating the relics] as has been done in many places for the sake of gain'. Moreover, 'old relics may not be exhibited outside of a vessel [i.e. outside reliquaries] or exposed for sale. And let no-one presume to venerate publicly new ones unless they have been approved by the Roman pontiff'. However, abuses relating to indulgences and relics continued right up until the time of the Protestant Reformation (and indeed constituted one of the precipitating causes of that movement), being harshly satirized in the late fourteenth century by William Langland and Geoffrey Chaucer and, in the sixteenth century, by the playwright John Heywood.

Another group of Lateran canons is concerned with education, of both the clergy and layfolk. Toughening up a decree of the Third Lateran Council, canon 11 orders that not only in every cathedral church but also in every other church which can afford it, there should be a master who shall instruct the clerics of those and other churches, at no cost to them, 'in the art of grammar and in other branches of knowledge'. Furthermore, the metropolitan church should appoint a theologian to instruct priests in sacred Scriptures and especially in those things pertaining to the cure of souls. Educational issues are also raised by the famous canon 21 (*Omnis utriusque sexus*), which decrees that 'all the faithful of both sexes' who have reached the age of discretion should 'faithfully confess all their sins at least once a year to their own (parish) priest and perform to the best of their ability the penance imposed, receiving reverently at least at Easter the sacrament of the Eucharist . . . '. (In this case, as Alexander Murray has cogently argued, the Lateran decree was giving 'universal stamp to a duty' of annual confession which 'anyone acquainted with theology' was 'well aware of'; 'it confirmed an existing momentum'.)[12] The obvious implication is that the clergy should be well prepared to give lay folk adequate instruction in these matters, and that layfolk themselves should seek education in the mysteries of their faith, so they could participate in them successfully and to their own spiritual advantage.

The relationship between clerical competence and penitential self-consciousness is well brought out by one of the most significant English canons to have been inspired by *Omnis utriusque sexus*, namely Archbishop John Pecham's *Ignorantia sacerdotum* (*The Ignorance of Priests*), canon 9 of the 1281 Lambeth Council.[13] The ignorance of priests is castigated as casting 'the people headlong into the pit of error'; such 'folly and stupidity' means that the faithful can be led 'more to error than to sound teaching'. It is essential that 'sound teaching' be provided; thus Pecham commands that 'every priest with the care of souls shall four times each year . . . on one solemn day or several, either personally or by another, instruct the people using simple English' (Logan, *A History of the Church*, p. 200). A list of the requisite topics is then given – the Fourteen Articles of Faith, the Ten Commandments, the Seven Works of Mercy, the Seven Deadly Sins, and so forth. Here, then, is a recipe for the ideal priest's handbook. It reflects a trend in textual production already well developed by Pecham's time – and indeed, even before the Lateran Council. Staying with the English scene, one may cite as an excellent example Robert Grosseteste's highly popular *Templum Dei* (*The Temple of God*), which has as its central image a temple with faith as its foundation, hope as its walls, and love as its roof. This elaborately structured work is equipped with enough diagrams and tables to guide even the dimmest of priests through the processes of confession.[14] Although written in Latin, its material was meant to be taught in the vernacular, whether Anglo-Norman or English. The fact that *Ignorantia sacerdotum* specifies instruction in English indicates the fact that, by 1281, this was the dominant vernacular. For Grosseteste, writing several decades earlier,[15] Anglo-Norman seemed the better bet, for this was the language in which he penned a didactic poem of some 1770 lines, now generally known as the *Château d'amour*.

> We all are in need of assistance, and many will never be able to know the languages of Hebrew, Greek, or Latin in order to praise their Creator. . . . So that each in his own language might truly know his God and his redemption, I begin my account in French for those who have no acquaintance with learning or Latin.　　　(Mackie, 'Grosseteste's Anglo-Norman Treatise', p. 160)

R. W. Southern envisaged this poem being read aloud in aristocratic households.[16] More recently, Maura O'Carroll has suggested that, in producing it, Grosseteste may have been performing one of his duties as lector to the Oxford Franciscan community. We know from Thomas of Eccleston, chronicler of the early years of the Franciscans in England, that its first recruits included laymen and 'not a few knights'; here, perhaps, is the audience that Grosseteste was trying to reach (Mackie, 'Grosseteste's Anglo-Norman Treatise', pp. 155–6). At any rate, the *Château d'amour* offers a cogent (and at some points quite lively) account of salvation history for those lacking any formal theological training.

A few years after Grosseteste's death in 1253, a new wave of penitential *pastoralia* gained momentum. Penitential instruction was not just a matter of telling people how to confess properly; given the emphasis now being laid on true contrition, sinners had to do no less than 'build up the self', develop 'cleanness of heart' (as Boyle nicely puts it; 'The Fourth Lateran Council', pp. 34–5). And for most layfolk and no doubt for many clergymen also, that degree of intimate instruction, and the construction of self-knowledge that came with it, could only be attained by means of the vernacular. This helps to explain, for example, the profusion of translations and adaptations, in both Anglo-Norman and Middle English, of treatises like Guillaume Peyraut's *Summa de vitiis et virtutibus* (before 1250) and Laurent of Orléans' *Somme le roi* (1280): particularly noteworthy are William of Waddington's *Manuel des péchés* (c. 1260), Pierre d'Abernon of Fetcham's *Lumière as lais* (1267), Robert Mannyng of Brunne's *Handlyng Synne* (1303), the *Ayenbite of Inwit* (1340), and the *Speculum vitae* (*The Mirror of Life*) attributed to William of Nassington, who died in 1359. In such literature Boyle has detected a movement away from the virtues seen 'more as a means of combating vices than as things to be cultivated for themselves and in their own right'; subsequently the theme of 'the fostering of virtues' comes to dominate, the manifestations of which reach far beyond the above-mentioned *pastoralia* – to encompass, indeed, 'the remarkable flowering of spirituality and mysticism and expressions thereof, largely vernacular, in poetry and prose in the latter part of the thirteenth century and in the whole of the fourteenth'.

In England, as in Europe generally, this 'remarkable flowering' would have been impossible without crucial developments in higher education that resulted in a general raising of standards in the training of the country's intellectual elite. The origins of Oxford University go back to the twelfth century, from which period we have fragmentary evidence for the teaching of arts, theology, and law both civil and canon, by independent masters. The 1190s, however, seem to have been a period of rapid development, this being the era of Alexander Nequam, John Blund, and Edmund of Abingdon. A major setback occurred in 1209, when a suspension of studies and a student diaspora resulted from a bitter dispute between town and gown over who had legal jurisdiction over members of the university (who, as clerics, answered to ecclesiastical rather than civil authority). Some students fled to Cambridge, where (according to a tradition of long standing) their presence contributed to the founding of a university there; however, the patronage of the bishops of Ely, and the availability of teachers from nearby church institutions, were probably more crucial factors. What is perfectly clear is that the first Cambridge college, Peterhouse, was founded by Hugh Balsham, bishop of Ely, in 1284. Oxford's difficulties were settled by a papal decree of 1214, which made the town an attractive place for scholars once again, by promising them immunity from outside interference. From this date onwards the university thrived. During a fifty-year period between c. 1220 and 1270 the Friars arrived in Oxford – the Dominicans in 1221 and the Franciscans in 1224; they were soon followed by the Carmelites and Augustinians. The fact that the new orders of friars took to university life like the proverbial ducks to water – Thomas Eccleston claimed that, by 1254, the Franciscan school at Oxford had produced thirty licensed teachers together with some 'who taught without disputations'[17] – contributed hugely to the success of the new institutions.

Not everyone stood the course, however; the mystic Richard Rolle (d. 1349) left Oxford without taking a degree. But this may well have been due to a lack of funding rather than a conviction that the life of perfection could better be followed outside the lecture hall. Rolle's university training in hermeneutics certainly stood him in good stead; it can be seen in action in his Latin commentaries on Psalm 20, the first verses of the Song of Songs, and the Apocalypse, and also in his Middle English Psalter, which deploys glosses from Peter Lombard's commentary on the psalms.[18] The simplistic notion that, in the period under discussion here, a university training in theology was in some fundamental way antithetical to the contemplative life, is not to be entertained. In English universities, as at Paris, scholars debated the nature of the 'science' of theology, asking whether it was fundamentally 'affective' (i.e. appealed primarily to the *affectus* or disposition) or 'intellectual' (i.e. appealed primarily to the *intellectus*).[19] Many found in favour of the *affectus*, and even those (largely Dominican followers of St Thomas Aquinas, *c.* 1225–74) who preferred to champion the *intellectus* freely admitted that theology definitely had *some* 'affective' qualities. At the same time, some university-trained theologians were writing, for a wider audience, texts of 'affective piety', works that encouraged intense imaginative engagement with scenes from the Bible and saints' lives; thereby the human emotions were enlisted in the service of spiritual growth. The Franciscans in particular were interested in producing this kind of literature, one of the most popular instances being the *Meditationes vitae Christi* (*Meditations on the Life of Christ*), long attributed to the great Parisian theologian St. Bonaventure (*c.* 1217–74) but now believed to be the work of a lesser light, Johannes de Caulibus, OFM. A particularly sophisticated example produced by an English Black Friar is the 'Love Rune' of Thomas of Hales (discussed in the following chapter), which uses the vernacular discourse of secular love-poetry to direct a religious woman's longing towards God.[20] Thomas was an acquaintance of Adam Marsh, OFM (d. 1259), the first Franciscan regent at Oxford; Marsh was a friend (and had been the student) of Robert Grosseteste. And for Grosseteste, love (*amor*) is the superior function of the human mind, a belief which underpins his translation and exegesis of the 'negative' contemplative theology of Pseudo-Dionysius the Areopagite – supposedly the philosopher whose conversion by St Paul is recorded in Acts 17:34, but actually a Neoplatonic Monophysite who flourished *c.* 500.

Here Grosseteste stands square with the (more widely known) Dionysian scholarship of his French contemporary, Thomas Gallus, abbot of St Andrews, Vercelli (d. 1246).[21] James McEvoy, the most eloquent modern interpreter of Grosseteste's *via negativa*, is anxious to ensure that Grosseteste and Gallus should share the credit for the doctrine that downgrades the powers of the human reason and elevates the *principalis affectus* (Gallus's term) or *amor* (Grosseteste's term) as the supra-intellectual means by which the soul achieves union with God – a doctrine which had an 'immense influence... upon the history of Western mysticism till the close of the Middle Ages, and even beyond that'.[22] However, despite the superiority of Grosseteste's translations (he studied Pseudo-Dionysius in the Greek and thoroughly compared three previous Latin versions), it was Gallus who influenced those masterpieces of mysticism, the *Itinerarium mentis in deum* (*The Mind's Road to God*) of St. Bonaventure, the *Viae Sion lugent* (*The Ways of Sion Mourn*) which the Carthusian Hugh of Balma wrote probably between 1230 and 1290, and Middle English works by the author of the *Cloud of Unknowing*, including the *Cloud* itself (on which see ch. 7 below).

Indeed, it has been argued that the *Viae Sion lugent* directly influenced the *Cloud*[23] – a case which is difficult if not impossible to prove, given Hugh of Balma's use of Thomas Gallus. What we could be dealing with are the parallels which inevitably result from the independent use by two authors of one and the same source.[24]

Whatever the truth of that matter, the crucial point remains: scholarship on one of the most important late-medieval sources of contemplative theology, the Pseudo-Dionsyian corpus, found a home in the emergent universities. The legacy of the great Victorine exegetes of that corpus, Hugh and Richard, was nurtured in the later European schools, and many of the greatest minds of the time – including Alexander of Hales, Albert the Great, Thomas Aquinas, Bonaventure, Ulrich of Strasbourg, and Henry of Ghent – were profoundly influenced by 'Saint Denis'. Such scholarship found an English audience, and English thinkers made a substantial contribution to it.

Among the many matters which the first Oxford masters of theology[25] discussed – and one of particular import for female mystics – was the question, can women be ordained as priests? The answer was, predictably enough, in the negative. Thus in the *Sentences* commentary which he produced in the period 1240–5 (the first by a Dominican at Oxford), Richard Fishacre insisted that the 'masculine sex' was essential for the reception of the sacrament of ordination, 'and it follows from this that a woman is incapable of receiving orders'.[26] If anyone attempted to ordain a woman, Fishacre continues, this simply would not work; the imprint or *character* of the sacrament cannot be impressed on the female body. Canon law is quoted as prohibiting women from touching sacred vessels or linens, and from teaching in a male assembly. Further, 'abbesses are not able to preach, or bless, or to communicate or to absolve, or to give penances, or to judge, or to exercise the office of any order'. But what of those 'deaconnesses' who are known to have existed in the early church? They were simply nuns who were allowed to read out a homily at Matins, Fishacre explains. And the title *presbyterae* did not designate female clergy, but rather the wives of priests (in the days when clerical marriage was possible) or widows who performed a quite menial role as the caretakers of churches. In fact, these arguments are highly dubious; there is some evidence, for instance, that in the tenth century women functioned as deaconesses, whether as the spouses of deacons or in their own right.[27] But Fishacre, along with the canonists he is quoting, will have none of this; their objective is to undermine and refute any historical precedents for female ordination. If Christ had wanted women priests, Fishacre continues, surely he would have ordained the Blessed Virgin. In fact, He did not give his mother the 'power of the keys', even though 'she was more excellent than the Apostles'. The inference is clear – no ordinary woman can possibly hope for what the most perfect of all women was denied.

This discussion may be taken as part of a process, powered by the Gregorian Reform movement of the eleventh and twelfth centuries and consolidated by successive Church councils, wherein the clergy was distinguished more sharply from the laity than hitherto. (One may recall the Fourth Lateran Council's clear sense of the parameters of the *officium praedicatoris*, as discussed above, with which may be compared its emphasis on the priest 'who has been duly ordained in accordance with the keys of the Church' as uniquely empowered to confect the Eucharist (canon 1). This process is here called 'transubstantiation' – an attempt to draw a line under centuries of debate on the issue, which is consonant with the empowerment of the priest as the sole minister of this great mystery.) One consequence was a narrowing of the concept of ecclesiastical 'ordination', with the privileges of women within the western Christian Church being reduced. Up until the end of the twelfth century, 'abbots, abbesses, deaconesses, nuns, monks, emperors empresses, kings and queens' were considered sacramentally ordained, just as were priests, despite the obvious differences in function and role.[28] After that time came the firm imposition of a (re-)definition which confined sacramental ordination to the priesthood and the deaconate. Not everyone was willing to move with the times. Peter Abelard eloquently made the case that present-day abbesses were the direct successors of deaconesses, and hence could claim the privileges of the diaconate.[29] He had history on his side, given the abundant evidence that, in the early Middle Ages, abbesses heard nun's confessions, imposed penances, read from the Gospels, gave blessings to layfolk, and in effect preached. But this history was being erased, and a new one constructed, the outline of which we see in Fishacre's excursus.

Fishacre's refutation of the idea of female ministry was apparently an innovation in a *Sentences* commentary. After *c.* 1250, however, a substantial number of theologians felt obliged to pronounce on the matter, including two of Fishacre's Dominican successors at Oxford, Simon of Hinton (whose lectures may be dated to the late 1240s) and William Rothwell (writing *c.* 1255). However, the most comprehensive treatments were produced by Parisian masters, or at least by masters who spent a substantial amount of time at Paris, studying and teaching, namely Thomas Aquinas, Bonaventure, Henry of Ghent, and John Duns Scotus (who also lectured on the relevant part of the *Sentences* at Oxford in 1304).[30] Two distinctions frequently drawn in this literature are of crucial importance: one between the divine gift of prophecy and the sacrament of ordination, and another between 'public' and 'private' teaching. Thomas Aquinas will be our guide to the first one (Aquinas, *Summa theologiae* (*The Sum of Theology*),

2a 2ae, qu. 177, art. 2). Noting the presence of prophetesses in both the Old and New Testaments (Huldah, Deborah, and the four daughters of Philip mentioned in Acts 21:9), Aquinas concludes that women may indeed receive the gift of wise and 'scientific' (i.e. knowledgeable) speech. However, being a wise prophetess, enjoying direct communication with the divine, does not give a woman the right to preach in church. (One may recall here Richard Fishacre's comment on the Virgin Mary: the fact that she was the most perfect of all women did not mean that she was ordained. Neither had she the specific authority which is necessary to perform those functions exercised by ordained clergymen.) As far as the reception of divine revelation is concerned, there is no impediment of sex; the minds of both men and women may be inspired without hindrance. But in the case of the instruction of persons, bodies *do* matter. Teaching in church must be done by superiors and not by inferiors, Aquinas declares; since women are the inferior sex, they cannot occupy such a position of pedagogic authority. Moreover, women's speech would lead men into lecherous thoughts (cf. Ecclesiasticus 9:11). This rules out women teaching an audience of men, or a mixed audience which includes men. It is true that at Proverbs 4:3–4 Solomon says that he was taught by his mother. But that, Aquinas concludes, is a case of private teaching, whereby a mother teaches her son, and hence is quite permissible.

This brings us to our second crucial distinction, between the two kinds of teaching. Wise and knowledgeable 'speech may be employed in two ways', explains Aquinas. First, one may speak 'privately (*private*), to one or a few people, in familiar conversation (*familiariter colloquendo*)'. Women are allowed to do this. Secondly, one may speak 'publicly (*publice*)', as 'when addressing the whole church, and this is not permitted to women'. In his application of this distinction, Henry of Ghent claims that the female prophets referred to in the Bible were given their gift for private rather than public instruction. Public preaching or teaching by women, he emphasizes, is acceptable only in special cases. It was granted that Martha and Mary Magdalen should preach, and that Philip's daughters should prophesy publicly. But this, in Henry's view, was due to a shortage of skilled labour in the early days of the church: since there were many harvests (of converts) to be made and a small number of labourers (cf. Luke 10:2) the aid of women was necessary. The clear implication is that, when there are enough men to do the job, the assistance of women should be dispensed with. It cannot be assumed that those Biblical figures provide role-models for contemporary women.

Given such discourse, it is evident why Julian of Norwich was careful to assert that she was not setting herself up as a teacher, but rather conveying the truth she had received from Christ the Teacher (here appealing to the 'prophecy justification' of uttering wise and knowledgeable speech), and why Margery Kempe should declare, 'I preche not, ser; I come in no pulpytt. I use but comownycacyon and good wordys.'[31] On this occasion Margery did well to tell the archbishop of York and his familiars what they wanted to hear. Current in her day was the belief that Lollard women priests (followers of the arch-heresiarch or proto-Protestant – depending on one's point of view – John Wyclif, c. 1330–84), were actually preaching to mixed audiences of men and women, and even daring to consecrate the sacraments. This was largely a paranoid fantasy, as Margaret Aston's study has made quite clear.[32] But such creatures lived at least in the minds of some of Wyclif's supporters and opponents. Wyclif himself briefly entertained the possibility of women priests in a (highly polemical and somewhat inconsequential) discussion in his *De potestate pape* (*On the Power of the Pope*),[33] and his ideas were developed by at least two of his followers, John Purvey and Walter Brut. A series of *quaestiones* against female preaching and confection of the Eucharist was compiled, presumably by the theologians who had been enlisted by John Trefnant, bishop of Hereford, in his proceedings against Brut (in 1391–3).[34] They drew heavily on the refutations of women priests which had been devised a hundred years previously by Aquinas and Henry of Ghent.

To return to that previous time: Richard Fishacre may well have been the first *Sentences* commentator to treat of the ordination of women, but, generally speaking, in the later thirteenth century no English educational institution rivalled the University of Paris for distinction in theology. The case altered dramatically in the early fourteenth century. Then Richard de Bury, bishop of Durham (d. 1345), could boast, with some justification, that 'admirable Minerva . . . has passed by Paris, and now has happily come to Britain'.[35] The Dominican Nicholas Trevet was regent master in Oxford from 1303 to 1307 – an exceptional scholar who was equally at home with King Alfred's Anglo-Saxon translation of Boethius's *The Consolation of Philosophy* (one of the sources of his highly popular exegesis of that text) as he was with the tragedies of Seneca (on which he was to produce the first extensive commentary). His younger contemporaries, the Dominicans Robert Holcot, Thomas Waleys, and Thomas Ringstead, together with the Franciscan John Ridevall, put their classical learning to different use, in Biblical exegesis replete with 'poetic pictures' which enlisted antique (and pseudo-antique) imagery in the service of Christian truth. This was also the time of the great logicians Walter Burley (c. 1274/5–1344) and William of Ockham OFM (c. 1285–1347), the 'Merton School' of brilliant physicists and mathematicians,[36] and Thomas Bradwardine (who died in 1349, shortly after having been appointed archbishop of Canterbury), whose attacks on what he saw as a dangerous revival of Pelagianism led him into a theory of future contingents which has the appearance of strict determinism. Geoffrey Chaucer was to cite 'Bisshop Bradwardyn' alongside 'the hooly doctour Augustyn' as thinkers who had thoroughly separated out the valid from the invalid arguments concerning necessity, divine foreknowledge, and the freedom of the will (*Canterbury Tales*; Nun's Priest's Tale, VII. 3240–50). Given Bradwardine's Neo-Augustinian theology, Chaucer's coupling is a shrewd one.

Even from this brief sketch, it should be evident that the new orders of friars continued to contribute substantially to the universities as centres of learning. Their participation was not always valued, however. In the second half of the thirteenth century a major power struggle erupted within the University of Paris between the mendicants and the secular clergy. Having first supported the friars, Pope Innocent IV proceeded to take away their privileges. Alexander IV suspended his predecessor's rulings and, in his bull *Quasi lignum vitae* (1255), annulled the university statutes which were detrimental to the mendicants' interests. The university initially refused to accept this solution, and matters became even more heated due to the popularity of William of St Amour's treatise *De periculis novissimorum temporum* (*On the Perils of the Most Recent Times*). Published in 1256, this heaped ridicule on the friars (through a listing of thirty-nine 'signs' by which 'false Apostles' might be known) and attacked the principle of mendicancy as savouring of Antichrist rather than of Christ. The friars counterattacked, with plangent defences of their position being produced by such formidable thinkers as Thomas Aquinas and Bonaventure. The Franciscan John Pecham (whose reformist agenda as archbishop of Canterbury we mentioned above) contributed a treatise *De perfectione evangelica* (*Concerning Evangelical Perfection*) to the controversy. But, generally speaking, attitudes were far less bitter in England than in France – despite the fact that the Dominicans ruffled feathers by seeking recognition in Oxford for the privileges they were enjoying in Paris, a matter substantially settled in 1314–16. The situation deteriorated when Richard FitzRalph (*c.* 1300–60), who had served as chancellor of Oxford University during the period 1332–4 and was consecrated archbishop of Armagh in 1346, devoted the last years of his life to turning himself into, so to speak, the British equivalent of William of St Amour. FitzRalph's *De pauperie salvatoris* (*On the Poverty of the Saviour*; 1356) argued that Christ had neither lived nor advocated a life of voluntary begging, thereby rejecting the mendicants' claim that they were following in the Saviour's footsteps, while his 1357 sermon *Defensio curatorum* (*The*

Defence of the Curates; dubbed 'the most influential piece of anti-mendicant polemic published during the later Middle Ages') mounted a thorough-going attack on the friars' pastoral privileges – going dangerously close to implying, as Katherine Walsh puts it, that 'the power to bind and loose, and therefore to absolve, was greater in a secular priest than in a friar authorized by the papacy'.[37] The harsh words of 'Armachanus' were long remembered.

> Of thes Frer Mynours me thenkes moch wonder,
> That waxen are thus hauteyn, that som tyme weren under.
> Among men of Holy Chirch thai maken mochel blonder . . .
>
> . . .
>
> With an O and an I, one sayd ful still,
> Armachan distroy ham, if it is Goddes will. . . .[38]

Wyclif and his followers quoted FitzRalph with great respect, on account of not only his antimendicant views but also his biblical literalism and theory of dominion, designating him as 'Saint Richard'.

All of these squabbles pale into relative insignificance when we consider the horrors which the Black Death inflicted on the English church – or, at least, on certain English churchmen. Many prominent figures died of the plague. In 1349 Robert Holcot and Thomas Bradwardine, opponents in theological debate, were united in death; Richard Rolle perished in the same year. The chronicler Henry Knighton follows his obituary for Bradwardine with the general statement that 'At that time there was such a great short-age of priests everywhere that many churches were widowed and lacked the divine offices, matins, vespers, and the sacraments and sacramentals.' Whereas previously there had been a 'glut' of chaplains and priests, now there was an acute shortage (trans. Horrox, *Black Death*, pp. 78–9). In sim-ilar vein, in 1349 Ralph of Shrewsbury, bishop of Bath and Wells, spoke of how the plague had 'left many parish churches and other benefices' in the 'diocese without an incumbent, so that their inhabitants are bereft of a priest', and therefore 'many people are dying without the sacrament of penance' (p. 271).

However, and I hope without sounding in any way dismissive of such terrible suffering, it may be argued that, considered as an institution, the English Church proved remarkably robust and resilient. Let us consider Shrewsbury's statement in more detail. Because of the emergency caused by the abovementioned lack of priests, he orders his clergy to publicize the fact that, in these extreme situations, confession to a layman, 'even to a woman if a man is not available', is perfectly valid. 'Confession made in this way to a lay person can be wholesome and of great benefit to them for the remission of their sins' (pp. 271–2). Can we find here a dangerous breakdown of orthodox church practice, which presaged the subsequent turning-away from the ordained clergy that characterized the age of Wyclif, when the Lollards adumbrated a doctrine of the priesthood of all believers? Christopher Harper-Bill makes the point quite acutely: 'a Catholic bishop had authorized a practice the advocacy of which half a century later would be regarded as one of the more obnoxious tenets of the Lollard heretics'.[39] Here one may recall the arguments of the abovementioned Walter Brut, to the effect that layfolk, including women, can – at least in certain circumstances – perform all the sacraments, including the sacrament of the altar. On the other hand, it may be emphasized that there is nothing theologically dubious or subversive about the bishop's decree. Confession to a layman in an emergency situation had long been deemed a permissible course of action; for instance, this doctrine is included in that theological textbook *par excellence*, Peter Lombard's *Sentences*. Further, it should be noted that Shrewsbury goes on to say that 'all those who confess their sins to a lay person in an emergency, and then recover, should confess the same sins again to their own parish priest'. That doctrine also is to be found in the Lombard's *Sentences*. So, then, it is probably imprudent to find in the bishop's words an undermining of the power of the priesthood and a foretaste of Lollardy. Harper-Bill's statistical analysis of ordination levels in the period leads to what he confidently terms an 'obvious' conclusion: 'the initial impact of the Black Death did not cause a crisis of faith or deter men from entering the priesthood'; the plague certainly 'did not initiate a decline in clerical numbers which continued unabated until the Reformation' (Harper-Bill, 'The English Church', p. 89). Men pursued careers in mother church rather than seeking spiritual comfort in heresy.

But what about the *quality* of recruits to the priesthood, did that not decline? Many contemporary commentators certainly thought so, and modern historians have been tempted by the vision of a 'frenzied quest for inflationary rewards' led by a 'poorly motivated clergy with an eye to the main chance' (Harper-Bill, 'The English Church', pp. 90–1). The increased demand for indulgences and masses to ensure the prompt progress of souls through purgatory cannot simply or easily be reduced to that cause, however; an inflationary spiral there certainly was, but many factors contributed to its making.

Then there is the widely held perception that the second half of the fourteenth century saw 'a real decline in the intellectual vigour' of English university life in general and Oxford in particular.[40] Was the Black Death in some way responsible for that; did it nip in the bud the work of brilliant young schoolmen? The problem with such a theory is that the period 1340–50, apparently a moribund time in Oxford, 'was one of the most intellectually active decades of the century' in Paris, where the plague also wreaked havoc.[41]

Did such work as was produced by the Oxford masters fail to survive because it was not deemed worthy of preservation, and was that because of a diminution in quality of the students being recruited, as a consequence of the Black Death? Once again, no clear correlation is possible, though it seems reasonable to assume that plague reduced the size of the pool from which good scholars emerged. Part of the problem is that such treatises on logic and theology as did survive have not yet received the attention they deserve in modern scholarship. The statistics seem encouraging. William J. Courtenay has concluded that, 'when compared with the high productivity of authors from the 1330s and the survival rate of their works, the number of *Sentences* commentaries declines slightly, but not drastically. Far more has survived from the 1350s than from the previous decade...' (Courtenay, *Schools and Scholars*, p. 339). However, he also notes that the arguments in the 1350s commentaries 'sometimes appear incomplete, chaotic, or rambling', whether 'as a result of imperfect revision, poor scribes, or simply the style and reasoning of the authors' (p. 340). If there was indeed some decline in quality of 'style and reasoning' this may have been due, at least in part, to the fact that, following their studies in the arts, the brightest and best students were choosing a career in law rather than in theology – an excellent example being afforded by Ralph Strode (*fl.* 1350–1400), the 'philosophical Strode' honoured by Chaucer at the end of his *Troilus and Criseyde*. Ambition to follow the career path which would bring the most prestige and power can hardly be blamed on the plague.

What the method of analysis practised above cannot possibly reach, of course, are the agonies of soul-searching and self-recrimination which the Black Death induced in many conscientious Christians, both clerical and lay. Writing in 1348 to the senior churchmen in his diocese of Winchester, just before the plague hit that region, Bishop William Edendon commented that, while 'it is not within the power of man to understand the divine plan', a 'likely explanation' is to hand.

> It is to be feared that... human sensuality... has now plumbed greater depths of evil, producing a multitude of sins which have provoked the divine anger, by a just judgment, to this revenge. But because God is benign and merciful, long-suffering, and above malice, it may be that this affliction, which we richly deserve, can be averted if we turn to him humbly and with our whole hearts, and we therefore earnestly urge you to devotion.[42]

With humility and with their whole hearts, the contemplatives of late-medieval England sought to transcend all the contagion of the quotidian world, to rise towards union with a God in whose justice and mercy they tried to have total faith.

NOTES

1 Trans. C. Fasolt in Julius Kirshner and Karl F. Morrison (eds.), *Medieval Europe* (Chicago, IL, and London: University of Chicago Press, 1986), pp. 371–2. For the original text, see S. Kuttner and A. Garcia y Garcia, 'A New Eyewitness Account of the Fourth Lateran Council', *Traditio* 20 (1964), 115–78 (125).

2 On these events see F. M. Powicke, *Stephen Langton* (Oxford: Clarendon Press, 1928), pp. 75–128.

3 F. Donald Logan, *A History of the Church in the Middle Ages* (London and New York: Routledge, 2002), pp. 193–201.

4 From Thomas Walsingham's *Historia anglicana*; Rosemary Horrox (trans.), *The Black Death* (Manchester and New York: Manchester University Press, 1994), p. 66.

5 Brenda Bolton, 'A Show with a Meaning: Innocent III's Approach to the Fourth Lateran Council, 1215', *Medieval History* 1 (1991), 53–67 (53).

6 Constance Hoffman Berman, *The Cistercian Evolution: The Invention of a Religious Order in Twelfth-Century Europe* (Philadelphia, PN: University of Pennsylvania Press, 2000), pp. xi, xiii. *Pace* the earlier scholarly tradition, houses of Cistercian nuns *do* date from the twelfth century; see Berman, *Cistercian Evolution*, esp. pp. 39–45.

7 'The Fourth Lateran Council and Manuals of Popular Theology', in Thomas Heffernan (ed.), *The Popular Literature of Medieval England* (Knoxville: University of Tennessee Press, 1985), pp. 30–60 (pp. 30–1).

8 Innocent hoped to revitalize the Benedictine ideal, the order having been in decline for centuries. In Europe generally his canon was widely ignored; in England, where attempts were made to enforce it, considerable opposition was voiced by those who saw it as imposing dangerous novelties on ancient and well-established practices. See R. W. Southern, *Western Society and the Church* (Grand Rapids, MI: Eerdmans, 1970), pp. 236–7.

9 Here and elsewhere in this chapter I draw on the translation of the Lateran Canons by H. J. Schroeder, *Disciplinary Decrees of the General Councils: Text, Translation, and Commentary* (St Louis, MO, and London: Herder, 1937), pp. 236–96.

10 See especially Jean Leclercq, 'Le Magistère du prédicateur au XIIIe siècle', *AHDMLA* 21 (1946), 105–47.

11 See the examples quoted by Arnold Williams, 'Some Documents on English Pardoners, 1350–1400', in John Maloney and J. E. Keller (eds.), *Mediaeval Studies in honor of U. T. Holmes* (Chapel Hill, NC: University of North Carolina Press, 1965), pp. 197–207 (esp. pp. 201, 203).

12 Alexander Murray, 'Confession before 1215', *TRHS* 6th ser. 3 (1993), 51–81 (65).

13 Here the decrees of the Fourth Lateran Council were read aloud, to reinforce the polemical point that the English Church was in a sorry state due to its

failure to observe such decrees; see Decima Douie, *Archbishop Pecham* (Oxford: Clarendon Press, 1952), p. 133. However, the Lambeth Council was but one of a series of substantial English responses to the Lateran Council; cf. in particular the preceding decrees of Salisbury and Oxford, emphasized by Logan, *A History of the Church*, p. 199.

14 This treatise survives in no fewer than ninety manuscripts, written between the thirteenth and the fifteenth centuries. It has been edited by J. Goering and F. A. C. Mantello, *Robert Grosseteste: Templum Dei* (Toronto: Pontifical Institute of Mediaeval Studies, 1984).

15 The *Château d'amour*'s date of composition is a matter of scholarly controversy. A review of opinions is included in Evelyn A. Mackie's study, 'Robert Grosseteste's Anglo-Norman Treatise on the Loss and Restoration of Creation, commonly known as *Le Château d'amour*: An English Prose Translation', in Maura O'Carroll (ed.), *Robert Grosseteste and the Beginnings of a British Theological Tradition*, Bibliotheca seraphico-capuccina 69 (Rome: Istituto storico dei Cappuccini, 2003), pp. 151–79. On the four Middle English translations (two of which focus on the allegory of the Four Daughters of God), see Kari Sajavaara, *The Middle English Translations of Robert Grosseteste's 'Chateau d'Amour'* (Helsinki: Société Néophilologique, 1967).

16 R. W. Southern, *Robert Grosseteste: The Growth of an English Mind in Medieval Europe* (Oxford: Clarendon Press, 1986), pp. 225–30.

17 *De adventu fratrum minorum in Angliam*, cap. 11; trans. Leo Sherley-Price as *The Coming of the Franciscans* (London: Mowbray, 1964), p. 42.

18 See H. R. Bramley (ed.), *Richard Rolle of Hampole, The Psalter or Psalms of David* (Oxford: Clarendon Press, 1884), and Robert Boenig (ed.), Richard Rolle, *Biblical Commentaries* (Salzburg: Edwin Mellen Press, 1984). See further J. P. H. Clark, 'Richard Rolle as a Biblical Commentator', *Downside Review* 104 (356) (1986), 165–213.

19 For translations of relevant texts, and introductory discussion, see ch. 7 of Alastair Minnis and A. B. Scott with David Wallace (eds.), *Medieval Literary Theory and Criticism c.1100–c.1375: The Commentary Tradition* (Oxford: Clarendon Press, 1991; repr. 2001).

20 Susanna Greer Fein (ed.), *Moral Love Songs and Laments* (Kalamazoo, MI: Medieval Institute Publications, 1998), pp, 11–56.

21 The above-mentioned Adam Marsh was the mediator in an exchange of Dionysian commentaries between the two scholars. Marsh sent Gallus a copy of Grosseteste's exposition of *The Celestial Hierarchy*, and requested on Grosseteste's behalf a copy of Gallus's *Extractio* on *The Mystical Theology*. Here I follow the interpretation of one of Marsh's letters by D. A. Callus, 'The Date of Grosseteste's Translations and Commentaries on Pseudo-Dionysius and the *Nicomachean Ethics*', *Recherches de théologie ancienne et médiévale* 14 (1947), 186–210.

22 James McEvoy, *The Philosophy of Robert Grosseteste* (Oxford: Clarendon Press, 1982), p. 308. This development has been described by Dennis D. Martin as 'the affective taming of Pseudo-Denis', a process which he sees as being continued by Hugh of Balma. Cf. the introduction to his translations, *Carthusian Spirituality: The Writings of Hugh of Balma and Guigo de Ponte* (New York: Paulist Press, 1997), pp. 38–47. The first Carthusian monastery or 'Charterhouse' in England

was Witham Priory in Somerset, a twelfth-century foundation whose success owed much to the efforts of St Hugh of Lincoln (prior to his appointment as bishop of Lincoln). A second house, Hinton, dates from the thirteenth century; others were founded in the fourteenth and fifteenth centuries.

23 Particularly by Rosemary Ann Lees, *The Negative Language of the Dionysian School of Mystical Theology: An Approach to 'The Cloud of Unknowing'*, *Analecta Cartusiana* 107 (Salzburg: University of Salzburg, 1983). Since the *Cloud* itself could be a Carthusian work it is tempting to suppose that it was inspired (at least in part) by one of the most important and influential of Carthusian theologians. See especially the discussions by John P. H. Clark, *The Cloud of Unknowing: An Introduction, Analecta Cartusiana* 119.4–6 (Salzburg: Institut für Anglistik und Amerikanistik, 1995–6), I.14–19, 71–3, and James Walsh, in the introduction to his modern English translation of *The Cloud of Unknowing* (New York: Paulist Press, 1981), pp. 2–9, 19–23.

24 Cf. Alastair Minnis, 'The Sources of *The Cloud of Unknowing*: A Reconsideration', in *MMTE I*, pp. 63–75.

25 For an excellent summary account of the activities of those masters see J. I. Catto, 'Theology and Theologians 1220–1320', in J. I. Catto (ed.), *The History of University of Oxford*, vol. 1, *The Early Schools* (Oxford: Clarendon Press, 1992), pp. 471–517.

26 John Hilary Martin, 'The Ordination of Women and the Theologians in the Middle Ages', conveniently repr. in Bernard Cooke and Gary Macy (eds.), *A History of Women and Ordination*, vol. I: *The Ordination of Women in Medieval Context* (Lanham, ML, and London: Scarecrow Press, 2002), pp. 31–160 (pp. 52–4).

27 Gary Macy, 'The Ordination of Women in the Early Middle Ages', in Cooke and Macy (eds.), *History of Women and Ordination*, pp. 1–30 (pp. 8–9).

28 Gary Macy, 'The "Invention" of Clergy and Laity in the Twelfth Century', in M. H. Barnes and W. P. Roberts (eds.), *A Sacramental Life: A Festschrift honoring Bernard Cooke* (Milwaukee, 2003), pp. 117–35 (p. 119). Yves Congar has demonstrated that considerable diversity existed concerning what constituted an 'ordination' and which 'orders' should be considered 'clerical'. 'Note sur une valeur des termes *ordinare, ordinatio*', *Revue des sciences religieuses* 58 (1984), 7–14.

29 See Gary Macy, 'Heloise, Abelard and the Ordination of Abbesses', *JEH* 57.1 (2006), 1–17, and also Mary Martin McLaughlin's pioneering study, 'Peter Abelard and the Dignity of Women: Twelfth Century "Feminism" in Theory and Practice', in *Pierre Abelard, Pierre le Vénérable: Les Courants philosophiques, littéraires et artistiques en Occident au milieu du XIIe siècle* (Paris: Editions du Centre National de la Recherche Scientifique, 1975), pp. 287–333.

30 See Martin, 'The Ordination of Women', pp. 56–73, 75–7, 78–83, and also Alastair Minnis, '*De impedimento sexus*: Women's Bodies and Medieval Impediments to Female Ordination', in Peter Biller and Alastair Minnis (eds.), *Medieval Theology and the Natural Body* (York: York Medieval Press with Boydell and Brewer, 1997), pp. 109–39.

31 'A Vision Showed to a Devout Woman', ed. Nicholas Watson and Jacqueline Jenkins, *The Writings of Julian of Norwich* (Turnhout: Brepols, 2006), p. 75.

Barry Windeatt (ed.), *The Book of Margery Kempe*, I.52 (Cambridge: D. S. Brewer, 2000, repr. 2004), p. 253.

32 'Lollard Women Priests?', in Aston, *Lollards and Reformers: Images and Literacy in Late Medieval Religion* (London: Hambledon Press, 1984), pp. 49–70.

33 See Alastair Minnis, 'John Wyclif – All Women's Friend?', in Bonnie Wheeler (ed.), *Mindful Spirit in Late Medieval Literature: Essays in honor of Elizabeth D. Kirk* (Houndmills: Palgrave Macmillan, 2006), pp. 121–33.

34 See Alastair Minnis, '*Respondet Walterus Bryth*... Walter Brut in Debate on Women Priests', in Helen Barr and Ann M. Hutchinson (eds.), *Text and Controversy from Wyclif to Bale: Essays in Honour of Anne Hudson* (Turnhout: Brepols, 2005), pp. 229–49.

35 E. C. Thomas (ed. and trans.), *Philobiblon* (1888; repr. Oxford: Blackwell, 1960), pp. 106–7. On this period, see especially J. A. Weisheipl, 'Ockham and the Mertonians', in *History of the University of Oxford*, vol. 1, pp. 607–58.

36 Or 'The Oxford Calculators', as Edith Dudley Sylla more prudently calls them; see her chapter, with that title, in Norman Kretzmann, Anthony Kenny, and Jan Pinborg (eds.), *The Cambridge History of Later Medieval Philosophy* (Cambridge: Cambridge University Press, 1982), pp. 540–63.

37 Katherine Walsh, *A Fourteenth-Century Scholar and Primate: Richard FitzRalph in Oxford, Avignon and Armagh* (Oxford: Clarendon Press, 1981), p. 413, pp. 423–4.

38 'I wonder much about these Friars Minor [Franciscans]; previously they were humble but now they have grown proud. Among men of Holy Church they cause great confusion... With an 'O' and an 'I' [a refrain formula], one said very quietly, may "Armachan" [FitzRalph, Archhishop of Armagh] destroy them, if it is God's will!' *Of Thes Frer Mynours* (dated 1382 by Thomas Wright), in James M. Dean (ed.), *Medieval English Political Writings* (Kalamazoo, MI: Medieval Institute Publications, 1996), pp. 53–4.

39 Christopher Harper-Bill, 'The English Church and English Religion after the Black Death', in W. M. Ormrod and P. G. Lindley (eds.), *The Black Death in England* (Stamford: Paul Watkins, 1996), pp. 79–123 (p. 84).

40 J. A. Robson, *Wyclif and the Oxford Schools* (Cambridge: Cambridge University Press, 1961), p. 97.

41 William J. Courtenay, *Schools and Scholars in Fourteenth-Century England* (Princeton: Princeton University Press, 1987), p. 330.

42 *Vox in Rama*, trans. Horrox, *Black Death*, p. 116.

5

DENIS RENEVEY

1215–1349: texts

The previous chapter suggests that the canons issued under the authority of Pope Innocent III on the occasion of the Fourth Lateran Council of 1215 officially licensed, codified, and reinforced newly emerging trends in the clerical practice of pastoral theology. This foundational moment in the history of the western church had a lasting effect on the way the medieval self was to be shaped. The Lateran documents shaped medieval religious psychology and its attendant literature by encouraging the production of pastoral manuals and manuals of confession to assist priests in the exercise of their new responsibilities in the care of souls (*cura animarum*). Canon 10 of the Fourth Lateran Council acknowledges that bishops may require the support of capable men who, in lieu of the bishop, will preach in his diocese.[1] The continuing implementation of this legislation in England produced further constitutions, including influential sets by Bishop Richard Poore (d. 1237) of Salisbury in 1222, and Bishop Robert Grosseteste (*c.* 1170–1253) of Lincoln in 1239. These diocesan constitutions were codified for the whole of Canterbury Province (and in effect for the whole of England) in the 1281 Lambeth Constitutions of Archbishop John Pecham (d. 1292). Through such routes basic catechetical material was circulated for the use of parish priests in the pastoral care of their flock. This material was glossed and the needs of priests supported in newly composed Latin pastoral manuals, such as William of Pagula's (*c.* 1290–1332) *Oculus sacerdotis* (*The Eye of the Priest*), written in the 1320s and used, for example, by Richard Rolle.[2] Religious vernacular textual production between 1215 and 1349 bears witness to this increased insistence on penitential self-introspection as encouraged by the official church. If it is indeed a hallmark of several of the vernacular theologies written from 1215 onwards, such a characteristic blends with, and gives new impetus to, the affective tradition which marked twelfth-century monastic spirituality.

Vernacular theologies from the period 1215 to 1349 typically address the emotional, affective side of the human psyche in order to move it to a greater desire for the divine. Appealing to human emotions in order to direct the medieval self towards a better self-knowledge and help understand the nature, and experience of, a personal relationship to God, such texts generated a form of 'contemplative feeling' whose growth will be explored in the course of this chapter.[3]

Anchoritic texts

The most far-reaching vernacular religious texts to emerge in the decade or so following the Lateran Council are a group of highly specialized works originating in the West Midland area, which promoted this form of 'contemplative feeling'. *Ancrene Wisse* initially addressed an audience of three female anchorites. Anchorites lived solitary lives in cells or group of cells near or adjacent to a church. In the latter case, a window would allow the anchorite to peer into the church and attend, from the cell, the church services. Anchorites led a life based on the model of the desert fathers, although their desert was understood metaphorically to signify their isolation from the world and their attempt to commit themselves to a life of reading, prayer, and devotion. Practical and spiritual aspects of the anchoritic life are a major concern of *Ancrene Wisse*. Structurally divided into eight books, or 'destinctiuns', *Ancrene Wisse* reflects developments in contemporary intellectual and academic thought in its layout and careful division of its material. The text was composed after 1215, possibly by a Dominican friar engaged in the implementation of the Lateran Council's new pastoral priorities, notably the need for all Christians to confess annually. The first and the last 'destinctiuns' address external aspects of the life of an anchorite, and form the outer rule, while 'destinctiuns' two to seven focus on aspects of the inner life and form the inner rule.[4] Part One provides for the three sisters who make the primary audience of *Ancrene Wisse* an adjustable devotional template and useful information about their suggested daily devotional routines. The last book, itself subdivided into seven branches, deals with the regulation of the anchorhold as a religious household, with such diverse concerns as the reception of visitors, handling of material goods and animals, circulation of knowledge from the anchorhold to the outside world, and the general behaviour of the anchoresses, their spiritual guide and confessor, and the anchoresses' maidservants. The central part of the inner rule deals with the technology of confession, laid out in a most detailed fashion, and also apparently intended for the use of a wider audience. Indeed Parts Four to Six ('Temptations', 'Confessions', and 'Penance') are all potentially universal in their address and share similar concerns with other pastoral theologies written following the Fourth Lateran Council:

Al thet ich habbe i-seid of flesches pinsunge nis nawt for ow, mine leove sustren – the other-hwile tholieth mare then ich walde – ah is for sum thet schal rede this inoh-reathe, the grapeth hire to softe.

All that I have said of the mortification of the flesh is not meant for you, my dear sisters, who sometimes suffer more than I would like; but it is for anyone who handles herself too gently who reads this willingly enough.[5]

In the Corpus manuscript, which may have been revised by the author himself, reference is made to a much larger community of anchoresses living throughout the whole of England (*Ancrene Wisse*, p. 270; *Anchoritic Spirituality*, p. 141). The author therefore seems to assume a multiple anchoritic audience. However, considering the significant confessional material that makes the core of the treatise, it may be that, from the onset, *Ancrene Wisse* was not exclusively designed for an anchoritic audience. For instance, while the following passage has literal applicability to real anchoresses, there is also always the possibility of a more metaphorical meaning, addressing a non-anchoritic audience who are equally interested in the exploration of the interior life:

Ant nes he him-seolf reclus i Maries wombe? Theos twa thing limpeth to ancre: nearowthe ant bitternesse, for wombe is nearow wununge ther ure Laverd wes reclus, ant tis word "Marie," as ich ofte habbe i-seid, spealeth "bitternesse." Yef ye thenne i nearow stude tholieth bitternesse, ye beoth his feolahes, reclus as he wes i Marie wombe. Beo ye i-bunden in-with fowr large wahes? – ant he in a nearow cader, i-neilet o rode, i stanene thruh bicluset hete-feste! Marie wombe ant this thruh weren his ancre-huses.

And was he not himself a recluse in Mary's womb? These two things belong to the anchoress: narrowness and bitterness. For the womb is a narrow dwelling, where our Lord was a recluse; and this word "Mary," as I have often said, means "bitterness." If you then suffer bitterness in a narrow place, you are his fellows, recluse as he was in Mary's womb. Are you imprisoned within four wide walls? – and he in a narrow cradle, nailed on the cross, enclosed tight in a stone tomb. Mary's womb and this tomb were his anchorhouses.

(*Ancrene Wisse*, p. 370, *Anchoritic Spirituality*, p. 186)

Such images of confinement and enclosure are semantically loaded: considered more loosely, they could be used more generally by an audience wanting to experience the spiritual pregnancy of contemplation. Reference to the humanity of Jesus invites comparison with one's own life: the immediate and implied parallel is with the anchoritic mode of life, but it does not exclude other possible comparisons. The anchorhold in *Ancrene Wisse* is defined as an extension of the body, a necessary container of the soul, as the author reminds us when talking about the anchoress living, like Christ, in those confined spaces: 'thet schal beon hwen the gast went ut on ende withuten bruche ant wem of his twa huses: thet an is the licome. Thet other is the utter hus, thet is as the uttre wah abute the castel.' ('That will be when the spirit goes out in the end, without break or blemish, from its two houses. One of them is the body, the other is the outer house, which is like the outer wall around a castle') (*Ancrene Wisse*, p. 370; *Anchoritic Spirituality*, p. 187).

Ancrene Wisse's organized structure and general rational approach to the anchoritic/contemplative life aims to lead its readership to the pinnacle of the Christian life, achieved only after contemplating or even experiencing rigorous ascesis (self-discipline, usually achieved by rigorous bodily discipline). While highly specialized, *Ancrene Wisse* is nevertheless influenced by contemporary pastoral theology in whose diffusion the friars, and especially the Dominicans, took an important role. In that respect, if one reads beyond its pervasive anchoritic asceticism, the spirituality of the text moves towards that advocated by the twelfth-century Cistercians such as Bernard of Clairvaux on the Continent and Aelred of Rievaulx in England. Part Seven of *Ancrene Wisse* suggests, for example, a form of spiritual love that is enacted via the erotic and sensuous representation of Christ as the wooing lover/knight. It points to a mystical moment which one reads as the culmination that one attains if the doctrine expounded in the rest of the treatise has been well digested. Imagery from the world of romance is fused with images borrowed from the Song of Songs or its commentaries. Although brief, it alludes to the potential of ecstatic experience and thus depicts contemplative feeling:

'Thi luve,' he seith, '- other hit is for-te yeoven allunge, other hit is to sullen, other hit is to reavin ant to neomen with strengthe. Yef hit is for-te yeoven, hwer maht tu biteon hit betere then up-o me? Nam ich thinge feherest? Nam ich kinge richest? Nam ich hest i-cunnet? Nam ich weolie wisest? Nam ich monne hendest? Nam ich thinge freoest? For swa me seith bi large mon the ne con nawt edhalden, thet he haveth the honden, as mine beoth, i-thurlet. Nam ich alre thinge swotest ant swetest?'

'Your love,' he says, 'is either to be wholly a gift, or it is for sale, or it is to be taken and captured by force. If it is to be a gift, where could you bestow it better than upon me? Am I not the fairest one? Am I not the richest king? Am I not highest born? Am I not the wisest among the rich? Am I not the most courteous of men? Am I not the most generous one? For one says of a generous man who can keep nothing back, that his hands are pierced – as mine are. Am I not of all things the gentlest and sweetest?'

(*Ancrene Wisse*, pp. 385–6, *Anchoritic Spirituality*, pp. 193–4)

Ancrene Wisse looks like a multi-purpose text. Its generic complexity (is it a rule, a confessional manual, a pastoral treatise?), its indebtedness to traditional Augustinian monastic practices and its borrowings from thirteenth-century academic discourses (especially its use of *distinctio* structure) probably contributed to making it a popular, multi-functional religious text. It is also a strong reminder of the cultural diversity of England, with French and Latin taking a significant role in the making of English religious identity. Its comfortable after-life is attested by seventeen extant manuscript versions, in English (nine), French (four), and Latin (four). Further evidence of popularity is attested by the number of borrowings from *Ancrene Wisse* in devotional and contemplative texts in the fourteenth and fifteenth centuries. The nature of the borrowings and their new contextualization show how the anchoritic model (used metaphorically) became a trademark for exemplary religious life, both for the more laicized and urban devout public and the (male) monastic public of this later period.

'Loke, Lauerd, to me, mi lif, mu luue, mi leofmon, ant milce me, þi meiden,' *Seinte Margarete.*

'Lord, watch over me, my life, my love, my lover, and have mercy on me, your maiden', *Saint Margaret.*[6]

As with the metaphorical appropriation of anchoritic culture for a diverse public, vernacular literature extolling the spiritual benefits of virginity also bears a metaphorical dimension which should not be underestimated when considering its functions, and the various linguistic conduits (Anglo-Norman, English, and Latin) which serve for its circulation. The virginity texts associated with the West Midland dialect and early manuscript circulation of *Ancrene Wisse* display exemplary female lives as models to be used for the direction of one's own life. Faith and virginity are inextricably linked: the extremes of pain and suffering which female characters are ready to undergo to preserve their virginity stand as the measure of the intensity of their faith.[7]

In the case of *Seinte Margarete*, the female heroine is depicted as a passive and suffering virgin, physically enduring a form of *imitatio Christi* (imitation of the life of Christ, more specifically the Passion events) by having her body tortured through the creative perversity of her male tormentor Olibrius. That heroic moment of passive endurance is counterbalanced by a second phase which depicts a warrior-like Margaret governing and annihilating the power of demonic visitations in the form of a dragon or other devilish creatures. Like those of St Katherine of Alexandria and St Juliana of Nicomedia, this saint's life portrays a combative female character whose life calls for affective empathy. Even an anchoritic audience would not aspire to a literal imitation of those deeds. But a metaphorical or allegorical reading of the lives could strengthen any religiously committed audience in the face of adversity. These saint's lives point to virginity as the spiritual condition most favoured by the deity. A treatise on holy virginity, *Hali Meiðhad*, travelling with these female saints' lives, and written in the same dialect, make virginal lives the spiritual condition most favoured by the deity. The spiritual quality-gap between matrimony/motherhood and virginity is unequivocal:

Hwenne schulde Ich al habben irikenet þet springeð bituhe þeo þe þus beoð igederet? ȝef ha ne mei nawt temen, ha is icleopet gealde; hire lauerd luueð hire ant wurðgeð þe leasse, ant heo, as þeo þet wurst is þrof, biwepeð hire wurðes, ant cleopeð ham wunne ant weole fulle þe temeð hare teames. Ah nu iwurðe hit al þet ha habbe hire wil of streon þet ha wilneð, ant loki we hwuch wunne þrof hire iwurðe. I þe streonunge þron is anan hire flesch wið þet fulþe ituket, as hit is ear ischawet; I þe burðerne þrof is heuinesse ant heard sar eauer umbe stunde: in his iborenesse, alre stiche strengest, ant deað oþerhwiles; in his fostrunge forð, moni earm-hwile.

When should I have finished an account of everything that comes between those who are joined in this way? If she cannot have children, she is called barren: her lord loves her and honours her less, and she, as the one who has the worst of it, bewails her fate, and calls those women who do bear children full of happiness and good fortune. But now suppose that it turns out that she has all she wanted in the child that she longs for, and let us see what happiness she gets from it. In conceiving it, her flesh is at once defiled with that filth, as has been shown before; in carrying it there is a heaviness and constant discomfort; in giving birth to it, the cruellest of all pains, and sometimes death; in bringing it up, many weary hours.   (*Medieval English Prose for Women*, pp. 28–31)

The case for the superiority of virginity is here based on the physical constraints of its opposite, matrimony and motherhood. But this gender-based discourse encodes a message with which male readers could also identify: virginity is, on one level, a state of mind. The virgin martyrs of the Katherine group exemplify the androgynous-feminine type of holy life, which is characterized by penitential asceticism. These stories repeatedly stage a contrast between male power and feminine subjection, which is characterized by passive forbearance and obstinate constancy. Because those qualities were typically gendered as feminine in the medieval period, it can be initially shocking to find that the medieval Passion narratives attribute those qualities to the person of Christ. But the feminization of Christ allows for those narratives of female subjection to resonate with Christ's passion. Therefore the lives of the female martyrs potentially read as active re-enactments of the Passion: their performance by a female or male audience allows for a closer and soundly orthodox apprehension of the experience undergone by God in his humanity. The female saint's subjection to barbaric power makes them ungendered heirs to Christ.

The three sisters for whom *Ancrene Wisse* was written had not experienced monastic enclosure and its way of life before entering their anchoritic cells. Their ability to read in the vernacular, as well as their apparent literacy in liturgical Latin, reflect the degree of competence reached by female lay readers of gentle birth in the thirteenth century. Because the number of postulants for entry into anchoritic cells was always limited, one can assume that many lay people of gentle birth would have had some of the same hermeneutic skills assumed in the anchoresses. These texts would have been suitable for an audience beyond the enclosure of the anchoritic cell: this specialized literature had a decisive impact on the making of religious books for the attention of the laity. Canon 13 of the Fourth Lateran Council prohibited the foundation of new religious orders and as a consequence some individuals were prevented from joining orders that could have catered for their affective religious needs. The scarcity of new institutional contexts for the practice of affective piety accounts in part for the surge of lay devout activity in the thirteenth century, in parallel to monastic and anchoritic practices. The transmission of spiritual material from the monastery to the anchorhold and beyond into the lay world at large is concurrent with, and dependent on, the use of vernacular languages for their dissemination.

The texts which constitute 'The Wooing Group', for example, resonate with the imagery developed in the Cistercian commentaries of the Song of Songs, while at the same time addressing the reality of anchoritic life. But, they also have an affective quality with which a lay readership would have felt comfortable. That the text called *Þe Wohunge of ure Lauerd* survives in only one manuscript is counterbalanced in terms of possible popularity and dissemination by the fact that it eventually found its way into two late fourteenth-century bulky devotional anthologies of vernacular spiritual material, the so-called Vernon and Simeon manuscripts, as a compilation called *A Talking of the Love of God*.[8] Few other medieval vernacular poems vibrate with the affective intensity of *Þe Wohunge of ure Lauerd*, the central piece of 'The Wooing Group'. The 658-line alliterative prose text abounds in imagery derived from the commentary tradition of the Song of Songs, *fin' amor* literature, the conventions of chivalric behaviour, and the lexis of kinship and exile. The imagined exchange between an I-persona and Christ is so craftily designed that it privileges an emotional performative reading in which the reader engages dialogically with Christ. This narrative tour-de-force reaches its climax towards the end of the poem, which describes the Passion of Christ:

> A hwat schal i nu don? Nu min herte mai to breke, min ehne flowen al o water. A nu is mi lefmon demd for to deien. A nu mon ledes him forð to munte caluarie to þe cwalm stowe. A lo he beres his rode up on his bare schuldres – and lef þa duntes drepen me þat tai þe dunchen ant þrasten þe forðward swiðe toward ti dom . . . A swete iesu þu oppnes me þin herte for to cnawe witerliche ant in to redden trewe luue lettres; for þer i mai openlich seo hu muchel þu me luuedes. Wið wrange schuldi þe min heorte wearnen siðen þat tu bohtes herte for herte.

> Ah! What shall I do now? Now my heart can break apart, my eyes all overflow with water. Ah! now is my lover condemned to die! Ah! now they lead him toward Mount Calvary, to the death-place! Ah! see, he bears his cross upon his bare shoulders – and, beloved, would that those blows would fall on me with which they strike you and thrust you so violently forward toward your doom . . . Ah! sweet Jesus, you open your heart to me, so that I may know it inwardly, and read inside it true love-letters; for there I may see openly how much you loved me. Wrong would it be to refuse you my heart, since you have bought heart with heart.
>
> (*The Wohunge of Ure Lauerd*, pp. 33–5 (with modern punctuation); *Anchoritic Spirituality*, p. 255)

The re-enactment of the Passion events is assimilated by the narrator in a most personal, emotional manner, through brief sentences, affective outbursts and present tense exclamations expressing surprise, shock, and outrage, so as to bring the reader closer to the events themselves. There is both an a-temporal quality and blending of the voices in this passage that allows for complete fusion into the sequence on the part of the meditative reader. Much of the relationship between the I-persona and the person of Christ is based on the language of economic and social difference to express the spiritual inequality and imbalance between them. In this particular setting, Christ takes on the role of the exile, without an abode in the created world, whereas economic wealth and social benefits negatively mark the I-persona in the context of salvation history. Elsewhere, the I-persona mentions kinship as an important aspect of its life before their current devotion to the person of Christ. Class awareness is also pertinent to this theme, with references to men of gentle birth winning too easily women's hearts and depriving them of their virginity:

Ah noble men ant gentile ant of heh burðe ofte winnen luue lihtliche cheape, for ofte moni wummon letes hire mensket þurh þe luue of wepmon þat is of heh burðe.

But noblemen, gentlemen, men of high birth, frequently win love at little cost, for often many a woman loses her honor through the love of a man of high birth. (*The Wohunge of Ure Lauerd*, p. 24; *Anchoritic Spirituality*, p. 250)

In the economy of salvation there is no better gain than to become Christ's beloved. *Þe Wohunge of ure Lauerd* is ambitious in scope and aspires to bring the reader to an elevated affective level of empathy with, and indebtedness to, the person of Christ. It reflects the penitential concerns of the post-Lateran world by combining the theme of Christ as lover with a detailed and anxiety-ridden description of the crucifixion which forces a guiltily self-aware re-positioning of the reader-performer as an unworthy sinner.

Thomas of Hales

These anchoritic works have for long been used as evidence for linguistic continuity between the Old and Middle English periods. However, on the religious front, the apparent specialization of the material for a regional anchoritic audience has until relatively recently pre-empted investigations into the impact of this material upon the larger late medieval religious context. Although there is no space to offer an extensive argument for the influence of anchoritic literature on the language and description of late medieval contemplative experience, one of the first recorded Franciscan lyrics shows how religious themes partake of a large tradition that is shared by different religious orders over different genres and over an extended period of time.

Recent evidence has shown that the Franciscan friar Thomas of Hales had contact with the Queen Eleanor of Provence, wife of Henry III.[9] Queen Eleanor seems to have had a penchant for Franciscan friars as confessors and spiritual confessors. William Batale, Thomas of Hales, and Adam Marsh were all connected to the queen. Thomas of Hales, who seems to have had a powerful influence upon her, wrote in Latin, French, and English. His Latin life of the Virgin is his most popular work. Another of his extant works is a sermon written in Latin with short prayers written in French. But Thomas of Hales turned to English for the third of his surviving works, the 'Love Rune', composed between 1234 and 1272. The poem claims that it was written at the instigation of a young maiden, and it is filled with an emotional dimension that would appeal to a girl inexperienced in matters of love and religion. This female character may have decided for a religious life, either as a nun or as an anchoress, and the poem shows a mild didacticism in its goal to lead the reader to an exclusive desire for God. The narrator assumes she has already undergone outer *conversio* (turning away from the physical world) and her apparent request for the 'Love Rune' may characterize her need to be strengthened in her new life devoted to Christ in order to reach inner *conversio* (psychological transformation to achieve complete absorption in the divine).

Franciscan spirituality broadly belongs to the affective and cataphatic tradition. This tradition works on the emotions of its audience to move their attention from the material to the spiritual world. But even at the higher reaches of the contemplative life the need to respond emotionally is considered to be of the utmost importance in leading the listener to develop contemplative feeling. The first stanzas of the 'Love Rune', set as *ubi sunt* formulae, lamenting the transience of earthly power and beauty, consider common themes, such as the transience of material wealth, power, and human love. The emotional instability generated by absorption with such issues is pointed out, with a particular focus set on the lovers of the classical and medieval traditions:

Hwer is Paris and Heleyne	
That weren so bryht and feyre on bleo?	beautiful and fair in face
Amadas and Ideyne,	Idoine
Tristram, Yseude, and alle theo?	those
Ector with his scharpe meyne,	powerful strength
And Cesar riche of wordes feo?	wordly wealth
Heo beoth iglyden ut of the reyne	they have vanished; dominion
So the schef is of the cleo (ll. 65–72).[10]	just as the sheaf is (cut) by the scythe

The reference to legendary heroes of the romance tradition suggests that the recipient may formerly have been a keen reader of such texts herself, and one perhaps familiar with the conventions and practices of secular *fin' amor* (refined love). But such models and practices no longer fit the role she has now taken for herself as bride of Christ. Now her will must be turned towards other models and practices, even if such a conversion does not imply a complete negation of her former outlook. The romance heroes are instead used as a springboard to the love of Christ. The technique used by Thomas of Hales has its roots in Bernardine spirituality, in which carnal love is transferred from the physical to the spiritual sphere, and is transposed to become spiritual itself. The humanity of Christ and the events of his Passion often serve as the intermediary moment for this transference. Most medieval Passion narratives deploy those events with the specific aim of making possible for the audience a transfer from a carnal to a spiritual concern. The *ubi sunt* formulae serve as a means of denying the physical world and the use of *fin' amor* vocabulary expresses a form of eternal and abstractly idealized love. In stanzas 12–19, the charms of Christ, and the invitation to the maiden to become his bride are followed by a description of the glories and bliss of Christ's eternal abode. Stanza eighteen describes the bliss of the sight of Christ and stanza nineteen concludes this moment of the poem with the gift to the maid of the precious treasure, her virginity. The poem tactfully builds a generous portrait of her new spiritual lover, so that from an initial desire to set her will towards God it moves to triggering a strong desire for his sight:

A! Swete, if thu ikneowe	knew
The gode thewes of thisse childe –	qualities
He is feyr and bryht on heowe,	in appearance
Of glede chere, of mode mylde,	countenance, temperament
Of lufsum lost, of truste treowe,	amorous desire
Freo of heorte, of wisdom wilde –	noble; strong of wisdom
Ne thurhte the never reowe	you would never regret it
Myhtestu do the in His ylde! (ll. 89–96)	were you to put yourself; protection

To concepts of a highly abstract, almost Neo-Platonic-like nature, comparison is made with individuals of this world, and the power of this ethereal practice of love is even measured against that of the king of England himself:

He is ricchest mon of londe,	
So wide so mon speketh with muth;	as far as men speak with mouth
Alle heo beoth to His honde,	all are at his command
Est and west, north and suth!	
Henri, King of Engelonde,	
Of Hym he halt and to Hym buhth.	
Mayde, to the He send His sonde,	you; message (or messenger)
And wilneth for to beo the cuth (ll. 97–104)	desires to be known by you

Henry III (reigned 1216–72) was a great benefactor of the church, with the building of the new gothic church of Westminster Abbey as the most ostentatious sign of his religious devotion. Thomas of Hales may have written his poem after the queen turned to him for spiritual direction and while or after Westminster Abbey was built in a record time of twenty-four years (1245–69). While the building of Westminster Abbey is not specifically mentioned in the poem, references to Solomon's temple (ll. 113–20) and other building imagery recall the construction of an English *templum dei* whose magnificence echoed that of Solomon's temple.

In the poem, the expression 'bolde' (l. 113) alludes to Solomon's temple, the Heavenly Jerusalem, Christ's body and, more importantly here, the human body. But 'bolde' refers also to a lady's bower, an image used repeatedly in *Ancrene Wisse*, and one that becomes the structural metaphor for the anchoritic text *Sawles Warde*. Further the use of 'mote' (l. 121) in the 'Love Rune' refers also to a contemporary castle, perhaps of Norman design (motte-and-bailey type) and the use of this enclosed space at this moment in the poem, invites a deeper focus on the interior life with a further development of the trope of enclosure which characterizes anchoritic literature. Recognition of the significance of one's own interiority makes possible a reference to an experience of love that is beyond the duality of the everyday world:

Ne may no mon Hine iseo	see Him
Al so He is in His mihte	entirely as
That may withuten blisse beo;	who
Hwanne he isihht ure Drihte,	sees
His sihte is al joye and gleo!	gladness
He is day wythute nyhte!	
Nere he, Mayde, ful freo	privilege
That myhte wunye myd such a knyghte? (ll. 137–44)	dwell with

Such moments of bliss are only possible through the preservation of the maiden's literal and metaphorical virginity. Indeed, towards the end of the poem, virginity becomes its main topic. Spiritual bliss will be delivered only upon condition of the preservation and protection of this most marvellous gem.

This stress on the value and importance of virginity within the 'Love Rune' does not preclude a movement which culminates in making possible a strong contemplative feeling for the audience, characterized by a desire for the experience of union with the divine. Indeed the force of virginity as metaphor for purity makes possible this desire through a fine-tuning of *fin' amor* values which are transformed so as to catalyze the spiritual potential of the audience. Such an approach is however not without some ambiguities. Indeed, in a few passages of the 'Love Rune', the persona of the narrator is rather ambivalent. First, his answer to the maiden's request for a 'love rune' is not clear. What is the maiden really asking for? A love song, a piece of wisdom on love, or perhaps a private message between lovers? Friar Thomas seems to play with linguistic ambiguity and to transfer that ambiguity to the role which he enacts with the maiden. For lines 185 to 192 refer once again to the request of the maiden for a 'luve rune' and the narrator's words could be suggesting that the maiden had a choice between the narrator himself and Jesus. This is of course a reading which plays with the possibly literal and secular meanings of the amorous language used in the poem and it may be that the poet wishes to exploit such an ambiguity to coerce the reader to calibrate his contemplative feeling when reading the text. The maiden, or any other reader, should turn back to the text, memorize it, and sing it 'mid swete stephne' (l. 203). The 'Love Rune' is not to be read for pleasure but in order to focus correctly one's own will and spiritual direction. It makes an intelligent and strategic use of the affective spirituality whose precursors were, among others, Anselm of Canterbury, Bernard of Clairvaux, Francis of Assisi and the early Franciscans. The 'Luve Rune' and the anchoritic works make strong claims for the preservation of virginity and thus they obviously address, in the first instance, a readership of female virgins. If contemplative claims are therefore intimately linked to the preservation of this privileged female condition, evidence is plentiful for attesting to later male interest in those texts.

John of Howden

The texts from the *Ancrene Wisse* group were written in the West Midland dialect and attest to a very active vernacular literary activity in remote regional settings. However, as has been shown with Thomas of Hales, the devotional demands of the court of Henry III and his queen Eleanor of Provence also played a significant role in triggering the composition of vernacular pieces. The writings of the Northerner John of Howden, chaplain to Queen Eleanor, owe much to the appetite for devotional literature in the queen's court.[11] We know very little about John of Howden, (and even less if he is not, as recent scholarship argues, the John of Howden who was prebendary of the church of Howden in Yorkshire). But, the works which are attributed to him, like those of his contemporary Thomas of Hales and the later major Yorkshire author Richard Rolle, display a multilingual flexibility. There is a body of Latin texts, such as his *Philomela* (*Song of Love*); *Canticum amoris* (*Song of Love*); *Cythara* (*Cittern*); *Quinquaginta cantica*, *Quinquaginta salutationes* (*Fifty Songs; Fifty Salutations*), and several other shorter Latin poems. But he also wrote in Anglo-Norman: *Li Rossignos* (*The Nightingale*) is a re-working of Howden's own Latin *Philomena*, with borrowings from the anonymous *Desere iam anima* (*Abandon Now O Soul*).[12] This account of the life of Christ is dedicated to the queen mother Eleanor (*c.* 1223–91), 'Mere au roi Edward', which means that the dedication, at least, was written after the death of Henry III in 1272 and his son's accession to the throne as Edward I.[13] Internal evidence also suggests that the poem was written before 1282. One of the characteristics of this 5,272-line poem is the emphasis placed on the developing devotion to the Name of Jesus, suggesting that, like other Yorkshire writers, Howden was knowledgeable in, and influenced by, Cistercian spirituality.[14] Section XXX of the poem is entirely devoted to the Name, with a coda on this theme in Section XXXII. The enormously popular and influential hymn *Dulcis Jesu memoria* (*Jesus the Memory is Sweet*), composed in England by a Cistercian author, inspired an extensive meditation on this theme in *Li Rossignos*.[15] Stanzas ten and eleven make direct allusion to the sweetness of the name celebrated in the Cistercian hymn:

> Douz Noun 'jhesu'! fai que te chante
> Quant la Mort mordra la plante!
> Vien en ma langue et la te plante,
> Que li pleidur ne me sosplante!
> 'Jhesu', douz Noun! Se je te troeve
> En ma lange quant Mort m'esproeve,
> Ce me serra lors droite proeve
> D'avoir la joie toz tenz noeve.
>
> Douz Noun! Pur celi qi te porte,
> Vien lors a moi et me conforte,
> Kar si de toi lors me desporte,
> Tote ma peine serra morte!
> En toi, douz Noun, est alejaunce
> Et de la mort et de grevaunce,
> Vigor qui ja n'avra faillaunce,
> Et joie qui n'ad esmaiaunce!

Sweet Name 'Jesus'! Do that I sing it when death bites the plant! Come on my tongue and put yourself in there, so that the pleader does not uproot me! 'Jesus', sweet Name! If I find you on my tongue when Death tests me, it will be then for me direct proof that I will have new joy for ever.

Sweet Name! for the one who carries you. Come to me; comfort me, because if I am then removed from you, all my effort will be lost! In you, sweet Name, is my relief, against death and grievance. It is unfailing strength and joy without dismay.[16]

The poetic meditation on the Name digresses from the general intention of the poem which offers a detailed account of the life of Christ. It partakes of the same affective tradition which saw the making of such influential texts as the late thirteenth-century *Stimulus amoris* (*Goad of Love*) by James of Milan, the *Meditationes vitae Christi* (*Meditations on the Life of Christ*), probably written by the Franciscan friar Johannes de Caulibus in the early fourteenth century, and Ludolph of Saxony's (d. 1377) *Vita Jesu Christi*, also known as the *Speculum vitae Christi* (*Mirror of the Life of Christ*). *Li Rossignos* had a significant impact on later English devotional writers.[17] The Middle English *Meditations on the Life and Passion of Christ*, probably written during the second half of the fourteenth century, was influenced by both Howden's *Philomela* and his *Rossignos*, together with passages clearly indebted to some of the writings of Richard Rolle.[18] The way that this text is adapted from Latin into Anglo-Norman for a royal female audience, only to find its way later into yet another significant transformation into Middle English, well describes the ways in which medieval English contemplative writings are part of a multilingual textual exchange which manifests itself in Latin, Anglo-Norman, and English.

Richard Rolle

There is no evidence that Richard Rolle (*c.* 1300–49) wrote in Anglo-Norman. He owes his modern-day fame to his contributions in English, with his three letters (*The Commandment*, *Ego dormio* (*I Sleep*) and *The Form of Living*) written for the attention of female recipients, his lyrics and his two Passion meditations as his most well-known pieces.[19] But, like John of Howden, Rolle wrote far more in the Latin language than in the vernacular during the course of his literary career. A brief biographical sketch of Richard Rolle may provide us with a partial explanation for this.[20] Rolle was born at Thornton, near Pickering in Yorkshire. He was the son of William Rolle. Thanks to the financial support of Thomas de Neville, he went to study at Oxford, which he left without a degree at the age of nineteen. Some time after his return to Yorkshire, he led the life of a hermit and found an abode in the estate of John de Dalton, whose son had met Rolle during his Oxford days. After leaving the Dalton estate, Rolle for some time moved from one abode to another, finally finding a more permanent dwelling near the nunnery at Hampole in Yorkshire. There he acted as spiritual guide to at least one of its nuns, Margaret Kirkeby, who had already chosen the anchoritic life when Rolle worked as her spiritual advisor. He died near Hampole in 1349. Although Rolle's own account of devotional and contemplative experience is based on the long-established western tradition which the Cistercian and the Franciscans circulated and popularized in the twelfth and thirteenth centuries, he is today better known for some of the idiosyncrasies of his contemplative programme. For instance, Rolle makes the daring claim of living in a permanent state of union with the deity, of hearing heavenly melody at all times, and of experiencing particular physico-contemplative feelings such as *fervor*, *dulcor*, and *canor* (heat, sweetness, song). In some of his autobiographical moments, he also shows the importance that the devotion to the Name of Jesus has in his contemplative system. However, an overall study of Rolle's substantial corpus shows his great linguistic, generic and devotional versatility. The English writings comprise only a quarter of the surviving works, and are much shorter than those composed in Latin. Alongside books of ascetic guidance, handbooks for parish priests, commentaries of the Psalter and other biblical books, his strictly contemplative writings, in Latin or Middle English, are a relatively small part of his output. One must take into consideration this generic and textual versatility in order to offer a credible account of Rolle's career. In contrast to other contemplative writers, Rolle explores medieval religious generic variety profusely, with the writing of commentaries, postils, religious autobiographies and visions, pastoral manuals, epistles, rules and lyrics.[21] His generic versatility, his pastoral concerns and the emotive nature of several of his writings contributed to his popularity in the fourteenth and fifteenth centuries.[22] Rolle belongs first and foremost to the post-Lateran Latin tradition which stresses the *cura animarum* (care of souls). Some of his writings, like the *Judica Me* (*Judge Me*) and some of his earlier commentaries, cover pastoral purposes. They would have empowered parish priests by giving them the necessary material to ruminate on when searching the soul of their parishioners during the sacrament of confession. Rolle himself seems to have moved from a gradual sense of his own sinfulness in his early pieces, to a greater sense of spiritual identity in his middle works. His late Middle English works show the degree of confidence he has reached in his activity as spiritual guide for nuns and female anchorites.[23]

Many of Rolle's texts are deeply affective in nature, appealing to the emotion of his audience in order to move it to a stronger desire for God. The ways in which Rolle suggests the soul is moved to the love of God have sometimes been considered controversial by scholars. At times Rolle overtly projects himself and his experiences as a superior model of the spiritual life. Also he makes contemplative claims that some of his contemporaries deemed excessively ambitious. The Latin *Incendium amoris* (*The Fire of Love*) is autobiographical at times and it shares many of the weaknesses and qualities which are hallmarks of his textual output, such as the apparent desire for self-promotion and the construction of an authoritative narratorial presence, but these are also mixed with moments of great sincerity. Of the five 'Middle English mystics', Rolle is perhaps the one who insists more on touching the affection in order to trigger contemplative feeling. For that reason, he belongs to a tradition marked by the impact of pastoral theology and spiritual psychology as spread by the friars.

The Latin *Melos amoris* (*Song of Love*) is a postil (an expository discourse inspired by a biblical book) on the Song of Songs. *Melos* stands as a pivotal text, in which pastoral and more contemplative passages cohabit. The generic form of this piece is occasionally thwarted by the insertion of autobiographical passages which convey Rolle's personal views about the religious life. It is revealing of Rolle's own concept of the religious life, and shows that, together with contemplative aspirations, he was also very much aware of the need for basic instruction. The extract below is made up of a patchwork of contemplative and contempt-for-the-world passages which is characteristic of the entire piece:

O Spiritus specialis, inspira spiramen: quemadmodum cupio carnem calcare et carere cupidine squalore cooperta, ita et integre animer amore Auctoris et ambulem ad alta ardens amore. Forma feminea non flectet firmatum nec puritas pacifica pectoris pii putredini patebit, sed spreta spurcicia Speciosum in splendore cernere suspiro et interna intendo intente intueri, audacter aspiciens ad oculos Amati. Sanctus secernitur a seculi singultu, et singulare solacium, scilicet celeste, sumit incessanter, corporale contagium continue conquassans. Terror tristicie trahetur a tali et thronus Trinitatis in thalamo tuetur tacite triumphans tormenta tiranni.[24]

O friendly Spirit, send me your inspired breath: I wish to scorn the flesh and deprive myself of this sordidly clothed concupiscence and, vivified by the love of my Author, I want also to walk towards the peaks in the ardor of this love. Woman's beauty will not make me tremble, because I am now strong. In its purity and peace, my heart full of tenderness cannot let corruption invade it. Showing contempt for impurity, it is the God of Beauty which I wish to see in its splendor. I try to gaze at its depths, boldly setting my eyes into those of the Beloved. The saint is protected from the weeping world and he enjoys ceaselessly a singular consolation – that is that of heaven – as he wins constant victories over carnal attraction. Fear of unhappiness is banished from such a soul. Protected by the Trinity, of whom she is the throne and nuptial chamber, without noise she triumphs from the persecutions of the Tyrant.

In other passages *Melos* disengages itself from the carnal-spiritual dichotomy to focus more on the metaphorical potential of the vocabulary of love. It is, however, illuminating to see in a text praised for its autobiographical and contemplative qualities traces which show the influence of pastoral literature. The world, the flesh, and the devil are the enemies against which the sinful soul has to engage its fight in its journey towards union with God. Rolle incorporates and accommodates such pastoral concerns in his most ambitious religious pieces, be they written in Latin or the vernacular.

This ongoing concern for pastoral material, with which Rolle possibly first acquainted himself during his Oxford days, may account for his success as a religious author. Even the pieces written towards the end of his career, such as *Ego dormio*, display a concern for all the stages of the religious life. This piece shows how triggering contemplative feeling can be achieved in the context of early fourteenth-century religiosity. *Ego dormio* is an epistle addressed to a nun and it offers a systematic approach to the contemplative life, based on three degrees of love which correspond to different states of spiritual consciousness and religious engagement. The first degree of love is experienced when one follows the Ten Commandments and avoids committing one of the seven deadly sins. The second degree of love is achieved when one forsakes the world completely, including parents and siblings. The third degree of love corresponds to a state that Rolle defines as the contemplative life. He defines this first in rather pragmatic terms as a solitary mode of life, marked by a thought process in which prayers deliquesce into joyful song and thoughts transform into heavenly melody. This epistle is marked by a high degree of performativity. It attempts to lead its reader/listener to an affective feeling which will prompt and encourage spiritual performance. Each progressive level of consciousness is encapsulated in a lyrical outburst that crowns and defines the degree of the religious experience.[25] In each lyric, Rolle addresses and analyses the particular feeling that one is likely to experience when living in one of the three degrees of love. The epistle ends with a lyric corresponding to the third, i.e. highest, degree of love, which defines a pure spiritual form of love directed in this particular case at the person of Jesus. For the third degree, he writes:

> In þis degree of loue al drede, al sorrow, al wo, al ydel ioy and al wicked delites is put fro vs, and we lyve in swetnesses of heuyn. Thynk euer to lest, and to be bettyr and better, and þat wil gif þe grace to love hym, as he doth another.
>
> (Ogilvie-Thomson, *Richard Rolle*, p. 32)

The lyric, which Rolle calls 'a songe of love', is to be performed when one is being focused into an intense state of love for Jesus Christ. The Latin verse which begins the epistle, *Ego dormio et cor meum vigilat* (*I sleep and my heart is vigilant*) (Song of Songs 5:2), is only one of the instances of borrowing and influence of the Song of Songs for the making of this piece. The kind of feeling that Rolle tries to trigger with his request for the performance of his modern version of the Song of Songs is contemplative. But of course the lyric itself does not provide the feeling without a genuinely participatory performance. This is possible only if the performer apprehends it with a pure intention. One has to love Jesus Christ in order to experience contemplative feeling:

Ihesu my savyour, Ihesu my confortour, of fairnesse þe floure,
My helpe and my sokour, when may I se þi toure?
When wil þou me kale? Me langeth in to þi halle
To se þe and þyn alle. Thi love let hit nat falle...   (p. 33)

The strikingly strong sensuality of the piece is inspired by the Song of Songs and *fin' amor* vocabulary. Further, the narrative voice calls for Jesus' mercy so that union be made possible now:

When wil þou rewe on me, Ihesu, þat I myght with þe be,
To loue and loke on þe? My sete ordain for me,
And set þou me þerin, for þan may we never twyn,
And I þi loue shal synge þrogh syght in þy shyninge
In heuyn withouten endynge. Amen ...   (p. 33)

Rolle's strategies cannot be properly understood without appreciating his stress on the necessity of a proper performance of the song of love. Some scholars have argued that the sexual double-entendres between lovers, largely derived from the Song of Songs, contribute to the making of the Rolle-persona as messenger between lovers, guiding the female recipient to direct her love message through him to Jesus. In this case, Rolle's epistle would have the same kind of linguistic ambivalence as Thomas of Hales's 'Love Rune'. But although the early part of the epistle functions in a dialogic fashion, with the narrator fashioning himself as an expert in love and spiritual guidance, and asking the female recipient to surrender to his advice, the later, more lyrical parts of the epistle work to delete this dialogic exchange, effacing the narrator and giving the lover the initiative for a direct dialogue with Christ. The lyrics are for the recipient to be performed on uniquely direct personal terms. Rolle does not write down the experience of contemplative feeling, he only offers a textual rendering which may or may not trigger it in the performer.

These texts are only a small fraction of the enormous output of religious texts written during the period 1215 to 1349. *Ancrene Wisse*, Thomas of Hales's 'Love Rune', are written by friars (probably a Dominican friar in the case of the *Ancrene Wisse*, definitely a Franciscan friar in the case of the 'Love Rune'). With Rolle's *Ego dormio*, they are all influenced by the affective mystical tradition that the Cistercians spread in the twelfth century, and which the friars developed for lay use in the thirteenth century as part of their pastoral mission following the Fourth Lateran Council. Another characteristic shared by these texts is their high degree of performativity. The 'Love Rune' is clearly a text to be performed, as is indicated in the last stanza: 'Hwenne thu sittest in longynge,/ Drauh the forth this ilke wryt:/ Mid swete stephne thu hit singe,/ And do al so hit the byt. (ll. 201–4). The lyrics which make an integral part of *Ego dormio* are also to be performed, as in Rolle's other English epistles which use similar lyrics. Contemplative experience cannot be confined to a textual setting: the latter necessarily points to its own performative qualities. Performativity may be part of the answer in our aim at qualifying contemplative texts and the kind of feeling they hope to generate on the part on their performers in their requirement for active engagement. Many of the vernacular devotional and mystical texts written during that period initially address a female readership: three anchoresses in the case of *Ancrene Wisse* for instance, a young maiden just having become a nun in the case of the 'Love Rune', Queen Eleanor in the case of *Li Rossignos*, and a nun in the case of the *Ego Dormio*. But it would be too simplistic to conclude that affective religious literature was considered to appeal mainly or only to a female public. Some of Rolle's writings, written in the Latin language for a male clerical audience, show the same kind of affective tone as the pieces addressing female audiences. And after his death his vernacular works proved to have a hugely successful impact and spread beyond the nunnery and the anchorhold to an increasingly wider readership with the appetite for vernacular spiritual writings among literate lay men and women.

NOTES

1 For a translation of Canon 10, see the version offered in Siegfried Wenzel, *Latin Sermon Collections from Later Medieval England: Orthodox Preaching in the Age of Wyclif* (Cambridge: Cambridge University Press, 2005), p. 229.

2 Leonard Boyle, 'The *Oculus sacerdotis* and Some Other Works of William of Pagula', *TRHS* 5th ser. 5 (1955), 81–110; repr. in Boyle, *Pastoral Care, Clerical Education and Canon Law, 1200–1400*, pp. 81–110.

3 'Contemplation', from Latin 'contemplatio', translates the Greek word *theoria* in which the root *te* means to see, defines a limited, elitist form of interior life. See Santha Bhattacharji, 'Medieval Contemplation and Mystical Experience', in Dee Dyas, Valerie Edden, and Roger Ellis (eds.), *Approaching Medieval English Anchoritic and Mystical Texts* (Woodbridge: D. S. Brewer, 2005), pp. 51–59, esp. p. 51.

4 See Robert Hasenfratz (ed.), *Ancrene Wisse*, TEAMS (Kalamazoo, MI: Western Michigan University, 2000), p. 67.

5 *Ancrene Wisse*, p. 371. Anne Savage and Nicholas Watson (eds.), *Anchoritic Spirituality: Ancrene Wisse and Associated Works* (New York: Paulist Press, 1991), p. 187.

6 Bella Millett and Jocelyn Wogan-Browne (eds.), *Medieval English Prose for Women: From the Katherine Group and Ancrene Wisse* (Oxford: Oxford University Press, 1992), pp. 56–7.

7 For a study of medieval virginity in the Katherine group, see Sarah Salih, *Versions of Virginity in Late Medieval England* (Woodbridge: D. S. Brewer, 2001), esp. pp. 41–106.

8 The Wooing Group consists of the following texts: *þe Wohunge of ure Lauerd, On God Ureisun of God Almihti, On Lofsong of Ure Louerde*, and *On Lofsong of Ure Lefdi*. For an edition, see W. Meredith Thompson (ed.), *The Wohunge of Ure Lauerd*, EETS OS 241 (1958). See Salvina Westra (ed.), *A Talkyng of þe Loue of God, Edited from MS. Vernon (Bodleian 3938) and Collated with MS. Simeon (Brit. Mus. Add. 22283)* (The Hague: Martinus Nijhof, 1950).

9 See Margaret Howell, *Eleanor of Provence: Queenship in Thirteenth-Century England* (Oxford: Blackwell, 1998), pp. 92–4.

10 References by line number are to the following edition: Susanne Greer Fein (ed.), *Moral Love Songs and Lament* (Kalamazoo, MI: Medieval Institute Publications, 1998). I have used here the electronic version available at: www.lib.rochester.edu/camelot/teams/lovefrm.htm. See also Betty Hill, 'The "Luve Ron" and Thomas de Hales', *Modern Language Review* 59 (1964), and 'The History of Jesus College, Oxford MS. 29', *Medium Ævum* 32 (1964), 203–13.

11 See Malcolm Robert Moyes (ed.), *Richard Rolle's Expositio super Novem Lectiones Mortuorum*, vol. I, (Salzburg: Institut für Anglistik und Amerikanistik, 1988), pp. 47–53. For a reconsideration of the identity of John of Howden, the author, with John of Melton, prebendary of the church of Howden, see Glynn Hesketh (ed.), *Rossignos by John of Howden (a thirteenth-century meditation on the passion of Christ)*, ANTS (2006). I am grateful to Glynn Hesketh for having shared with me information about the author of *Rossignos*. For further evidence of the role played by Howden at the royal court, and especially for Queen Eleanor, see Margaret Howell, *Eleanor of Provence*, pp. 83, 97–8.

12 The reference to *Li Rossignos* is found in Cambridge, Corpus Christi College, MS 471, fol. 111r. For a description of the manuscript, see Nigel Wilkins, *Catalogue des manuscrits français de la bibliothèque Parker (Parker Library) Corpus Christi College Cambridge* (Cambridge: Parker Library, 1993).

13 Edward I's coronation ceremony took place on 19 August 1274, seventeen days after Edward's arrival in England on 2 August 1274. See Howell, *Eleanor of Provence*, pp. 287–91.

14 The poem makes direct reference to images and characters borrowed from the romance world. It also allows for significant meditative digressions on several devotional topics. For the influence of the hymn *Dulcis Iesu Memoria* on the devotion to the Name of Jesus, see Denis Renevey, 'Anglo-Norman and Middle English Translations and Adaptations of the Hymn *Dulcis Iesu Memoria*', in R. Ellis and R. Tixier (eds.), *The Medieval Translator/Traduire au Moyen Âge*, vol. 5 (Turnhout: Brepols, 1996), pp. 264–83.

15 See Moyes, *Richard Rolle's Expositio*, pp. 34–7. Stanzas 342 to 372 of *Philomela* have the devotion to the Name of Jesus as their main theme. (Information provided by Glynn Hesketh in private communication.)

16 Andrew Lawson King, 'A Critical Edition of Li Rossignos' (unsubmitted PhD thesis, University of Cambridge, 1984), p. 275. Translations are my own.

17 For a brief account of Ludolph of Saxony's *Vita Jesu Christi*, see Albert E. Hartung (ed.), *A Manual of the Writings in Middle English 1050–1500* (New Haven, CN: The Connecticut Academy of Arts and Sciences, 1993), pp. 3108–9. See also Elizabeth Salter, 'Ludolphus of Saxony and his English Translators', *Medium Ævum* 33 (1964), 26–35. For an account of the influence of Howden on Rolle, see Moyes, *Richard Rolle's Expositio*, pp. 47–53.

18 The *Meditations on the Life and Passion of Christ* is preserved in only one manuscript, London, British Library, MS Additional 11307. For an edition of this text, see Charlotte D'Evelyn (ed.), *Meditations on the Life and Passion of Christ. From British Museum Addit. MS. 11307*, EETS OS 158 (1921).

19 See S. J. Ogilvie-Thomson (ed.), *Richard Rolle, Prose and Verse*, EETS OS 293 (1988) and Ralph Hanna (ed.), *Richard Rolle: Uncollected Prose and Verse with Related Northern Texts*, EETS OS 329 (2007). For a modern English edition of Rolle's English writings, see Rosamund S. Allen (ed.), *Richard Rolle: The English Writings*, The Classics of Western Spirituality (New York: Paulist Press, 1989).

20 The *Officium et Miracula*, which were written in 1380 in hope of Rolle's canonization, provides most of the basic information about Rolle's life. There is no reason to doubt that kind of information. However, one needs to be careful about much else, as the documents were drawn in order to strengthen Rolle's case for canonization. The information above is borrowed freely from Nicholas Watson's own rendering of this document. See Nicholas Watson, *Richard Rolle and the Invention of Authority* (Cambridge: Cambridge University Press, 1991), pp. 31–53.

21 For a consideration of generic variety in Rolle's corpus, see Denis Renevey, 'Richard Rolle', in Dyas *et al.*, *Medieval English Texts* (Woodbridge: D. S. Brewer, 2005), pp. 63–74. For a consideration of the way in which the commentary tradition of the Song of Songs shaped Rolle's mysticism, see Denis Renevey, *Language, Self and Love: Hermeneutics in the Writings of Richard Rolle and the Commentaries on the Song of Songs* (Cardiff: University of Wales Press, 2001).

22 For an example of accommodation of Rolle's writings, see E. A. Jones (ed.), *The 'Exhortacion' from Disce Mori*, Middle English Texts 36 (Heidelberg: Universität Verlag Winter, 2006); see also by Jones, 'A Chapter from Richard Rolle in Two Fifteenth-Century Compilations', *Leeds Studies in English* n.s. 27 (1996), 139–62.

23 For a chronology of Rolle's writings and the works belonging to the early, middle and late categories, see Watson, *Richard Rolle*, pp. 273–94.

24 For a brief discussion of *Melos*, see Renevey, *Language, Self and Love*, pp. 91–102. François Vandenbroucke (ed.), Richard Rolle, *Le Chant d'amour (Melos Amoris)*, vol. 1, Sources Chrétiennes 168 (Paris: Cerf, 1971), p. 226. The English translation, based on the Latin text and the French facing translation, is my own.

25 For further discussion on Rolle and performance, see Denis Renevey, 'Mystical Texts or Mystical Bodies? Peculiar Modes of Performance in Late Medieval England', in Peter Halter (ed.), *Performance*, Swiss Papers in English Language and Literature 11 (Tübingen: Günter Narr, 1998), pp. 89–104.

6

JEREMY CATTO

1349–1412: culture and history

The death of Richard Rolle, probably on 29 September 1349, marks the beginning of a new period in the practice of the contemplative life in England. A recluse latterly resident at Hampole in the south of Yorkshire, he would be noted in the district for his miracles and would be the focus of a local cult, playing a traditional and respected part not greatly changed, perhaps, since the seventh century. On the other hand, he was among the first European contemplatives to combine the description of his religious experiences, previously a literary genre characteristic of female enthusiasts like Mechtild of Magdeburg, with a grasp of mystical theology which enabled him to direct the spiritual life of nuns and recluses. His English successors Walter Hilton and the author of the *Cloud of Unknowing* would direct their readers in the contemplative art with the authority of personal experience, correcting in the process the undisciplined religious emotion which they associated with Rolle. He was the pioneer of an art which would cease to be the exclusive practice of monks and recluses and would by stages enter the mainstream of lay religious practice, a process far from complete by 1412.

Rolle's works of instruction, notably the *Incendium amoris* (*Fire of Love*), the *Emendatio vitae* (*The Amending of Life*) and the *Form of Living*, were written largely though not exclusively for nuns and hermits; they were composed both in Latin and English, and it is likely that at first they were known only to a small circle of Yorkshire admirers: Margaret Kirkeby, for whom more than one of them were written, the nuns of Hampole, and other recluses of the vicinity (a hermit of Tanfield owned a Rolle text in 1409), together with their lay patrons of the Scrope and FitzHugh families.[1] After 1390 they seem to have become known in the circle of Thomas Arundel, archbishop of York (1388–96) and to have enjoyed wide popularity in the fifteenth century, being copied and translated systematically for an increasingly lay readership both in England and abroad. Their fate illustrates a dominant theme in the development of the contemplative art in this period: its emergence from the structured world of religious houses and reclusories where spiritual advice from the learned was available through personal instruction, into a larger literary world in which texts were scrutinized, licensed, and proliferated systematically for the edification of a sophisticated and independent-minded laity. The subject of this chapter is the reading of spiritual literature in this rapidly changing period. The nature of the genre, the cultural formation of its authors, and the development of its readership are topics which will need some consequent attention.

The quiet gestation of Rolle's writings, followed by their rapid proliferation in the last part of this period, illustrates the coming of age of a literary genre new in England: guides to the art of contemplation, now becoming distinct from sermons, exhortations to a better life, expositions of the Decalogue, and other instruments of moral and pastoral religious teaching. It was a literature of which the common ground was the development of *conscientia* (self-awareness) as the starting point of contemplation. This was a notion grounded in the moral and pastoral theology of the later fourteenth century; it had come to be articulated as the great speculative questions of the mid-century, the relation of God's omnipotence to human free will and that of divine grace to human merit, and had been subtly refocused in more personal terms, on the issue of salvation, or justification as it would be termed in the following century. These great questions had never been purely speculative, and as developed by Thomas Bradwardine in his *De causa Dei contra Pelagianos* (*The case of God against the Pelagians*), the doctrine of God's gratuitous grace and predestination of the saved became a source of consolation and a spur to steadfast faith for the sinner, and therefore a powerful influence on confessors (like Bradwardine himself) by whom men of action sought to be absolved. Though philosophical speculation on such topics, exhausted by fifty years of discussion, was at a discount in the later years of the century and dismissed by theologians such as Jean Gerson in Paris as useless and insubstantial, it underpinned the discussion in theology faculties of consequent questions which touched on the moral life of the individual: the nature of the state of innocence before the Fall; the salvation of non-Christians; the constitution and destiny of the community of the faithful, the Church; and the character of public religious cult and private devotion. John Uthred of Boldon, a monk of Durham, raised the question of the salvation of unbaptized infants, and in the 1370s John Wyclif, the leading theologian of Oxford, seeking a legitimate basis for ecclesiastical authority, found the only reliable criterion of truth to be the word of Scripture, leaving its specific meaning to the interior judgement of its readers.

In all these questions, the *forum internum* of individual conscience was the touchstone of practical moral judgement.

The spread of the practice of private confession with its concomitant examination of conscience was a potent instrument of moral self-awareness, at least among the circle of Edward III's companions in war. A confessor's precept probably prompted Henry, duke of Lancaster, to write his *Livre de seyntz medicines* (*c.* 1355), effectively the examination of a military commander's conscience; similar advice, perhaps, impelled his unmilitary colleague Humphrey Bohun, sixth earl of Hereford to keep a French translation of Grosseteste's *Confession* in his Book of Hours.[2] Numerous guides to the conduct of confession suggest that the practice was already widespread by the third quarter of the century. One of the most popular was the *Oculus sacerdotis* (*The Eye of the Priest*) of William of Pagula, compiled in the 1320s but recommended officially for use in parishes in the northern province in the 1360s; though its moral guidance was not limited to the work of confessors, its detailed precepts for pastoral care had obvious applications in the confessional.[3] A compendious digest, the *Pupilla oculi* (*The Pupil of the Eye*), was made by John de Burgo, a Cambridge theologian, about 1385. The voluminous questions on Matthew 1–5 of William Woodford, OFM, given as doctoral lectures in Oxford in 1373–4, were directed, as he explicitly remarked, for 'those who had confessions to hear'.[4] New pastoral manuals such as the *Cibus anime* (*Food of the Soul, c.* 1380–1400) found a ready audience; the latter was adapted about 1400 for a simpler use, with part of the text turned into mnemonic verses in English, in the popular work *Speculum Christiani* (*A Christian's Mirror*).[5] In this period, expositions of moral theology were beginning to be compiled in English, in language carefully adapted to avoid unorthodoxies, and sometimes in verse, presumably so that passages could be read out and committed to memory by the illiterate. This may have been the use to which the especially popular text *The Pricke of Conscience* was put: this verse tract, written perhaps about 1370, was arranged around the stages of human life and final destiny, making the operation of conscience as transparent as possible.[6] *Dives and Pauper* is a more extensive and rather discursive exposition of the Ten Commandments, compiled about 1405 apparently by a friar, which turns from general moral instruction to consideration of the 'mixed life', the art of contemplation practised within an active way of life.[7] Books of moral guidance such as *Dives and Pauper* or the *Speculum Christiani* were, it seems, more likely to be found in the hands of pastors and confessors, and their contents administered in confession, or in sermons; their objective, however, was the refinement by examination of conscience of the individual. Their purpose was distinct, of course, from that of guides to the art of contemplation like the *Cloud of Unknowing*; but they marked out conscience and moral self-awareness as the starting point for the more arduous journey set out by its author.

Most pastoral manuals and their derivatives are anonymous. Where they are ascribed, they show unmistakeable evidence that their authors had a university training in theology, like the Cistercian William Rimington, author of a *Stimulus peccatoris* (*The Goad of Sinners*), or John de Burgo, compiler of the *Pupilla oculi* (*The Pupil of the Eye*); or in canon law, such as John Acton, the author of *Septuplum commentatum de peccatis* (*Seven-part Exposition of Sins*). This is equally true of writers in English, such as William of Nassington, a canonist who composed the long English poem *Speculum vitae* (*The Mirror of Life*), Richard Lavenham, O Carm, the author of a *Litil Tretys* on the Seven Deadly Sins, or Richard Maidstone, O Carm, whose verse paraphrase of the penitential psalms became a popular devotional text. The two latter had degrees in theology; that they were both Carmelite friars may well imply that the mendicant orders, or at least their university-trained members, were active in preparing pastoral material for the direct instruction of the unlettered. Where they are not ascribed, the wide range of sources and reliance on learned works which is characteristic of both Latin and English pastoral texts indicates clearly that their compilers had a theological or canonical education. They were not however speculative theologians in the mould of Duns Scotus; theologians of the later fourteenth century had become, and canonists had always been, involved in the service of church and government, and their widely circulated digests of moral theology were at least congruent with and possibly an instrument of government's increasing aspiration to influence or control the moral life of its subjects.

Theologians and canonists, whose learning had always overlapped and whose shared concerns were now largely identical, were the vanguard of the movement of university graduates into the leadership of the Church, and enjoyed the lion's share of its patronage; and as bishops and other high ecclesiastical dignitaries were essential to the running of temporal government, together with a militarized nobility, their opportunities in the service of the English crown were correspondingly increasing. Something of their culture and outlook can be gleaned from the letter books of John Lydford and Gilbert Stone, graduates who served in a variety of bishops' households between 1360 and 1410, writing letters on their masters' behalf and sometimes on their own business. In these letters the careerists' constant search for patronage and benefices, their friendship networks, which often originated at university, and their lightly borne but thorough Latin culture come to life.[8] Their more proactive and intelligent service of secular and ecclesiastical government must have transferred the argumentative style of university disputation to the world of government. If they had new opportunities of advancement, they also had new anxieties, heightened by the uncertain prospects inseparable from life at the top.

The emergence of the graduate careerist would have a direct bearing on the practice of the contemplative art. Several of its proponents, most notably Walter Hilton, had first sought and then had given up the rewards of their calling; and further, concern for the active life and its responsibilities prompted some of them, Hilton again to the fore, to seek ways of accommodating it to contemplative practice. But the most immediate consequence of this development was the overflow of university debates on theological and ecclesiological questions into the public domain, making the later fourteenth century a period of sharp and sometimes violent religious controversy in which theologians deliberately sought to engage lay sympathy, sometimes to the displeasure of government but occasionally with its connivance. It is necessary, therefore, to consider how this public debate about religion was related to the quickening appeal of the contemplative life outside the monastic orders. Implicit in theologians' public activity was the recognition of the independent judgement of the lay world as a valid form of Christian witness: a recognition that authors of works like Henry of Lancaster's *Livre de seyntz medicines* (*Book of Holy Medicines*) were responding to their call for moral self-awareness and therefore had a new status in the life of the Church. A harbinger of the era of public controversy appeared in 1356, in the shape of the popular sermons of Richard Fitzralph, archbishop of Armagh, against the friars, preached in London and elsewhere. FitzRalph was, or had become, one of the new breed of theologians whose public employment, in his case by the Roman curia to discuss reunion with Armenian prelates, had fed his theological ideas and writings, and whose pastoral work as an Irish archbishop had similarly sharpened his eschatological perception of the friars as agents of destruction of proper ecclesiastical order.[9] This was a challenge to the established masters of evangelizing the laity, the mendicant orders who had moulded the popular religion of the time; like the friars' preaching, it was a challenge founded in theological expertise and debatable in the schools; but in intention at least it aimed to draw in the laity, the listeners to Fitzralph's sermons at St Paul's Cross, and thus to open a public debate, at once intellectual and popular, of a kind hitherto unknown in England. Fitzralph's ally John Grandisson, the powerful bishop of Exeter, in his diocesan letter against the friars of 1358–9, ordered to be read to congregations, and their allies among monastic preachers also aspired to raise lay opinion on their side. They do not appear to have succeeded: the affair went unmentioned in the contemporary political record, though Edward III took some notice: he inhibited preaching against the friars and tried to prevent either side from taking the case to the Roman curia.

The laity were perhaps still unprepared to express opinions on religious issues. In the next decades religious questions were occasionally aired in controversial sermons preached to the laity. In 1367 the Dominican William Jordan seems to have denounced from the pulpit up and down the country the opinions of the monastic scholar John Uthred of Boldon (expressed in the Oxford schools on a variety of points), perhaps in retaliation for Uthred's earlier support for Fitzralph. This debate too was prohibited by the church authorities when Archbishop Langham forbade discussion of the matter and then censured propositions made by both parties, without naming either: whether the public character of this controversy influenced him is not certain, but it is consistent with the authorities' response to Fitzralph ten years earlier.[10] The most notable effect of the debate on the friars and clerical dominion was a settled bias against the mendicants and their activities among graduates and officials active in government; it is virulently and repeatedly expressed in the encyclopaedia *Omne Bonum*, compiled by the exchequer clerk James le Palmer about 1375, and echoes are found in the works of Chaucer and Gower and especially in *Piers Plowman*, a poem whose author was familiar with the exchequer and its officials.[11] While these ideas were commonplace in the *bienpensant* world of the graduate careerist, they do not seem at this time to have affected the bulk of the laity, who continued to make charitable bequests to friars and to take them as confessors. But in the 1370s, when a more formidable and much more prestigious scholar, John Wyclif, raised another variation on the theme of clerical and lay dominion, or authority, and its relation to grace, religious controversy would enter the bloodstream of public life irreversibly.

Wyclif was a theologian careerist in the contemporary mould: he had made his name, about 1370, as a great Oxford logician and philosopher; but he was as ready for government service, and as ambitious for its rewards, as any contemporary, and was prepared to allow his experience of representing the government in its diplomatic battle with the Roman curia over papal taxation (1374) to inform further theological writings on the urgent practical questions of the era, the authority of the clergy, the independent judgement of lay Christians, and the idolatries of popular religion exhibited most scandalously, as he saw it, in the cult of the eucharist. If the format of his career and its interpenetration by his writings approximated to that of immediate predecessors such as Fitzralph or such contemporaries overseas as the Franciscan Peter Philargi of Candia, later Pope Alexander V, or Pierre d'Ailly the chancellor of Paris, its outcome was quite different, in spite of strong if sporadic support from patrons at court. Too controversial for preferment, his opinions were ineffectively condemned by the pope in 1377 and more conclusively by the English church in 1382, and he remained teaching in Oxford until impelled to retire to the country for the last, defiant phase of his career (1381–4). But by then he had changed for ever the nature and scope of religious controversy in England, forcing it out of university lecture rooms into the pulpit, the market place, and the residences of the nobility. His attack on clerical property rights, launched in Oxford lectures in 1375–6, was broadcast in a series of London pulpits with full government support in the autumn of 1376, and he preached again in defence of the government's breach of ecclesiastical sanctuary rights in 1378. As a beneficiary of the church's privileges, his strictures were in part directed against himself (as he disarmingly pointed out): they were another example of the sense of guilt and anxiety exhibited also by Hilton, in a very different way; Wyclif showed no sign of interest in the interior devotional practice by which the art of contemplation was nurtured.

Wyclif's activities won him the support of numerous Oxford colleagues, some of whom such as Nicholas Hereford and Philip Repingdon preached his views up and down the country, and cooperated in producing a vernacular Wycliffite sermon-cycles, numerous moral tracts, and above all an English translation of the Scriptures in the last twenty years of the century. These unorthodox or 'Lollard' works resembled in form, and often in learning, contemporary didactic literature, and sometimes circulated in their company. The resemblance is superficial, however: the burden of the sermon-cycle and of tracts such as *Vae octuplex* (*The Eightfold Woe*) or *Speculum de Antichristo* (*The Mirror of the Antichrist*) is not the refinement of personal conscience but the identification of enemies of true believers and of the religious or superstitious practices which they fostered. They were therefore, like Wyclif's polemical work, a contribution to the reform of public religion. This is not to say that individual Lollard masters, careerists like their contemporaries, did not eventually feel the call of the religious life: Repingdon, having submitted and risen to occupy the see of Lincoln, resigned it to live more simply in retirement; and Hereford, another deserter from the Lollard cause, would become a Carthusian in old age. Nevertheless, the preaching of the Lollards had little in common with the interior direction of the religious life as set out by the *Cloud of Unknowing* or Hilton's *Scale of Perfection*. Wyclif and the Lollard masters urged a form of interior independence on the laity quite different from the self-awareness engendered by contemplation. The lay Christian was to exercise his own judgement on external religion: 'we may not yit wite for certeyn which persone is of Cristis spouse of alle the men that wandren heere, but we may gesse and that is ynow'.[12] Scripture alone was the one indefeasible authority in the church, but its physical manifestations, the texts in which it was read, could be corrupt, and ultimately 'intellection in the mind is more truly scripture than lines on a membrane', and its authority therefore resided in individual conscience and judgement.[13] Wyclif, then, focused in common with the author of the *Cloud* and Walter Hilton on the lay Christian, but on his judgement in a public forum, not on his interior life. The Lollards appealed to the same educated lay cadre as Hilton, but their call was to action, not to contemplative thought. Lollard literature, like the works of Wyclif himself, carried no hint of a devotional disposition.

If Wyclif and his followers, albeit of the same university milieu, had only a negative impact in this context, three letters of Walter Hilton from the 1380s throw a more direct light on the various ways in which the new breed of graduate careerists could be called to the contemplative life, and it is worth paying them some attention. They are replies to three correspondents after he had himself thrown up his legal practice, but before he made up his mind to join the Augustinian community at Thurgarton: an unhappy period, probably in the early 1380s, during which he tried to live the life of a recluse. One of his letters was apparently addressed to the canon lawyer John Thorpe, a Cambridge graduate who probably practised, as Hilton had, in the Ely consistory court.[14] Like that of Gerard Groote of Deventer, inspirer of the 'the modern devout' (*devotio moderna*) and another canonist, Thorpe's spiritual crisis occurred after illness, and in his case imprisonment for debt; under pressure, he had made an unrealistic vow, and sought to enter a religious house in expiation. Hilton's reply is a mixture of consolation and dissuasion: he advised Thorpe to lead a virtuous life in his current avocation, though to give up civil law and the consistory courtroom. In the event Thorpe continued to practise as a lawyer, perhaps mixing 'þe werkes of actif liyf wiþ goostli werkes of lif contemplatif', as Hilton would later prescribe for men of business.[15] As a professional colleague Hilton knew, and wrote with revulsion about the life Thorpe proposed to leave behind, its 'honours, favours, riches, pleasures' and the anxieties they engendered. If Thorpe's tender conscience needed bolstering, Hilton could write with more straightforward encouragement to Adam Horsley, Foreign Apposer in the Exchequer and formerly Controller of the Great Roll of the Pipe, who wished to join the Carthusian order. Horsley seems to have risen through the ranks of the Exchequer clerks; as Apposer and Controller he must have acquired the widespread skill of accounting in its specialized Exchequer form, and some legal knowledge which may have brought him into contact with Hilton.[16] Exchequer and chancery clerks normally acquired their expertise in the course of their office work; there is no reason to think that Horsley was a university graduate. His mid-life conversion to the religious vocation seems to have been of the same kind as Hilton's and his other graduate correspondents, however; in England, the common law and the service of government had created at least a metropolitan professional world parallel to that engendered by graduates of the higher faculties in Italy and France. The clarity of Horsley's intention diminished occasion for Hilton to say much in his reply about his correspondent's state of mind: references to the 'security of conscience and tranquillity of mind' he will experience in the Carthusian life, and to the 'fear of worldly cares in his earlier duty and responsibility' which have perhaps impeded his transition to the religious life may indicate that Horsley had both been an uneasy occupant of his post and had taken his responsibilities too seriously for a clean break with them (Hilton, *Epistola de utilitate et prerogativis religionis* (*A Letter on the Utility and Prerogatives of Religious Life*), Latin Writings I.119–72 (all translations are my own unless otherwise stated)). Horsley entered the Carthusian Priory of Beauvale in Nottinghamshire in 1386 and lived until 1424, apparently in good standing. In the following century, several other successful careerists would follow him in maturity into the order.

Hilton is more severe and more revealing in his letter to his third and perhaps earliest correspondent, who is unnamed, but who had enjoyed church benefices, honours, wealth, the favour of the great and the praise of his family, and who had lived in some style (*De imagine peccati* (*On the Image of Sin*), Latin Writings I.75–6). He was now, like Hilton, a solitary, and had written for advice in distress. Hilton dealt savagely with his complaints: he had not rid himself of his worldly desires, but had translated them into spiritual pride. 'How do you see yourself? For sure, you see yourself like some idol on high, superior to other people, propped up on your precious virtue... you say to yourself, I am better than them...' (*De imagine*, I.76). His correspondent's illusions are swept away: 'I know what you want: you want to be humble, and to be respected for it. The truly humble man does not want to be thought humble.' His life as a recluse is just idleness, in contrast to the secular and regular clergy, who have work to do (I.89, 86–7, 90). Hilton's ruthless dissection gained depth and power because, as gradually becomes clear, he was really castigating himself, another solitary. 'What are we doing, the two of us and our like, lazy and useless men standing idle all the day long? We are not labouring in the Lord's vineyard by administering the sacraments, nor do we preach the word of God abroad or manifest the spiritual works of mercy... we are like children, having taken leave of our senses and our will-power, we are under no rule of life' (I.90–1). The theme of this letter is the image of sin in the soul, the invisible thread which tied him to his past life. He has not shed the burden of guilt accumulated in his professional career, but merely transmuted its desires and illusions into spiritual pride. Unless the soul be purged of pride, it can only operate sluggishly and with trepidation (*cum gravedine et anxietate*) (I.81). We do not know how Hilton's correspondent took this advice, but Hilton himself eventually abandoned his unhappy existence as a recluse and accepted the discipline of the Augustinian Rule. His later works in English, and especially the *Scale of Perfection*, were written with a confidence and serenity which contrast sharply with *De imagine peccati*. His painful journey from the consistory courtroom seems to have found its final destination in a small religious house, under not too onerous a Rule, at Thurgarton.

The transition of the contemplative art from monasteries and reclusories to a wider world where it could be cultivated by secular clerks and by the laity was effected by university-trained men of affairs like Hilton and his correspondents. Even monastic works of devotion seem to have been written by religious with university training. It is fairly clear that at least some of the great Benedictine and Cistercian houses experienced a revival of their monastic vocation in the later fourteenth century, and made serious efforts to understand the origins of monasticism and to reinterpret it as a distinct way of life comparable – or contrastable – with the life of secular clergy, friars or the laity. In this process the masters of novices, the nurturers of the monastic vocation, seem to have played the major part: at Bury, where the monastic past weighed heavily but fruitfully upon an ancient corporation, Henry Kirkestede was an active novice master after his probable period of study at Oxford, and is likely to have composed the *Speculum coenobitarum* (*The Mirror of Monks*) for the novices' instruction in the origin and purpose of the monastic life. He may also be the author of a number of brief tracts on progress in a contemplative vocation, addressed to novices, as well as a bibliographer of heroic status who tried to sort out the whole of the Latin literary tradition primarily for their use.[17] At Durham, an even older foundation, the monk of Farne (almost certainly John Whiterig), a Durham monk who had been at Oxford about 1350, was a novice master whose *Meditaciones* (*c.* 1363–71) aimed primarily in the Bonaventuran tradition to evoke pity for the sufferings of Christ; there is no hint of the stripping out of thought and feeling prescribed in the *Cloud of Unknowing*. The same is generally true of the *Meditacio devota* of Uthred of Boldon, another Oxford theologian monk of Durham, and of the *Stimulus peccatoris* (*The Goad of Sinners*) of William Rymington, O Cist, a third Oxford monastic theologian.[18] A university education seems to have sharpened the monastic scholar's sense of the contemplative purpose of cenobitic life.

It is salutary nevertheless to remember that however much the doubts and anxieties of the professional world may have been the starting point for many who set out on the difficult stages of a contemplative life, monastic houses following a regular rule tended to be where they came to rest. With the foundation of more Carthusian houses in this period, the available options increased. There were no communities living the 'common life' such as Gerard Groote had founded at Deventer after experimenting with a Carthusian vocation, but there were small houses of Austin canons, like Thurgarton, following the freer Rule of St Augustine which suited Walter Hilton, Carthusian monasteries which offered a more solitary life to Adam Horsley and many other refugees from secular cares, and of course the great Benedictine houses in whose remote cells, like that on Farne Island, it was possible to follow a way of life of great austerity. Nunneries were almost equally various, though the Brigittine rule which especially fostered the contemplative life was followed in only one great house at Syon, and there only after 1415. The vocation of the enclosed recluse seems to have been popular with spiritual women of this period, including Rolle's disciple Margaret Kirkeby and of course Julian of Norwich. Recluses seem to have generally had some spiritual direction, often perhaps from friar confessors, and to judge by Julian's encounter with Margery Kempe, the opportunity to offer spiritual advice; her *Book of Showings*, describing in two separate versions her vision of Christ and revelation of divine love, was intended for the guidance of contemplatives, and the short version was circulated with other spiritual literature by Carthusians and others. Her remarkable learning, of a generally monastic kind, and her familiarity with rhetorical colours, also throw light on what the life of a recluse could achieve, free from secular cares yet unburdened by the demands of a community.[19]

Some of the literature of contemplation was addressed to monks and then adapted for the laity, but increasingly the lay reader was its target audience and forms of the mixed life its primary subject. It is now necessary, therefore, to consider who read these works and how they were circulated. The *medelid lijf*, or 'mixed life' which Hilton described, was designed for lay aspirants as well as for clergy active in affairs, and it brings into focus the increasingly sophisticated and educated lay officers of government, primarily the nobility but including to varying degrees the gentlemen who kept the king's business going in the English provinces. Hilton envisaged the mixed life as appropriate for clergy active in business, and also for 'sum temporal men the whiche have sovereynte with moche avere of wordli goodis, and have also as it were lordschipe overe othere men for to governe and sustene hem' (*Walter*

Hilton's Mixed Life, pp. 14–15). It is fairly clear that in the earlier fifteenth century 'temporal men' of this kind were receptive to devotional literature like *Donatus devocionis* (*Manual of Devotion*) or Simon Wynter's *Life of St Jerome*, and might be invited to copy them as a religious exercise.[20] The evidence for the later fourteenth century is more ambiguous; it shows some members of the high nobility habitually examining their conscience, like Humphrey Earl of Hereford mentioned above, or the member of the Hungerford family who owned the missal with additional prayers which is now in the University Library at Cambridge (Cambridge, University Library, MS Add. 451), but the degree of independent religious life among officials and the county gentry who performed much of the government's work remains obscure. Such rare survivals as the late fourteenth-century Book of Hours in York Minster Library made before 1396 for Joan Mountenay of Shercliffe near Doncaster, with its additional psalms and aids to devotion, may indicate that their personal religion may easily be underestimated.[21] A similar pattern emerges from the inventories, uncommon though they are, of forfeited property, which in the three known cases of this period list books. All three of them relate to noblemen and courtiers condemned for treason: Sir Simon Burley in 1388, Thomas of Woodstock, duke of Gloucester in 1397, and Henry, Lord Scrope of Masham in 1415. In all three cases devotional works in Latin or English have a prominent place: Gloucester's *Speculum humane salvationis* (*Mirror of Human Salvation*), Scrope's collection of Rolle texts and books of meditation, Burley's two expositions of the Ten Commandments, one of them new, were probably familiar texts to their owners and must imply some religious individuality and receptivity to the practice of the mixed life, however sporadic under pressure of business it may have been.[22] But they refer to the world of the court and the high nobility, some of whom in all likelihood were the first lay persons to have an idea of the mixed life and its implications.

The mixed life was prescribed by Walter Hilton not only for the laity but for the 'men of holi chirche, as to prelates and othire curates which have cure and sovereynte over othere men, for to kepe and for to rule hem' (*Walter Hilton's Mixed Life*, p. 14). One particular clerical circle, the household and intimates of Thomas Arundel as archbishop of York in the early 1390s has been identified as the initial milieu in which Rolle's works, confined as they hitherto seem to have been to his immediate disciples and their patrons, were copied and circulated. Arundel had surrounded himself with vigorous proponents of an enhanced pastoral care which could outface the attraction of the Lollards: Richard Scrope, rector of Ainderby when Margaret Kirkeby was a recluse there, was Arundel's official at Ely, bishop of Lichfield (1386–98) and finally Arundel's second (and martyred) successor at York; William

Noion, his receiver at Ely and treasurer at York; John Newton, master of Peterhouse, Cambridge, and his vicar-general at York and several others.[23] Lawyers and scholars by training, they made the chapter at York a centre of devotional and pastoral activity which outlasted Arundel's tenure of the see (1388–96), continuing under those of Richard Scrope (1398–1405) and Henry Bowet (1407–23). Their experience in the Ely consistory court implies that they must have known Walter Hilton well; they were natural subjects for his notion of the mixed life. But his *Scale* did not circulate among them, in contrast to Rolle's works, whose popularity can be detected by the first bequests of his books from associates of Arundel and from York clergy in 1396 and 1398.[24] Newton went to the trouble of correcting a text of Rolle's *Incendium Amoris* in his own hand, by reference to a text alleged to be Rolle's autograph.[25] This may be only one of several attempts to establish good texts of the Rolle canon by reference to accessible autographs of the master, which could only have been undertaken within a limited distance of Hampole or West Tanfield where autographs survived.[26] The process of ascription to Rolle of both old and new didactic or devotional texts had already begun in these early collections. A note of criticism could also be heard: the author of the *Cloud of Unknowing* warned against 'a fals hete wrouȝt by þe feende', and another critic, apparently a Carthusian prior, was sharply taken to task by Thomas Basset, perhaps another Carthusian, for his detraction of Rolle.[27] But the rapid circulation of Rolle's writings by Carthusians from exemplars provided by Richard Scrope and his circle shows that his defenders had the best of the argument.

In the end both detractors and defenders had their eye on the ultimate readers and hearers of Rolle's or Hilton's teaching, the educated laity. One way of bringing the written word to them was by providing exemplars of accessible devotional literature from which appropriate texts could be copied for lay use. In the 1430s one Carthusian compilation, the *Donatus devocionis* and another from the associated house of Syon, Simon Wynter's *Life of St Jerome*, were put together for copying by lay persons for their own use: the first was partly copied by Jean d'Orléans, a prisoner in England, while the author suggested that Margaret duchess of Clarence should copy the second as a spiritual exercise.[28] While there is no clear instance of this practice in the late fourteenth century, the great 'libraries' of texts in the enormous Vernon manuscript, originally of 404 separate texts, and its less bulky sister codex, the Simeon manuscript, seem to have been designed for selections to be copied for private use. The Vernon text in particular must have been made to rest on a lectern or reading-stand; as many texts are of northern origin, while the two scribes can be located to north-west Worcestershire and there is a reference to Newark as not too far away, it is tempting to speculate that it was made to be consulted at Lichfield Cathedral, about 1395, at the instigation of bishop Richard Scrope.[29] It is headed *Salus anime* and *Sawlehele* (*Health of the Soul*); the text of the Southern Legendary is modified for private reading rather than preaching; its purpose, therefore seems to focus on the encouragement of inward devotion in persons of various needs and capacities who could at least read the texts. F. 91v of the Simeon manuscript bears the name of Joan Bohun, countess of Hereford, the matriarch of a notably devout family, though whether she owned it or merely consulted it is not clear. A third miscellany, Oxford, University College MS 97, which contains some of the Simeon manuscript's texts, belonged to William Counter, the chaplain and perhaps confessor of Sir William Beauchamp, once a fellow-traveller of the 'Lollard knights' and devotee of the cult of the Holy Name; one of the texts is headed 'heere begynneth a full good meditacion for oon to seie by himself al oun'.[30] It would seem that William Beauchamp and Joan Bohun, educated and thoughtful members of the high nobility, were characteristic examples of the target readership sought for the new style of devotional tract.

At some point shortly after 1400, the lead in the diffusion of spiritual texts seems to have been taken by members of the Carthusian Order. While Carthusians by no means had a monopoly over the distribution of texts, they had distinct advantages: the creation of a spiritual library in both Latin and vernacular languages from texts which might have originally been written in French, Italian, Dutch, German, or English was a task prefigured by the instruction of an early prior, Guigo II, to copy and circulate devotional texts. The systematic translation of texts, however, seems to have marked a new project in which Carthusians in many parts of Europe needed to cooperate.[31] Though no direct evidence of any plan survives in the archives of the Order, it is likely that much of the original impetus came from Stephen Maconi, Prior of the Order from 1398 to 1410, who had been an early associate of Catherine of Siena and was instrumental in the Latin translation and circulation of her letters and *Dialogo* throughout the Order.[32] Significantly, these were not written by a Carthusian; texts by both Carthusians and outsiders were adopted, translated and diffused without distinction. Among works by English authors, the Latin version of Hilton's *Scale of Perfection* was translated by a Carmelite contemporary, Thomas Fishlake, O Carm, but both versions were probably circulated by the Carthusians.[33] By contrast, it seems that a Carthusian translated *The Cloud of Unknowing*, itself probably a Carthusian work, into Latin.[34] It was presumably due to Carthusian action that the *Cloud*-author's desire to restrict access to his book was respected while other texts more suited to a wider public were circulated. Among the latter, the *Mirror of the Blessed Life of Jesus Christ*, a rendering of the *Meditationes vitae Christi* attributed to Bonaventure, written sometime before 1410 by Nicholas Love, Prior of Mount Grace, was particularly noteworthy in attracting the imprimatur of Archbishop Arundel, probably in 1409, when Arundel was both the leader of the English Church and the king's principal minister. Love's version gave a sacramental framework to Bonaventure's text through passages on confession and the Eucharist, thus placing the practice of contemplation in the context of public religion, and incidentally criticizing Lollard notions of religious practice. Arundel's positive commendation of the work gave it a favoured status among other Carthusian-circulated contemplative texts, and ensured that copies would be in the hands of the educated laity.[35] The archbishop's constitutions, published originally in January 1407 but reissued definitively in April 1409, about the same time as his adoption of Love's *Mirror* as the standard text for personal devotions, provided firm definition to the permitted bounds of initiative in matters of religion. Besides prohibitions on unauthorized preaching, translating texts of scripture and expounding the works of Wyclif, Arundel forbade theological speculation in university arts faculties and reaffirmed his predecessor's procedure of inquiry into the orthodoxy of Oxford students; he explicitly commended popular devotional practices, 'the adoration of the glorious Cross, the veneration of images of the saints, and pilgimages to their shrines or relics ... by means of processions, genuflexions, bowing the head, incensing, making offerings, kissing [the relics], and burning lights before them'. The practice of private contemplation was to be firmly located in a public religious context, its devotional prompts repeated in the liturgical prayers of the Use of Sarum, the ever more widely accepted voice of the fifteenth-century church of England.[36]

The achievement of the English writers and compilers of contemplative texts in this period was undoubtedly greater than that of any previous generation since the time of Richard of St Victor. Without separating the art of contemplation from its roots in the moral teaching and sacramental life of the Church, they had begun to explore its specific character; they had developed several distinctive approaches to it; and they had made it more accessible to the active clergy and the laity. They were no longer primarily monastic by profession: though some were monks, their common experience was the university world and its professional training; they were familiar with the techniques of argument, with the disciplines of theology or canon law and with the wealth of Latin religious texts which were available at Oxford and Cambridge. Even Julian of Norwich, whose sex precluded her from sharing the university experience, was clearly familiar with a rich literature in Latin and had some rhetorical training. For Walter Hilton and some others, a privileged career in the law created anxieties which eventually forced him to seek a form of claustral discipline, but gave urgency thereafter to his reflection on the active and the mixed life. His suffering is comparable to that of Jean Gerson in Paris and Gerard Groote in Utrecht, both of them like Hilton trained in a professional discipline at university; like them he was able in the end to see it as a tribulation sent by God. These writers commonly underwent individual spiritual experiences: they were also able to articulate them for readers aware of the difficult process of spiritual ascent, and willing to be instructed. Their readers were still, ideally, under some monastic or reclusory life. Increasingly, however, they included clergy and laity active in affairs, and Hilton at least was prepared to meet the aspirations of his new readers with advice on the mixed life. The Carthusians, finally, seem to have created an international library of spiritual texts in both Latin and several vernaculars, which included compilations and miscellanies directly for lay use. In this period, the art of contemplation had begun to be practised outside the monastic life, *de cella in seculum*. If the process was a long way from completion in 1412, the first essential stages had already been achieved.

NOTES

1 Hope Emily Allen, *Writings Ascribed to Richard Rolle Hermit of Hampole* (New York: MLA and London: Oxford University Press, 1927), pp. 28–9, 504–8; Jonathan Hughes, *Pastors and Visionaries* (Woodbridge: D. S. Brewer 1988), pp. 202–8.

2 E. J. F. Arnould (ed.), *Le Livre de Seyntz Medicines*, ANTS (1940); The Bohun Book of Hours, London, British Library, MS Egerton 3277, ff. 166–168v.

3 L. E. Boyle, 'The *Oculus Sacerdotis* of William of Pagula', *TRHS* 5th ser. 5 (1955), 81–110.

4 William Woodford, *Super Matthaeum*, Cambridge, University Library, MS Additional 3571, f. 213r.

5 On these two texts, see esp. Vincent Gillespie, 'The *Cibus Anime* Book 3: A Guide for Contemplatives?', in James Hogg (ed.), *Analecta Cartusiana* 35, *Spiritualität Heute und Gestern* 3, 3 (Salsburg: Institut für Anglistik und Amerikanistik, 1983), pp. 90–119, and 'The Evolution of the *Speculum Christiani*', in A. J. Minnis (ed.), *Latin and Vernacular: Studies in Late-Medieval Texts and Manuscripts* (Woodbridge: D. S. Brewer 1989), pp. 39–62.

6 R. Morris (ed.), *The Pricke of Conscience* (London: Philological Society 1863).

7 P. H. Barnum (ed.), *Dives and Pauper*, 3 vols., EETS OS 275, 280 323 (1976–2004).

8 Dorothy M. Owen (ed.), *John Lydford's Book* (London: Historical Manuscripts Commission JP 22, 1974). Stone's letters have not been edited; see Oxford, Bodleian Library, MS Bodley 859, ff. 1–42v.

9 See Katherine Walsh, *A Fourteenth-Century Scholar and Primate: Richard FitzRalph in Oxford, Armagh and Avignon* (Oxford: Clarendon Press, 1981), pp. 406–21; Penn R. Szittya, *The Antifraternal Tradition in Medieval Literature* (Princeton: Princeton University Press, 1986), pp. 123–51.

10 See David Knowles, 'The Censured Opinions of Uthred of Boldon', *PBA* 37 (1951–3), pp. 305–42; J. I. Catto, 'Wyclif and Wycliffism at Oxford, 1356–1430', in J. I. Catto and I. A. R. Evans (eds.), *The History of University of Oxford*, vol. II, *Late Medieval Oxford* (Oxford: Clarendon Press, 1984), pp. 184–6.

11 L. F. Sandler (ed.), *Omne Bonum: Fourteenth-Century Encyclopedia of Universal Knowledge*, 2 vols. (London: Harvey Miller, 1996).

12 *De officio pastorali*, in F. D. Matthew (ed.), *The English Works of Wyclif hitherto unprinted*, EETS OS 74 (1880), p. 422, quoted by Anne Hudson, *The Premature Reformation: Wycliffite Texts and Lollard History* (Oxford: Clarendon Press, 1988), p. 315.

13 John Wyclif, *De veritate sacrae scripturae*, ed. R. Buddensieg, 3 vols. (London: Wyclif Society), 1905–7, I, 189.

14 *Epistola ad quemdam seculo renunciare volentem*, in J. P. H. Clark and Cheryl Taylor (eds.), *Walter Hilton's Latin Writings*, 2 vols., Analecta Carthusiana 124 (Salzburg: Institut für Anglistik und Amerikanistik, 1987), II, 249–98. The attribution was made in a lost manuscript, probably from Bury, cited by Bale; for Thorpe, see A. B. Emden, *Biographical Register of the University of Cambridge to 1500* (Cambridge: Cambridge University Press, 1963), pp. 586, 684.

15 S. J. Ogilvie-Thomson (ed.), *Walter Hilton's* Mixed Life *edited from Lambeth Palace MS 472*, (Salzburg: Institut für Anglistik und Amerikanistik, 1986), p. 10; cf. *Latin Writings*, II, 290, 262.

16 Horsley was appointed Controller in 1375, and promoted to Apposer in 1382; he gave up his post at the end of Hilary Term (about mid-March) 1385. On Horsley's appointments and emoluments see J. C. Sainty, *Officers of the Exchequer*, List and Index Society Supplementary Series 18 (1983), pp. 69, 73, 78, 81; on his duties in both posts, which largely concerned the reception of sheriffs' accounts, see W. H. Bryson (ed.), L. Squibb, *A Book of all the several Officers of the Court of Exchequer (1641)*, Camden Miscellany 27, Royal Historical Society 4th ser. 14 (1975), pp. 111, 115.

17 See Richard H. Rouse and Mary A Rouse (eds.), *Henry of Kirkstede, Catalogus de libris autenticis et apocrafis*, Corpus of British Medieval Library Catalogues 11 (London: British Library, 2004), pp. xxxii–xlii, cxxvi–clxxiii;

18 D. H. Farmer (ed.), 'The Meditations of the Monk of Farne', *Analecta Monastica* 4, *Studia Anselmiana* 41 (1956), pp. 141–245; D. H. Farmer (ed.), 'The Meditacio devota of Uthred of Boldon', *Analecta Monastica* 5, *Studia Anselmiana* 43 (1958), pp. 187–206; R. O'Brien (ed.), William Rymington, *Meditationes sive Stimulus Peccatoris*, Cîteaux 16 (1965), pp. 278–304.

19 Edmund Colledge and James Walsh (eds.), *A Book of Showings to the Anchoress Julian of Norwich*, 2 vols. (Toronto: Pontifical Institute of Mediaeval Studies, 1978), esp. I, 43–71.

20 See A. I. Doyle, 'Publication by Members of the Religious Orders', in Jeremy Griffiths and Derek Pearsall (eds.), *Book Production and Publishing in Britain 1375–1475* (Cambridge: Cambridge University Press, 1989), pp. 109–23, esp. 114–16.

21 York, Minster, MS Additional 54; see J. Hunter, *Hallamshire*, Victoria County History: Yorkshire (London, 1869), p. 391; Hughes, *Pastors and Visionaries*, p. 16.

22 M. V. Clarke, *Fourteenth Century Studies* (Oxford: Clarendon Press, 1937), pp. 120–2; Viscount Dillon and W. H. StJ. Hope, 'Inventory of the Goods and Chattels Belonging to Thomas Duke of Gloucester', *Archaeological Journal* 54 (1897), 275–308, esp. 300–3; C. L. Kingsford, 'Two forfeitures in the year of Agincourt', *Archaeologia* 2nd ser. 70 (1918–20), 71–108, esp. 82–3 (books in Scrope's will) and 93–4 (books in the inventory).

23 See Margaret Aston, *Thomas Arundel* (Oxford: Clarendon Press, 1967), pp. 305–6, 313–16.

24 Sir William Thorpe (1396), in A. Gibbons (ed.), *Early Lincoln Wills* (Lincoln: J. Williamson, 1888), p. 79; Edmund Daldirston (1398) in Borthwick Institute, York, Probate Register 3, f. 16; Thomas Monkton in Borthwick Institute Probate Register 1, f. 81; Hughes, *Pastors and Visionaries*, pp. 203–5.

25 Cambridge, Emmanuel College, MS 35; see Allen, *Writings*, pp. 215–16.

26 Oxford, Bodleian Library, MS Bodley 861 is a scholarly corpus of Rolle's writings made in 1409–11 which refers several times to autographs; Cambridge, University Library, MS Dd.v.64 has unique information on the original recipients of Rolle's works. See Allen, *Writings*, pp. 22–34, 37.

27 Phyllis Hodgson (ed.), *The Cloud of Unknowing and the Book of Privy Counselling*, EETS OS 218 (1944, repr. 1981), p. 86; Thomas Basset, *Contra oblatratores Ricardi*, partially ed. in Allen, *Writings*, pp. 529–37, and in full in M. G. Sargent, 'Contemporary criticism of Richard Rolle', *Analecta Cartusiana* 55, *Sonderdruck aus Kartäusermystik und -Mystiker* 1, 1 (Salzburg: Institut für Anglistik und Amerikanistik, 1981), pp. 160–205, cf. pp. 188–205.

28 Doyle, 'Publication by Members of Religious Orders', pp. 114, 116.

29 Oxford, Bodleian Library, MS Eng. poet. a.l and London, British Library, MS Additional 22283. See Doyle, 'The Shaping of the Vernon and Simeon Manuscripts', in B. Rowland (ed.), *Chaucer and Middle English Studies in honour of Russell Hope Robbins* (London: Allen and Unwin, 1974), pp. 328–41, esp. 334.

30 Oxford, University College, MS 97, f. 153r. See Doyle, 'University College Oxford MS. 97 and its Relationship to the Simeon Manuscript' in M. Benskin and M. L. Samuels (eds.), *So Meny People, Longages and Tonges, Philological Essays in Scots and Medieval English Presented to Angus McIntosh* (Edinburgh: Middle English Dialect Project, 1981), pp. 265–82.

31 See M. G. Sargent, 'Transmission by the English Carthusians of Some Late Medieval Spiritual Writings, *JEH* 27 (1976), 225–40, and 'Contemporary Criticism of Richard Rolle', esp. pp. 170–6. Caution over the omnipresence of Carthusians in the process of diffusion of texts is expressed by A. I. Doyle, 'Carthusian Participation in the Movement of Works of Richard Rolle Between England and Other Parts of Europe in the Fourteenth and Fifteenth Centuries', in James Hogg (ed.), *Analecta Cartusiana* 55, *Kartäusermystik und -Mystiker*, 2, 2 (Salzburg: Institut für Anglistik und Amerikanistik, 1982), 109–20.

32 See E. Dupré Theseider (ed.), *Epistolario di Santa Caterina da Siena* (Fonti per la Storia d'Italia, Rome 1940), pp. xxiii–xli.

33 Vincent Gillespie, 'Vernacular Books of Religion' in Griffiths and Pearsall (eds.), *Book Production and Publishing*, pp. 317–44. Fishlake, who was evidently coeval with Hilton, is likely to have made his translation during Hilton's lifetime or not long after his death in 1396. See Emden, *Biographical Register*, p. 231.

34 See J. P. H. Clark (ed.), *Nubes Ignorandi, Analecta Cartusiana* 119 (Salzburg: Institut für Anglistik und Amerikanistik, 1989).

35 Michael Sargent (ed.), *Nicholas Love. Mirror of the Blessed Life of Jesus Christ. A Reading Text* (Exeter: Exeter University Press, 2004), and S. Ogura, R. Beadle, and M. C. Sargent, *Nicholas Love at Waseda* (Woodbridge: D. S. Brewer, 1997).

36 D. Wilkins, *Concilia magnae Britanniae et Hiberniae*, 4 vols. (London, 1737), III, 315–19.

7

ROGER ELLIS AND SAMUEL FANOUS

1349–1412: texts

This chapter opens with the death of Richard Rolle, who perished in the Black Death (1348–9), which decimated the population of the British Isles. It coincides with what was to become known as the Hundred Years' War with France, and ends in 1413 with the death of Henry IV. In 1399 Henry had deposed his cousin Richard II, who had become king as a 10-year-old boy in 1377, when his grandfather, Edward III, died. The reigns of the two grandsons witnessed periods of enormous social, political, and religious turmoil. Paradoxically, Richard's reign coincided with a brilliant flowering of secular vernacular literature, for which John Burrow first coined the term 'Ricardian', and whose major figures include Chaucer, Gower, Langland, and the so-called *Gawain*-poet.[1] No less prestigious are developments, both original and translated, in religious vernacular writing, where what Nicholas Watson has called 'vernacular theology' took energetic root.[2] The major figures to be considered here are Walter Hilton (d. 1396), the anonymous author of *The Cloud of Unknowing* (*fl.* 1380s?), and Julian of Norwich (*c.* 1343–*c.* 1416). Hilton and the *Cloud* author are represented principally by their major works, *The Scale of Perfection* and *The Cloud*; Julian by both versions, short and long (ST, LT), of her *Showings*. Other major works to be discussed in this chapter include the anonymous *Chastising of God's Children*, produced between 1391 and 1408,[3] and *The Mirror of the Blessed Life of Jesus Christ* by Nicholas Love *c.* 1409. By way of suggesting a context for these writings, the chapter begins with brief reference to two anonymous texts from the later years of Edward III: the *Speculum vitae* (*Mirror of Life*) (1360s?);[4] and the *Book to a Mother* (1370s).

Generally the writers we are considering make little direct reference (unlike, say, Langland or Gower) to the social and political upheavals of their time. They are more involved, though generally only obliquely, in the major religious upheavals of their day. On mainland Europe, the Papal Schism (1378–1417) saw Italian and French ecclesiastics laying claim to the papacy and splitting Catholic Europe into two factions. Abroad, and at home, the spread of heretical movements gave cause for alarm. Recent scholarship has emphasized the threat felt by Church officials from the heresy of the Free Spirit which flourished on the Continent.[5] At home, the movement originating with John Wyclif and his followers came to be known as Lollardy. Wycliffite opposition to the Church's structures and teachings (shared with many orthodox thinkers in the period) came clearly into focus in the later years of the 1370s. The last twenty years of the century saw the production, by Wyclif's academic supporters, of ambitious and large-scale vernacular texts: a cycle of sermons, and the so-called Wycliffite Bible. The Wycliffites were condemned by successive archbishops of Canterbury in 1382 (the Blackfriars Council, convened by William Courtenay) and, more importantly, in 1407 (the Oxford Council, convened by Thomas Arundel, which resulted in the draconian Constitutions of 1409) that sought to assert episcopal control over vernacular translation, preaching and theological speculation.[6] The Wycliffites feature regularly in this chapter as a way of explaining some of the distinctive emphases of the contemplative authors, who regularly make unintentional (and occasionally intentional) common cause with their heretical neighbours.

Pastoral texts

Ironically, orthodox and heretical Ricardians were joint beneficiaries of over 150 years of highly successful religious instruction.[7] The deliberations of the Fourth Lateran Council (1215) were a response to the challenge of the Cathar heresy. The Council's pastoral imperatives led directly in England to the Lambeth Constitutions of 1281, which legislated for priests to foster a religiously literate laity by instructing them in the basic doctrines of the faith. Those constitutions were reworked in 1357 by John Thoresby, archbishop of York and were translated into the vernacular by his chaplain John Gaytryge to secure their wider circulation and use. The continuing vibrancy of the Church's teaching programme at this time is suggested by the appearance of the *Speculum Vitae* (*The Mirror of Life*), the last of the great catechetic verse handbooks, a 16,000-line poem which survives in more than forty copies. A later version, the *Myrour to Lewde Men and Wymmen*, survives in four copies.[8]

The *Speculum* grows out of the tradition of clerical teaching manuals noted elsewhere in this volume (see ch. 4). It comes bristling with Latin marginalia and Bible quotations. The treatment of sin and virtue proceeds in a conventionally exhaustive and systematic fashion. The teaching seems aimed at beginners in religious understanding, on the face of it far removed from those who have reached 'þe heght of perfeccioun/ And þe ende of contemplacioun' (II, 484, ll. 14625–6). In this text, these are generally identified with members of religious orders (II, 421, 12725–6, *Myrour* p. 183) rather than with laity. Yet this opposition of active and contemplative lives (II, 74–6, 2165–229) in practice dissolves into a 'medled' [mixed] life (*Myrour* p. 91) which shares the qualities of both. Similarly, a text which spells out, in considerable detail, the circumstances and remedies for sin also shares with the Middle English contemplative writers some of their most arresting understandings: with Julian, her understanding that 'synne is called noght in Holy Writt for God made it neuere' (I, 27, 693–4); with the *Cloud*-author, his sense that of the many names given to God – 'right gode . . . right wys or . . . right myghty', names conventionally appropriated to the different persons of the Trinity – none suits him (her/it/them) so well as the one implied in the first phrase of the Our Father: 'þis worde "Es"' (I, 27–8, 693–4, 748).

The *Speculum*'s acknowledgement of the contemplative option, then, is part and parcel of its drive to offer a comprehensive account of Christian life from its catechetic foundations upward. Because for the most part the *Speculum* draws on thirteenth-century French materials, any sense of the increasingly choppy waters through which the ship of England was sailing is largely absent. The later history of the *Speculum* reveals them, though: according to a Latin note preserved in three manuscripts, it was investigated for heresy at Cambridge in 1384, by which time, clearly, vernacularity was seen as part of a religious problem, not its solution. The *Speculum* passed the test with flying colours: but the examination shows how unstable the boundary dividing orthodox and heretical literary production was to become, and the difficulties with which more openly contemplative writing might have to contend.

A Book to a Mother, produced in the 1370s, probably before 1377 and hence too early to show reaction to either the Papal Schism or the growth of the Wycliffite heresy, serves as a useful bridge to that contemplative writing.[9] This completely orthodox (but orthodoxly reformist) text provides a very thorough witness to the upheavals of the 1370s; to the success of the Church's teaching programmes; and to the way in which texts of instruction themselves prepared for, and contributed to, the burgeoning literature on contemplation, which remained closely linked to the catechetical imperatives of the English church.

The *Book* presents an intimate relationship between writer (a priest) and first reader (his widowed mother). The writer makes little of the building blocks of the Christian faith so vital to the *Speculum*, and routinely spiritualizes for his mother the circumstances of her own life, suggesting an expectation of greater spiritual awareness and commitment on her part than the *Speculum* seems to have had of its first readers/hearers. She is encouraged to see her religious observance as a laywoman as the spiritual equivalent of membership of a religious Order, and to observe vows appropriate to a Benedictine (pp. 124–5). And she is offered a large number of (mainly) biblically derived metaphors as a way of encouraging a spiritual understanding of her own situation. More importantly, the writer provides a patchwork of carefully translated Bible passages, strikingly anticipating the Wycliffite Bible. Easily the most important of these (pp. 151–6) is taken from Christ's discourse at the Last Supper (John 13–17). At this point metaphor becomes literal: the reader is encouraged to hear Christ speaking to her directly. We are not far, here, from the divine voice heard by Margery Kempe, ventriloquized by Julian, and fictionalized by Walter Hilton in later chapters of the *Scale*, all of which arguably draw confidence (see further below) from the pervasive voice of Christ in contemporary lyrics and para-liturgical texts.

'Contemplation' is routinely assumed to be both the process and end of this religious observance. Like Mary at the Annunciation, the soul can conceive Christ; as Mary went to the mountains to visit her cousin Elizabeth, the soul is to raise her love 'into contemplacioun and hiȝe . . . into hilles, þat Dauid clepiþ holi saintes of heuene' (p. 46). The collocation of mountains, sanctity, and contemplation is a commonplace: Rolle's Psalter, for example, makes it routinely. But, challengingly, holiness and contemplation come at a price. For example, family relations are encouraged only insofar as they accord with the will of God; consequently, 'but a man hate his wife and forsake hure', he cannot be Christ's disciple (p. 94, cf. Luke 14:26).

The writer has a strong sense of the catastrophic decline of the morals of contemporary secular and religious estates. Consequently, the work ends with translated materials from the New Testament epistles (pp. 157–90), which, addressing the 'last days' of their own times, like the 'now' of the writer's, roundly condemn bad faith and practice. The apocalyptic colouring of this stringent call to perfection, although it has ample parallel in contemporary writing, both orthodox (especially Langland) and heretical, is not much in evidence in Middle English contemplative texts.

This work, then, goes much further, in several directions, than the teaching manuals which made it possible. It reminds us that contemplative writing may represent an urgent reaction to the prevailing religious and social trends of the time, and argues for contemplation as a natural outgrowth and the fullest expression of the Christian life which the Church's teaching programmes sought to develop.

Lyrics

Around the time *Book to a Mother* was written, the medium favoured by writers of vernacular expository texts shifted from verse to prose. Prior to this, the genre which best reflected the diversity and vitality of contemplative and meditative aspirations was probably the lyric. The Middle English religious lyric is a manifestation of a distinctive late medieval tradition, where writers provided vernacular texts for use in contemplative exercises. The immediate quality of the lyrics and their suitability for use in a range of devotional contexts, from liturgical to private prayer, is witnessed by their scattered and incidental survival: they were copied into the margins of commentaries, on the flyleaves of books of hours, and into commonplace books such as those of Robert Raynes, a fifteenth-century churchwarden from East Anglia. The corpus of lyrics carefully copied out early in the 1390s, in the final quires of the monumental Vernon and Simeon manuscripts, seems to represent an institutional attempt to compile and present a large number of lyrics for a single audience alongside as wide a range of other orthodox religious texts as the compilers could lay hands on. The position of the lyrics at the end of both volumes suggests that they were intended as dramatic manifestations and explorations of the ways in which the teachings of the rest of the book could be worked out in daily life and devotions.[10]

The Middle English religious lyrics inhabit a broad spectrum of writing which draws on a number of textual traditions, including the liturgy, sermons, and, most importantly, the Psalms, often taking the form of improvisations or paraphrases of these texts. The link between the Psalms and the lyrics is fundamental. The large-scale lyric versions of penitential psalms, such as that of Richard Maidstone, O Carm, effectively demonstrate the ease with which the Psalms could be adapted to lyric discourse.[11] Within this broader genre, the contemplative lyric is firmly part of the spectrum of contemplative texts, all of them potentially performative. The Psalms, particularly the penitential Psalms, are the first Scriptural psychodramas. In this reworking of King David's turbulent relationship with God, the king's experience is universalized, allowing medieval readers to insert themselves into the drama working out between the soul and its maker.

The development of the dramatic quality of the Middle English contemplative lyric owes much of its impetus to the pioneering work of Richard Rolle, to whom a large number of lyrics is attributed. While Rolle is more fully studied in an earlier chapter of this volume, he casts so long a shadow on the late fourteenth century and has so great a pioneering role in the development of the Middle English lyric that he warrants mention in this context. Drawing on the thirteenth-century tradition of Yorkshire Cistercian spirituality reaching as far back as Aelred of Rievaulx, Rolle sought to blend spiritual song with lyrical expressions of yearning and devotion to the person of Christ. For Rolle, who wrote two popular commentaries on the Psalms, the lyrics were analogous to the Psalms in providing a text for a spiritualized psychological drama, serving specifically to prepare readers for the exercise of contemplation. The lyrics do not define the contemplative experience itself; rather, they describe its context, and provide a script which encourages affective yearning and leads to the experience. In his *Incendium amoris* (*The Fire of Love*), translated into English in the 1430s, a work with pronounced autobiographical elements, Rolle describes how he warms his heart, when it grows spiritually cold, with songs of love and longing, lyrics which define the readiness, the hope, and the waiting for the gift and grace of contemplative experience, and which bring him to the threshold of union with God. Rolle's lyrics draw on the erotic language of the Song of Songs, or Canticles, to provide a vocabulary of desire for and delight in the love of Christ.[12] In his vernacular epistles, lyrics embedded in the prose enact and formulate the appropriate stage of spiritual development reached by the aspirant contemplative (see, for example, *The Form of Living* and *Ego Dormio*). One lyric expresses this objective at the outset:

> Ihesue swet, nowe wil I synge
> To the a songe of loue-langygne.
> Do in my hert a wel to sprynge,
> The to loue ouer al thynge.[13]

This sense of progression is brilliantly captured in 'In a vaile of restles mynd', a fifteenth-century lyric which seamlessly bridges the world of romance, where Christ is cast as a Lover-Knight, and the Song of Songs, which gives him his repeated refrain from Song of Songs 2:5. 'Quia amore langueo' ['Because I languish for love']. In the series of encounters enacted in this lyric, the narrator is drawn from his initial 'restles mynd', by way of an increasing recognition of Christ's love for the soul, to the threshold of the bridal chamber of the Song of Songs, where he finds that the soul has at last become Christ's 'owne dere wyfe'.[14]

One of the finest descriptions of the contemplative processes charged by the religious lyrics survives not in a lyric but in a treatise closely linked to Rolle's style of intense affective meditation, but in fact a reworking of thirteenth-century texts of the so-called Wooing Group (see above pp. 97–9), *A Talkyng of þe Loue of God*:

> Hit falleþ for to reden hit.esyliche and softe. so as men may mest [most] in
> inward felyng.and deplich [deeply] þenkyng. sauour fynden. and þat not beo

dene [straight through]. but biginnen and leten [leave off] in what paas [pace].
so men seoþ [see]. þat may for þe tyme ȝiuen mest lykynge. And whon men
haþ conceyued.þe maters wiþ redyng. inward þenkyng.and deoplich sechyng
[seeking]. wiþouten eny redyng vppon þe selue maters. and of such oþere
þat God wol senden. hose [whoever] wole sechen.schal ȝiuen inward siȝt
and felyng in soule. and swetnes wonderful. ȝif preyere folowe. But hose
wole in meditacion swete fruit fynden. hit mot [must] be taken in wone [as a
custom]. wiþ þreo [three] poyntes þat folewen.affyaunce.and continuance.and
louh herte and clene. þat he truste sikerliche [certainly] to fynden þat [what]
he secheþ And þat his þouȝt beo [be] harde iset.and ful bisyliche ikept, and
holden himself vnworþ.out [unworthy of any] of godes ȝifte.and wlate on
[feel loathing for] himseluen.þorw [through] siht of his fulþȝ [filth]. Men
schal fynden lihtliche [easily] þis tretys in cadence [rhythmical form].after þe
bigynninge. ȝif hit beo riht poynted. and rymed in sum stude [place].to beo
more louesum.[agreeable] to him þat hit reden. God ȝiue vs grace.so for to
rede. þat we mowen [may] haue heuene to vre [our] mede.[15]

Reading at the appropriate pace brings one to the threshold of delight in
inward feeling and deep thinking ('inward þenkyng. and deoplich sechyng'),
the sweet fruit of meditation. The self-characterization of a prose text as written rhythmically ('in cadence'), and urging its readers to observe its metre,
punctuation, and rhyme ('ȝif hit beo riht poynted. and rymed'), is extraordinary. As in the lyrics, self-consciously heightened language expresses and
encourages unusual states of spiritual attention and aspiration. It is this manner of spiritual attentiveness, which the lyrics teach by sustained imaginative
focus on particular images, or sustained ruminations on the love of Jesus,
or scripted narratives of the gospel sequence. Like the *Meditationes Vitae
Christi* (see further below), which present the contemplative with a series of
narratives from the life of Christ scripted for the purpose of imaginary performative engagement, many Middle English religious lyrics employ rhetorical strategies expressly to bring the contemplative to a heightened state of
affective fervour. They provide a vantage point over a meditative mental
landscape, which the contemplative is encouraged to survey and traverse.
The narrator facilitates this process by speaking for all contemplatives, creating an empty 'I'-space which provides a highly immediate and powerful point
of entry for the reader. The variety of approaches to this common end in the
lyrics is quite astonishing. Some lyrics are little more than mnemonics; others
develop the scholastic *distinctiones* and lists favoured by medieval preachers.
Still others, like some in the Vernon collection, use the same unusual stanza
form favoured by the *Gawain*-poet in *Pearl*, a poem that explores the fail-
ures of visionary ambition and the limitations of contemplative aspiration
without the necessary humility and obedience to the will of God.

Once learned, the discipline of meditation through the lyrics could be applied to other scenarios and in other contexts. The lyrics present ways of seeing and participating in the drama of salvation which could be directed to a single image, to wide-ranging, systematic imaginative re-working of the entire gospel story, or to a range of spiritual exercises used by private devout lay people in their daily devotions. Viewed collectively, the lyrics perform a function somewhere between a mantra and a route map. They represent and enact a process of formation or training in which the contemplative trains his or her reflexes and instincts, recalling St Ambrose's description of the psalms as a gymnasium of the soul. The process is not exclusive, nor is it restricted to the situations described in the lyrics.

Julian of Norwich

The religious lyrics and the *Speculum* represent responses to two different sets of imperatives: on the one hand, the personal and the devotional, on the other the institutional and the pedagogic. Contemplative writers respond in varying ways to these two sets of imperatives. The writings of Julian of Norwich respond clearly to the former:[16] her work is acutely attentive to the registers and rhetorical gestures of the devotional writings of her own time.

At a young age, possibly while still a secular (later she becomes an anchoress) she asks God for three gifts: first, for a 'mind' (active recollection) of the Passion of Christ; then for a bodily sickness severe enough to make her think she is dying; lastly, for three 'wonndys' of contrition, compassion, and willed longing for God. In so praying she shows how far, even then, she has internalized the common teachings of the Church. She makes her prayer for the first two gifts conditional on the will of God, since she knows they pass the 'comene course of prayers' (ST I, 204). These requests witness to her familiarity with the devotional practices recommended to spiritually ambitious laity. Both seek identification with the crucified Christ: the first, by creating an imaginative re-enactment of the Passion into which the devout person can insert herself emotionally; the second, by literalizing, in and upon the body, pains identifiable with those of the Crucifixion. Julian's world is immediately recognizable from the countless representations of the Passion in the visual and verbal arts of the period. These are the standard expressions of late medieval affective piety. Hilton in *Mixed Life* thought them a safe route to God for seculars; in his *Mirror*, Nicholas Love recommends them to his readers; as previously noted, religious lyrics embody their strategies and gestures.

Even at this early stage of her narrative, though, we see Julian passing beyond the limits of the religious models available to her. Her third wish (for contrition, compassion and wilful longing for God) spiritualizes the literal conditions of the first two requests. It represents an embodiment of the spiritual state which the other two symbolized and for which they were supposed to predispose her. Julian requests this gift unconditionally; although she forgets about the other two, the third remains with her constantly.

When she is thirty years old, in about 1373, the first two requests are, as she sees it, answered unexpectedly, with an apparently terminal illness. Her miraculous cure from this allows her to ask for and receive over two days a set of revelations (1, 2, 4, 8) about the Passion. Interspersed with these are revelations about the Virgin Mary and the Trinity, and about other elements of the Christian life, notably sin and prayer (3, 13–14). They culminate with a revelation (16) which shows Jesus as a ruler in the 'cite' of the soul. Others focus on the actual contemplative experience as a mixture of 'wele and . . . woo' (7) or consider the problems of their own interpretation (2). In both the Short Text and the Long Text, though much more in the latter, these revelations become the launch-pad for theological speculation and interpretation of an extremely advanced nature.

In the later Middle Ages, revelations were a routine expression of and response to popular piety. It is an indication of the adventurousness of Julian's writing that, unlike her near-contemporaries Margery Kempe and St Birgitta of Sweden, both of whose revelations on the Passion fit comfortably in the traditions popularized by pseudo-Bonaventura and his English translator Love, Julian offers readers a series of visual fragments, isolated from the narrative sequence, allowing her to home in on specific details like a cinematic close-up. This approach is not without parallel, especially in the visual arts. Her account of the buffeting of Christ, in the second revelation, focuses on the face of Christ enduring 'despite, spittynge in, sowlynge [soiling] . . . and buffetyng', much like the painting by Fra Angelico in St Mark's Florence (cell 7), where the humans, reduced to their disembodied heads and hands, spit at and smite the blindfolded Christ, and provide a shorthand account of the whole narrative.[17]

However, Julian's Passion revelations boldly rework even these figures. No image in the visual or verbal arts, for example, matches in vividness the Long Text's reworking of the eighth revelation, where the skin on Christ's head, torn by the crown of thorns, dries and curls about the thorns 'as it were garland vpon garland' (LT ch. 17, II, 363). This extraordinary moment links an instrument of the Passion (the crown of thorns) and its principal human agent (Christ) as joint expressions of divine purpose, and, in the metaphor of the garland, makes the Passion the locus not just of suffering but also of triumph and festivity. The crucifix is central to Julian's early thinking about the divine purposes. Especially in the Short Text, it enjoys a free-standing existence as the sign of salvation. In the Long Text this understanding, still omnipresent in Julian's thought, undergoes a dramatic modification. The Passion, a principal object of devotion (the faithful pray to God for the sake of Christ's 'holy passion'), has become merely one (admittedly, the major) means for God to communicate his goodness to humans (LT ch. 6).

Julian laboured to situate her understanding of her visions within the context of the teaching programmes of the Church, but it seems that she was not as directly engaged with the religious controversies of the time as were the other major writers discussed in this chapter. She once refers to the Church being troubled in the future 'as men shakyth a cloth in the wynde' (LT ch. 28, II, 408), a phrase whose apocalyptic colouring very possibly expresses her sense of the dangerous times in which she was living. Generally, though, neither version addresses its own wider context other than allusively. To discover the pressures of the time in the writings of Julian thus calls for a readiness to read, if not against, certainly through, the grain of her work.

Granted, the lost exemplar of the surviving copy of the Short Text, produced in 1413, may have been designed as a shot in the arm for orthodoxy. In the same way, Julian's text insists obsessively on its own orthodoxy. In the Short Text, for example, her desire for a 'mynde' of the Passion is, she tells us, of a piece with the Church's teaching on the Passion and 'the payntyngys of crucyfexes... made be the grace of god aftere the techynge of haly kyrke to the lyknes of crystes passyonn als farfurthe as manys witte maye reche' (I, 202).

What are we to make of this apparently seamless linking of the grace of God, the power of the imagination ('witte') of painter (and, by implication, writer) to produce a 'lyknes' of the Passion, and the teaching of the Church in defence of the image?[18] One reading would make the Church an unproblematic mediator of divine grace to the faithful. All references to the Church in the Short Text – and there are many – can be read in this way, and might consequently function as a defence of the Church's mediatory role against heterodox criticism.

Julian's insistence on her own orthodoxy has another, more urgent trigger. Especially in the Short Text, she feels the need to defend herself against possible criticism for writing as a woman 'leued, febille, and freylle' (I, 222, a phrase cut in LT). The likeliest source of such criticism, of course, is churchmen. Julian's assertion of her own orthodoxy may represent an attempt to neutralize potential opposition from inside the Church, which she might have good reason to fear, given that many women, including nuns and anchoresses, had already embraced Lollardy.

Not that the priest who enters her sickroom, after her first fifteen visions have passed, dismisses her as a 'leude' woman. When she tells him she has been raving, he bursts out laughing; but when she adds that 'the crosse that stode atte my bedde feete, it bled faste', he is reduced to marvelling silence (I, 266). Here Julian, with that same fine instinct for the psychological to-and-fro of spiritual experience displayed earlier in the showings (especially in the seventh, and at the end of the eighth), dramatizes in her own person the limited imagination and understanding which require the Church's intervention: the priest, acting as the Church's representative, opposes her unbelief with his faith. Immediately she concludes that, having abandoned God in denying her previous experiences, she has sinned, and needs to go to confession.

Fortunately, religious scruple does not win the day, though what frees her from what she sees (and subsequently literalizes) as a diabolic temptation is a determination to hold fast to the truth of her revelations 'with alle the fayth of hali kyrke, for I holde it as bathe ane' (I, 267). A second devilish temptation, after the sixteenth showing, is met in a subtly different way: Julian fixes her eyes on the crucifix, and talks to herself about the Passion, 'rehersynge... the faith of hali kyrke' (I, 270). Routinely invoked in other writings to counter diabolic temptation, these lower levels of the spiritual life – devotion to the crucified Christ; reciting the Creed – do not have to be abandoned by the spiritually advanced soul.

This implied identification of God and the Church is elsewhere explicit: Christ is the 'grownde of alle the lawe' of Christians (I, 257), God is 'haly kyrke, for he is the grownde' of it (I, 252). Divine grace can operate immediately in the soul, but the 'same grace' is also communicated by the external practices of the Church (I, 247). Yet there is nothing static about Julian's understanding of the relation of God, the Church, and the soul. When she talks about the sacrament of penance (I, 256), just possibly a rejoinder to Wycliffite rejection of the sacrament, she notes that the sense of contrition driving the soul to confession is produced by 'the towchynge of the haly gaste', by whose teaching (then or previously) the appropriate penance is delivered. Julian puts it like this: 'than he takes pennannce... eniewnyd [enjoined] be his domesmann, that is growndyd in haly kyrke be the techynge of the haly gaste'. Who or what is grounded in Holy Church: the sinner, the penance, the priest? Or all of them? Julian makes no effort to unpick this question; probably she intuits that only a creative ambiguity with language can properly represent the dynamic of her spiritual experiences. Her failure to unpick the question does not mean, though, that she could not have done so.

Addressed to 'ilke saule contemplatyfe' (I, 215, 243), ST possibly envisages a conventional monastic readership, equating it straightforwardly with the contemplative option. The Long Text widens the perspective to include all 'faithfull lovers' of God, in the words of the colophon to the copy in BL MS Sloane 2499. In several other respects, too, even while using most of the Short Text and keeping close, especially in the early revelations, to its overall structure, the Long Text generates important new understandings.

The most striking of these considers the role of the Church in relation to the visionary and to God. The Short Text formally identifies God and the Church, and subordinates any special graces to the common practices of Christian living. Julian's reaction to the apparent cessation of the revelations confirms this understanding: though God's teaching in the revelations gives her all she then needs, his withdrawal leaves her still needing instruction and dependent on 'the techynge of haly kyrke' (I, 244).

The Long Text cuts this last detail. It also, in chapters 45–6, introduces a new and radically different emphasis. Julian is talking about her experience of the unqualified love of God for the whole of creation, such that 'betwen God and oure soule is neyther wrath nor forgevenesse in hys syght' (II, 493). At the same time, she knows the 'comen teching' of the Church (cf. *Scale* II.3), that those who die in sin or unbaptized will be damned. Initially Julian presents the two teachings in a hierarchical relationship: that of the revelations is higher, that of the Church lower, and the visionary struggles to see 'in God' how the Church's teaching 'is tru in his sight' (II, 488), given that both need to be 'savyd [preserved], so as it ware wurschypfulle to God and ryght wey to me'. Higher and lower understandings are to be kept in mind simultaneously, 'for the hygher...kepyth vs in gostly solace...the lower...kepyth vs in drede' (ch. 82, II, 721).

On the other hand, the identification of God and the Church means that, for the duration of the visionary experience, God does not need the Church to communicate with the visionary. Hence, LT comes up with an altogether more radical understanding than ST of the sacrament of penance: 'alle this [or Thy] lyvynge is pennannce profytable' (ch. 77, II, 693); our natural yearning for God is 'kyndly pennance, and þe hyghest to my syght' (ch. 81, II, 716). Thus, if we are not to leave 'the knowyng of the lower' we should aim to 'holde vs moche more in þe beholdyng of the hygher' (ch. 82, II, 721).

A later chapter (50) presents the relationship of the two teachings even more uncomfortably, as 'two contraryes' (II, 511), a term whose adversarial colouring can be clearly glimpsed from its regular use, in later chapters, to describe the relation of love and hate or the devil (52, 77, 82), faith and ignorance (70), bliss and pain (72), wisdom and folly (76). If God's presence in the vision passes away without giving Julian an answer, it does not seem as if the Church will provide it. When, therefore, Julian professes to submit her limited understanding to that of the Church (ch. 46), at the start of her major quest for answers, we can hardly see this as the end of the matter. One answer to the question, though not conclusive, is the 'mervelous example of a lorde and of a seruaunt...full mystely shewed' (ch. 45, II, 488; the revelation is ch. 51). More important than the failure to answer the question is the fact of its asking, at a time when the Church was responding in ever more draconian ways to the growing Wycliffite challenge to its authority. After all, if we accept Watson's dating of the Short Text, Julian in producing that text had reason to fear that she might herself be labelled a heretic.[19] When she composed the Long Text, the dangers of her situation must have felt much greater. Yet she goes much further than she did in the Short Text to set her vision up in tension with the teaching of the Church.

She was certainly aware of the need to fit her visions to the standard taxonomy of such visions as physical, spiritual (or imaginary), and intellectual. This was first propounded by St Augustine, and recycled, in her own time, in the 1370s, in his *Epistola solitarii ad reges* (*The Letter of the Solitary to the Kings*), by Alfonso of Jaén, confessor of St Birgitta of Sweden, editor-in-chief of her revelations, and enthusiastic supporter of her canonization; it was adapted in the vernacular (see further below) by the author of *The Chastising of God's Children*. Strikingly, as she does elsewhere so often, Julian accommodates the pattern to her own experience: the teaching came to her, she writes, 'be bodylye syght, and be worde formede in myne vndyrstandynge, and be gastely syght' (I, 224, 272).

Walter Hilton

With Walter Hilton (d. 1396) we seem to return to the second of the two imperatives noted earlier, the institutional and the pedagogic. A canon lawyer trained at Cambridge, Hilton was, at some stages of his life, close to leading religious figures of his day like Archbishop Arundel. He attempted life as a hermit before settling for membership of the Augustinian Canons, an order with a distinctive double vocation to contemplation and pastoral work.[20] In his major work, *The Scale of Perfection*, and in his Latin epistles and vernacular translations, he explores and develops an orthodox response to contemporary challenges to religious authority. His world is one of clear religious certainties without fuzzy edges: one strikingly at odds with that of many of his contemporaries. (We might contrast his approach to Islam, for example, with the cultural curiosity and occasional approval revealed in the translation by an anonymous contemporary of Mandeville's *Travels*.)

For Hilton, the heretic's rejection of the Church's sacramental system is the product of settled choice and moral failure. Like Jews and Saracens (I.56), the heretic's besetting sins are pride and self-will (I.58, II.26); in such a person, the stirrings of pride are damnable. For Hilton, every 'leste ordenaunce of general techynge of al Hooli Chirche' is to be preferred to any unauthorized teaching or expression of the imagination (I.21, p. 54).[21]

Of a piece with this rigorous insistence on orthodoxy is Hilton's insistent laying out, especially in *Scale* I, of the building-blocks of the faith, as transmitted by the legislative programmes and pastoral initiatives of the English hierarchy over the previous 150 years. Unlike the *Speculum Vitae*, he makes little in *Scale* I of the articles of the Faith and the sacramental system; like the *Speculum*, though, he goes into considerable detail about the sins (they occupy the latter half of *Scale* I) from which his reader needs to be protected. He categorizes these as energetically as any confessor's manual, writing, for example, of the two kinds of pride (I.57), of the role of the senses (I.78), of the ways in which eating can be sinful (I.72); and strikingly, of the limbs and branches of sin (I.64, 85).

In another respect, too, Hilton's work stresses its own orthodoxy more strongly than either Julian or the *Cloud* author. Virtually every page comes with extensive quotations from the Latin Vulgate which are translated, sometimes literally, but more often with a spiritualizing gloss. In so using Latin, Hilton may be responding to the growing academic debate about vernacular biblical translation.[22] For Hilton, Latin remains the language of authority.

Hilton has another reason for emphasizing the basics of the faith. The intended first reader of *Scale* I is a newly professed anchoress. The processes of her internalization of the disciplines of the anchorhold parallel, at least metaphorically, those of the Christian life. In line with this general emphasis, Book I routinely talks of practices disposing a person to contemplation (I.2, 14, 60). The movement between active and contemplative states can then be mapped straightforwardly, if intricately. *Scale* I.9 insists that the full expression of contemplation requires 'solitarie... liyf' (p. 39). Therefore, the life of vowed religious ought to offer a straightforward correlation between their religious status and their vocation to and experience of contemplation. For the anchoress to become contemplative, she has only to become what she has professed (I.16).

Unlike their religious counterparts, the laity must settle for the lower reaches of contemplative experience. This understanding is confirmed in another of Hilton's works, *Mixed Life*, addressed to a secular lord who wishes to renounce worldly duties and embrace the contemplative life. 'Mixed life', a term originally coined to describe the life, partly contemplative and partly active, of bishops and prelates, refuses him the option, requiring him instead to continue with a life of good work, devout meditation and verbal prayer. Here, as in *Scale* I, Hilton views his secular reader through monastic lenses, and the resulting picture (not surprisingly, given the upheavals of the time when he is writing) is extremely traditional and unyielding.

Nevertheless, the clear outline Hilton tries to draw for his readers is in practice blurry at the edges. Social status and vocation do not map straightforwardly onto one another. Though the anchorhold provides the best place to prepare for contemplative life, its primary requirement, the love of God, may on occasion be better met by seculars than by professed religious (*Scale* I.61–2).

Moreover, the teacher's authority is regularly challenged by the inscribed reader's questions. This rhetorical device derives from the methods of scholastic debate and pulpit oratory. Hilton's use of this dialogic device parallels similar strategies in *The Cloud of Unknowing* and *The Chastising of God's Children*. It is particularly noticeable in passages interpolated into the *Scale* (eg. I.44 and I.71). In the addition to I.44, for example, the disciple speaks of 'summe hooli menn . . . ' (p. 80) whose view of the conditions necessary for salvation is more stringent than Hilton's. Scholars understand this to refer to Richard Rolle, an important if mostly unacknowledged presence in much later fourteenth-century contemplative writing. Here, Hilton's disciple forces him to define himself against Rolle's views and to argue that Rolle's doctrines square with his, if each is understood spiritually.

Scale I ends with an invitation to its first reader to emend the text where the writing is too terse. Instead, this first, or a later, reader requests further elucidation of a central element of the teaching of *Scale* I, the reformation of the image of God in man, which triggers the altogether more ambitious writing found in the second Book. *Scale* I had paid little attention to salvation history or the sacramental system of the Church, focusing instead on the active presence of sin. The opening of *Scale* II accounts for such sin, both original and actual, by appealing to salvation history, as interpreted by St Anselm, and to the two sacraments which root out original sin (baptism) and actual sin (confession and penance). These opening chapters revisit the catechetical and penitential imperatives of the late medieval Church and insist on annual confession as part of the necessary technology of self-knowledge developed through the examination of the conscience (II.7).

They also introduce subtle differences of emphasis from *Scale* I. The programme for reformation of the human soul is addressed in two stages: first, 'in feyth'; then, 'in feelynge' (the latter also labelled 'feith and felynge' to imply the continuance of the lower state in the higher, e.g. pp. 142, 190). The vital importance of baptism is dramatized by the walk-on part accorded once more to Jews and infidels, who are damned if they die unbaptized. Heretics appear here only, by implication, as holders of mistaken views, though the greater doctrinal emphasis of these opening chapters may suggest growing anxiety about the challenge they represent. In striking contrast, though, with the interlocutor of *Scale* I, who questioned the means but not the fact of her spiritual quest, the unspecified questioner(s) in this section raise difficulties central to the faith: that following one's own conscience guarantees salvation (II.3); that confession is neither necessary nor useful (II.7); that God's mercy will not permit anyone to be damned (II.10); and that people cannot be damned for the grace not given them (II.14) and need not work to acquire grace (II.20). The second of these could certainly have the Wycliffites in its sights. Others seem to refer to the heresy of the Free Spirit. All of them show significant doctrinal and argumentative development of similar material in *Scale I*.

Much greater developments are to come. Easily the most important is Hilton's treatment of the crucial question of the relationship between divine grace and human effort in the contemplative process. The importance of this question can be gauged by the amount of time Hilton devotes to opposing two contrasting and differently erroneous views: that grace does away with the need for human effort; and that readers may confuse means and end (e.g. II.19), and set too great store by their own efforts.

Hilton offers two broad accounts of the relation of grace and human effort. In the first, grace co-operates with human effort to bring about the desired result (ch. 20): God 'formeth [creates] oonli by Hymsilf, but he reformeth vs with vs . . . ' (II.28, p. 199). Consequently, the exercises required for reformation in faith, and the experiences accompanying reformation in feeling, can be referred respectively to human and divine agents. But the second view, introduced as early as ch. 20, is altogether more radical: when an individual is truly reformed in feeling, through grace he or she sees Jesus and understands how Jesus 'doeth al, and hymsilf [the human] dooth right nought' (p. 174). This paradoxical understanding centrally informs the rest of the work: for example, 'this desire [for Jesus] sotheli it is Jhesu . . . he it is that desireth in thee and he it is that is desired' (II.24, p. 183). No stage of the spiritual life is free from God's engagement with the soul. Hence, when Hilton quotes a Pauline proof-text (Romans 8:29–30) to argue for the verse's special relevance for contemplatives, he acknowledges that it also applies in its entirety to 'alle chosen soulis in the lowest degree of charite that aren oonly reformed in feith' (p. 199).

Yet even here, Hilton does not leave behind his reader's religious beginnings. The final chapters of book II consider how the soul, its spiritual eye opened, will be able to see for itself what previously it has depended on teachers of the Church to know about (II.46): the divinity and humanity of Jesus; the nature of rational souls and of angels; the Trinity (II.45–6). Hilton makes no attempt at this point to create a language rhetorically commensurate with these heightened understandings, as Rolle had done.[23] In keeping with the plain and sober style that characterizes most of his writing, he simply returns to the catechetical formulations with which he had started. When writing about the opening of the spiritual eye, for example, he does not attempt his own definition of the experience but gestures towards its nature in a series of juxtaposed doublets 'in holi writynge by dyvers men': 'purite of spirit and gosteli reste, inward stillnesse and pees in conscience, highnesse or deepnesse of thought and oonlynesse [solitude] of soul' (II.40, p. 236).

Much more striking are the words Hilton puts into Christ's mouth in II.36 by way of glossing Ps. 45:11 ('be still and know that I am God'):

> Seeth onli hou I, Jhesu God doo...I am love, and for love I doo al that I do; and ye do nought... There is no good deede doon in yow... but yif it be doon thorugh me... And yit neverthelesse are thise good deedis... called your: not for yee wirken hem principali, but for I geve hem to you for love that y have to you.
>
> (pp. 224–5)

Echoes of Christ's voice in Julian's showings are probably accidental, but they point to the ground of contemplative experience that Hilton's writing shares with her.

The Cloud of Unknowing

Like Hilton, the late fourteenth-century author of *The Cloud of Unknowing* was a priest, probably a member of the rigorously contemplative Carthusian order, who were, with the Birgittines, a major force in the production and dissemination of vernacular religious literature in the fifteenth century.[24] He has, however, a very different take to either Julian or Hilton on the contemplative quest, incorporating both less and more of his immediate context than either. He takes the beliefs and practices of the Church much more for granted than Hilton. And he takes for granted Julian's starting point in the traditions of affective piety, expecting his readers to be well versed in those traditions, and to leave them behind as they embrace the contemplative option (chs. 7–8). Among these 'means' (such as oral prayer, the liturgy, the use of images and other similar devices), they must even leave behind – what had been crucial for Julian – the idea of God's goodness (ch. 7). The author also views with suspicion the 'counfortes, sounes, and...swetnes þat comyn fro wiþoute sodenly' (ch. 48, p. 50). Among these extraordinary graces of the spiritual life (which he sees, again, as means) he might well have included the whole of Julian's showings.

In one striking respect, he makes more of his immediate context than either Hilton or Julian. He tackles the question of heresy head-on in ch. 56, and identifies heretics as people whose 'pride and corioste of kyndely witte and letterly kunnyng' have led them to abandon 'þe comoun doctrine and þe counsel of Holy Chirche' and to 'lenyn ouermoche to þeire owne knowyng'. In the end they 'brestyn up and blasphemyn alle þe seyntes, sacramentes, statutes and ordenaunces of Holy Chirche'. They attract a following of 'fleschly leuyng' men who reject the teachings of the Church, thinking them too hard, and support the heretics, with whom they reckon to find a 'softer wey' (p. 58). All this – along with other details – could well be an account of the origins of the Wycliffite heresy, and is, if so, uncannily accurate. Wyclif's first followers were academics associated with his College (The Queen's) and University (Oxford). In the early stages of their movement's growth, the Wycliffites were also supported by powerful laymen, including John of Gaunt. If Gaunt were one of the 'fleschly leuyng' men' here referred to, this might provide a date for the composition of the work. Gaunt's interest in Wyclif, dating from soon after 1376, lasted at least until the Blackfriars Council of 1382.[25] If this interpretation is correct, the *Cloud*-author was engaging with the politics of his own time more directly than Hilton or Julian: more directly even than the author of the *Book to a Mother*.

The context does not suggest, however, that the author's real quarry in his work is the Wycliffites. The phrase 'coriouste of . . . witte', allied disapprovingly with words like 'vnkyndely' and 'ymaginatif', or, as in the first quotation, with 'pride', occurs repeatedly in his works, usually as a marker of academic (not simply heretical) interest. Academics generally are one of the author's principal targets. Where they should be 'meek scolers and maystres of deuinite or of deuocion', they often become 'proude scolers of þe deuel and maysters of vanite and of falsheed' (ch. 8, p. 16), pursuing worldly advancement as energetically as the ecclesiastics castigated in the *Book to a Mother*. Their procedures needlessly sophisticate the simplicity of the gospel and of the writer's own message. In relation to the 'oueraboundaunt loue and þe worþines of God in himself' they are 'foles' (ch. 13, p. 22). Consequently, they are routinely warned off the author's works, which aim to get readers beyond mental speculation, even about their own, or God's, nature, so as directly to connect their own and God's 'naked' beings.

The energy of the author's attack on 'vnordeyned' academic speculation points, in fact, elsewhere. Crucially, heresy appears first, in the *Cloud*, in the context of those who embraced the contemplative option but refused to follow spiritual direction and turned into hypocrites or heretics, falling into 'frenesies and many oþer mescheues, in sclaundre of alle Holy Chirche' (ch. 18, p. 27). These false contemplatives share the Wycliffite refusal to accept religious authority, but, unlike the Wycliffites, whose starting-point and besetting sin is the undisciplined exercise of the intellect – a failing shared with orthodox academic contemporaries – theirs originates in undisciplined and overactive imaginations.[26] Naïve spiritual enthusiasts, they read literally what they should understand figuratively. (Elsewhere, orthodox writers make this literal/figurative dichotomy a feature distinguishing heretic from orthodox, and/or laity from clergy.)[27]

The dangers of literalism are crystallized in a passage (ch. 45) which describes how neophytes, told to lift their hearts up to God, may immediately imagine that a physical action is being spoken about, 'and trauyalen þeire fleschly hertes outrageously in þeire brestes', experiencing a false and unnatural warmth. They, however, call this 'þe fiir of loue, getyn and kyndelid by þe grace... of þe Holy Goost'. Their obstinate refusal to correct their error generates 'moche ypocrisie, moche heresye, and moche errour' (p. 47). Rolle is the likeliest English source of the distinctive label they give to their experience ('þe fiir of loue'), though parallels abound in European writings. It is unclear that the author knows at first hand of any neophytes who have so perverted sound doctrine, or how far he thinks of Rolle as a spiritual enthusiast whose example needs careful interpretation if it is not to prove misleading. His covert criticism of Rolle is shared by a contemporary, anonymous Carthusian, whose objections to Rolle's teachings are preserved in a defence of Rolle by a hermit, Thomas Basset, in a text written before 1391.[28]

Bystanders are also prone to misunderstand what they have not experienced. 'Into þis day' people living the active life react unfavourably to a person's decision to become contemplative, even if the person's own motives have been approved by 'prouid werchers'. They immediately tell stories of 'fallyng of men and wommen... ʒouen... to soche liif before' (ch. 18, p. 27). Or they scorn 'horrible synners' who have become contemplatives, and treat others 'as aungelles' because of their apparent holiness, not realizing that some presently, 'worschepid of men', who 'neuer ʒit synned deedly, schul sitten ful sory amonges helle calues' (ch. 29, p. 36).

The *Cloud*-author, then, is keenly aware of human proneness to error, regardless of state or vocation, especially in spiritual matters. Truth and error co-exist at every stage of the spiritual process. What contemplatives think they understand may, on closer scrutiny, turn out to be an illusion. This understanding contrasts strongly with that of Hilton, for whom the contemplative experience of God confirms the doctrines of the Faith. The

Cloud's account of heightened spiritual experiences reflects their unpredictable occurrence and problematic interpretation:

> þan wil he sumtyme parauenture seend oute a beme of goostly liȝt, peersyng
> þis cloude of vnknowing...and schewe þee sum of his priuete, þe whiche man
> may not, ne kan not, speke. þan schalt þou fele þine affeccioun enflaumid wiþ
> þe fiire of his loue, fer more þen I kan telle þee...at þis tyme.
>
> (ch. 26, p. 34)

Unlike the generality of people, practised contemplatives *know* their own ignorance.

The contemplative option is, in fact, a commitment to the ongoing experience of failure. In the context of an account of the soul's powers, the author notes that, just as the works of the senses cannot provide information about spiritual things except negatively ('by þeire failinges'), so the understanding cannot access an 'vnmaad goostly þing' except 'by þe failing' (ch. 70, pp. 70–1). Understanding, that is, gestures beyond itself to what it can express only brokenly, allusively, metaphorically. We are here in the apophatic world of pseudo-Dionysius, whose *Mystical Theology* the *Cloud*-author later translated (as *Hid Diuinite*). Human language needs to be stretched to the limits in order to find the least unsatisfactory way to talk about God. The *Cloud*-author routinely acknowledges his failure adequately to represent the divine: he produces two later works, *Priuy Counseling* and *Hid Diuinite*, in an attempt to get closer to the truths he is writing about. All the same, the author's certainty of failure accompanies an extraordinarily careful and thorough determination to find the least unsatisfactory ways of talking about God to his first readers.

The author is also keenly aware of the network of relationships which fosters and expresses spiritual purposes. Thus, for example, writing of a 'childish' analogy he has just used, he continues: 'I haue ben sterid many day...to fele...and þink þus..., as weel to som oþer of my specyal freendes in God, as...now vnto þee' (ch. 47, p. 49). The bystanders at Julian's sickbed offer a rough parallel for these unnamed 'specyal freendes'; nothing in Hilton's work does.

Consequently, to return to the place where we started, the *Cloud* is as relaxed about the means of the quest as it is rigorous in its insistence on the process, understanding the Church itself, by implication, as just such a means. Of course, the author is not dismissing outright the practices of 'Holy Church the Less' (in Marguerite Porete's phrase), any more than Julian was doing when she similarly spiritualized penance. Rather, he is insisting on their subordination, for the duration, to contemplative practice and experience.

The Chastising of God's Children

It may not be entirely accidental that the final works to be discussed in this chapter seek to limit the exercise of the contemplative option, albeit in two very different ways. As noted above (n. 3), *The Chastising of God's Children* may have been written not long before the promulgation of Arundel's Constitutions (though probably in the 1390s); Love's *Mirror of the Blessed Life of Jesus Christ* was published in their immediate aftermath. There is a clear difference in the original readerships of the two works. Like *Scale* I and several other texts, the *Chastising* was written at the request of a woman religious by her male spiritual adviser; the *Mirror* was written for a lay readership. But, in both, the need to combat heresy and defend orthodoxy comes to override such expressions of the contemplative option as Julian, Hilton, and the author of the *Cloud* were willing to encourage.

The *Chastising* achieved popularity and was widely read and owned by the laity, as external evidence shows (pp. 37–40). Its theme is the value of the '*gostli chastisynges*' of spiritual and physical suffering, a topic which had not been tackled in a single work before in English. But the *Chastising* is not a road map to the heights of contemplative ascent. It offers no formulae for systems of contemplation, like those in the *Scale* or the *Cloud*. It is rather a series of markers laid down and warning against the adoption of practices which can lead the unwary into heresy, and offering strategies for recognizing the dangers and avoiding them. The text is peppered with warnings and admonitions against error and heresy: 'þus haue I shewed 3ou o grete errour þat sum tyme falliþ amonge gooslie lyuers. Wakeþ þerfor and preieþ, þat 3e entre nat into temptacion' (p. 134). The voice of sobriety and restraint runs throughout, even when the author discusses popular themes of devotion, such as the Holy Name, the Five Wounds, and the Sacred Heart.

The work draws heavily on a wide range of patristic and Continental texts, several relatively new to English readers: primarily Henry Suso's *Horologium sapientiae* (*The Hourglass of Wisdom*), but also Jan Ruusbroec's *Spiritual Espousals*; and, most importantly, Alphonse of Jaén's *Epistola solitarii*. The *Chastising* knits these works together in a very sophisticated and highly selective way so as to bring clearly into focus the author's over-arching, and closely related, preoccupations: the detection and prevention of heresy, the suppression of religious fervour, the dangers of seeking 'sweetness of devotion' during the performance of the canonical hours, and the 'discernment of spirits' (*discretio spirituum*). In some of these matters, the author is much of a mind with the *Cloud*-author: there are numerous similarities between the *Chastising* and the *Cloud*.

Spiritual advisers frequently cautioned contemplatives against the desire for 'special gifts' – in the words of the *Chastising*, 'myraclis, or visions, eiþer reuelacions, or sum oþer specialte' (ch. 10, p. 135). These were particularly to be avoided, since they could be counterfeited by the devil (cf. *Cloud*, ch. 52). Also to be avoided are physical phenomena of mysticism, treated under the description of physical drunkenness: excessive tears (though in ch. 1 the author cites with approval the traditional formulation of tears of contrition, compassion, and compunction); stirrings of the body which result in an irrepressible desire to skip, run, or dance; handclapping from sheer joy; crying aloud with a high voice; even a stillness which takes away a person's power of speech (ch. 2). These 'gifts' are dangerous, since they may easily lead their recipient to pride and vainglory. Moreover, they are not always present, raising the risk of 'vndiscrete heuyness' in their absence (ch. 4, p. 112).

The theme of diabolical temptation runs through monastic literature from St Anthony onwards, and it is a danger particularly associated in the late Middle Ages with contemplative ecstasy or *raptus*. ('Ravishing', the English equivalent, occurs many times in the works of the *Cloud*-author.) The question how true *raptus* could be discerned from demonic visitation was the business of the 'prouid wercher' who had the power of 'discernment of spir-its'. The author of the *Chastising* drew heavily on an extremely up-to-date work (the *Epistola solitarii*) for this purpose, which had codified in an almost scientific classification of signs the distinction between demonic possession and divine manifestations of contemplation. Its author had rehearsed these themes together with their biblical and patristic antecedents, applying them to St Birgitta in a series of simple questions designed to prove her orthodoxy and the divinely inspired nature of her visions.[29] Is the visionary spiritually minded, or is he or she attached to the world? Does the visionary submit his or her visions to the judgement of a spiritual director? Does he or she rejoice in the works of virtue? Is the visionary experienced or a novice? Is he or she intellectually sound? Are the visions received when awake, asleep or dream-ing? Are they attended by spiritual favours or physical signs? Alphonse had the evidence of his own senses to support his appeal to standard authorities like St Augustine: he reports, for example, how he had seen Birgitta

> in oracione totam absortam et quasi exanimem, alienatam a sensibus corporis, raptam in extasi spiritus, nichil videntem nec audientem de his que agebantur in loco illo vbi ipsa corporaliter erat [totally absorbed in prayer and like one lifeless, alienated from her bodily senses, ravished in a spiritual ecstasy, and seeing and hearing nothing of those things that were done in her physical presence]. (p. 136)

Quite remarkably, the *Chastising*-author strips the *Epistola* of every com-mendation of genuine contemplatives, turning the text on its head to produce a sermon on the dangers of diabolical deception for the unwary. He keeps only one reference to St Birgitta, and that as a clear recommendation to his readers: Alphonse's praise of her obedience to her religious superiors. He also adapts Ruusbroec's earlier 'condemnation of heretics in the Low Countries... so as to allude to and delineate the social impact of Lollardy in [his] own times'.[30]

Like Hilton's *Scale*, the *Chastising* reached a much wider audience than the professed religious for whom it was first intended (pp. 37–40), and provides striking evidence of the growing appetite for treatises on the spiritual life among the laity, who were probably envisaged from the outset as part of the work's readership. The author's attitude to this wider readership contrasts with that of the *Cloud*-author, who also wrote initially for a professed religious, but knew that his work would be taken up by others whom he judged unsuited for it. Like the *Cloud*-author, the author of the *Chastising* is concerned, given the spread of heresy, about the uses to which such materials might be put. The Church was clearly responding to a ground-swell of interest in contemplation in the vernacular while seeking to retain its mediating role, shaping and adapting contemplative literature and setting the guard of clerical authority on texts loaded with the potential for heresy and excess.

The Mirror of the Blessed Life of Jesus Christ

While the author of the *Chastising* was prepared to countenance English versions of the Gospels, or even the whole Bible, as a supplement to the Latin of the Vulgate (p. 221), such was the growth of the Wycliffite heresy and Bible that less than a decade later, unauthorized translations of the Bible were banned. To feed the growing appetite for biblical texts, the church sanctioned the translation of the *Meditationes Vitae Christi*, one of the most popular devotional texts of the late Middle Ages.[31] *The Mirror of the Blessed Life of Jesus Christ* was translated, with Archbishop Arundel's explicit blessing and *imprimatur* – perhaps at his instigation – by Nicholas Love, the Carthusian prior of Mount Grace, Yorkshire.[32] This remarkable text brought together the mystical theology of St Bernard and various strands of Franciscan piety, together with teachings of St Bonaventura, to whom the *Meditationes* were regularly attributed. It offered not a structured regime of contemplation, such as the Hours of the Passion provided, but a series of scripted exercises for imaginary participation in the life of Christ, frequently counterpointed by a moral, in a manner traditionally intended for religious novices and women. While this required readers to disengage their critical faculty ('kyndely reson') and to satisfy themselves with a diet of 'mylke of lyȝte doctryne', rather than with what Love called 'the sadde mete of grete clargye [learning] and of hye contemplacion' (p. 10), it also, at the same time, fed the desire for affective piety focused on the humanity of Christ.

Love's re-working of the *Meditationes* returns us to the world of the religious lyrics, to whose strategies of rumination it is indebted, and creates, like them, a psychological space for readers to engage imaginatively in the drama of their own salvation. This engagement was predicated on the exercise of a fecund imagination, or what Love called 'gostly chewyng' (p. 156). The process which runs through the entire tradition – from the *Meditations* of St Anselm to St Thomas à Kempis' *Imitatio Christi* (*The Imitation of Christ*) – demands that the devout step out of the historical present and into the timeless drama of biblical narrative. Whereas the *Cloud*-author had warned his readers against the perils of *fantasye*, 'whiche is nouȝt elles bot a bodely conseyte of a goostly þing' (ch. 65, p. 65), Love admonished readers: 'Now take hede, and ymagine of gostly þinge as it were bodily, and þenk in þi herte as þou were present in þe siȝt of þat blessed lord' (p. 21). Expanding this rubric, Love instructs his readers to immerse themselves completely in the narrative events of the Gospels:

> Wherefore þou þat coueytest to fele treuly þe fruyt of þis boke, þou most with all þi þought & alle þin entent, in þat manere make þe in þi soule present to þoo þinges þat bene here writen seyd or done of oure lord Jesu, and þat bisily, likyngly and abydyngly, as þei [if] þou herdest hem with þi bodily eres, or sey þaim with þin eyen don, pyttyng [putting] awey for þe tyme, & leuyng alle oþer occupacions and bisynesses. (pp. 12–13)

The central episodes from Christ's life best suited to stimulate the emotions ('certayne parties most deuoute') were amplified, embellished, and pre–packaged into set meditative exercises which the devout could then reconstitute at will according to their own devotional regime. To facilitate this process, the text was loaded with extraordinary attention to the physical setting, the characters' physical gestures, and even their spatial relations to one another.[33] The dramatic element of the narrative is further heightened by the deployment of literary devices such as metaphor, paradox, and hyperbole. In each exercise, the devout reader is presented with explicit instructions for appropriate posture, gesture, actions, and speech in the *Meditationes*. The devout reader speaks to Christ, his mother, and the disciples, eats and drinks with them, engages in the most ordinary and minute details of their daily lives, becoming their constant companion and experiencing the Gospel events from the perspective of a contemporary. To make the characters more accessible, they are presented not as saints surrounding an incarnate deity but as ordinary individuals enjoying the intimate familiarity appropriate to close friends, subject to all the vicissitudes of the human condition. Their tenderness and vulnerability render their sufferings supreme. Moreover, the Passion story is told largely from their perspective: they suffer through their exposure to Christ's sufferings. This viewpoint gives the narrative vividness and the sense of immediacy, allowing the devout to experience the story through sharing the emotions of the central characters.[34]

Through imaginative participation in the gospel events, the devout reader was drawn into a stronger sense of identification with Christ and the central characters of the narrative. Identification was intended to stimulate compassion, which would in turn lead to love of Christ and moral imitation. But in transforming the mystery of salvation into a homely drama, we may wonder if the text infantilizes the devout rather than empowering them to practise meditation as the gateway to contemplation.

Most texts from this period do not attempt to describe contemplation: rather, they consider the processes that lead up to it (Julian's revelations constitute a striking exception to this generalization). In a short treatise by Rolle, the author defines the second stage, meditation (which he prefers to call, in 'propyr Inglysch', thinking) as follows:

> Bot qwhoso wyll trauell [labour] besily in thynkyng of frutefull thynges, I trowe þat Gode of his gudenesse wyll lyghten his saule with sum of his gracyus gyftes, þat all þe trauell þat euyr was in þis lyffe a man walde thynke itt in comparyson of þat inwarde reste bot a chyldes play. Bot þou schall wytte well, þoff-all of [although] þow haue grett trauell [labour] in meditacyon or thynkyng, þat þis swete gyfte of þe grace of Godd is noght geuyn to þe þerfore, bot of þe free gyfte of Godde, qwen and howe he wyll do and take it away as hymselfe lyste. And þerefore, þoff-all þow haue grett trauell, and yf þow be visytt any seldun tyme with þe souereyn swetenesse, gyffe þerefore grett louyng [praise] to Godde. And wytt þow wele, þe more ioy þat þow feles, þe more arte þow behaldyn [enjoined] to trauell in prayer and thynkyng and louyng to God day and nyght.[35]

Meditation, or thinking about appropriate mental images to stimulate contemplation, is as clearly Nicholas Love's primary concern as it is that of the authors of the lyrics. True contemplation, a freely given gift of God that can never be acquired by what Hilton calls 'purchase', cannot really be taught. What can be communicated is the necessary stillness and attentiveness to the moving of the Holy Spirit without which the winds of inspiration and understanding will never be discerned. So the preparatory processes and devotional disciplines by which meditation leads to true prayer and contemplation are the vital linking tissue in all the texts of this period. In his consistent attention to this preparatory work, and in the popularity that his meditative and para-mystical texts achieved among lay and clerical readers of vernacular texts in the fourteenth and early fifteenth centuries, Rolle's authentic texts and the increasing numbers of anonymous works attributed to him serve as inviting book-ends for the period.

It is worth drawing attention to the long afterlife of several of these texts. The *Scale, Chastising*, and *The Mirror* all made it into print, along with *The Seven Points of True Wisdom*, an anonymous translated reworking of Suso's *Horologium sapientiae* which this chapter has not had space to consider.[36] Arundel's Constitutions were still being read in the sixteenth century: in 1529 Thomas More cited them in the form of their later, fifteenth-century, elaboration by the canon lawyer William Lyndwood, in the course of his debate with Tyndale (his *Dialogue concerning Heresies and Matters of Religion*).[37] More also cited Love and Hilton with approval as writers of unimpeachable orthodoxy, who could be safely used by the laity. In giving Love his seal of approval he was echoing Arundel 120 years previously. In recommending Hilton he probably had in view not only Hilton's endorsement for seculars of the option of the 'mixed life' but also the insistent orthodoxy of the *Scale* and its handling of the bread-and-butter issues of sin and salvation history (especially in *Scale* I and the beginning of *Scale* II). At a time when a Catholic identity was beginning to seem problematic, More could recommend Love and Hilton as safely orthodox: much as Julian would prove useful, in their maintaining of their Catholic identity, to recusant Catholics, upon whose interest in her work we are dependent for all but one of the surviving copies of her Long Text. The close links between the contemplative writers of the Ricardian age and the religious literature directly and indirectly inspired by the teaching programmes of the fourteenth-century Church easily justify their enlistment in the cause of orthodoxy. Fortunately, they offer us much more. It is a tribute to Julian and the *Cloud*-author that their texts have transcended their immediate historical and religious environments and continue to speak to and inspire contemporary readers.

NOTES

1 See John Burrow, *Ricardian Poetry* (London: Routledge and Kegan Paul, 1971).
2 Nicholas Watson, 'Censorship and Cultural Change in Late-Medieval England: Vernacular Theology, the Oxford Translation Debate, and Arundel's Constitutions of 1409', *Speculum* 70 (1995), 822–64.
3 For this dating, see Roger Ellis (ed.), *The Liber Celestis of St Bridget of Sweden*, EETS OS 291 (1987), p. xii. For an earlier offered dating (the 1380s) see Joyce

Bazire and Eric Colledge (eds.), *The Chastising of God's Children* (Oxford: Blackwell, 1957), p. 35.

4 For this dating, see Vincent Gillespie, 'Religious Writing', in Roger Ellis (ed.), *The Oxford History of Literary Translation in English*, vol. 1, *To 1550* (Oxford: Oxford University Press, 2008), p. 249. For further information about dating and authorship – the work is usually ascribed to William of Nassington – see Ralph Hanna (ed.), *Speculum Vitae: A Reading Edition*, 2 vols., EETS OS 331–2 (2008), I, lx–lxiii. Quotation from the *Speculum* is from this edition, cited by volume, page, and line number.

5 The Heresy of the Free Spirit allowed for the possibility of reaching perfection on earth through a life of austerity and spirituality and of communicating directly with the Divine without the agency of the Church. See Kathryn Kerby-Fulton, *Books Under Suspicion: Censorship and Tolerance of Revelatory Writing in Late Medieval England* (Notre Dame, IN: University of Notre Dame Press, 2006), and below, chs. 8 and 9.

6 For recent comment on the Constitutions, see Gillespie, 'Religious Writing', pp. 234–9.

7 See further Gillespie: 'Religious Writing', pp. 244–54; 'Vernacular Books of Religion', in Jeremy Griffiths and Derek Pearsall, *Book Production and Publishing in Britain 1375–1475* (Cambridge: Cambridge University Press, 1989), pp. 317–44; and Leonard E. Boyle, 'The Fourth Lateran Council and Manuals of Popular Theology', in Thomas Heffernan (ed.), *The Popular Literature of Medieval England* (Knoxville: University of Tennessee Press, 1985), pp. 30–43.

8 Venetia Nelson (ed.), *A Myrour to Lewde Men and Women: A Prose Version of the 'Speculum Vitae'*, Medieval English Texts 14 (Heidelberg: Winter, 1981).

9 For a modern edition, used for quotation, see Adrian James McCarthy (ed.), *Book to a Mother: An Edition with Commentary* (Salzburg: Institut für Anglistik und Amerikanistik, 1981). See also Elisabeth Dutton, 'Christ the Codex: Compilation as Literary Device in *Book to a Mother*', *Leeds Studies in English* 35 (2004), 81–100, and Nicole R. Rice, 'Devotional Literature and Lay Spiritual Authority: *Imitatio Clerici* in *Book to a Mother*', *Journal of Medieval and Early Modern Studies* 35 (2005), 187–216.

10 For recent comment on Vernon and Simeon manuscripts, see David Lawton, 'The Bible', *The Oxford History* vol. I, pp. 211–18 *passim*.

11 Valerie Edden (ed.), *Richard Maidstone's Penitential Psalms*, Medieval English Texts 22 (Heidelberg: Winter, 1990), pp. 9–12.

12 On this point, see Denis Renevey, *Language, Self and Love: Hermeneutics in the Writings of Richard Rolle and the Commentaries on the Song of Songs* (Cardiff: University of Wales Press, 2001).

13 S. J. Ogilvie-Thomson (ed.), *Richard Rolle: Prose and Verse from MS. Longleat 29 and Related Manuscripts*, EETS OS 293 (1988), p. 50.

14 Douglas Gray (ed.), *A Selection of Religious Lyrics* (Oxford: Clarendon Press, 1975), no. 61.

15 M. Salvina Westra (ed.), *A Talkynge of þe Loue of God* (The Hague: Martinus Nijhoff, 1950), p. 2. In this quotation, capitalization and word-division have been modernized.

16 The *Showings* survive in two versions: the Short Text and Long Text (ST and LT), both in Edmund Colledge and James Walsh (eds.), *A Book of Showings to the Anchoress Julian of Norwich*, 2 vols. (Toronto: Pontifical Institute of Mediaeval Studies, 1978), here used for quotation, and cited by volume and page number, and Nicholas Watson and Jacqueline Jenkins (eds.), *The Writings of Julian of Norwich: A Vision Showed to a Devout Woman and A Revelation of Love* (University Park, PA: Penn State Press, 2006).

17 For reproductions, see Luciano Berti, *L'Angelico a San Marco*, Forma e Colore 13 (Milan: Rizzoli, 1965), pl. 13, and *Fra Angelico* (London: Faber, 1968), pl. 68.

18 For comment on Julian's possible appeal in this phrase to contemporary orthodox teaching on the use of the image as an aid to devotion, see Nicholas Watson, 'The Composition of Julian of Norwich's *Revelation of Love*', *Speculum* 68 (1993), 637–83.

19 For Watson's dating of ST, see 'The Composition'; see also Barry Windeatt, 'Julian of Norwich', in A. S. G. Edwards (ed.), *A Companion to Middle English Prose* (Woodbridge: Boydell and Brewer, 2004), p. 71.

20 For brief comment on Hilton's life and career, and fuller comment on the *Scale*, see John H. P. Clark and Rosemary Dorward (trans.), *Walter Hilton: The Scale of Perfection*, (Mahwah, NJ: Paulist Press, 1991).

21 Quotation from the *Scale*, by Book, chapter and page number, is from Thomas H. Bestul (ed.), *Walter Hilton: The Scale of Perfection* (Kalamazoo, MI: Medieval Institute Publications, 2000).

22 First studied in Anne Hudson, 'The Debate on Bible Translation, Oxford 1401', *English Historical Review* 90 (1975), 1–18.

23 On this point, see Nicholas Watson, 'Translation and Self-Canonization in Richard Rolle's *Incendium Amoris*', in Roger Ellis et al. (eds.), *The Medieval Translator* I (Woodbridge: D. S. Brewer, 1989), pp. 167–80.

24 For a modern edition, used for quotation, see Phyllis Hodgson (ed.), *The Cloud of Unknowing and Related Treatises on Contemplative Prayer*, Analecta Cartusiana 3 (Salzburg: Institut für Anglistik und Amerikanistik, 1982).

25 On Gaunt and Wyclif, see K. B. McFarlane, *John Wycliffe and the Beginnings of English Non-conformity* (London: English Universities Press, 1966), pp. 117–19, 125, and May McKisack, *The Fourteenth Century 1307–1399* (Oxford: Clarendon Press, 1959), p. 514.

26 These false contemplatives could also be a reference to the heresy of the Free Spirit. See further, n. 5 above.

27 See Roger Ellis, 'Figures of English Translation 1382–1407', in Ellis and Liz Oakley-Brown (eds.), *Translation and Nation: Towards a Cultural Politics of English* (Clevedon: Multilingual Matters, 2001), pp. 22, 30.

28 For an edition of the defence, see Michael Sargent, 'Contemporary Criticism of Richard Rolle', in James Hogg (ed.), *Kartäusermystik und -Mystiker*, Analecta Cartusiana 55.1 (Salzburg: Institut für Anglistik und Amerikanistik, 1981), pp. 160–205.

29 For a modern edition of the *Epistola*, see Arne Jönsson (ed.), *Alfonso of Jaén, His Life and Works*, (Lund: Lund University Press, 1989). For comment, see Eric Colledge, '*Epistola Solitarii ad Reges*: Alphonse of Pecha as Organizer of Birgittine and Urbanist Propaganda', *Mediaeval Studies* 18 (1956), 19–49; and for

more general comment on the theme of discernment of spirits, Rosalynn Voaden, *God's Words, Women's Voices: The Discernment of Spirits in the Writing of Late-Medieval Women Visionaries* (Woodbridge: York Medieval Press, 1999), and Claire L. Sahlin, *Birgitta of Sweden and the Voice of Prophecy* (Woodbridge: Boydell, 2001).

30 Gillespie, 'Religious Writing', p. 269.

31 On lay literacy generally, see Margaret Aston, 'Devotional Literacy', in her *Lollards and Reformers: Images and Literacy in Late Medieval Religion* (London: Hambledon, 1984), pp. 101–33.

32 For a modern edition, used for quotation, see Michael G. Sargent (ed.), *Nicholas Love. The Mirror of the Blessed Life of Jesus Christ. A Reading Text* (Exeter: University of Exeter Press, 2004). Secondary literature on Love includes Elizabeth Salter, *Nicholas Love's 'Myrrour of the Blessed Lyf of Jesu Christ'*, (Salzburg, 1974) and Shoichi Oguro, Richard Beadle, and Michael G. Sargent (eds.), *Nicholas Love at Waseda* (Woodbridge: D. S. Brewer, 1997).

33 M. Twycross, 'Books for the Unlearned', in J. Redmond (ed.), *Drama and Religion*, Themes in Drama 5 (Cambridge: Cambridge University Press, 1983), pp. 70–3.

34 On this general point, see Emile Mâle, *Religious Art in France: the Late Middle Ages* (Princeton, NJ: Princeton University Press, 1986) pp. 136–46; Millard Meiss, *Painting in Siena and Florence after the Black Death: The Arts, Religion, and Society in the Mid–Fourteenth Century* (Princeton, NJ: Princeton University Press, 1964), pp. 126–31; H. van Os (ed.), *The Art of Devotion in the Late Middle Ages in Europe 1300–1500*, trans. M. Hoyle (Princeton, NJ: Princeton University Press, 1995), p. 165.

35 Ralph Hanna (ed.), *Richard Rolle: Uncollected Prose and Verse With Related Northern Texts*, EETS OS 329 (2007), p. 85

36 For a modern edition, see Carl Horstmann (ed.), '*Orologium Sapientiae* or *The Seven Poyntes of Trewe Wisdom* aus MS Douce 114', *Anglia* 10 (1888), 323–89.

37 For a modernized version of relevant sections of the *Dialogue*, see Douglas Robinson, *Western Translation Theory From Herodotus to Nietzsche* (Manchester: St Jerome Publishing, 1997), p. 77.

8

VINCENT GILLESPIE

1412–1534: culture and history

> For of old custom it longith unto kynges
> First holy chirche to meyntene and goverene
> And for ther sogetys in al maner thynges
> For to prouyde and prudently discerne
> To showe themseylf lyk a clere lanterne
> With lyght of verteu ther sogettys tenlumyne
> Both by example and vertuous doctryn.
>
> John Lydgate, *Cartae versificatae*[1]

Strong kings with a mission to reform their national churches mark the beginning and end of this period. The two Henries (V and VIII), both lavishly gifted and devout sons of usurping monarchs, sought to reform their ecclesiastical inheritances as part of a policy of buttressing their own imperial power. But whereas Henry V aligned his church more closely and immediately with the international struggle against heresy and schism, and with a movement for radical reform of the institutions and life of Christianity, Henry VIII, despite closely and deliberately imitating the political and religious example of his illustrious namesake, ended up isolated from the universal church and from most of its Protestant offshoots. The defender of the faith (*defensor fidei*) became known as the destroyer of faith (*destructor fidei*). Yet the different outcomes should not cloud the very real similarities between their attitudes to the *ecclesia anglicana* (the English Church, a phrase that would have been familiar to both).

Henry V succeeded his father on 21 March 1413, and soon showed himself as astute in matters of ecclesiastical policy as he was in diplomacy and warfare. His short reign (he died in September 1422) is marked by a remarkable efflorescence in national self-confidence, accompanied by an equally remarkable change in the way that the English church presented itself at home and abroad. Both changes had their efficient causes abroad, even if the personality of the king was the primary cause. An alliance with Sigismund, effective Holy Roman Emperor, was fundamental to both. The great (and unlikely) English victory at Agincourt in 1415 allowed a surge of national pride that was rapidly mythologized. Equally Henry's decision to support Sigismund in the reforming Church Council held at Constance between 1414 and 1418 seems to have had an energizing effect on the English church, which was already responding to the twin stimuli of a dynamic new king and an astute, long-serving, and far-sighted new archbishop of Canterbury, Henry Chichele. After being installed in the Order of the Garter in May 1416, Sigismund is reported to have caused bills praising king and country to be thrown from his carriage as he headed for the coast:

> Farewel, with glorious victory
> Blessid Inglond, ful of melody.
> Thou may be cleped of angel nature,
> Thou servist God with so bysy cure
> We leve with the this praising,
> Whech we schal evir sey and sing.[2]

In the Emperor's eyes, England was militarily victorious and orthodoxly devout in equal measure. Both outcomes were the result of a curious mixture of luck, judgement, and good timing.

In his *Chronica maiora* entries for 1414, Thomas Walsingham, a Benedictine monk of the great and powerful Abbey of St Alban's, juxtaposes three events with far reaching impact on the temper of English spirituality in the fifteenth century:

> In this year on 20 February there collapsed and died that lofty tower of the English church and its never defeated champion, Sir Thomas Arundel. As primate of all England he had waged the Lord's wars time after time against the Lollards, and it was thought that he would never have been defeated if only his suffragan bishops had determined to fight with equal devotion. His successor as archbishop of Canterbury was the bishop of St David's, Master Henry Chichele, the king's confessor. Master Stephen Patrington, brother of the order of Carmelites, a man learned in the Trivium and Quadrivium, was made bishop of St David's . . .

> In this year King Henry began the foundation of three religious houses near to his manor commonly known as Sheen. One was for the order of Carthusian monks; another for the monks called the Celestines (these profess the Rule of St Benedict, which they say they follow to the letter, and going beyond it, they bind themselves to perpetual seclusion); the third for the Brigittines, who follow the rule of St Augustine, which, with other rites added to it, they now call 'the rule of the Saviour' . . .

> At this time indeed the archbishop of Canterbury was holding a great council of clergy there [i.e. London], at which there was a discussion about the

abolition of the privileges enjoyed up to now by those who had been granted exemptions by the popes of Rome. This was the first of the signs given by the new metropolitan to indicate his anger. Also at this council, representatives for the clergy of England were chosen to attend the general council that was to be held in the German city of Constance... the representatives sent to the council from England were the most venerable bishops of Salisbury [Robert Hallum, d. at Constance 1417], Bath [Nicholas Bubwith, d. 1424] and Hereford [Robert Mascall, d. at Constance 1416] and together with these the abbot of Westminster [William Colchester, OSB, d. 1420], the prior of the cathedral church of Worcester [John Malvern, OSB, d. 1423] and several other high powered individuals famous for their piety and learning... [3]

Together, the events reported by Walsingham represent a fundamental paradigm shift in the English church's view of itself, and of its relationship to the rest of the Universal Church.

These entries tell of a series of fresh starts. Walsingham's comments perhaps suggest a hint of disappointment with the Arundelian regime and its effects on the state of the English church. Arundel's suffragans – if not the man himself – are seen to have failed in the vigour of their pursuit of heresy. He was not alone in his view that Arundel's pastoral policies were flawed and ineffective. Dissenters, like the preacher of the sermons in MS Longleat 4 (who also wrote the important treatise *Dives and Pauper*) passionately defended their right to instruct the laity in the vernacular (and the laity's right to be so instructed), while the arch-conservative Thomas Gascoigne, an Oxford contemporary and opponent of Reginald Pecock, argued that the unintended consequence of Arundel's 1409 decrees was that the orthodox stopped preaching and the heterodox carried on as before. [4]

Walsingham also notes Chichele's plans (sanctioned and perhaps urged by Henry V) for significant English involvement in the pan-European movement to reform and strengthen the Universal Church, which manifested itself in the first thirty years of the fifteenth century in what has become known as the Conciliar movement. The leaders of the Universal Church, afforced by secular rulers and diplomats, met in session at Pisa in 1409, at Constance between 1414 to 1418 (a meeting that finally resolved the Schism by the election of Martin V as an agreed unity candidate for the papacy, largely through the alliance between the English and Sigismund), Pavia-Siena in 1422, and finally (and much less successfully) at Basel in the 1530s. Because of the power vacuum created by rival claimants to the papacy, these meetings developed a theory of conciliar power that challenged the absolute authority of the pope in matters of doctrine and policy, and therefore empowered the representatives of national churches to think deeply and creatively about the ways to address the Church's troubles.

Church historians tend to see the Conciliar movement as a missed opportunity, which fizzled out and produced no policies of lasting value. But the active role played by the English delegates at the first two meetings meant that, after a period of relative isolation because of the Schism (when England supported the Roman candidate against their opponent supported by the French) and the ongoing effects of the Hundred Years' War, the leading figures in the English church could meet, talk to, and learn from their continental colleagues. The genuine and fast developing humanism of the English episcopate in the first half of the fifteenth century owes much to the contacts and experiences (not to mention the book exchanges and purchases) made by Englishmen at these meetings. Pisa, and especially Constance, opened a window onto a wider intellectual world. It placed the local difficulties experienced by the *ecclesia anglicana* into a much bigger picture. Most importantly it allowed English church leaders to develop a plan for the reform and renovation of the national church in the context of what was acknowledged as an international crisis of self-definition and mission in Christianity as well as in response to the continuing challenges of Lollardy. The councils were a showcase and a platform for some of the brightest reforming minds in Europe: men such as Pierre d'Ailly and his pupil Jean Gerson, whose treatises on the necessary reforms became required reading for the leaders of the English church, despite the cultural, theological and political disagreements that remained between England and France. The Council of Constance described its mission as the reform of the church 'in head and members' and recommended a return to the apostolic simplicity and missionary zeal of the early church. It also addressed the problem of burgeoning heresy, retrospectively condemning Wyclif, and trying and executing the Bohemian Jan Hus as an alleged disciple of the arch-heresiarch. Although many of the reforms agreed at these councils were either ignored or watered down in Europe as a whole, the intellectual and cultural impact on the English church should not be underestimated. Henry V became the figurehead and the inspiration for an English church that speedily acquired new confidence and a new sense of direction and purpose. The sermons of Oxford, Bodleian Library, MS Bodley 649 refer to Henry as 'our master mariner', steering the ship of church and state through the stormy waters of contemporary life.[5]

Walsingham also reports a palpable sense of a generational shift underway. Under Chichele, the episcopate that had laboured through the fiercest heat of the battle against Schism and Lollardy was speedily replaced by a new team which remained relatively stable until after Chichele's death in 1443. The new king, Henry V, had signalled a break with the past with the symbolic reburial of Richard II in Westminster Abbey. His coronation on Passion Sunday 1413 had been accompanied by heavy snowfall that generated a variety of interpretations, as Walsingham notes:

> Everybody was surprised by the severity of the weather. Some people connected the climatic harshness with the fate that awaited them at the hands of the new king, suggesting that he too would be a man of cold deeds and severe in his management of the kingdom, while others who knew of a gentler side to the king took the unseasonable weather as the best of omens, suggesting that he would cause to fall upon the land snowstorms which would freeze vice and allow the fair fruits of virtue to spring up, so that his subject would be able to say of him: Winter is now past/The rains are over and gone. [Song of Songs 2:11]
>
> (*Chronica maiora*, p. 389)

The death of Arundel, within a year of the new king's accession, and his succession by Henry Chichele, a career diplomat from a leading mercantile family, and with experience of the papal curia, whose reign would last for a remarkable twenty-nine years, is paralleled by the sense of an extensive changing of the guard among the English episcopate and the heads of major religious houses. Stephen Patrington, O Carm, the bishop who succeeds Chichele at St David's signals both the high esteem of eremitical orders with pastoral vocations and contemplative aspirations in Henrician England, and a respect for learning and education. Chichele's bishops, and the cadre that succeeded them in the 1440s, valued learning and sound doctrine to an unusual degree. In one of his sermons at the Council of Constance, Richard Fleming, who later founded Lincoln College Oxford to train orthodox men as a clerical bastion against heresy, calls for a proper valuing of scholarship and scriptural learning among the episcopate, noting that although many learned doctors and professors are present at the Council 'ultra duos prelates in sacra theologia doctores non video' ('I do not see more than two prelates who are doctors of theology').[6] No doubt some of this was special pleading from an academic, but it does seem to reflect a wider recognition among the English episcopacy of the need to reinforce *sana doctrina* by the promotion and strategic placing of theologically trained scholars in positions of influence inside English dioceses, and, in the same year that Fleming's sermons were preached at Constance, the University of Oxford successfully lobbied Chichele for a mechanism for the promotion of graduates. Another Oxford academic, Henry Abingdon, in a surviving sermon to the Council delivered in October 1417 argued that 'true prelates before everything else took care of *doctrina*, the craft of instructing the people in religion'. *Doctrina* was an art, he argued, that no cleric in authority should scorn to learn 'though too many . . . cared little for the science of morals and the struggle for heresy'. And the humanistic interests manifested by a small sub-group of them showed that their intellectual horizons were broadening, and their interests in education and humane letters deepening. Chichele's church took preaching and catechetic instruction exceptionally seriously: this was the basis for a 'back to basics' campaign of pastoral instruction, of which Reginald Pecock's mid-century experimentations with re-imagining the catechetic syllabus was an eccentric but by no means isolated manifestation.

Under Chichele, the English church is asserting itself as a distinct, individual, powerful, and above all ultra-orthodox player in the Universal Church. There is a palpable sense of things needing to change. Chichele's convocation statute of 1416 against heresy commits him to blow away 'the dust of negligence' from the feet of the English church.[7] At the Council of Constance in March 1417, Thomas Polton, at that stage a papal diplomat, and later to be bishop of Worcester under Chichele, delivered a fascinating defence of the English church's growing ability to think of itself as an *ecclesia anglicana* that reveals some of the vectors of change that make Henry Chichele's church rather different from Thomas Arundel's. The French delegates at Constance had claimed that the English church, consisting of only two provinces, was tiny in proportion to other nations (which covered much larger geographical areas). Moreover, they stressed the sanctity of the French monarchy and pointedly, in view of England's recent troubles over heresy, asserted 'the length of time since it received the faith of Christ, from which it has never deviated as compared with the kingdom of England.'

In his reply, Polton, referring to himself as speaking on behalf of the English nation 'also known as the British nation', asserts the greater antiquity of the faith in England; the higher Christian dignity of the English dynasty and the larger size of the church in England, as well as stressing the size and linguistic diversity of the British dominions. He argues that England 'is superior in the antiquity of its faith, dignity and honour and at least equal in all the divine gifts of regal power and numbers and wealth of clergy and people'. The royal house had emerged during the second age of the world and enjoyed an unbroken continuity. Many saints and pilgrims had been born in England, most notably St Helena (daughter of the old king Coel) and her son Constantine the Great, 'born in the royal city of York', so that the power, influence, and riches of the Roman church and the religious enlightenment it had brought to the world might be attributed directly to the blessed realm of the English. The conversion of the Empire, the endowment of the church, the building of St Peter's, and the finding of the true cross were all the consequence of the act of an English man and woman. Polton argues, using the Glastonbury legends, that Joseph of Arimathea came to England with twelve companions, 'and converted the people to the faith'. This means that England was Christian long before St Denis converted France. Moreover:

> that puissant English royal house never strayed from the obedience of the church of Rome, but until this day has always fought for it in exemplary Christian fashion.[8]

At Constance, the English church under Chichele was repositioning itself very visibly. This was signalled not only by Thomas Polton's powerful defences, but also by the high profile use of the full glory of the Sarum liturgy in public events conducted by the English delegation, its use in sermons preached by the English there, and also by the performance of religious dramas in front of Council delegates, including Emperor Sigismund. The Sarum liturgy, developed and elaborated in the diocese of Salisbury, was one of the grandest and most elaborate rites in the western Church. So elaborate and high profile were these liturgical and para-liturgical events that they were recorded in diaries and chronicles as among the greatest wonders of the gathering.

The *Ecclesia Anglicana vel Brittania* may in some senses have been reborn at Constance. But its greatest changes would inevitably be felt at home. In the first few years of Chichele's and Henry's reign, the Sarum rite was extended across the whole province of Canterbury, new patronal feasts for George, David, Cedd, Chad, and John of Beverley were raised in stature to encourage lay devotion, and processions and public prayers for the king's wars were encouraged, alongside the continuing bearing down on heresy and heterodox thought and activity. The sermons preached by Englishmen at Constance provide a key to the new lexis of orthodox reform found echoing through vernacular religious texts by John Lydgate, Thomas Hoccleve, John Audley, along with the Benedictine author of the lyrics in Oxford, Bodleian Library, MS Digby 102, and of the macaronic sermons in MS Bodley 649, almost certainly the same monk, and certainly from the same milieu of orthodox reform.[9] New ideas flowed into the English church, and its sense of its historical anchorage was reinforced by the two greatest texts of institutional self-definition produced in this period: *Doctrinale fidei antiquitatum ecclesiae catholicae* (1427), a systematic reply from Thomas Netter, the Carmelite delegate at Constance, to Wyclif and Lollardy by appeal to the precedents and history of the English and the Universal Church; and *Provinciale* (1429), by John Lyndwood, a codification of English episcopal legislation for the province of Canterbury by one of Chichele's right hand men.[10] Works like this created a sense of historical antiquity and doctrinal stability that was much needed in Chichele's church.

Walsingham's comments on the choice of orders to occupy the King's new monastic houses send a more subtle and significant signal. The king was making a clean break with the monastic past. No house of Birgittines or Celestines had ever before been founded in Britain (in the event the Celestine house failed). Nor had the Carthusians ('never reformed because never deformed') featured prominently in either side's arguments about the merits of monasticism. None of these orders had therefore been tainted by the in-fighting, self-preservation, and name-calling that had characterized the campaigns run by the orders of friars and the older monastic orders to defend themselves against, first, the anti-fraternalism of Richard FitzRalph and, then, Wyclif's increasingly strident calls for clerical disendowment and the abolition of 'private religions'. More importantly, as Walsingham's account of the Celestines suggests, they were all characterized by eremitical inclinations, contemplative aspirations, seclusion from the world, and high standards of spirituality. They were to be public avatars of the new reformist orthodoxy that was to characterize Henry V's and Chichele's church. They were the outward and visible sign of an inward and invisible reformation in the way that the English church thought and wrote about itself, and were to serve as a fountainhead, powered by prayer and contemplation, from which would flow the grace of renewal and reform. And in the eremitical houses of Carthusians and the Birgittines fifteenth-century England was to find its greatest institutional centres of interest in contemplative writing and contemplative experience. The role of the Carthusians as collectors of contemplative literature is well known, though it is less clear how energetic or comfortable they were in circulating such texts outside of their own order. The unique copy of the Short Text of Julian of Norwich survives in the Amherst manuscript (BL, Add. MS 37790), which offers graduated guidance in the contemplative life from Rolle's English epistles through to a version of Marguerite Porete's *Mirror of Simple Souls*. But such books were needed by members of the order themselves, who spent twenty-two hours a day in solitary contemplation and work, and by those in the order charged with discerning the authenticity of the contemplative experiences reported by their colleagues.[11] It may be that the unusually rich concentration of copies of contemplative texts held by the Carthusians (which included the *Book of Margery Kempe* and a Latin version of the 1465 *Vision of Edmund Leversedge*, as well as the Rhineland visionary texts preserved in MS Douce 114 (discussed below) owes more to their need to calibrate their own spiritual discernments and to advise other monks and clergy on their spiritual lives, than to a desire to promulgate such materials to the laity. Those texts that did reach lay hands may more plausibly have done so through the agency of other monastic and clerical intermediaries.

The relationship between Sheen Charterhouse and the Birgittines at Syon is one of the most well-documented synapses in the textual history of (especially vernacular) religious books. *The Mirror to Devout Men and Women*, or *Speculum devotorum*, for example, written by a Carthusian at Henry V's new house at Sheen, probably sometime around 1430, although it reflects in its agenda and style some of the changes in vernacular theology in the English church under Chichele, is primarily addressed to a 'gostely suster in Ihesu cryste', or 'relygiouse sustre' (f. 5r), whose command of Latin is limited.[12] The ghostly sister is likely to be a nun of Sheen's twin foundation, the Birgittine house at Syon. Indeed, the *Speculum devotorum* may have been commissioned by Syon for the use of its nuns, and then released by them into a wider, if limited, circulation among its powerful lay supporters, to whom its learned priestly community sometimes served as spiritual advisors. It survives in two copies (both perhaps related to Syon) but while one remained in a religious milieu, the other was made for a high-born laywoman who belonged to two famous book-loving families in the north of England.

From the outset, Syon's and Sheen's textual and spiritual lives were profoundly intertwined. Henry V left books in his will to both houses (though they never seem to have been delivered), stipulating that the books of contemplation should go to Sheen and the preaching books to Syon. This is because Syon, as well as being an enclosed house of nuns and contemplatively inclined priests, also had an outward-facing function as a place of public preaching, confession and, in time, generously indulgenced pilgrimage (Margery Kempe visits Syon for its indulgence at the end of her *Book*). As an order founded by a visionary woman whose authenticity was frequently and repeatedly challenged, even at the Council of Constance, Syon also had a particular interest in contemplative, prophetic, and visionary materials, and in the processes of their discernment (one of the most serious faults to be confessed by the brethren was 'If any afferme the reuelacions of saynte birgitte as dremes, or els detracte hem', so the issue remained live even inside the house).[13] Its massive brethren's library, and the documented book holdings of the nuns show a systematic and continuing interest in contemplative experience and its discernment.[14] Syon's involvement in the 1530s with the political visionary Elizabeth Barton was a late (and politically highly perilous) example of a constitutional fascination that had marked the house throughout its life.

It was in the 1530s that a major Syon text, the *Myroure of Oure Ladye*, Syon's in-house handbook of liturgical guidance for its nuns, was printed, though it had been composed in the early decades of the house's life.[15] It talks about the nuns' need for supported access to the Latin of their liturgy, and provides careful versions of the core texts of the Office. In one of the few explicit orthodox references to Arundel's restrictions on Bible translations, the author comments that they can consult Rolle's vernacular exposition of the Psalms and 'Englysshe bibles if ye haue lysence therto'; he has 'asked and haue lysence of oure bysshop to drawe suche thinges in to englysshe to your gostly comforte and profyt' (ed. Blunt: 3, 71). The *Myroure* includes an important discussion of the uses of reading religious books. Devout reading is called one of the parts of contemplation, for it causes much grace and comfort to the soul if it is discreetly used. When you read alone, you should not be hasty and read too much at once, but should sometimes read a thing twice or three times. Books can be dipped into, tasted, savoured, and used as meditative stimuli. The advice on reading in the *Myroure* is designed to be applied to any kind of book encountered by the nuns. But singled out for comment are those books that:

> ar made to enforme the vnderstondynge. & to tel how spiritual persones oughte to be gouerned in all theyr lyuynge that they may knowe what they shall leue. & what they shall do. how they shulde laboure in clensyng of theyr conscyence. & in gettyng of vertewes how they shulde withstonde temptacyons & suffer trybulacyons & how they shall pray. & occupy them in gostly excercyse. with many suche other full holy doctrines.   (*Myroure*, ed. Blunt, 68)

The reader of such books should seek to assess the extent to which their own life conforms to these models and precepts and, where deficiencies are identified:

> besely to kepe in mynde that lesson that so sheweth you to youre selfe & ofte to rede yt ageyne. & to loke theron. & on your selfe. with full purpose & wyll to amende you & to dresse youre lyfe therafter.

This repertoire encompasses pretty much the full spectrum of the religious books being translated into English in the fifteenth century. And in its printed circulation in the 1530s such orthodox and austere guidance would have been a valuable part of Syon's role as a bastion of sound doctrine in the turbulent political and religious weather that began to buffet the English church.

Birgitta's order had from its foundation a clear role of fostering sanctity of life and orthodox aspiration for union with God. The translator of the *Myroure* refers to 'eny other [boke] of oure drawyng' (p. 8) suggesting it was part of a series of works by him or his team. Indeed Syon probably emulated the example of the Swedish mother house (Vadstena), a notable centre of vernacular translation of Latin religious texts. It may deliberately have functioned as a source of copies of orthodox and approved texts of vernacular devotional and para-mystical materials, whose impacts would have been enhanced by the abbey's close links with Westminster and London, and its popularity with gentry and noble clients who turned to the house for spiritual guidance. This enduring connectedness, and high public profile, which later manifested itself in its links with the devotional printing output of Wynkyn de Worde, and which encompassed the patronage and support of Lady Margaret Beaufort, made the preaching and confessional activities of the house a major target for Thomas Cromwell's campaigns against the monasteries in the 1530s.[16] From the outset, works, including many translations, were composed explicitly for the community (such as the *Myroure* and *The Orchard of Syon*, both later printed; probably also the *Speculum devotorum*); others may have been composed for them by, or commissioned by, the brethren. In the sixteenth century we have names of several Syon translators: Thomas Prescius (on his translation of the *Formula noviciorum* (*Rule for Novices*)), Thomas Betson, Richard Whitford, John Fewterer, and William Bonde. The brethren's library contained a whole section stuffed with rare and valuable copies of visionary and contemplative materials, including a copy of Rolle's *Melos amoris* (*Song of Love*) allegedly in his own hand. Both brothers and sisters owned copies of Hilton's *Scale of Perfection*, including copies of the early printed edition sponsored by Lady Margaret Beaufort that also contained the *Epistle on the Mixed Life* as a third book.[17] Translations of or from Latin works of guidance, perhaps made at or for Syon, include texts such as *The Manere of Good Lyuyng* in Oxford, Bodleian, MS Laud Misc. 517, or *The Doctrine of the Heart*, or *Disce Mori* (*Learn to Die*). The English translation of Mechtild of Hackeborn's visionary text the *Liber specialis gratiae*, which calls itself *The Book of Ghostly Grace*, is probably also closely associated with Syon, and the 1422 *A Revelation of Purgatory*, which uses Birgittine materials, may well be connected to the house in some way and certainly reflects the orthodox reform agenda of the English church and the house that became its metonymy.[18]

Many of the textual productions by or for the nuns of Syon found their way in due course, by accident or design, to readers outside the enclosure. A notable early instance is a series of saints' lives, including the translation of the *Life of St Jerome* by Simon Wynter (d. 1448), for his particular friend, benefactor, and spiritual client, Margaret, duchess of Clarence (d. 1439), instructing her: 'that hit sholde lyke youre ladyshype first to rede hit and to doo copye hit for youre self and syth to lete other rede hit and copye hit, whoso wyll'.[19] The *Life* included material from the revelations of St Birgitta, and its prologue also translates material from the Rhineland mystic Henry Suso's *Horologium sapientiae* (*The Hourglass of Wisdom*).[20]

All surviving copies have associations with Syon, even when they have documented lay circulation. This permissive attitude probably reflects that found more widely through the textual communities of the fifteenth century, especially as the textual competencies and tastes of nuns and lay readers markedly narrowed in the course of that century. Contemplative aspiration and orthodox doctrine exist in fertile tension against each other.

Despite the changes in attitudes to vernacular religious books after Arundel's decrees, the prosperous, urban literate laity wanted guidebooks to the mount of contemplation (or at least usable maps of its foothills), directions for their prayer lives, and exemplars for an evolving form of living that allowed them to stay in the world but to live lives of holy aspiration. One of the unintended consequences of Arundel's decrees may have been a new impetus to the translation into English of older texts with an impeccably orthodox pedigree or an unimpeachable authorial reputation, and Syon was probably a leading centre in the production of such texts. It had the library resources, the connections with opinion formers in the church and laity, highly qualified and intelligent members, access to scribal, textual and translatorial resources over the river at Sheen, and the status and brand name to be figured as a leading centre of orthodox spirituality and devotion.

Syon's centrality to the religious life of later medieval England is attested not only by the pattern of bequests and donations that made it one of the best endowed monasteries in the country at its suppression in 1539, but also by the connections that it developed with major gentry and nobility families (such as the Boleyns and Hungerfords), its strong pattern of recruitment from the universities (especially Cambridge), and its high visibility in the religious life of the capital through its connections with rectors of the city churches (many of whom went on to join Syon or to give it books or money) and its other religious institutions, and its later connections with early printers as both a major purchaser of printed books from the 'Latin trade' and the supplier and commissioner of vernacular religious books.[21]

The religious life of London in the fifteenth century was marked by a notable campaign to improve the standard of parish clergy (by the establishment of in-service training facilities at Whittington College and by the foundation of the Guildhall library of theological books), to improve general levels of education and literacy by the foundation of new grammar schools, to foster fraternities and sodalities, and to improve the quality of preaching and teaching in the city. There is also mounting evidence of probable links between Syon and the fraternities and sodalities (both formal and informal) out of which emerged the so-called 'common profit books'. Several key laymen involved in the development of these shared anthologies are associated with the foundation of the Guild of All Angels on the edge of the domain at

Syon, and increasingly closely connected to it. One of the surviving common profit books is a clone of a manuscript known to have been in the library at Syon. These books, refracting a stable but variable canon of short works by and extracts from Hilton and Rolle alongside other para-mystical texts such as *The Mirror of St Edmund* and *Pore Caitif*, are important tokens of lay initiative in, or support for, the making of religious books among the mercantile and professional classes of mid-fifteenth-century London.[22] This is substantially the same group for whom Reginald Pecock was to seek to provide instructive and edifying vernacular books, drawing on his own experiences as Master of Whittington College in London and as a London rector. Pecock was himself named in the foundation charter of the All Angels Guild at Syon, and his views on the translation and circulation of religious texts may well have been honed in such a milieu. In the *Book of Faith*, Pecock urges prelates and 'othere myȝty men of good' to cause books 'to be writun in greet multitude, and to be wel correctid, and thanne aftir to be sende, and to be govun or lende abroad amonge the seid lay persoonys'. This is described as a ghostly alms giving, and Pecock argues that it is not adequate to hope that listening to such vernacular books will reform the laity:

> But forsothe that these writyngis now spokun, and othere mo maad in the lay peplis langage, take her effectis into reforming of the lay peple now erryng, it is not ynouȝ that the seid bokis be writen and made and leid up or rest in the hondis of clerkis, thouȝ fame and noise be made greet to the seid lay peple of suche bokis... but tho bokis musten be distributid and delid abrood to manye where that nede is trowid that thei be delid: and that the seid erring persoonys take long leiser forto sadli and oft overrede tho bokis unto tyme thei schulen be wel aqueyntid with tho bokis and with the skilis and motives therynne writen, and not forto have in oon tyme or ii tymes a liȝt superficial overrideng or heering oonly.[23]

Oxford trained, reformist in outlook, and aware of and sympathetic to many of the critical discourses that swirled and eddied around the fragmented and often incoherent Lollard discourses of the first half of the fifteenth century, Pecock is a key avatar of reform orthodoxy, occupying one wing of that movement. When seen in this context, he is both less intellectually and culturally isolated than he can sometimes appear, and more intellectually radical, innovative, and rigorous than many of his peers and contemporaries.

With his strongly expressed preference for 'the doom of resoun' over the more intuitive affectivity popular in a lot of contemporary devotional and meditative writing, Pecock was no great fan of contemplative experience, though he uses a philosophical vision as the starting point for one of his own missionary texts (*The Reule of Cristen Religioun*). Preferring the active life to the contemplative, his primary concern was for the effective religious instruction of the laity, arguing that most engaged Christians managed complex concepts and abstract ideas in their own commercial and professional lives (he is clearly thinking of the urban mercantile classes and the gentry with whom he interacted most extensively, and who showed great eagerness for devotional and para-mystical books). He wanted a radical rethinking of the Church's catechetic programme. One of Pecock's major works, *The Repressor of Overmuch Blaming of the Clergy* appeared in 1443, the year of Henry Chichele's death. Had he not fallen foul of his ecclesiastical and secular opponents, it is likely that he would have been one of the intellectual leaders of the next generation of English bishops. Although Pecock's campaign was to founder on the rocks of political and institutional disapproval and censure, there is plenty of evidence to show that merchants, gentry, and nobility (and perhaps especially their wives, widows, and daughters) shared a common appetite for, and interest in, devotional books.

Books produced in London (such as London, British Library, MS Harley 1706 and Oxford, Bodleian Library, MS Douce 322) often show an even more elaborate and sophisticated range of sources, and may well have been compiled to order by professional stationers or commissioned by religious guilds or well-motivated groups of laymen. Booklets of moral and religious verse seem to have been available to professional and private copyists both as copy texts and as a source from which selections and adaptations of material could be made.[24] Such bespoke anthologies often and easily carried contemplative and devotional materials to a much wider audience. The collections of religious texts made in the fifteenth century by provincial gentry or merchants like Robert Thornton, Richard Heege, Rate, or Richard Hill show similar devotional tastes, and probably derive from similarly mixed clerical and lay sources.[25] Increasingly lay and religious readers used the same vernacular texts, and inevitably developed similar spiritual ambitions. The burgeoning lay market for books of hours demonstrates the desire of literate and prosperous laity to share in the public liturgy of the Universal Church, and to develop their own distinctive but orthodox para-liturgical devotions.

Multiple vernacular theologies were emerging to cater for the needs and abilities of an increasingly diverse range of religious competencies. The growing dominance of the Sarum rite, which developed one of the most gloriously elaborate ceremonial frameworks in medieval Europe, and which acquired sumptuous musical settings in many venues, allowed the addition of new feasts that reflected and fostered changing vectors in popular religious culture. The introduction of special votive masses in honour of the Five Wounds and the Name of Jesus parallel and support the growing popularity of para-mystical cults among the laity, and this is reflected in changing patterns of post-mortem benefactions in their support.[26] After the royal foundation of Sheen and Syon in 1415, no major new monastery was established in England before the dissolutions began in 1534. Instead, lay benefactions increasingly flowed into colleges, chantries, grammar schools, fraternities, and other 'mixed life' institutions, and these new institutions offered fresh contexts for the fostering of good devotional practices and sound teaching. Chichele's own family came from the mercantile gentry, and he shared and fostered one of the growing interests of the nobility and wealthy gentry in his support for education and high quality pastoral care through the foundation of new colleges, most notably All Souls in Oxford, but also a college in his home town of Higham Ferrers (Northamptonshire).

The institutional landscape of England changed in the course of the fifteenth century to reflect the desire and the increasing financial ability on the part of well-motivated laity to create new institutions that brought spirituality decisively out of the cloister. Chantries, such as those developed by the Hungerford family, borrowed from and imitated the liturgy and spirituality of great spiritual centres like Syon.[27] The proliferation of such institutional foundations in the fifteenth century, and the growing importance of chantries in parish churches, changed the centre of gravity of the English church, creating, for those who could afford to be part of it, a flatter, more spiritually democratic structure where spirituality, prayerful intercession, and 'the life of soul' were no longer sequestered in the great abbeys and monasteries, but could be replicated more locally and be more immediately tailored to the needs, tastes, and resources of local communities. Merchants could aspire to contemplation as legitimately as monks. The 'mixed life' is as distinctive a manifestation of the spirituality of fifteenth-century reform orthodoxy as the anchorhold and eremitic seclusion had been in previous centuries.[28]

When texts of interior religion came to be produced or adapted for laymen in later medieval England, they often borrowed as their dominant spatial allegory the structure and architecture of a monastic community:

> Blessid is þat religioun of whiche þe temple is holynes, þe scole sooþnes, and þe cloister stilnes, þe chapilte of equite, þe dortoir of chastite, and þe fermary pitee, þe fraitir sobirnes and þe hostrie largenes and charite. þerfore who þat haþ þese viij placis goostly in his soule and outward in hise werkis, his religioun is perfi3t.
> (*The Eight Ghostly Dwelling Places*)

As anchoritic and monastic texts reached a wider readership and were adapted for laymen and women, the notion of monastic or eremitic enclosure as the physically metaphorical representation of a superior state of spiritual and mental commitment becomes superseded by the sense that spiritual commitment is imaginatively and allegorically comprehensible without physical claustration.[29]

These changes and extensions in popular devotional practice and taste are marked by a growing curiosity for meditative and contemplative spirituality, allowing even modestly wealthy laymen and women to develop contemplative prayer practices in the contexts of their own homes and parishes. Popular vernacular compilations such as the *Pore Caitif*, or *Contemplations of the Dread and Love of God*, often use the catechetic syllabus as the starting point for explorations of spirituality that go far beyond rote learning of the basic teachings to encompass much more ambitious explorations of, and exhortations to, their readers to immerse themselves in the fullest understanding of what it is to love God.[30] Texts such as these often passed into lay as well as clerical ownership. New forms of religious association emerged. Women took the mantle and ring as vowesses in increasing numbers. Usually such women were widows (an important category of devout reader), but there are records of married women (such as Margery Kempe and her major role model Birgitta of Sweden) vowing chastity and giving themselves to religion while their (consenting) spouses were still alive.[31] Fraternities and guilds proliferated in the fifteenth century, often bringing together influential and prosperous laymen and clergy from local parishes and religious orders in a sodality that was meant to be mutually beneficial as well as spiritually supportive and stimulating.[32] Such associations, often tied to particular devotional practices and with distinctive liturgies or paraliturgical observances, emerged in this period as one of the most powerful vectors of urban spirituality and innovative religious engagement. Alongside them, morality plays and single religious dramas develop as a locus where contemplative aspiration could be explored, guided and, where necessary, warned against.

Cycle plays like the York *Nativity*, or the *Dream of Pilate's Wife* often address issues of contemplative potential and achievement, while the (probably East Anglian) N-Town *Mary Play* is introduced and commented on by an interlocutor character called *Contemplacio*.[33] *The Mary Play*, drawing on the *Legenda aurea* (*Golden Legend*), and the *Charter of the Abbey of the Holy Ghost*, draws most of its spiritual force from the Pseudo-Bonaventuran tradition's presentation of the Virgin as a paradigm female contemplative, also found in vernacular versions such as Love's *Mirror* and the *Speculum devotorum*. In the play *Wisdom who is Christ*, which bristles with locations from the heartland of London legal life, and uses contemplative and para-mystical materials from Hilton and Suso, it is Lucifer himself who acts as a persuasive advocate in favour of laymen pursuing the mixed life of

action and contemplation, perhaps reflecting official concerns at the potential abuse of such spiritual ambition. The late fifteenth-century *Croxton
Play of the Sacrament*, which survives in a copy possibly made during the
Marian restoration of the mid-sixteenth century, addresses mercantile spirituality and clerical slackness, stressing the ineffability of the real presence,
and the core role of the clergy in policing orthodoxy and in mediating sacramental absolution and mercy.[34] The early sixteenth-century texts in Oxford,
Bodleian MS e. Mus 160 preserve 'acted meditations', closet plays to be used
in private rumination and drawing from a range of learned sources, probably
by Carthusians whose solitary lifestyle needed guided sustenance. The mid-
to late fifteenth-century Carthusian anthology, London, British Library, MS
Additional 37049 similarly offers contemplative and meditative paradigms
(often accompanied by images to create composite texts for rumination).
Although these contemplative texts probably did not circulate outside of
the order, they reflect the importance of dramatic enactment of meditative
modellings every bit as vividly as Nicholas Love's injunctions to mediators
to imagine themselves present at the foot of the Cross or in the upper room
awaiting the resurrection.[35] Such dramatic enactments (or reenactments) are
central to the English tradition of contemplative writing from Rolle, through
Julian of Norwich, Margery Kempe, and onwards.

Celebrations of the lives of saints provided a rich and productive seam of
preaching material and of safe and edifying reading material for increasingly
voracious vernacular readers and listeners, both clerical and lay (audiences
that are often increasingly undifferentiated and increasingly inseparable in
the address and in the circulation of these texts). Lydgate's hagiographic
texts often work to fuel popular national or local pride in the achievements of the English church, as with his prayers to Thomas Becket and
his legends of St George and St Augustine at Compton. His various Lives
and Legends (including his very popular *Life of Our Lady*) help to establish
the saint's life as one of the characteristic genres of the post-Arundelian
English church eager to reform itself and to foster right religion and proper
devotion. To approve of saints and the efficacy of their prayers was one way
of marking out the orthodox from the heterodox in the fifteenth century.
But of course saints' lives also taught lay and religious readers how to live
their lives in emulation, and the most popular lives in the later medieval
period often showed heroic laymen and (even more often) women aspiring
to profess, protect, and preserve their special relationships with God, even
to the point of martyrdom and death.

The *Legenda aurea* was the dominant collection of saints' lives in medieval
England. It offered succinct, authoritative, accessible, and clearly structured
accounts of most leading figures in the hagiographical pantheon. It was the

first port of call for many sermons and exemplary narrative discourses. In the fifteenth century it was faithfully translated as the *Gilte legende*, with the addition of some supplementary new lives drawn from more recent hagiography. It was also later supplemented by a new, specifically English, group of lives, addressed to the 'Peple of this realme', and this collection may have been produced under the auspices of the hyper-orthodox Birgittines at Syon (the initials of the abbess are hidden in the border of the Birgittine woodcut at the front of the book).[36] John Capgrave and Osbern Bokenham, both working in the middle decades of the century, produced sequences of lives for nuns, religious, and male and female secular readers. Bokenham is writing for young gentry and noble readers, of both genders, who are not only the patrons and audience for his lives, but who often find reflected in those lives a similar social status, devotional literacy, and spiritual ambition in the saints who are their subjects. This is hagiography for the 'mixed life', and illustrates the tastes and abilities of mid-century English readers.

These collections of legendary lives were powerfully supplemented by smaller, bespoke collections of lives, often of holy women of more recent vintage than those in the usual legendaries. These women, largely of European extraction and often alive not far beyond living memory, and therefore perhaps of more immediate interest to a vernacular readership, are usually marked with contemplative aspirations or verified visionary experiences. Many were vowed religious, or aspired to become nuns or recluses, and their lives often record at much greater length and in much greater detail the accounts of their dynamic and developing mystical relationship with Christ. The English market for such lives seems initially to have been circumscribed by (and was probably always largely supplied from) the great contemplative orders of the Carthusians and Birgittines. But their readership soon spread out into the ranks of pious and well-born laywomen and men and from them into wider circulation, though often only in extracted and episodic versions drawn from the whole life. This spread coincided with a more engaged and active interest in some sections of the gentle and noble laity in the cultivation of the kinds of interior spiritual growth exemplified in books written for nuns and anchorites, a process of creating an interior para-monastic spirituality that became known as 'religion of the herte'. This interest can be vividly observed in Oxford, Bodleian Library, MS Douce 114, a fascinating if idiosyncratic volume of translations from Latin, containing a life of Catherine of Siena and the lives of Elisabeth of Spalbeck, Christina Mirabilis and Marie of Oignies (the latter, of course, a great influence on one of Margery Kempe's priestly supporters, and probably on Margery herself). In addition, the book contains the English redaction of

Henry Suso's Latin *Horologium sapientiae* (itself a text of likely Carthusian provenance in both its Latin insular circulation and its vernacular manifestation), known in the English vernacular as *The Seven Points of True Wisdom*.[37] The book carries an *ex libris* mark for the Charterhouse at Beauvale in Nottinghamshire, but it is by no means clear that it was produced there. Indeed, there were Latin versions of these lives preserved at another nearby Nottinghamshire monastery, the Augustinian house at Thurgarton where Walter Hilton had eventually become prior, and other versions are associated with John Blacman, sometime chaplain to the contemplatively inclined Henry VI, and eventually himself linked with the Carthusians. The Thurgarton connection is especially interesting as the Augustinian canons often served in parishes, as well as writing for nuns and recluses (as Hilton had done). The lives found in Douce 114 offer fascinating exemplars for a new kind of intense and expressive spirituality, perhaps useful for priests engaged in the pastoral care and spiritual direction of nuns, and of devout and contemplatively aspirant laywomen.

Although these lives reflect the normalizing techniques of late medieval hagiography, this does not mean that they are in any way homogenized. The extreme physicality of Elizabeth of Spalbeck's *imitatio Christi*, for example, replaces the liturgy of the canonical Hours with a violent re-enactment of the Passion of Christ and transfigures meditation on an image into a near-death experience of real force and contemplative otherness. Unlike many of the later English practitioners of such affective techniques, whose 'ymagynacouns' could sometimes get out of hand or prove doctrinally or psychologically problematic without proper spiritual guidance, Elizabeth's real life was always enacted within the confines of her monastic community (of Cistercian nuns at Herkenroode) and under the spiritual and canonical guidance of male clerics. Her written life was always already inscribed within the interpretative confines of the hagiographic tradition:

> Wherfore this virgyne, whos lyfe is alle mirakil, 3e moor-ouer alle hir selfe is but myrakil, . . . figures and expounes not allonly Cryste, but Cryste crucifyed in hir body, and also þe figuratif body of Cryste, þat is holy chirche.
>
> (p. 118/ p. 50)

This hagiographic inscription into the world of the *magisterium* (the teaching authority of the church) and its interpretative tradition of *probatio* (testing) and *discretio spirituum* (discernment of spirits) is an essential safety precaution and such lives become both models for emulation for aspirant contemplatives and also cautionary tales of the need for clerical support and spiritual guidance. This dualism is perhaps one of the reasons for making these materials available in the vernacular: their carefully orthodox, if often racily mystical, lives are acted out within the context of the nurturing and validating ethos of the institutional Church.

Christina Mirabilis's near-death experience of judgement and return to life is blended with her ability to produce what is described as 'angel's song':

> Cristyn was atte matyns euery nyghte, and whanne alle oþere were goon out of þe chirche and þe dores lokked, she dwellynge in þe chirche paument made a songe of so grete swetnesse, þat hit semyd raþere aungels songe þan mannes. þat songe was so merueilous to hir þat hit passed alle þe noyses and Instrumentis of musikers or mynstralles, but lesse and ferre vnlike to þe swetnesse of þat melodye þat sownyd by-twix hir þrote and hir brest. But þat songe was latyne and feyre sette to-gadir wiþ many clauses of acordauns.
>
> (p. 129/ p. 74)

Angelic song had become something of a *topos* in fourteenth-century English contemplative writings. Richard Rolle had alluded to his own experience of it, the *Cloud of Unknowing* expresses its unease about such signs, and Walter Hilton had felt moved to write a short vernacular treatise warning against the spiritual dangers of such kinaesthetic manifestations. Aural disturbances were a common feature of contemplative or visionary experience, such as in Margery Kempe's flutterings and twitterings (probably the result of frontal lobe epilepsy).[38] But in Christina's case this charismatic ability to 'speak with the tongues of men and of angels' is grounded and earthed in her ability to sing complex Latin hymns and chants, and to expound Scripture, despite the fact that 'sche neuer knewe lettir syþen she was borne'. Unlike those 'great reasoners in Scripture' among the Lollards who claimed the authority as well as the ability to engage in exegesis, Christina's life (translated into English when such Lollard claims were still fresh in the memory if not still being made) stresses her reluctance to exercise her gift:

> whan she was asked moost dyuyne questyons of holy wrytte, she wolde declare hem moost openly to summe of hir spiritual freendes. But ful gretely ageyns hir wille & ful selden she wolde so do, seyynge þat hit byfelle to clerkys to expoune holy writte, & þat siche mater felle not to hir.　(p. 129. p. 74)

She is also tactful in the exercise of her office of clerical correction, admonishing sinful priests and clerics 'esely and priuely with a wonder reuerens'(*ibid.*). Christina's authority, her life demonstrates, comes not just from her charism, which transcends her avowed limitations of language and understanding, but also from her willingness to exercise that charism within the sheltering, monitoring, controlling, and ultimately validating arms of the institutional Church. Such lives, therefore, even when they are critical of the Church, add lustre to its claims of spiritual hegemony. Subliminally, the message of such translations is that spiritual aspiration is best expressed in and through communion with the wisdom of the *magisterium* rather than in solipsistic rejection of it.

Subversive and radical as such lives might appear, they in fact provide templates for orthodox contemplation. As with Margery Kempe, who translates and internalizes many of the tropes of these continental visionaries into her own spiritual praxis, the texts dramatize spiritual ambition, love of the Church and its sacraments, eagerness for a properly functioning clerical cadre, and desire for discernment, approval and approbation. Even more like Margery, unsurprisingly, is the life of the great weeper Marie of Oignies. Marie's life comes with its own health warning not to imitate the various excesses of her life too readily. She too has a remarkable ability to remember and interpret Holy Scripture (we are told that she was always reading the Psalter as she worked or spun), even expounding new teachings and interpretations on her deathbed 'in rime & romayne tunge' (p. 179/ p. 179), in a curious swansong that ranges from the Trinity, through the Old and New Testaments and the liturgy down to the sins of individual men. Like Margery, Marie is something of a clerical groupie, prone to kiss the feet of effective preachers until she has to be physically prised off them, and eager always to be in earshot of preaching:

> Sooþly, þe wise and discrete womman was suffyciently byshyned wiþ holy writte; for often she herde goddes wordes and kepte and bare in hir herte wordes of holy writte, and hauntynge holy chirche she hidde holy hestes wysely in hir herte . . . þat atte she herde deuoutly she bisyed hir to fulfille hit more deuoutly in dede. (p. 163/ p. 146)

Here again, the particular appeal of this life for a fifteenth-century translator is probably the stress on Marie's hearing (rather than reading) the words of Scripture, and her 'haunting' of the church building, rather than abandoning it for private conventicles.

> And þof she were taughte wiþ-in forþe þurghe vnxione of þe holy goste and goddes reuelacyons neuerþeles sche gladly herde wiþoute forþe wordes of holy writte, þe whiche accordid fully to þe holy goost. For oure lorde, þof hee myghte haue taughte his disciplis þurgh inwarde lighte wiþouten voys, neþer þe les outewarde techynge wiþ worde expouned to hem scriptures to whom hee seyde: 'Now are ȝee clene for þe worde þat I haue spoken to ȝow.' þerfore sche fro daye to daye was more wasshen in clennessse wiþ þe wordes of goddes writynge, was edifyed to exhortacyone of vertues, was enlumynid to þe feiþ, neþerles if feiþ may propirly be seyde in hir þe whiche by reuelacyoune of oure lorde perceyued inuisibil þinges as visibil wiþ an open feiþ. (p. 164/p. 148)

This passage enacts a fascinating balancing act between her independent revelation and her continued dependence on the word of God mediated through the teaching office of priests. Both processes require her to listen (not read, or indeed talk) with humble obedience and an open faith. By equating her with the disciples she is being empowered, and simultaneously modelled as an exemplum of open and obedient faith. This is a fascinating illustration of complex negotiations necessary between revelatory enlightenment and obedience to the Church. No wonder this text was so influential for the priest seeking to understand Margery Kempe. Marie and the others validate the ecclesiastical status quo by showing its efficacy in developing their own spiritual and contemplative potential.

The lives of such 'approued women' (as the author of *Speculum devotorum* revealingly calls Mechtild of Hackeborn, Elizabeth of Töss, Catherine of Siena, and Birgitta of Sweden in his own work) enact a careful balancing act between the celebration of a special charism that brings, on the one hand, renown (and pilgrims) to a particular religious house and, on the other, confirmation, reinforcement and potentially model behaviours for those living and journeying in faith and in the hope of grace; and between a style of writing and encoding of that life that reinforces and re-enacts the centrality of the institutional Church and its clergy in interpreting, validating, and transmitting that life to others, and in seeking to control and police its subsequent significations. Margery's clerical scribe, though more uncomfortable and uncertain of touch than many of his hagiographical predecessors, is certainly not without precedent in his ungainly attempts in his officiously added prologue to classify her book as a treatise on the uses of tribulation, and he is not alone among clerics in wishing to inscribe Margery's life into the formats and formulae of hagiography:

> Sum proferyd hir to wrytyn hyr felyngys wyth her owen handys, and sche wold not consentyn in no wey, for sche was comawndyd in hir sowle that sche schuld not wrytyn so soone. And so it was twenty ʒer and mor fro þat tym þis creatur had fyrst felyngys and revelacyons er than sche dede any wryten. Aftyrward whan it plesyd ower Lord, he comawnded hyr and chargyd hir that sche xuld don wryten hyr felyngys and reuelacyons and þe forme of her leuyng that hys goodnesse myth be knowyn to alle the world.[39]

But given the climate of uncertainty surrounding revelatory materials in the fifteenth century, and the tendency of East Anglian women claiming religious teaching authority or heterodox views to be arraigned on heresy charges, it is hardly surprising that Margery waits until the 1430s before finally committing her experiences to writing, and that, initially at least she did so to a (semi-)literate layman, probably her own son.[40]

After Chichele's death in 1443, he was succeeded by John Stafford (d. 1452), who had served under Chichele for many years as bishop of Bath and Wells. The gradual changing of the episcopal guard around the middle of the century saw Chichele's cadre of sound administrators and incipient humanists succeeded by a new raft of appointments, largely of theologians. In these years, national concerns came to focus increasingly on the anxieties of civil war and political instability. Although ecclesiastical historians rarely have much to say about the Church in the second half of the century, it is clear that Chichele's generation had steadied the ship, that parochial and public religious culture continued to thrive, and that the growing number of laity able and willing to exercise their pragmatic and devotional literacies kept the spirituality of the Church afloat and alert. It fell to the embattled and pragmatic William Warham, translated to Canterbury from the see of London in 1503 to lead the Church through the increasingly stormy waters of the early sixteenth century until he was succeeded in 1532 by the protestant reformer Thomas Cranmer. But the great scholar bishops of the early sixteenth century like John Fisher of Rochester (first appointed in 1504), spiritual advisor to Lady Margaret Beaufort, or Richard Fox of Durham and Winchester (first appointed in 1494), founder of colleges and sponsor of printing, did not emerge from a spiritual and cultural vacuum. The diurnal life of the English church at the end of the fifteenth century was rich, diverse, and variegated. The thriving market for psalters and books of hours, and the notable array of printed works of devotional and para-mystical spirituality produced, in particular by Wynkyn de Worde's press, suggests that the audience for such materials continued to expand beyond the limits of enclosed religious.

Syon, for example, continuing its role as a fountainhead of works of vernacular theology and contemplative aspiration, seems to have been involved with printed vernacular books from at least as early as the 1483 *Quattuor sermones* (*Four Sermons*) (*RSTC* 17957), issued by Caxton with an edition of Mirk's hugely popular sermon cycle, the *Festial*. In 1487, the *Directorium sacerdotum* (*The Directory of Priests*) (*RSTC* 17720), a liturgical guide by one of their own early brethren Clement Maydestone, was published, perhaps through their agency. In 1499, Simon Wynter's early fifteenth-century life of Jerome also appeared in print from Wynkyn de Worde (*RSTC* 14508). In 1500, Wynkyn printed Syon librarian Thomas Betson's *Ryght Profytable Treatyse* (*RSTC* 1978), the first printed work to emanate from identifiable Syon authorship, made up of translations of ascetic and patristic materials, and carefully aimed at an audience 'that ben come & shall come to relygyon'. This seems to have initiated a substantial and ongoing commercial relationship between Wynkyn and Syon, who may have supplied him with

materials to print and commissioned editions from him and other later printers (such as the printed texts of *The Orcherd of Syon* in 1519 (*RSTC* 4815)
and *The Myroure of Oure Ladye* in 1530 (*RSTC* 17542)). The size of the
Syon community (sixty nuns and twelve priests at full complement) would
have given some guarantee of a minimum sale, and printers and importers
of books probably used an association with Syon as a valuable advertising
aid. Books with Syon-related woodcuts clearly seek to associate the works
they contain with the reputation of the order and its foundress.[41]

In the 1530s, Richard Whitford, (self styled 'wretch of Syon') and probably the most prolific author among the Birgittines, William Bonde, John
Fewterer, and other Syon brethren published texts though printers in the
metropolis, perhaps as part of a deliberate campaign to produce doctrinally orthodox materials for a reading public increasingly threatened with
Lutheran and other protestant ideas. A man of cultured experience, friend
of Erasmus, and an early figure in the development of the New Learning
in England, Whitford's marketability was such that his works continued to
appear in print after the suppression of the community at Syon in 1539
(when he was styled 'late brother of Syon'). He seems to have welcomed the
advantages that the new technology brought. In his 1537 *A Dayly exercyse
and experyence of dethe* (*RSTC* 25414) he explains the provenance of his
text:

> This lytle tretie or draght of deth dyd I wryte more than xx yeres ago at the
> request of the reuerende Mother Dame Elizabeth Gybs whome Jesu perdon
> then Abbes of Syon. And by the oft calling vpon and remembraunce of certeyne
> of hyr deuout systers. And nowe of late I haue been compelled . . . to wryte it
> agayne and agayne. And bycause that wrytynge vnto me is very tedyouse
> I thought better to put it in print whereunto I was the rather moued that I
> perceyued by the printers you haue thankfully taken suche other poore labours
> as we before haue sende forth. Rede this I pray you ones ouer and after as you
> lyke it is but very short and therefore haue I not deuyded it into chapytours
> but only into ii partes. (sig. ai^v–aii^r)

Part blurb, part apologia, part begging letter, such prefatory remarks are
common in Whitford's books. Typically they explain the reason for his
activity, the provenance of the text and the target audience for them. The
sense that these prologues allow lay readers as well as religious to share
vicariously in the spiritual and contemplative life of a vibrant and prestigious
house like Syon was no doubt a major part of the appeal of his books:

> But late I sende forth a lytle worke of the lyfe of perfecttyon named the pype
> or tunne of the same lyfe. And here nowe one of my brethren brought vnto me
> a treatise or lytle draght in latyn of an vncerteyn auctor whiche he founde by

chaunce of certen impediments or lettes of the spirituall profite, profotynge, good spede & goyng forwarde in the iourney to obtain & come unto the same lyfe whiche tracte or draght I thought shuld frame wel vnto the same worke. And therefore I put hyt into Englysh and added thereunto many thynges that I thought conuenient for the same. (*A worke of dyuers impedimentes and lettes of perfection*, 1541 (*RSTC* 25420, sig. Ni^r))

Whitford became a brand name himself, a metonymy of the merits of his house. Here the fact that the text he has translated was 'of an uncerteyn auctor' (and therefore of uncertain authority) is controlled and turned to advantage by stressing the orthodox quality control offered by Whitford's role as translator and advocate. Elsewhere, Whitford's prologues allow the reader glimpses of the processes by which his texts come into being and of the internal dynamics of Syon at work:

Here be many good and profetable lessons ascribed vnto saynt Isodor whiche maye be rather called & taken for notes gadred then for any worke digested and ordered...A deuout brother of ours instantly requirynge forsed me to translate the mater which I haue done more after the sens and meaning of the auctour then after the letter, and somewhere I haue added vnto the auctour rather than mynished any thynge...Your assured bedeman the olde wreched brother of Syon Rycherd Whytforde. (*An instrucyon to auoyde and eschewe vices and folowe good maners*, 1541 (*RSTC* 25420, sig. Rii^r))

The authority of Isidore is reinforced by the editorial re-ordering and augmentation that Whitford has undertaken, which gives the work added value.

Whitford recognizes that materials that he had originally produced for his fellow Birgittines would by virtue of his translation soon fly out into much wider circulation. But unlike his largely anonymous predecessors, Whitford decides that he must put his name to his authentic translations as a guarantor of their worth, having found other, potentially heterodox material bound in with and passed off as works from his own pen:

And that I do charitably to gyue you warnyng to serche well and suerly that none suche other workes be put amonge them that might deceyue you. For (of a certente) I founde nowe but very late a worke ioyned and bounde with my pore labours & vnder the contentes of the same volume and one of my workes that was named in the same contentes lefte out in sted wherof was put this other worke yat was not myne...An the other worke hathe no name of any auctour and all such workes in thys tyme be euer to be suspected for so the heretykes do vse to sende forthe theyr poyson amonge the people couered with sugar...Be you ware therfore of all suche fatherless bokes that nother haue the name of the auctour nor of the translatour. Knowe what you rede and what you suffre your chyldren to lerne. Specially (after my pore aduise) medle not with the workes of nameles and vnknowne auctours. I haue shewed you why. (*A deuoute worke of pacience*, 1541 (*RSTC* 25420, sig. Ai^v–Aii^r))

In an age of renewed anxiety over heresy, and under the darkening clouds of an increasingly hostile state apparatus, fatherless books about devotion and contemplative aspiration would soon be a thing of the past. Perhaps John Fewterer's 1534 translation of *The Mirror or Glass of Christ's Passion*, a work avowedly in the Bonaventuran mould and using the contemplative techniques and structures of earlier centuries, is the last native flowering of a para-mystical and contemplative tradition of vernacular translation that had blurred the boundaries between professed religious and motivated lay-men and women. Soon the precious inheritance of contemplative literature would be largely entrusted to the recusant English religious communities that cherished the memory and example of the English tradition in their foreign exile. The leaders of the new English church would relegate and seek to suppress visionary and contemplative activity as a branch of the poten-tially subversive activity of political prophecy. Commenting on the Elizabeth Barton affair, in a letter to the soon to be martyred John Fisher, bishop of Rochester, Thomas Cromwell said that:

> If credense shuld be gyven to every suche lewd person as wold affirme him self to have revelations from God, what redyer way wer ther to subvert al common welths and good orders in the world?[42]

In his words we hear the authentically ruthless tones of the religious realpoli-tik which would govern the rest of Henry VIII's reign.

NOTES

1 Cited from the *Memorials of St. Edmund's Abbey* by Jennifer Summit, '"Stable in Study": Lydgate's *Fall of Princes* and Duke Humphrey's Library', in Larry Scan-lon and James Simpson (eds.), *John Lydgate: Poetry, Culture, and Lancastrian England* (Notre Dame, IN: University of Notre Dame Press, 2006), pp. 207–31, p. 216.

2 This Middle English version comes from Francis Charles Hingeston (ed.), *The Chronicle of England by John Capgrave* (Rerum Britannicarum Medii Ævi Scriptores: London, 1858), p. 314, but the story is also told in many contem-porary Latin sources such as Adam Usk's *Chronicle*, The *Chronica maiora* of Thomas Walsingham, Elmham's *Liber metricus*, the *Gesta Henrici quinti* and in Capgrave's *De illustribus Henricis*.

3 David Preest (trans.), Thomas Walsingham, *The Chronica Maiora of Thomas Walsingham, 1376–1422*, with Introduction and Notes by James G. Clark (Woodbridge: Boydell and Brewer, 2005), pp. 396–7, 398, 399–400.

4 Priscilla Heath Barnum (ed.), *Dives and Pauper*, 2 vols. EETS OS 275, 280, 323 (1976–2004), II, xviii–xxxi; Anne Hudson and Helen Leith Spencer, 'Old Author, New Work: The Sermons of MS Longleat 4', *Medium Ævum* 53 (1984), 220–38. On Thomas Gascoigne, see *ODNB*; James Edwin Thorold Rogers (ed.), *Loci E Libro Veritatum. Passages Selected from Gascoigne's Theological Dictionary, Illustrating the Condition of Church and State, 1403–1458* (Oxford: Clarendon Press, 1881), pp. 34–5, 180–1.

5 Patrick Horner (ed.), *A Macaronic Sermon Collection from Late Medieval England: Oxford, MS Bodley 649*, Studies and Texts 153 (Toronto: Pontifical Institute of Mediaeval Studies, 2006), pp. 518–31; Roy Martin Haines, *Ecclesia Anglicana: Studies in the English Church of the Later Middle Ages* (Toronto: University of Toronto Press, 1989).

6 Chris L. Nighman, '"Accipiant Qui Vocati Sunt": Richard Fleming's Reform Sermon at the Council of Constance', *JEH* 51 (2000), 1–36, (29).

7 The detailed legislation of Chichele's early years is contained in Gerald Lewis Bray (ed.), *Records of Convocation* (Woodbridge: Boydell, in association with the Church of England Record Society, 2005), V: Canterbury 1414–43. This comment, p. 33.

8 For a full translation of Polton's fascinating speech, which prefigures (and perhaps supplies) many of the claims made by Henry VIII's ministers during the break with Rome), see C. M. D. Crowder, *Unity, Heresy and Reform, 1378–1460: The Conciliar Response to the Great Schism* (London: Edward Arnold, 1977), pp. 110–26; J.-P. Genet, 'English Nationalism: Thomas Polton at the Council of Constance', *Nottingham Medieval Studies* 28 (1984), 60–78. James P. Carley, 'A Grave Event: Henry V, Glastonbury Abbey and Joseph of Arimathea's Bones', in James P. Carley (ed.), *Glastonbury Abbey and the Arthurian Tradition*, Arthurian Studies 44 (Woodbridge: D. S. Brewer, 2001), pp. 285–302.

9 Roger Ellis (ed.), *'My Compleinte' and Other Poems*, EMTS (Exeter: University of Exeter Press, 2001). On Hoccleve's engagement with reform orthodoxy, see Sebastian James Langdell, '"What World Is This? How Vndirstande Am I?": A Reappraisal of Poetic Authority in Thomas Hoccleve's *Series*', *Medium Ævum* (2009), 281–99. Ella Keats Keating (ed.), *The Poems of John Audelay*, EETS OS 184 (1931), but see now Susanna Fein (ed.), *John the Blind Audelay: Poems and Carols (Oxford, Bodleian Library MS Douce 302)*, TEAMS (Kalamazoo, MI: Medieval Institute Publications, 2009); Susanna Fein (ed.), *My Wyl and My Wrytyng: Essays on John the Blind Audelay* (Kalamazoo, MI: Medieval Institute Publications, 2009). On MS Digby 102, see J. Kail (ed.), *Twenty-Six Political and Other Poems*, EETS OS 124 (1904), and Helen Barr (ed.), *The Digby Poems: A New Edition of the Lyrics* (Exeter: University of Exeter Press, 2009); P. Horner (ed.), *A Macaronic Sermon Collection*. David Lawton, 'Dullness and the Fifteenth Century', *English Literary History* 54 (1987), 761–99, presents a remarkably prescient argument that benefits from re-reading in the light of our developing understanding of English reformist orthodoxy.

10 On Netter, see *ODNB*, and Johann Bergstrom-Allen and Richard Copsey (eds.), *Thomas Netter of Walden: Carmelite, Diplomat and Theologian (c.1372–1430)*, Carmel in Britain 4 (Aylesford: St Albert's Press, 2009), which reproduces an early printed text of the *Doctrinale* on CD-ROM. On Lyndwood, *ODNB*;

Christopher Robert Cheney, *Medieval Texts and Studies* (Oxford: Clarendon Press, 1973), pp. 158–84.

11 Marleen Cré, *Vernacular Mysticism in the Charterhouse: A Study of London, British Library, MS Additional 37790* (Turnhout: Brepols, 2006).

12 All quotations are from the copy now preserved as Notre Dame, Indiana, University of Notre Dame, MS 67. See the useful collection of essays on this text in Jill Mann and Maura Nolan (eds.), *The Text in the Community: Essays on Medieval Works, Manuscripts, Authors, and Readers* (Notre Dame, IN: University of Notre Dame Press, 2006).

13 Ch. 4 of the *Additions to the Rule*: James Hogg, *The Rewyll of Seynt Savioure and Other Middle English Brigittine Legislative Texts*, 3 vols. (Salzburg: Institut fur Anglistik und Amerikanistik, 1978–80), 3. 27.

14 For the brethren's library, see Vincent Gillespie (ed.), *Syon Abbey*, Corpus of British Medieval Library Catalogues 9 (London: British Library, 2001); Vincent Gillespie, 'The Book and the Brotherhood: Reflections on the Lost Library of Syon Abbey', in A. S. G. Edwards, Vincent Gillespie, and Ralph Hanna (eds.), *The English Medieval Book: Studies in Memory of Jeremy Griffiths* (London: British Library, 2000), 185–208. For the nuns, see Ann M. Hutchison, 'What the Nuns Read: Literary Evidence from the English Bridgettine House, Syon Abbey', *Medieval Studies*, 57 (1995), 205–22. On Syon as an important textual community, see the essays by Katherine Zieman and Elizabeth Schirmer in Linda Olson and Kathryn Kerby-Fulton (eds.), *Voices in Dialogue: Reading Women in the Middle Ages* (Notre Dame, IN: University of Notre Dame Press, 2005); Cathy Grisé, 'The Textual Community of Syon Abbey', *Florilegium* 19 (2002), 149–62.

15 John Henry Blunt (ed.), *The Myroure of Oure Ladye*, EETS ES 19 (1873).

16 See, for example, George Keiser, 'The Mystics and the Early Printers: The Economics of Devotionalism', in *MMTE IV*, pp. 9–25; Susan Powell, 'Lady Margaret Beaufort and Her Books', *The Library* 6th ser. 20 (1998), 197–240.

17 Vincent Gillespie, 'Walter Hilton at Syon Abbey', in James Hogg (ed.), *'Stand up to Godwards': Essays in Mystical and Monastic Theology in honour of the Reverend John Clark on His Sixty-Fifth Birthday*, Analecta Cartusiana 204 (Salzburg: Institut für Anglistik und Amerikanistik, 2002), 9–61. For a detailed account of Syon and Sheen's role in the fifteenth-century London transmission and elaboration of Hilton's *Scale of Perfection*, see Michael G. Sargent, 'Walter Hilton's *Scale of Perfection*: The London Manuscript Group Reconsidered', *Medium Ævum* 52 (1983), 189–216.

18 *The Manere of Good Lyuyng* is still unedited. Denis Renevey, Christiania Whitehead, and Anne Mouron (eds.), *The Doctrine of the Hert*, EMTS (Exeter: University of Exeter Press, 2009), Theresa A. Halligan (ed.), *The Booke of Gostlye Grace of Mechtild of Hackeborn* (Toronto: Pontifical Institute of Mediaeval Studies, 1979); Mary Erler, '"A Revelation of Purgatory" (1422): Reform and the Politics of Female Visions', *Viator* 38 (2007), 321–47. On *Disce mori* and its links with Syon, see E. A. Jones (ed.), *The 'Exhortacion' From Disce Mori: Edited from Oxford, Jesus College, MS 39*, Middle English Texts 36 (Heidelberg: Winter, 2006).

19 George Keiser, 'Patronage and Piety in Fifteenth-Century England: Margaret, Duchess of Clarence, Symon Wynter and Beinecke Ms 317', *Yale University*

9

BARRY WINDEATT

1412–1534: texts

It is a modern commonplace that the English fifteenth century – although an age of such flamboyant achievements in many of the arts – was a time of intellectual and spiritual repression, regulation and censorship, fearful of heresy and of innovation alike. Within this overstated larger picture of the age, modern assessment of contemplative life and literature in the fifteenth century becomes comparably distorted. The very accomplishment of mystical writing in English in the fourteenth century – so the standard literary history runs – is underlined by a lack of successors. In its pursuit of the contemplative life, the fifteenth century is hence nowadays characterized – in neglect of much contrary evidence – as conservative, insular, and without originality.

Emblematic of modern interpretation of fifteenth-century spirituality has been the ambivalent reception of *The Book of Margery Kempe* since its rediscovery in the 1930s. Soon judged an embarrassment – whether as some pooterishly unselfaware 'Diary of a Nobody', or because a sadly self-deceived mimicry of more authentic mystical experience – the *Book* embarrasses still, for all the achievement of recent commentary that variously seeks to neutralize the challenges of its embarrassments. The terms of the *Book*'s current celebrity – its recruitment as witness to modern-day preoccupations with dissent, gender, authority, and empowerment – attain invaluable insights but evade the embarrassment of facing what centrally concerns and fills Kempe's *Book*: her revelatory conversations with Christ, in a stream of consciousness that constitutes the only biography that Kempe felt worth recording. What unites most reception of the *Book* is disinclination to value its spiritual content and purpose, the sophistication of contemporary contemplative culture that it evidences, and hence the counter indicators it provides for the limited modern evaluation of fifteenth-century devotion. Kempe's sheer audacity fits strangely with a current insistence on her struggles that rather overlooks how she recounts these difficulties only to celebrate her triumphs over them. Recent enlistment of Kempe as witness to an England in the grip of ecclesiastical repression and persecution of heresy overlooks the unprobing mildness with which she is ever questioned and the bumbling officialdom that she so easily obfuscates in order to pursue the inner life that becomes her sole reality.

From the *Book*, as from a wider survey, there emerges a picture of fifteenth-century contemplative culture that in its variety and profusion is both in vibrant vitality and yet essentially self-regulating according to context and ability. Within the expanding availability in English of a much broader devotional literature, the more specialized pursuit of contemplation also developed a wider appeal to lay as well as religious readerships, although such laicization in contemplative readership develops alongside, and in interaction with, continuing pursuit of contemplation at a high level among the religious.[1] Whereas a monk at Canterbury – affronted by Kempe's freelance role as a holy woman at large – irritably wishes she were 'closyd in a hous of ston' (ch. 11),[2] and hence incommunicado, spiritual advisers adumbrated for their lay readers an inner life pursued in a kind of metaphorical cloister: the *Book to a Mother* urges 'Modur, ȝif þou kepe wel þis cloister and holde þe þerinne to þi liues ende, Crist, þat is Abbot and Priour of þis cloister wol euer be þerinne wiþ þe where-euere þou be...' (p. 122).[3] Kempe's facility in absorbing and applying recent contemplative literature from home and abroad is symptomatic of fifteenth-century confidence in re-reading the English contemplative classics, often in radically edited selections, rearrangements, and compilations which represent forms of critical interpretation through recontextualization. Latin works are translated into English (Rolle's succinctly useful *Emendatio vitae* (*The Amending of Life*) is translated and excerpted a number of times), and English works are translated into Latin. English reception of continental works – usually characterized nowadays as cautiously censoring foreign daringness into anodyne piety and conventional edification – instead may represent shrewd judgement of what is worth adding to an already accomplished native tradition. The *Treatise of the Seven Points of Trewe Wisdom*, a radically edited and reassembled English version of the Rhineland mystic Henry Suso's *Horologium sapientiae* (*The Hourglass of Wisdom*), is evidently unconcerned to transmit the more mystical fervours of Suso's original, but in so doing it reveals much about the mature judgement of what was considered worth reading for contemplation in fifteenth-century England. From Thomas Hoccleve's translation in his *Lerne to Dye* of Suso's section on the *ars moriendi* (art of dying) to Wisdom's opening speech in the morality play of *Wisdom* (whose author also knew and variously echoes Hilton's *Scale*, Book II), many pious rather than mystical appropriations were made from Suso's text, as too in the extracts included in devotional compendia.

In making his case for Rolle against a detractor Thomas Basset cites the *Horologium* in his defence, and to English readers, long schooled in Rolle's life and work, Suso's preoccupation with his experience, his overwrought idiosyncrasies and attacks on his persecutors may not have promised to add much to what native tradition could already offer ('in þe forseyde boke þere beþ manye maters and long processe towchynge him þat wrote hit and oþere religiose persones of his degre, þe whiche... were lytel edificacione to write to 30we', as the English version puts it).[4] In a market already saturated by the fervid Rolle brand, it was more the insights attained and validated by Suso's fervours that were widely marketable than the fervours themselves.

With its native tradition of Rolle, Hilton, and the *Cloud*-author to draw on (even assuming Julian was not widely known), English contemplative culture in the fifteenth century could afford to be fastidious in its reception of continental mysticism. The hindsight of literary history had not yet defined these contemplatives (oversimplifyingly) as any kind of group, movement, or school, and in the fifteenth-century English view they towered as distinctively different giants who filled the contemplative landscape – even if reception of Rolle and Hilton would long be swayed by variously plausible and implausible misattribution to them of a whole hinterland of apocryphal works, fakes, and pastiche. Indeed, as the Carthusian annotators at Mount Grace demonstrate, in their marginal commentaries to the extant manuscript of Kempe's *Book*, readerships can prove more adventurous and insightful than might be predicted: few would have imagined the *Book* read so sympathetically in a male cloister. For the contemplatively minded seek out counsel and example where they may find it, indifferent to later categorizations, so that what may now seem merely didactic works (such as *The Desert of Religion* or *Disce Mori* (*Learn to Die*)) can address contemplation in passing as part of their general discourse on piety. Or again, and tellingly, *The Tree & XII Frutes of the Holy Goost* – in three late fifteenth-century manuscripts and one printed edition of 1534–5 (*RSTC* 13608) – includes discussion of contemplation only in its section on joy, but within its broader treatment of a pursuit of spiritual perfection ('he openith to þe eye of þe soule þe yates of heuen so þat þe eygh may loke into heuen', pp. 59–61), while the third English recension of William Flete's Latin *De remediis contra temptaciones* (*Remedies against Temptation*) – which borrows from Hilton's *Scale*, the *Chastising of God's Children* and the *Stimulus amoris* (*Goad of Love*) – may not treat advanced contemplation as such, yet it does address the vicissitudes of pursuing a spiritual life.[5] This very diversity of late-medieval texts containing some contemplative material suggests a coexistence of both spread and depth of understanding, so that increasing familiarity with contemplation as a theme did not necessarily mean that contemplation was being pursued to its higher reaches by large numbers.

In the dynamism with which Kempe pursues her inner life, and the boldness with which she appropriates models, texts, and authorities to her purpose, the *Book*, however singular and inimitable, is symptomatic of fifteenth-century contemplative culture. When a young priest reads to her 'many a good boke of hy contemplacyon and other bokys, as the Bybyl wyth doctowrys therupon, Seynt Brydys boke, Hyltons boke, Boneventur, *Stimulus amoris*, *Incendium amoris*, and swech other' (ch. 58), Kempe's *Book* identifies some of the key influences that connect her own inner life – and that of many contemporaries – with contemplative culture. 'Not lettryd' she may have been, but nor was Kempe a passive audience for the young priest, because she 'causyd hym to lokyn meche good scriptur and many a good doctowr, whech he wolde not a lokyd at that tyme, had sche ne be'. Here is a glimpse into fifteenth-century contemplative culture that Kempe reflects throughout her *Book*, mediated to her through her interchanges with sympathetic spiritual advisers, whose own reading has its influence upon her, for it is not only in her interview with the anchoress Julian of Norwich that the *Book* records how Kempe sought out the spiritually minded to consult and confer with them. Kempe's named authors and texts – the revelations of St Birgitta of Sweden, the native English contemplative tradition as exemplified in Rolle and Hilton, the Pseudo-Bonaventure, taken in connection with related works – can offer a way to understanding the continuing renewal of thinking, reading, and writing on the spiritual life in fifteenth-century England.

'Seynt Brydys boke' is mentioned in the *Book* in ways that suggest how emboldening a model the Englishwoman found for herself in both the life and visionary experience of St Birgitta of Sweden (1303–73). When (in ch. 20) Kempe sees a marvel during mass, the Lord tells her that St Birgitta never saw him in such a way, but that he speaks to her just as he spoke to St Birgitta, and that the truth of Birgitta's book will be recognized through Margery Kempe. Latin texts of St Birgitta's revelations were available in England before 1400 (e.g. Oxford, Merton College, MS 215), and the English cult of St Birgitta and the influence of her life, visions, and devotions extended throughout the fifteenth century.[6] Pivotal in this was Henry V's foundation of the Birgittine house of Syon Abbey, to which the *Book* records Kempe's pilgrimage (probably in August 1434) seeking the 'Pardon of Syon', an indulgence available to pilgrims at Lammastide.

St Birgitta's *Liber celestis* (*Book of the Heavenly [Emperor to the Kings]*) is a voluminous ragbag of some seven hundred revelations, many in the form of prophecies, warnings and admonishments, dictated to amanuenses as they occurred. Although two early fifteenth-century Middle English translations of the whole text of the *Liber celestis* survive, English audiences encountered Birgitta's work just as influentially in the form of selected extracts and in compilations.[7] The *Liber*'s relative indifference to form and structure, and its repetitiveness in theme and mode, invited the excerpting and rearrangement of its contents into new compilations and anthologies, both in Latin and English. Compilers, on the evidence of their compositions, were particularly interested to draw out three aspects of Birgitta's original: her prophetic warnings; her disquisitions on the requirements of the spiritual life; and her visionary elaborations on the lives of Christ and Mary. With regard to her prophetic writings, no small reason for Birgitta's status in fifteenth-century England was that her revelations were so obligingly right-minded as to support the English claim to the throne of France in the Hundred Years' War. In one volume of Middle English selections (Princeton University, MS 1397) are found prophetic judgements on the estates of society, ecclesiastical authorities, and unfortunate individuals, arranged together with chapters on the requirements of the spiritual life, and including a lengthy exposition of the active and contemplative lives through the traditional symbolism of Martha and Mary.[8]

Perhaps because of this very conformity and traditional focus, St Birgitta's teachings on the spiritual life were invested by English readers with great authority and were absorbed by means of excerpts into such widely-read works of spiritual instruction as William Flete's *De remediis* (*Remedies Against Temptation*), *The Pore Caitif*, and *Contemplations of the Dread and Love of God*. Birgitta's revelations about the lives of Christ and Mary can be found excerpted and repackaged either into sequences assembled exclusively from her revelations (as in Oxford, Bodleian Library, Rawlinson MS C.41), or interspersed with material from other sources to form such new texts promoting meditation as the 'Meditaciones Domini Nostri' (in Oxford, Bodleian Library, MS Bodl. 578 and Cambridge, Trinity College, MS B.v.42), the *Speculum devotorum* (*Mirror of the Devout*), or *The Fruyte of Redempcyon* by Simon of London Wall (printed four times by Wynkyn de Worde between 1514 and 1532; *RSTC* 22557–60). Where St Birgitta's visions spoke to contemporary interests, as in her vision of the Virgin Mary giving birth instantly and painlessly at the Nativity, her revelation proved so popular as to influence enduringly the subsequent iconography of the scene: Birgitta sees Mary reverencing her newborn child as he lies on the earth surrounded by a glory of rays. Into the commonplace book of Robert Reynes, a fifteenth-century Norfolk man, has been inscribed Birgitta's devotion to the number of wounds suffered by the flagellated Christ,[9] although by contrast Birgitta's already old-fashioned vision of Christ being nailed to a previously erected cross had little appeal or influence. The respect accorded Birgitta as a prophet, together with her orthodox spiritual instruction, lent an authority as revelations to her affective meditations far beyond their intrinsic interest or originality. Perhaps because St Birgitta and her amanuenses were more concerned with the revelations' content than with stylistic or formal considerations, the *Liber celestis* represented a kind of vast lending library for subsequent readers and compilers. And since Kempe's mentor, the friar, Alan of Lynn, O Carm, had actually prepared indexes of the revelations (extant in Oxford, Lincoln College, MS 69), her access to Birgitta enjoyed the privileged guidance of an especially knowledgeable adviser.

For Margery Kempe the model provided by St Birgitta was a particularly powerful one, despite some evident dissimilarities: Birgitta's social status was altogether grander than Kempe's relatively modest middle-class station in life, for the saint was of the highest birth; in middle age she struggled at the divine command to learn Latin; she was divinely instructed to found a new order, to involve herself in great affairs, to denounce abuses. Notwithstanding such differences, the pattern of St Birgitta's life – her career as prophet and visionary, her transition from a wife and mother to a Bride of Christ, her pilgrimages, the sustainedly visionary experience of her life ('suspendid in extasy of gostely contemplacion', *Liber*, p. 366/11–12), her dictation of her revelations and prophecies – could lend endorsement to Margery Kempe's own experience, and in turn be endorsed by it, for as the *Book* acknowledges, the value of St Birgitta's legacy was not undisputed and uncontroversial during Kempe's lifetime. The writing of the *Book* is recorded to have begun on St Birgitta's Day in 1436, and parallels with St Birgitta's life recur. Like St Birgitta, Margery Kempe is given to frequent confession and communion, to fasting and wearing of a hairshirt, and to consultations with holy men. Mothers of large families, both persuade their husbands to live chaste; both mothers save the soul of a wayward son who predeceases them. As pilgrims both women journey to Santiago, Aachen, and the Holy Land; in Rome Kempe seeks out people and places associated with St Birgitta and, like the Swedish saint, lives a life of voluntary poverty there. Like St Birgitta, Kempe has a vision witnessing Christ's Nativity and perhaps remembered, in the Church of the Holy Sepulchre in Jerusalem, that St Birgitta had received a vision of Calvary in that place, although the *Book* shows no immediate influence by the iconographical features of St Birgitta's vision of the Nativity or Passion. Only fleetingly does the *Book* associate Margery Kempe with that wider concern and public role which St Birgitta's visions bring her – Birgitta's authority eludes Kempe in her own controversial attempts at teaching – but, like St Birgitta, Kempe undergoes a mystical marriage to the Lord which defines and endorses her vocation as visionary and prophet.

Although the *Book* does not mention them, English reception of St Birgitta is often recorded in association with that of two other continental women visionaries, St Mechtild of Hackeborn and St Catherine of Siena (whose spiritual director, Raymond of Capua, was in touch with the prior of Lynn, William Bakthorpe, in the 1390s). A fifteenth-century vicar of Swine in Yorkshire presented the Cistercian nunnery there with seven books, including works of St Birgitta and St Mechtild (as recorded in Cambridge, Kings College, MS 18, f. 104v). In the mid-fifteenth century Witham Charterhouse received from John Blacman (confessor of Henry VI) a donation of books including works by Birgitta of Sweden, Catherine of Siena, Elisabeth of Schönau, Rolle, and Mechtild of Hackeborn, and also a copy of Suso's *Horologium* (now London, Lambeth Palace, MS 436) with a note referring to Mechtild and Catherine.[10] The household ordinances of Cecily, Duchess of York (mother of Edward IV) record how during dinner she would listen to readings from Hilton's *Mixed Life*, 'Bonaventure' (presumably a translation of the *Meditationes vitae Christi*), the apocryphal *Infancy of the Saviour*, saints' lives from the *Golden Legend*, and works of women visionaries: Mechtild of Hackeborn, Catherine of Siena, and Birgitta of Sweden.[11]

As a prologue makes clear, an English translation of the revelations of St Catherine of Siena was prepared for the nuns of Syon, and according to the colophon of Wynkyn de Worde's handsome printed edition of 1519 (*RSTC* 4815), which entitles the translation *The Orcherd of Syon*, the Steward of Syon, Richard Sutton, found a manuscript there 'in a corner by itselfe' and had it printed at his expense for the benefit of 'many relygyous and deuoute soules', a wider readership inclusive of laity, which testamentary and other evidence shows the text had already attained.[12] The *Orcherd* presents a full and quite faithful version of *Il Dialogo* (or 'Boke of Diuine Doctrine' as the English text entitles it), which had been subsequently translated into Latin after St Catherine first dictated it to secretaries in her Tuscan dialect ('whiche was write as sche endited in her moder tunge when sche was in contemplacioun inrapt of spirit, and sche heringe actueli and in þe same tyme tellinge tofore meny what oure Lord God spake in her', p. 18). In his prologue the Syon translator adds his own allegorical framework and rationale for reader use, based on a new layout of divisions and sub-divisions articulating his English version (although the form of the text in one extant manuscript – New York, Pierpont Morgan Library, MS 162, possibly associated with another convent – may pre-date the elaborately schematized sub-division of the Syon version or represent a reversion to the original's format). The Syon text, now translated into seven parts each with five chapters, offers an orchard of thirty-five 'alleys' in which, as it were, to walk and to pick fruit and herbs. This goes back to the traditional monastic metaphor of reading as tasting and eating and of meditation as chewing. However, the *Orcherd* prologue – while urging readers first to absorb the book as a whole ('assaye & serche þe hool orcherd') – also envisages that readers will come back to chapters, picking and choosing ('o tyme in oon, anoþir tyme in anoþir').

How English readers, enclosed or lay, put into effect Catherine's concern to test visionary insights through active charity is now beyond retrieval, but accounts of her life and her book were evidently read, anthologized, and bequeathed throughout the fifteenth century.[13] Her colloquies with God were imbued with orthodoxy and evinced a settled authority and clarity of structure. For St Catherine contemplation was attainable by every soul as a continuing development of the life of grace ('How glorious is sich a soule þat so rialy can passe out of þis troublous see of þe world and come to me, þat am þe greet peesable see, and fille þe vessel of þe herte in þe see of myn euerlastynge souereyn Godheed', p. 196). What the saint – and her gifted English translator – so eloquently described of her own insights ('abouen hersilf wiþ a greet longynge desier out of coorse of þe bodily feelynge', p. 193) could be received as both report and model for the instruction, inspiration, and imitation of any reader ('And aftir tyme þei ben so goostly dronke wiþ þat blessid blood and be brennyd in þe fier of my loue, anoon þei taste in me þe eendelees Godheed, þe which is to hem as a pesible see, in þe which see þe soule haþ cauȝt sich an vnyoun and oonheed þat sich a soule haþ no maner of mouyng but in me', pp. 176–7).

In 1495 Cecily, Duchess of York, bequeathed to her granddaughter Brigitte (a daughter of Edward IV and nun at Dartford) a life of Catherine of Siena, a copy of the *Golden Legend*, and her 'Boke of Saint Matilde'.[14] Mechtild of Hackeborn (d. 1298) was a nun at the Cistercian convent of Helfta in eastern Germany whose revelations were recorded in Latin in her lifetime by Gertrude the Great and another nun at Helfta. This *Liber specialis gratiae* (*Book of Special Graces*) was then supplemented after Mechtild's death. Both spiritually orthodox and vividly descriptive, the account of Mechtild's visions and also an abridgement circulated widely in Europe, but no evidence remains of its reception in England before *c.* 1425. Here Mechtild's work was evidently promoted by the Carthusian and Birgittine orders and is cited in *The Myroure of Oure Ladye*, prepared *c.* 1420–48 for the Syon nuns ('And hereof ye haue a notable example in saynt Maudes reuelacions...'). Four fifteenth-century manuscripts of the Latin text are now extant in England, and two manuscripts survive of an English translation of the abridged version, *The Booke of Gostly Grace*.[15]

Extant evidence reveals a whole spectrum of different types and levels of reception, and great freedoms with the original: excerpts from the Latin original in compilations; paraphrase from the English *Booke*; brief references and snippets absorbed into amalgams of devotional or pastoral guidance in English, or simply association of the saint's name with such material. As early as 1438 Alianora Roos of York, who was to be buried at Mount Grace Charterhouse, left her 'Maulde buke' (presumably St Mechtild in English) to Dame Joan Courtenay, and surviving compilations containing material attributed to Mechtild often seem to have passed through female ownership, both lay and religious.[16] The sheer breadth and variety of English familiarity with Mechtild's revelations is a significant symptom of fifteenth-century interest in visionary writing for, despite lacking the celebrity of Birgitta and Catherine, Mechtild's work was savoured across the range from elite contemplative readerships to those for whom even invoking her name was a token of spiritual power and resource.

In contextualizing Margery Kempe's cries by recalling how 'Elizabeth of Hungry cryed wyth lowde voys, as is wretyn in hir tretys' (ch. 62), the *Book* refers to the *Revelations of Elizabeth of Hungary*, translated into an English version known in East Anglia in the 1430s and twice printed by Wynkyn de Worde (*c.* 1493 and *c.* 1500, with the *Lyf of Saynt Katherin of senis*).[17] The revelations were probably those of Elizabeth of Töss (*c.* 1294–1336), daughter of Andreas III of Hungary and an uncanonized Dominican nun in the Swiss convent of Töss, but were attributed to the very popular medieval saint, her great aunt, St Elizabeth of Hungary (1207–31, canonized 1235), daughter of Andreas II of Hungary. After the death on crusade in 1227 of her husband, the Landgrave of Thuringia, Elizabeth became a Franciscan tertiary, devoting herself less to contemplation than to the poor and sick and to a life of austerity, although Osbern Bokenham in his *Legendys of Hooly Wummen* (1443–7) mentions the tears associated with her contemplation. In her *Das Leben der Schwestern zu Töss* Elsbet Stagel, a nun at Töss and friend of Suso, gives an account of the lives of the nuns at Töss, in which the biography of Elizabeth is the longest and emphasizes her copious tears and passionate prayers. In her *Revelations*, largely of dialogues with the Virgin, praying and weeping go together and Elizabeth 'myte nawt wytholdyn here from owtwardys sobbyng and clamor of voys' (p. 60).

It is for a model of holy tears, cries, and clamourings that, along with Elizabeth of Hungary and Richard Rolle, the *Book* again refers to the *Stimulus amoris* (ch. 62), this time under its English title of *The Prick of Love*, presumably the vernacular version often attributed to Walter Hilton. The *Stimulus* – usually misattributed, like the *Meditationes vitae Christi*, to St Bonaventure – presents a series of passion meditations followed by a treatise on contemplation, and Kempe's references to this work are symptomatic of the immense influence on fifteenth-century English devotional life of these Pseudo-Bonaventuran works (a pattern in which, as ever, certain continental texts are enlisted to augment native contemplative traditions whilst other popular continental texts are ignored).[18] Although Nicholas Love, like Hilton or the *Cloud*-author before him, had allowed only a preliminary role in a contemplative life to such forms of meditation on the Manhood and Passion of Christ, this was a tradition that certain fifteenth-century texts could rework with some intellectual poise.

Part-translation from the *Meditationes* and part-compilation from other sources, the early fifteenth-century English prose *Speculum Devotorum* was composed by a Carthusian of Sheen. As his preface reveals, this fulfilled a promise made to a 'Gostly syster' (pp. 1, 9), probably of Syon Abbey, although a wider audience is envisaged of 'sympyl & deuout soulys þat cunne not or lytyl vndyrstonde Latyn' (p. 5) and so the book is entitled *A Myrowre to Devout Peple*.[19] The preface is open about how the author thought of abandoning his own project once aware of another English version of the *Meditationes* made by a fellow-Carthusian, Nicholas Love's *Mirrour*. That he has continued and completed his own version suggests he felt his aims and approach were different, as the preface obliquely indicates. Writing critically within a tradition of texts that both reflect and promote meditation, the author is alert to questions of authority posed by meditation's imaginative elaborations of what the gospel accounts may not explicitly detail. Such questions the *Speculum* author seeks to address by his claim to have included nothing 'of myne owen wytt but that I hope maye trewly be conseyvyd be opyn resun and goode conscyence, for that I holde þe sykerest' (p. 10). In a phrase reminiscent of Kempe's reference to hearing 'the Bybyl wyth doctowrys therupon', the author identifies his main sources as 'þe gospel and þe doctorys goynge thervpon' (p. 9), and specifies Peter Comestor's biblical history *Historia scolastica* and the biblical commentator Nicholas of Lyra to indicate his preferred emphasis on the literal sense of Scripture.

His preface also advertizes reference to 'sum revelacyonys of approvyd wymmen' (pp. 9–10), and the *Speculum* draws on the texts of Birgitta of Sweden, Catherine of Siena (on discernment of spirits), and Mechtild of Hackeborn (including her vision of a multitude of angels at Christ's sepulchre, reaching like a wall from earth to sky, p. 316). In writing initially for a Birgittine readership, the author allows to St Birgitta the authority of conveying what the Virgin Mary revealed to her of the Nativity in Birgitta's influential account ('ȝytt more opynly how oure lorde was borne & alle the manyr therof oure lady schewde to seyint Brygytt ful fayre be reuelacyon, the whyche sche tellyth thus', p. 73). Irreconcilable accounts of the Crucifixion by the gospel writers and St Birgitta can be set alongside each other as variant perspectives on the same actuality, with the most devotionally effective to be preferred by the reader depending upon experience ('Wherefore I wole telle ʒow too manyrys, whyche of hem maye beste styre ʒow to deuocyon, that takyth', p. 266). Even so, the Birgittine alternative comes recommended: 'anothyr wyse ʒe maye thynke hyt aftyr seyint Brygyttys reuelacyon & þat I holde sykyrer to lene to, & þat ʒe maye thynke thus' (p. 267). Indeed, the compiler only underlines the first-person immediacy of Birgitta's witness in noting that he has transposed testimony into narrative in translation, evidently from the Latin original ('sche tellyth hyt in here owen persone as sche seygth hyt doo, þe whyche I turne here into the forme of medytacyon, not goynge be the grace of god fro the menynge of here wordys', p. 267). Yet however self-conscious about the authority of meditation's variant insights, the compiler also includes graphic visualizations seen in his own mind's eye (as when at Christ's Flagellation his torturers 'drawe of angryly & fersly hys clothys & so strype hym sterte nakyd . . . And thanne happly they doo off here clothys also into here dublettys þat they myghte smyte the soryer & not be lettyd wyth here clothys', p. 249). The *Speculum* compiler's sense of himself as commentator on the literal sense can also interpolate his text with scholastic digression, as on whether Christ's crown of 'thorns' was actually made of sea-rushes so as to be more lacerating: Peter Comestor and Lyra are invoked, and even *Mandeville's Travels* ('Also Maundeuelde þat was a wel traueylyd knygthte seyth in hys boke I trowe þat our lordys crowne was of sueche ryischys of þe see', p. 250). The *Speculum* is written in an intriguing coexistence of intellectual unease – that attempts to write only 'be opyn resun' – and devout fascination with the continuing power of meditative tradition to develop independent insights into the Passion narrative. In flourishing his user-friendly table of chapter contents that will allow readers easily to identify and return to preferred chapters – while almost defeatedly adding that it would always be better to read his book as a whole – the compiler seems to acknowledge the enabling divisions between local insight and overall contemplative theory that the vibrancy of the meditative tradition in the fifteenth century was to promote.

If Kempe's meditations on Christ's Manhood and Passion lack the *Speculum*'s intellectual framework, both texts reflect how fifteenth-century contemplative culture draws deeply on its recent spiritual inheritance in order to renew it. By her reference to 'Hyltons boke' Kempe may simply mean the *Scale of Perfection*, and probably the more accessible Book I, although the *Mixed Life* had an evident relevance to Kempe's own vocation. Yet it may be that reference to 'Hyltons boke' expresses Kempe's sense of indebtedness to Hilton's broader oeuvre, perhaps encountered in a manuscript that collects together a number of Hilton's works or comprises selections and anthologies from them, for this is how the reception of Hilton often proceeded in the fifteenth century. No obvious verbal borrowings from Hilton mark the *Book*, unlike Rolle's distinctive idiom of fire, sweetness, and melody, which the Mount Grace annotator picks up on in Kempe's text and which reflects her exposure to Rolle's *Incendium amoris*, (*Fire of Love*) whether given a running translation by the young priest as he read to her, or more generally summarized and expounded in devout conversation.

One revealing measure of fifteenth-century reception of the fourteenth-century English mystics is the evidence provided over again by devotional compilations of the compilers' sheer familiarity with the native classics. This familiarity may be observed operating at all levels. There are texts in both Latin and English that are substantially constituted out of borrowed sentences from the earlier mystics. *De excellentia contemplationis* (*On the Excellence of Contemplation*) is a compilation made up from Rolle's Latin writings that weaves sentences and short extracts together so adroitly as to be easily attributable to Rolle himself. In such re-readings the earlier mystics are evidently known by heart and mentally stored in such a cherishing way that single sentences from the originals can be cut and pasted into quite altered sequences within new assemblages alongside borrowings from other texts. In the last part of the early fifteenth-century *Cibus anime* (*Food of the Soul*), which addresses the more advanced stages of spiritual progress for those in a religious life, there is a series of chapters piecing together quotations and paraphrases from Book II of Thomas Fishlake's (O Carm) Latin version of Hilton's *Scale*, from Rolle's *Encomium nominis Jhesu* (*Praise of the Name of Jesus*), *Emendatio vitae* (*Amending of Life*) and *Incendium amoris*, or interweaving material from the *Scale* and the *Stimulus amoris*.[20] In English, the short tract *Via ad contemplacionem* (*The Way of Contemplation*), like the very comparable *Of Actyfe Lyfe & Contemplatyfe Declaracion*, another Carthusian product, draws on the Carthusian Hugh of Balma's *De Triplici Via* (or *De mystica theologia*) to set out progress through the purgative, unitive and illuminative ways (a programme sparingly spelled out in English contemplative writings, although also reflected in the *Preisinges of Oure Lord God* in Cambridge, University Library, MS Add. 3042, ff. 116–25: 'First thou most purge the soule, and after lighte thi soule, and thanne oone him to gostly grace', f. 116v). Both these compilations are woven together, sentence by sentence, out of borrowings from the *Scale*, the *Form of Living* and, more unusually, from *The Cloud of Unknowing* and its satellite treatises, *The Epistle of Prayer*, *The Epistle of Discretion of Stirrings*, and *Treatise of the Study of Wisdom*.[21]

There is also a whole tradition of texts made up of selected excerpts edited and rearranged within new unities and presented as independent work, and there are compilations and anthologies within which indebtedness may be varyingly acknowledged and celebrated. The author's preface to the *Speculum spiritualium* (*The Spiritual Mirror*) – an early fifteenth-century compilation in Latin by an anonymous Carthusian – explains that the work is not merely for his own benefit but also for other contemplatives and persons in active life; he even invites readers to copy selections and declares that he has drawn on many sources 'with great labour and much study', so as to produce a compendium within one volume for those without the means for an extensive library of their own. Along with the predictable references to Augustine, Gregory, and Bernard, the *Speculum* draws on Rolle's *Emendatio vitae* and *Oleum effusum* (*Oil Poured Out*), extracted from his commentary on the Song of Songs, for the three degrees of love and devotion to the Holy Name (while citing the *Form of Living* in English), Edmund of Abingdon, Flete's *De remediis*, two of Hilton's Latin epistles and both books of the Latin *Scale*, as well as Suso's *Horologium*, St Birgitta, St Mechtild, and various other sources. A designedly eclectic but comprehensive guide to the spiritual life and its ascetic foothills, which reveals both the compiler's breadth of reading and what he could expect of his readers, the *Speculum* enjoyed some manuscript circulation and was printed in Paris in 1510 (*RSTC* 23030.7).

One later fifteenth-century anthology (London, Westminster Cathedral Treasury, MS 4) represents a strikingly ambitious attempt to distil something of the essence of texts as profound and copious as the *Scale* and Julian's *Revelations* and to position them (without attribution) as the third and fourth sections within a four-part disquisition on contemplative life.[22] Read as one whole, the four abridged texts imply a spiritually advanced audience – probably among female religious – and original concerns with resisting worldly temptations and material distractions are omitted (perhaps because no longer pressing), as are the original Latin quotations, but not their English translations.[23] The anthology contains an abridged text of *Qui habitat*, the contemplative-minded commentary on Psalm 90 often attributed to Hilton; a much shortened version of *Bonum est*, the associated commentary on Psalm 91; a synthesis of teachings drawn together from widely separated chapters of Hilton's *Scale*; and a text comprised of material selected from the longer version of Julian's *Revelations* and presented as a continuous text (of special value as the only medieval witness to reception of Julian's longer version). *Bonum est* is abridged radically so as to focus on Hilton's commentary on the dark night of the soul ('In this nyght þer is myche lyght, but it shynyth not; it shall shyne when þe nyght is passed and þe full day shall show', f. 29r). From the *Scale* this abridging reader weaves together a synthesis of some of Hilton's quintessential teaching, briefly referring to Book I but mostly moving selectively back and forth between the later chapters of Book II. Opening with and twice recurring in the keynote chapter II.30 (how the soul must have knowing of itself), the compiler has selected a series of excerpts from *Scale* chapters. It is one editing exercise to showcase the *Scale*'s contemplative project through a reassemblage of excerpts into what reads as a continuous essay on contemplative life, for some of the *Scale*'s address and its model of contemplative progress can still be reflected in the sampling. It is a very different exercise to shape selections from Julian's longer version into a continuous text which is still both a first-person narrative of witness to revelations and also of coming to understand what is shown, even though all sense has disappeared of who is seeing and when, along with reference to the author as a woman. Yet this is a discerning reading of Julian with its own logic, which does not aim to include all the showings, omitting some of Julian's more graphic Passion visions, while retaining many of the more challenging and abstractly spiritual showings.

As an example of a freer re-writing, the *Contemplations of the Dread and Love of God* (also entitled *Fervor amoris*) represents an unusually effective fifteenth-century repackaging of some fourteenth-century English contemplative literature within its own programme of the degrees of love, a structure laid open in an initial table of contents that allows for consultation of chapters at will and out of sequence. Directed at the needs and situation of a lay audience that feels itself drawn to contemplation within worldly life – it declares encouragingly 'for þay þou be a lord or a laidi, housbond-man or wif, þou maist haue as stable an herte and wil as some religious þat sitteþ in the cloistre'[24] – the *Contemplations* is focused on facilitating spiritual growth by analysing pragmatically what in the love and proper fear of God may further and hinder the inner life. The text represents a range of types and levels of allusion. Frequent borrowings from St Augustine and St Gregory, as also from St Bernard, Cassiodorus, and Peter Lombard, are flagged up by marginal references in the manuscripts, whereas indebtedness to passages from Rolle (especially his *Form of Living*), Hilton, and St Birgitta remains unacknowledged, although the debt to Rolle is so transparent that Wynkyn de Worde's printed editions of 1506 and c. 1519 (*RSTC* 21259, 21260) are entitled *Richard Rolle hermyte of Hampull in his contemplacyons of the drede and love of God*. The *Contemplations* was quite widely disseminated in manuscript and was in turn drawn on for excerpts in devotional compilations. However indebted to traditional sources, the *Contemplations* represents a stage beyond most contemporary devotional compilations in terms of how far it has absorbed its influences so as to redeploy them in a distinctive sequence of counsel on reaching towards a perfection of love in this life.

When books offer such a precious access to devotion their ownership – and its transfer – may be a special responsibility. As an instance of Kempe's special insights, the *Book* recounts how a shady character offers to sell a breviary to the priest who transcribes the *Book* (ch. 24). The sale is to be at a favourable price because the book's former owner, a priest, supposedly wanted his book to pass to a promising young priest, not least so that he might pray for the deceased owner. All this is reported as if a fraudulent degradation of how book ownership might be transferred in circles that Kempe knew. By contrast, in a 1402 York will, a chaplain of Coventry, William Wilmyncote, bequeathed seven very useful volumes for any parish priest to John Morele on condition that at his death the book collection would pass to Richard de Swayneby, a poor clerk expected to enter holy orders.[25] At Swayneby's death the library was to pass to other poor priests until the books wore out, except that if the possessors gained benefices with books they should pass the books on to other priests who needed them. This emphasis on use, where books are not to be clung on to as possessions but handed on to others who might benefit spiritually from them, is paralleled in a group of fifteenth-century manuscripts of devotional writings in English which all bear similar inscriptions that constitute them as 'common profit' books and witness to a lay readership for such devotional and contemplative texts. In Cambridge, University Library, MS Ff.6.31 – which includes Lollard tracts advocating lay knowledge of scripture, an English translation of a treatise *De pusillanimitate* (*On Small Mindedness*), misattributed to Hugh of St Victor, 'teching hou a man owiþ to have him in temptacions', together with *The Epistle of Prayer*, *The Epistle of Discretion of Stirrings*, and *The Treatise of Discretion of Spirits*, all associated with *The Cloud of Unknowing* – is this inscription:

> This booke was made of þe goodis of John Collopp for a comyn profite, that þat persoone þat hath þis booke committid to him off þe persoone þat haþ power to committe it haue þe vse þerof þe teerme of his liif prayng for þe soule of þe seid John. And þat he þat haþ þe forseid vse of commyssioun, whanne he occupieth it not, leene it for a tyme to sum oþer persoone. Also þat persoone to whom it was committid for þe teerme of lijf vnder þe forseid condiciouns, delyuere it to anoþer persoone þe teerme of his lijf, and so be it delyuered and committed fro persoone to persoone, man or womman, as longe as þe booke endureth. (f. 100r)

Four other manuscripts contain the same inscription, albeit with different donor names. London, Lambeth Palace Library, MS 472 – containing in itself a library of Hilton's works: *Scale, Eight Chapters on Perfection, Epistle on the Mixed Life*, the commentaries on Psalms 90 and 91, *Qui habitat* and *Bonum est*, and the *Benedictus* – was made from the goods (that is, funded out of the proceeds of the estate) of John Killum; British Library, MS Harley 993 – containing *Eight Chapters* and *The Treatise of Discretion of Spirits* – from the goods of Robert Holland; British Library MS Harley 2336 (*The Pore Caitif*) from the goods of John Gamalin; and Oxford, Bodleian Library, MS Douce 25 (Edmund of Abingdon's *Speculum ecclesie* (*The Mirror of Holy Church*) in English, 'þe bok sikerly þat techeþ to liuen parfytliche') from 'þe goodis of a certeyne persoone' (f. 72r).

There appear to have been personal links between John Colop and most of those whose estates funded the making of these manuscripts.[26] If attentive to the inscription, successive recipients of such a common profit book would pray for the donor's soul and be edified by the book. Another inscription in Lambeth Palace, MS 472 – directing that 'þis boke be deliuered to Richard Colop, Parchemanere [stationer] of Londoun' (f. 261v), perhaps a son or nephew of John Colop – suggests how personal links with the London booktrade may have been an enabling factor in promoting a network of pious lay readers of devotional and contemplative works in the mid fifteenth century ('fro persoone to persoone, man or womman . . . ').

An infinitely more extensive network for circulating devotional texts was provided by such religious orders as the Carthusians and Birgittines. Carthusian readership of the surviving copy of the *Book* is one of many pointers to the role of the English Carthusians in collecting and disseminating contemplative texts, albeit as only part of a contemplative order's larger mission to copy and circulate books. Even after allowance is made for circumstantial factors in what has chanced to survive, the evidence of books produced at the Charterhouse of Sheen, and especially of books produced there for the neighbouring Birgittines at Syon, has suggested a dynamic twin centre for the promotion and study of contemplative life and literature which sustained and renewed its impetus throughout the fifteenth century and until the Reformation, and was shared by other Carthusian houses. For some of the texts they collected, the Carthusians may have planned only a select and spiritually advanced readership. Through its excerpted absorption into the widely known *Chastising of God's Children*, Carthusian importation of Ruusbroec's *Die Geestelike Brulocht* achieved an extended audience, albeit in edited form.

By contrast, the Carthusian contemplative compendium in the Amherst Manuscript (London, British Library, MS Additional 37790) includes a more recherché import: *The Treatise of Perfection of the Sons of God*, the only extant copy of an English version of Ruusbroec's *Van den blinkenden Steen*

(*The Sparkling Stone*: the stone is that in Revelation 2:17 with 'a new name written, which no man knoweth saving he that receiveth it'), translated from its Latin version *De calculo* (*The Stone*), which itself occurs in a probably Carthusian manuscript (Heneage, MS 3083) alongside the Latin *Scale* and Rolle's *Incendium* and *Emendatio*. Taken as a whole the Amherst Manuscript represents a characteristically ambitious and distinctive range of Carthusian spiritual reading. Here is preserved the unique copy of the shorter version of the *Revelations* of Julian of Norwich. Here is one of three copies – all Carthusian – of the English translation of *The Mirrour of Simple Soules* (unattributed to, and presumably unaware of, its author Marguerite Porete, burned as a heretic in Paris in 1310). Into the literal translation are interpolated a series of glosses in a spirited English and signalled by their author's initials, M.N.[27] Evidently unaware of the French original's affiliations with the heretical 'Movement of the Free Spirit', M.N. is always concerned to set aside misleading and literal understandings, drawing out reservations and exceptions which he sees as implicit in the text, and so pursuing a benign and spiritually fruitful interpretation for his English readership, even when confronted – in the exchanges between Lady Love, Reason and the soul – with some of the original's more startling assertions.[28]

Alongside such texts, and brief selections from St Birgitta and Suso, the Amherst manuscript also promotes the English contemplative tradition by including Richard Misyn's (O Carm) painstakingly literal English translations of Rolle's *Emendatio* (1434) and *Incendium* (1435)[29] – the latter at the request of a recluse, Margaret Heslyngton – together with selections from *The Form of Living* and the short compilation *Via ad contemplacionem* (*The Way of Contemplation*), drawn from the *Cloud* corpus. The advanced contemplative techniques taught by the *Cloud*-author evidently found a ready readership amongst Carthusians. Hilton's writings were also much circulated, and although it is against a Carthusian detractor that Thomas Basset writes his defence of Rolle, various compilations (such as *De excellentia contemplationis*) may represent sympathetic Carthusian attempts to edit and re-read Rolle into more acceptable forms. It is surely no small endorsement that it was by Carthusian means – through circulation to their continental houses – that copies of Rolle's and Hilton's Latin works came to be disseminated widely outside England.[30] Carthusian compilers and editors of contemplative literature worked with various audiences in view, including works in English for religious women readers (such as the *Speculum devotorum*) or the trio of lives of Low Countries holy women and visionaries, completed by a letter about St Catherine of Siena, in a mid fifteenth-century manuscript from the Charterhouse of Beauvale (Nottinghamshire), translated by a monk for 'alle men and wymmen þat in happe rediþ or heriþ þis englyshe'.[31] Here is the life of that champion weeper beyond compare, Mary of Oignies, to whose example, as model and alibi, allusion is twice made in the *Book* by Kempe's clerical sympathizers, although they may well have known of Mary of Oignies' history of weeping from its excerpting in a widely circulated work, the *Speculum historiale* (*Historical Mirror*) of Vincent of Beauvais.[32]

This English version of the life of Mary of Oignies is the longest and most developed of these four accounts of holy women, being prefaced by the lives of St Elizabeth of Spalbeck and St Christina Mirabilis. Part of the fascination for fifteenth-century English readers of such holy lives from more than two centuries earlier, may have been their experience as beguines, for no English equivalent had developed to match this continental (and particularly Netherlandish) model of lay women organized into communities and leading strict religious lives of both practical and contemplative piety. Mary and her husband vowed themselves to chastity and worked in a leper colony; Mary committed herself to an ascetic life of exceptional austerities, while Christina trod the more isolated path of an ecstatic unattached to any order or beguine community. Such lives have evidently not been translated into English for the contents of these women's visionary experience – where mentioned, this seems conventionally affective and Christocentric – since the intensity of their inward lives is largely witnessed in outward tokens and extremes of asceticism. Christina Mirabilis – scarcely misnamed – apparently underwent a kind of mystical death but came back to life during her own requiem mass ('sodeynly þe body sterid and roos vp in þe bere, and anoon lifte vp as a bridde, steiʒh in to þe beemes of þe kyrke – þen alle þat þere were, fledde...' p. 120). Christina also made a habit of perching on turrets and steeples, lived in tree-tops like a bird, threw herself into bakers' ovens and boiling cauldrons, remained submerged beneath the surface of the River Meuse in winter for six days at a stretch, and was also resurrected a second time (perhaps luckily for Lynn, Kempe seems unaware of Christina's example).

Although Mary of Oignies's austerities, her epic feats in weeping spiritual tears, and Elizabeth of Spalbeck's extremes of empathy with Christ's passion are more domestic, the testimony presented by these beguine lives taken as a group is strikingly at variance with the much-repeated modern orthodoxy that medieval English spiritual advisers – sanely countering the unsettling influence of Rolle, not to mention excitable continentals – discouraged interest in extraordinary asceticism and contemplative exceptionalism. Moreover, the letter about the much more contemporary figure of Catherine of Siena even describes her preaching 'ful quykke and spedful sermons' to two popes and assorted cardinals, 'alle wiþ grete meruel seiynge þat neuere man spake so; and wiþ-outen doute, þis is no woman þat spekes, but þe holy goste' (p. 192). If this seems a world away from the clumsy clerical sus-picion of Kempe's discourse as preaching, it demonstrates – along with the larger interest in an intense para-mystical spirituality of the beguines – just how adventurously receptive and risk-taking might be some knowledgeable English Carthusian students of contemplative life. Concluding the collection with a letter about the modern Catherine of Siena, with its authenticity from personal acquaintance, serves to update how the three beguine lives are also presented as if from intimate knowledge and brings all these remarkable holy women's accomplishment into the present as a dynamic possibility and example for 'alle men and wymmen þat in happe rediþ or heriþ þis englyshe' and hence for a readership beyond the translator's circle and control.

Indeed, it is sympathetic Carthusian commentators on the *Book* who dis-cern parallels between Kempe's para-mystical behaviour and self-expression and that of two Mount Grace devotees of contemplation, Richard Methley, O Carth, and John Norton, O Carth. When Kempe grows weak after her loud cries over the Passion (ch. 28) the commentator remarks 'so fa RM & f Norton of Wakenes & of the passyon'. Three groups of texts by the Carthu-sian Richard Methley (1451/2–1527/8) survive to witness to his career of mystical experiences. Cambridge, Trinity College, MS O.2.56 (1160) con-tains a series of autobiographical spiritual treatises in Latin from the first period of Methley's monastic life and recording received graces: *Scola amoris languidi* (*The School of Languid Love*) (written August 1484); *Dormitorium dilecti dilecti* (*The Sleeping Place of the Dearly Beloved*, 1485); and *Refecto-rium Salutis* (*The Refectory of Salvation*), a kind of mystical diary recording a sequence of ecstatic experiences and spiritual presentiments day by day over several months in 1487. The London Public Record Office Collection SP 1/239 contains the second half (chs. 14–27) of *Experimentum veritatis* (*The Experiment of Truth*), which apparently dealt as a whole with the discretion of spirits and stirrings, and Methley's *Pystyl of Solytary Lyfe Nowadayes* addressed 'To Hew Heremyte' and responding with discreet wis-dom to a recluse's request for guidance.[33] Cambridge, Pembroke College, MS 221 contains Methley's glossed translations into Latin of *The Cloud of Unknowing* and *The Mirrour of Simple Soules*, the latter completed on 9 December 1491. Methley's extant texts also allude to some now-lost works, including a *Defensio solitarie sive contemplative vita* (*Defence of the Solitary or Contemplative Life*). The self-portrait emerging from Methley's earlier work points to engagement with enthusiastic sensory devotions, as in one occasion of mystical rapture recorded in the *Scola*:

> After I had finished celebrating Mass... God visited me with exceeding vehe-
> mence in meditation and prayer, and I yearned with such love that I nearly
> died... Love and desire for the Beloved raised me spiritually into heaven, so
> that nothing of the glory of God who sits on the throne would have been
> lacking to me except for death... Then I completely forgot all pain and fear
> and all meditation of any thing, even deliberate thought about my desire for
> the Creator... But as the languor of love grew stronger I was scarcely able to
> think, forming these words in my spirit: 'Love! Love!' And at last ceasing from
> this behaviour, I desired that I would give up my spirit totally in a manner
> more like singing than shouting in spirit out of joy, Ah! Ah! Ah!.   (f. 7r-v)

The rhetoric of love-drunkenness, celestial song, and sweetness, and the fire
and melting heart of love, expresses in highly sensory terms the urgent, compelling impetus of Methley's devotion, for which the Mount Grace annotator
found parallels in the *Book*. Methley was evidently well read in English spiritual writings of the previous century: in the *Refectorium* he distinguishes his
devotion from that of Rolle; he is aware of the problematic aspects of *The
Mirrour*; and in translating and commenting on *The Cloud* he reveals a
developing spiritual maturity.

Of Kempe's writhing about of her body during her cries, the Mount Grace
annotator remarks 'so dyd prior Nort[on] in hys excesse', and John Norton
(d. 1521/2), prior of Mount Grace from 1509, did practise an intensely affective devotion on the evidence of three treatises (surviving in Lincoln Cathedral, MS 57), which all describe Norton's dialogues with an angel, Christ
or Mary. *Musica monachorum* (*The Music of Monks*) deals principally with
obedience, and *Thesaurus cordium vere amantium* (*The Treasury of a True
Loving Heart*) with overcoming difficulties confronting the solitary, while
his *Devota lamentacio* (*Devout Lamentation*) recounts a heavenly vision
datable to 20 May 1485, when Norton saw in spirit the Virgin Mary in
the habit of a Carthusian nun and a vision of the salvation of a Carthusian
monk. Leaving her body levitating among the church rafters, the soul of
Christina Mirabilis had popped into purgatory and afterwards enjoyed a
vision of paradise. It is such a fascination with the fates of souls in the next
world that drives various fifteenth-century testimonies to revelations. While
not in itself necessarily mystical, such experience is very much part of the
cultural spectrum within which contemplation was pursued: Julian is dis-
appointed in her misguided attempt to discover the fate of a friend; Kempe
is troubled by what she does discover. Two fifteenth-century revelations
present themselves as reporting the singular experience of contemporary
individuals, while two others represent revisions of much earlier works.

A Revelation of Purgatory, or a 'Revelacyone schewed to ane holy wom-
ane now one late tyme', presents itself as a letter to a woman's confessor

recording a series of dreams ('me thoghte I was raveschede into purgato-rye') occurring in August 1422, but not a new experience for the author ('I sawe all the paynes whilke was schewed me many tyms byfore, als ye, fadir, knowe wel be my confessyone and tellynge').[34] In the dream the soul of her late friend, a nun, Margaret, shows the dreamer the sufferings of herself and others in a threefold purgatory of Righteousness, Mercy and Grace. Mar-garet is viciously mutilated by devils, while her arms and legs are gnawed by a dog and cat (because she in life, like Chaucer's Prioress, idolized her pets), but Margaret meticulously details the precise programme of prayers, masses, psalm recitation and hymns that will release her and others from purgatorial pains. The devil's last unsuccessful attempt – that Margaret failed to keep a vow to go on pilgrimage – is quashed by the news that another performed it for her. At the close the writer reports seeing Margaret's soul weighed in the balance, conducted over a bridge to a chapel, bathed, presented with the crown and sceptre of victory and led in procession to paradise's golden gate ('And anone, fadir, I woke and all thynge was vaneschede. No more, fadir, at this tyme...').

The Vision of Edmund Leversedge (1465) presents the English narrative of a layman's visionary experience, in this case the lord of the manor of Frome, Somerset.[35] Here is an account of a near-death experience: while ill from the 'pestylence' Edmund's soul is 'raveschyd and departyd fro my body' and led through a dark place into a valley at dawn by 'my good awngelle, like a chyld of þe age of.iiii. or.v. 3ere, þe which was wrapid alle in wyght' (p. 112), just as a child-angel shows Kempe her name written in the book of life (ch. 85). A group of devils modelling the latest high fashions – and Edmund has been a dedicated follower of fashion – come to tempt him. Guided by the angel to the summit of a hill, Edmund ascends a crystal ladder, and then another, stretching up into the sky and a region of brilliant light. A lady appears and instructs him to change his way of life: she imposes strict limits on his clothes shopping and hair styling; orders him never to kiss another woman (he protests and wins a reprieve on this), and to go and study theology at Oxford for eight years under the alias of 'William Wrech' (while at university he must not enter the washerwoman's house or let her into his chamber). The lady further divulges which of his relatives will have died by the time he returns home. The lady vanishes and the angel too, after various admonishments, and the soul returns to the body, thanking God for his deliverance and relating how a friend at Witham (the Carthusian house in Somerset) translated his text into Latin.

Leversedge's vision is found in London, British Library, MS. Add 34193 – alongside such otherworldly texts as *The Pylgrimage of the Sowle* and *De spiritu Guidonis* (*The Ghost of Guy*) – with *The Vision of William*

Stranton (1406/9), the account of a soul-journey in a dream through St Patrick's Purgatory at Lough Derg in Ireland which, according to legend, was an entrance to the other world.[36] Its author knew some version of the *Tractatus de purgatorio Sancti Patricii*, but the English version has a hortatory, sermonizing intent to attack sins and abuses, especially of the clergy and religious. William, a northerner, is guided by the northern saints St John of Bridlington and St Hild of Whitby, and a chill personal pang of guilty conscience is suggested by his encounter in the other world with his sister and her lover, whose wish to marry and have children he once heartlessly forbade. The landscape of this hellish purgatory displays nine numbered fires and five further places of torment including a high rock and stone wall, towers, more fires, a walled enclosure and river. At each point devils are observed energetically applying gruesome torments to malefactors, more often religious than lay. Once the earthly paradise is reached William witnesses the judgement of the newly arrived soul of a prioress addicted to luxury and ease. In one manuscript William's vision occurs on Easter Day; at its conclusion he is despatched homewards to warn others 'and say as þow hast herd and seen' (p. 116).

Occurring between the eve of Good Friday and Easter eve, and so coinciding with Christ's time harrowing hell, *The Revelation of the Monk of Eynsham* is another near-death experience. As the Middle English version (printed *c.* 1483; *RSTC* 20917) of a Latin account of a vision reported in 1196, the *Revelation* attests to the continuing interests of a fifteenth-century lay readership in such reported visions.[37] Feeling near his end after a yearlong illness, Edmund of Eynsham prays God 'to revele and schewe me in some manner of wise the state of the worlde that is to come and the condicion of the soulys that byn past her bodyes after this lyfe'. Guided by St Nicholas, Edmund traverses a threefold purgatory with variously desolate topography, during which the souls of sinners known to Edmund – including an alcoholic goldsmith – recount their stories and struggles. Also traversing the field of the earthly paradise and passing through a crystal wall and a brilliant light, the visionary sees stairs ascending to where Christ is enthroned, although the text carefully delimits its vision, stipulating that this is 'not the hye hevyn of hevyns where the blessid spiritis of angels and the holy sowlys of ryghtwys men joyin yn the seyghte of god seyng hym yn hys mageste as he ys'. Reminiscent of the liturgical setting of the close of Langland's eighteenth passus, Edmund's soul returns to his body as the bells of paradise ring out at Easter.

Just how strong was the interest in revelations and prophecies, and how continuingly influential were the models provided by the lives and works of

St Birgitta and St Catherine of Siena, is suggested by the career of Elizabeth Barton, 'The Holy Maid of Kent' (hanged for treason at Tyburn in 1534), although the destruction of almost anything but her enemies' testimony to her claims makes close textual comparison impossible. Barton, originally a household servant and later a nun at Canterbury, might have remained a visionary and prophet of local fame, like her contemporary Anne Wentworth, described by Sir Thomas More, who:

> prophesyed and tolde many thynges done and sayd at the same tyme in other places whiche were proued trewe and many thynges sayd lyenge in her traunce of suche wysdome & lernyng that ryght connyng men hyghly meruayled to here of so yonge an vnlerned mayden whan her selfe wyst not what she sayd suche thynges vttered and spoken as well lerned menne myght haue myssed with a longe study.[38]

Instead, like the Carthusian monk whose revelations prompted Edward Suffolk, Duke of Buckingham, to pursue his claims to the throne and hence to be executed in 1521, Elizabeth Barton strayed into more perilously political terrain. A later Elizabethan account described Barton's early visions as conventional enough:

> She tolde also, of heauen, hell, and purgatorie, and of the ioyes and sorrowes that sundry departed soules had, and suffered there: she spoke frankly againste the corruption of manners and euill life.[39]

However, the Holy Maid's visionary career also drew her into prophecies condemning Henry VIII's divorce and remarriage, which led to her execution. A sermon delivered on the occasion of Barton's public penance claims that her revelations were spawned by a daily diet of readings to her from St Birgitta and St Catherine by her confessor Edward Bocking, compiler of a lost book of the Maid's revelations, who

> daily rehearsed matter enough unto her, out of St Birgitta's and St Catherine of Senys revelations, to make up her fantasies and counterfeit visions, and moved her very often and busily to make petition to God to have revelations in manifold matter. And when she ceased any while of shewing new revelations unto him, he was wont to say unto her: 'How do you live now? Virtuously? Meseemeth God hath withdrawn His grace from you, that ye have no revelations this season.' Whose words caused her to feign many more revelations than she else would.[40]

Barton certainly developed personal connections with the religious at Sheen and Syon, and was surrounded by a circle of devoted adherents, as were Saints Birgitta and Catherine. Like St Birgitta, the Holy Maid was credited with discerning secret sins, performing miracles, and experiencing visions of hell, purgatory and heaven, and of the fate of dead souls. It was the model of St Birgitta and St Catherine as political prophets that empowered Barton to enter that more public sphere as a visionary and prophet – despatching warning letters to the pope and admonishing senior churchmen for their shortcomings – which was to be her undoing.

Thomas More had attempted unsuccessfully to warn Barton from political prophesying, and in his *Confutation of Tyndale's Answer* suggested that 'the people vnlerned' should content themselves with 'prayour, good medytacyon, and redynge of suche englysshe bookes as moste may norysshe and encreace deuocyon', of which he specifies 'Bonauenture of the lyfe of Cryste', *The Imitation of Christ* and 'the deuoute contemplatyue booke of Scala perfectionis wyth suche other lyke'.[41] More here commends what he sees as three works established in England as classics of devotional literature. Indeed, the long popularity of Love's *Mirror* and Hilton's *Scale* had found a wider readership through repeated printed editions, although, despite the burgeoning market for printed devotional works, relatively few other native contemplative classics made it into print.[42] Moreover, any popularity of *The Imitation of Christ* in England scarcely predated its first printed English translation, only thirty years before More wrote.

Thomas à Kempis probably wrote Book I of the *Imitation c.* 1420–4 and Books II, III, and IV by 1424, but he carried on developing his work until the extant autograph text, dated 1441. Well before this, versions of the text circulated, containing single books or groups of books under various editorial titles. The textual tradition of the *Imitation* circulating in fifteenth-century England normally contains Books I, II, and III, and sometimes Book I alone, but never Book IV, under the title *Musica ecclesiastica (Church Music)*. The earliest English copy of the Latin *Imitation* (Oxford, Magdalen College, MS lat. 93) – written by John Dygon, whose career as copyist and recluse presumably included both the transcribing and using of contemplative texts[43] – suggests that as early as 1438 he had access to the text of Book I and subsequently acquired texts of Books II and III. Possessing texts by Hilton and Birgitta of Sweden among others, Dygon was a discriminating reader of contemplative literature, and into the same manuscript in 1439 he copied another work of the *devotio moderna*, Gerard of Zutphen's *De spiritualibus ascensionibus (On the Spiritual Ascents)*, which was to have little circulation in England. This represents a remarkably early Carthusian importation into England of the *devotio moderna*, and variations between extant English *Imitation* texts suggest its English circulation derived from more than a single imported exemplar. Carthusians may well have been responsible as well for the earliest, mid fifteenth-century translation of the *Imitation* into English.[44] Of four surviving manuscripts two derive from the Sheen Charterhouse, including one commissioned in 1502 by Elizabeth Gibbs, abbess of Syon (where the library of the Birgittine brethren has four copies in Latin). A fairly literal version, this translation into the vernacular does not seem to have much expanded English readership of the *Imitation* before a second English translation of Books I–III by William Atkinson, Fellow of Pembroke College, Cambridge, was printed by Pynson in 1503, and then reissued in 1504 together with a translation of Book IV by Lady Margaret Beaufort from a French version. Before its appearance in printed editions the *Imitation* apparently enjoyed a limited circulation amongst cognoscenti: excerpts are not borrowed for manuscript compilations or circulated independently, and there are no popularizingly edited versions. By contrast, four editions of the second translation had appeared by 1530, and in 1531 a third translation was produced, probably misattributed to Richard Whytford, the self-styled 'Wretch of Syon'. By now, the *Imitation*'s simple piety, its distrust of scholastic philosophy and intellectual speculations about God, had found its moment and its audience ('Many hath lost their devocyon in sechynge so besily the hye inspekable thynges', as Lady Margaret put it).

When a seven-page pamphlet of extracts – *A shorte treatyse of contemplacyon... taken out of the boke of Margerie Kempe* – was published *c.* 1501 by Wynkyn de Worde, this selected certain sayings of Christ from his colloquies with Kempe, stripping away almost any sense of original context and occasion or of the personality of Kempe.[45] In 1521 the pamphlet – with Kempe by now identified as 'a devoute ancres' – was reprinted in an anthology of selections from six other mystical works, including excerpts of sayings from *The Orcherd of Syon* (entitled *The Divers Doctrines of Saint Katherin of Seenes*), Richard of St Victor's *Benjamin minor*, Hilton's *Of Angels' Song*, and three short works from the *Cloud* corpus, the *Epistle of Prayer*, the *Epistle of Discretion of Stirrings*, and the *Treatise of Discerning of Spirits*. Here, not found out of keeping alongside texts addressing how to discern truth from deception in mystical experience, was preserved all that was to be known of Margery Kempe until modern rediscovery of the *Book*, in a printed anthology that is symptomatic of late-medieval traditions of determined re-making of contemplative texts. If such re-made texts are less focused on authorial identity and the processes of mystical experience, that is only the measure of their focus on contemplative outcomes and the insights attained into 'the hye inspekable thynges' for those who *The Pylgremage of the Sowle* calls 'Spiritual men þat be contemplatif... and drawe hem self owt of this muddy erthe...'

NOTES

1 Of two versions of a translation into English of the first part (the *Formula novi-ciorum*) of the thirteenth-century *De exterioris et interioris hominis compositione* by David of Augsburg, one copy (Cambridge, University Library, MS Dd.2.33), written by Thomas Prestins or Prescius, recorded in 1539 as a brother at Syon, is adapted for an audience of Birgittine nuns, whereas another, late fifteenth-century, copy (Cambridge, Queens' College, MS 31) is addressed not only to religious but also suggests its usefulness to the laity ('And thought yt so be that thys booke aftyr hys name, and aftyr the matiers that he entretyth of, towche principally the religious persons, neuer the later euery seculer man or womman that desyreth to be the seruand of God may fynde herein sufficient instruccion and direccions to the performynge of hys seyd entente', col. 4). Indeed, an English extract from the *Formula Noviciorum* (in London, British Library, MS Arundel 197) omits those chapters particularly addressing the concerns of priests and religious.

2 All reference is to Barry Windeatt (ed.), *The Book of Margery Kempe* (Pearson: Harlow, 2000; repr. Woodbridge: Boydell and Brewer, 2004).

3 Adrian James McCarthy (ed.), *Book to a Mother: An Edition with Commentary*, (Salzburg: Institut für Anglistik und Amerikanistik, 1981).

4 For an overview, see Roger Lovatt, 'Henry Suso and the Medieval Mystical Tradition', in *MMTE II*, pp. 47–62. For a text, see C. Horstmann, '*Orologium Sapientiae* or *The Seven Poyntes of Trewe Wisdom* aus MS Douce 114', *Anglia* 10 (1887), 323–89. Michael Sargent, 'Contemporary Criticism of Richard Rolle,' *Kartäusermystik und –mystiker, Analecta Cartusiana*, 55.1 (Salzburg: Institut für Anglistik und Amerikanistik, 1981), pp. 160–205.

5 J. J. Vaissier (ed.), *A Deuout Treatyse called The Tree & XII Frutes of the Holy Goost*, (Groningen: J. B. Wolters, 1960); Benedict Hackett, Edmund Colledge, and N. Chadwick, 'William Flete's "De Remediis contra Temptaciones" in its Latin and English Recensions: The Growth of a Text', *Mediaeval Studies* 26 (1964), 210–30.

6 F. R. Johnson, 'The English Cult of St Bridget of Sweden', *Analecta Bollandiana* 103 (1985), 75–93.

7 For the version from London, British Library, MS Claudius B i, see Roger Ellis (ed.), *The Liber Celestis of St Bridget of Sweden*, EETS OS 291 (1987). See Roger Ellis, '"Flores ad fabricandum... coronam": An Investigation into the Uses of the Revelations of St Bridget of Sweden in Fifteenth-Century England', *Medium Ævum* 51 (1982), 163–86; and also Domenico Pezzini, 'Brigittine Tracts of Spiritual Guidance in Fifteenth-Century England: A Study in Translation', in Roger Ellis (ed.), *The Medieval Translator*, II (London: University of London, 1991), pp. 175–207.

8 W. P. Cumming (ed.), *The Revelations of Saint Birgitta*, EETS OS 178 (1929).

9 C. Louis (ed.), *The Commonplace Book of Robert Reynes of Acle: An Edition of Tanner MS 407* (New York: Garland Medieval Texts, 1980), pp. 264–8.

10 E. Margaret Thompson, *The Carthusian Order in England* (London: SPCK, 1930), p. 321.

11 See 'Ordinances and Rules of the Princess Cecill', in *A Collection of Ordinances and Regulations for the Government of the Royal Household Made in Divers*

Reigns (London: Society of Antiquaries, 1790), 37–9. For a study, see C. A. J. Armstrong, 'The Piety of Cicely, Duchess of York: A Study in Late Medieval Culture', repr. in his *England, France and Burgundy in the Fifteenth Century* (London: Hambledon, 1983), 135–56.

12 Phyllis Hodgson and Gabriel M. Liegey (ed.), *The Orcherd of Syon*, EETS OS 258 (1966), pp. i, 1–2, 16.

13 Wynkyn de Worde twice printed the life of Catherine by her confessor Raymond of Capua (in *c.* 1493 and *c.* 1500; *RSTC* 24766, 24766.3), and a letter about Catherine by one of her disciples is translated in a fifteenth-century Carthusian collection alongside three para-mystical lives (see below, pp. 211–13). A mid fifteenth-century English depiction of Catherine of Siena in the Carew Poyntz Hours (Cambridge, Fitzwilliam Museum, MS 48, f. 85v) presents a double image of the saint: above, standing in visionary rapture before a lectern with a book, and below, prostrate before an altar. The image has been painted over another, suggesting the saint's topicality, as does her depiction holding her burning heart, along with St Birgitta at her desk in rapture of revelation, on the 1528 roodscreen at Horsham St Faith, near Norwich. There is also evidence of some independent English translating and excerpting of sections from Catherine's *Dialogo* (as in London, British Library, MS. Harley 2409) and in an extract addressing 'doctrine schewyde of god to seynt Kateryne of seene. Of tokynes to knowe vysytacions bodyly or goostly vysyons whedyr þei come of god or of þe feende' (Oxford, University College, MS 14, f. 56v). See also Phyllis Hodgson, '*The Orcherd of Syon* and the English Mystical Tradition', *PBA* 50 (1964), 229–49.

14 To her granddaughter Anne de la Pole, prioress of Syon, the Duchess fittingly bequeathed 'a boke of the Revelacions of Saint Burgitte', as well as a book containing 'Bonaventura' and Hilton; see J. G. Nichols and J. Bruce (eds.), *Wills from Doctors' Commons*, Camden Society 83 (1863), pp. 2–3.

15 For Mechtild's text, context, and reception in England, Teresa A. Halligan (ed.), *The Booke of Gostlye Grace* (Toronto: Pontifical Institute for Mediaeval Studies, 1979). John Henry Blunt (ed.), *The Myroure of Oure Ladye*, EETS ES 19 (1873), pp. 38–9; for other references to Mechtild, see pp. 33, 276–7.

16 For the Roos will, see *Testamenta Eboracensia*, Surtees Society 30 (1855), p. 66; in 1491 Thomas Symson bequeaths his book 'de Revelatione Beate Matilde' to a fellow York secular priest (*Testamenta Eboracensia*, 45 (1865), p. 160). See also Rosalynn Voaden, 'The Company She Keeps: Mechtild of Hackeborn in Late-Medieval Devotional Compilations', in Rosalynn Voaden (ed.), *Prophets Abroad: The Reception of Continental Holy Women in Late Medieval England* (Cambridge: Cambridge University Press, 1996), pp. 51–69.

17 Sarah McNamer (ed.), *The Two Middle English Translations of the Revelations of St Elizabeth of Hungary, ed. from Cambridge University Library MS Hh.i.11 and Wynkyn de Worde's printed text of ?1493*, Middle English Texts 28 (Heidelberg: Winter, 1996).

18 Thus, the amplified and commented version of the *Meditationes* by Ludolph of Saxony (d. 1377) – immensely influential through its many translations into continental vernaculars – was evidently viewed at first as superfluous to English requirements already met by Love's *Mirror*, and only fragments of a late fifteenth-century English translation from a French version survive (in London, British Library, Additional MS 16609 and Edinburgh, University Library, MS 22).

19 James Hogg (ed.), *The Speculum Devotorum of an Anonymous Carthusian of Sheen, Analecta Cartusiana* 12–13 (Salzburg: Institut für Anglistik und Amerikanistik, 1973–4).

20 Vincent Gillespie, 'The *Cibus Anime* Book 3: A Guide for Contemplatives?', in James Hogg (ed.), *Spiritualität Heute und Gestern*, 3, *Analecta Cartusiana* 35.3 (Salzburg: Institut für Anglistik und Amerikanistik, 1983), 90–119.

21 For an edition that lays bare these tracts' composite nature, see Peter S. Jolliffe, 'Two Middle English Tracts on the Contemplative Life', *Mediaeval Studies* 37 (1975), 83–121.

22 For a modernized version of the manuscript's contents, see James Walsh and Eric Colledge (trans.), *Of the Knowledge of Ourselves and of God: A Fifteenth-Century Florilegium* (London: Mowbray, 1961).

23 On the readership of advanced contemplatives implied by this manuscript, see Barry Windeatt, 'Constructing Audiences for Contemplative Texts: The Example of a Mystical Anthology', in Stephen Kelly and John Thompson (eds.), *Imagining the Book* (Turnhout: Brepols, 2005), pp. 159–71.

24 Margaret Connolly (ed.), *Contemplations of the Dread and Love of God*, EETS OS 303 (1993), p. 40.

25 Jo Ann Hoeppner Moran, 'A "Common Profit" Library in Fifteenth-century England and Other Books for Chaplains', *Manuscripta* 28 (1984), 17–25.

26 As executor to Killum, a grocer (d. 1416), John Colop was entrusted with distributing in alms the residue of his estate; in 1441 Colop was granted administration of the estate of Robert Holland, shearman, who died intestate; Colop and Gamalin were both involved in settling the property of a London grocer, John Sudbury, in 1439. See Wendy Scase, 'Reginald Pecock, John Carpenter and John Colop's "Common-Profit" Books: Aspects of Book Ownership and Circulation in Fifteenth-Century London', *Medium Ævum* 61 (1992), 261–74.

27 M. Doiron (ed.), 'Margaret Porete: *The Mirror of Simple Souls*, A Middle English Translation', *Archivio Italiano per la Storia della Pietà* 5 (1968), 241–355, with appendix by E. Colledge and R. Guarnieri, 'The Glosses by M.N. and Richard Methley to *The Mirror of Simple Souls*', pp. 357–82.

28 For example: that the soul may take leave of virtues; scripture, knowledge, intellect alike become unnecessary; the soul desires neither masses, sermons nor prayers and gives to nature all that nature asks; the soul's name is oblivion; the soul has enough faith without works; all that men say of God is mendacious and deceptive; a soul in the true freedom of pure love does nothing against that which her inward grace requires; the soul on earth may have a constant perception and experience of the divine nature; the free soul does not pray; and so on.

29 R. Harvey (ed.), *The Fire of Love and the Mending of Life, or The Rule of Living of Richard Rolle*, EETS OS 106 (1896).

30 A. I. Doyle, 'Carthusian Participation in the Movement of Works of Richard Rolle between England and other parts of Europe in the 14th and 15th Centuries', in *Kartäusermystik und –mystiker, Analecta Cartusiana* 55.2 (Salzburg: Institut für Anglistik und Amerikanistic, 1981), 109–20.

31 Carl Horstmann, 'Prosalegenden: Die Legenden des MS Douce 114', *Anglia* 8 (1885), 102–96.

32 Roger Ellis, 'Margery Kempe's Scribe and the Miraculous Books', in Helen Phillips (ed.), *Langland, the Mystics and the Medieval English Religious Tradition* (Woodbridge: D. S. Brewer, 1990), pp. 161–75.

33 For editions of Methley in the following volumes of *Kartäusermystik und -mystiker, Analecta Cartusiana* (Salzburg: Institut für Anglistik und Amerikanistik, 1981–2), see: James Hogg (ed.), *Refectorium Salutis*, 55.1 (1981), 208–38; Michael Sargent (ed.), *Experimentum Veritatis*, and James Hogg (ed.), *Scola amoris languidi*, 55.2 (1981), 121–37 and 138–65; and James Hogg (ed.), *Dormitorium dilecti dilecti* 55.5 (1982), 79–103. For *To Hew Heremyte: A Pystyl of Solytary Lyfe Nowadayes*, see Barry Windeatt (ed.), *English Mystics of the Middle Ages* (Cambridge: Cambridge University Press, 1994), pp. 265–71.

34 Marta Powell Harley (ed.), *A Revelation of Purgatory by an Unknown Fifteenth-Century Woman Visionary* (Lewiston: Edward Mellen Press, 1985). See also George R. Keiser 'St Jerome and the Brigittines: Visions of the Afterlife in Fifteenth-Century England', in Daniel Williams (ed.), *England in the Fifteenth Century* (Woodbridge: D. S. Brewer, 1987), pp. 143–52.

35 W. F. Nijenhuis (ed.), *The Vision of Edmund Leversedge* (Nijmegen: Catholic University, 1990). For another vision of purgatory and paradise over three days in 1492 (recorded in a commonplace book), in which the visionary sees his dead wife and children, see Deborah Youngs, '*Vision in a Trance*: A Fifteenth-century Vision of Purgatory', *Medium Ævum* 67 (1998), 212–34.

36 For the *Vision of William Stranton*, see Robert Easting (ed.), *St Patrick's Purgatory*, EETS OS 298 (1991).

37 Robert Easting (ed.), *The Revelation of the Monk of Eynsham*, EETS OS 318 (2002).

38 T. C. Lawler, G. Marc'hadour and R. C. Marius (eds.), *A Dialogue Concerning Heresies: The Yale Edition of the Complete Works of Thomas More* (New Haven: Yale University Press, 1981), III.i, 87–8.

39 William Lambarde, *A perambulation of Kent* (1576), quoted in Diane Watt, 'The Prophet at Home: Elizabeth Barton and the Influence of Bridget of Sweden and Catherine of Siena', in Voaden, *Prophets Abroad*, pp. 161–76; see also Diane Watt, *Secretaries of God: Women Prophets in Late Medieval and Early Modern England* (Woodbridge: D. S. Brewer, 1997), ch. 3.

40 L. E. Whatmore, 'The Sermon against the Holy Maid of Kent and her Adherents, delivered at Paul's Cross, November the 23rd, 1533, and at Canterbury, December the 7th', *EHR* 58 (1943), 463–75.

41 Louis A. Schuster *et al.* (eds.), *Confutation of Tyndale's Answer, The Yale Edition of the Complete Works of Thomas More* (New Haven: Yale University Press, 1973), VIII.i, 37.

42 George R. Keiser, 'The Mystics and the Early English Printers: The Economics of Devotionalism', in *MMTE IV*, pp. 9–26.

43 See Ralph Hanna, 'John Dygon, Fifth Recluse of Sheen: His Career, Books, and Acquaintance', in Kelly and Thompson (eds.), *Imagining the Book*, pp. 127–41. The *Donatus devocionis* (a Latin compilation made in England and datable to 1430) includes pieces from Ruusbroec, Gerard of Zutphen, and the *Imitatio* and hence may represent the earliest English reception of the *Imitatio*: see A. I. Doyle, 'The European Circulation of Three Latin Spiritual Texts', in A. J. Minnis

(ed.), *Latin and Vernacular: Studies in Late-Medieval Texts and Manuscripts* (Woodbridge: D. S. Brewer, 1989), pp. 129–46.

44 Brendan Biggs (ed.), *The Imitation of Christ: The First English Translation of the 'Imitatio Christi'*, EETS OS 309 (1997). Roger Lovatt, 'The *Imitation of Christ* in Late Medieval England', *TRHS* 18 (1968), 97–121.

45 For the text of what de Worde introduces as 'a shorte treatyse of contemplacyon taught by our lorde Ihesu Cryste, or taken out of the boke of Margerie Kempe of Lynn', see Windeatt, *Book*, pp. 429–34. For an account, see Sue Ellen Holbrook, 'Margery Kempe and Wynkyn de Worde', in *MMTE IV*, pp. 27–46.

10

JAMES P. CARLEY AND ANN M. HUTCHISON

1534–1550s: culture and history

In 1534, one year after he had received a commission from King Henry VIII 'to peruse and dylygentlye to searche all the lybraryes of Monasteryes and collegies of thys your noble realme',[1] the Tudor antiquary John Leland saw a manuscript containing Richard Rolle's works at York Minster, and he recorded the titles: '[1] Hampole super Psalterium; [2] Idem super lectiones mortuorum; [3] Idem super Trenos; [4] Idem super aliquot loca Canticorum; [5] Idem super orationem dominicam et symbolum; [6] Idem de emendatione peccatoris; [7] Idem de amore; [8] Idem super Iudica me Deus; [9] Idem super Apocalypsim.'[2] It was not as a hermit and contemplative that Leland found Rolle worthy of note, however, but as an Englishman, one of those many predecessors whose writings he intended to bring 'out of deadly dark-enesse to lyvelye lyghte', so 'that thys your [Henry's] realme shall so wele be knowne, ones paynted with hys natyue colours, that the renoume therof shal geue place to the glory of no other regyon' (*The laboryouse Iourney*, sig. B.viiir, E.iiiir). This represents a fundamental shift from the concerns of Rolle's original readership, one that would become even more pronounced in Elizabeth's reign: by the end of the sixteenth century the writings of the English mystics would be considered in most circles (apart from the recu-sants) antiquarian curiosities at best rather than living witnesses to religious experience.

Although Leland himself may have seen his mission as an archival one, his patrons assumed that his examinations of the monastic libraries would bring 'profit' of a different sort to a regime whose theological perspectives were being radically revised, and Thomas Cromwell, appointed Master of the Jewels in 1532, then Chancellor of the Exchequer in 1533, no doubt viewed him above all as a member of his propaganda team. It is not surprising, therefore, that a matter of weeks before Leland set out on his first extended monastic tour in 1533 the verses he wrote conjointly with Nicholas Udall to celebrate Anne Boleyn's entry into London and progress to Westminster

Palace were publicly performed as part of the pageantry surrounding the coronation. What these verses emphasized was Anne's role as mother of future kings: 'Sic tibi progenies Annaeæ floreat instar / Stirpis, quae dextro numine sceptra gerat' (So may your lineage flourish like the stock of Anne, and bear the sceptre with propitious divinity).[3] They were meant to remind the London citizens of why the new marriage was necessary dynastically, and they thus formed part of the campaign to justify Henry's repudiation of his aging Spanish queen, Catherine of Aragon, in spite of threats of excommunication by Pope Clement VII.

By the time of Henry's second marriage the break with Rome was inevitable and Leland's ostensible mission over the next decade became, above all, to bring 'full manye thynges to lyght, as concernynge the vsurped autoryte of the Byshopp of Rome and hys complyces, to the manyfest and vyolent derogacyon of kyngely dygnyte' (*The laboryouse Iourney*, sig. C.vr). His efforts would culminate in a long prose work, the *Antiphilarchia*, begun in the late 1530s as a response to Albertus Pighius's *Hierarchiae ecclesiasticae assertio* (*A Declaration of Ecclesiastical Hierarchies*) (Cologne, 1538), but not presented to the king until the early 1540s. Leland's attack on the papacy did not mean, however, that he repudiated the traditional teachings of the Church on matters of basic doctrine: like the king himself, Leland held firm on the question of the Real Presence and the validity of works. Indeed, once thoroughly purged of 'all maner of superstycyon, and crafty coloured doctryne of a rowte of Romayne Byshoppes' (sig. C.ir), England would become more authentically Catholic in the view of the king and his supporters.[4] As we shall see, however, the reformed version of Catholicism of the later part of Henry's reign did not always accommodate itself comfortably to the contemplative tradition.

Long before the break with Rome, Henry considered himself an expert in theology. His *Assertio septem sacramentorum aduersus M. Lutherum* (*A Declaration of the Seven Sacraments, against Martin Luther*), printed by Richard Pynson in 1521 (*RSTC* 13078), was written as a defence of orthodoxy in response to Martin Luther's assault on four of the sacraments, the *De captiuitate Babylonica ecclesiae* (*The Babylonian Captivity of the Church*) (Wittenberg, 1520). As Henry had eagerly hoped, Pope Leo X rewarded him on 11 October 1521 with the title of *defensor fidei*. In subsequent years he and Catherine jointly sponsored tracts attacking heresy, her Spanish confessor Alphonsus de Villa Sancta portraying king and queen as a matched pair, Catherine the 'Fidei Defensatrix'. By 1527, however, Henry's conscience began to be troubled over his marriage to his brother's widow – a union prohibited in Leviticus 18:16 and 20:21 – even though the marriage had, in fact, received a papal dispensation from the impediment of affinity from

Pope Julius II. Soon a major campaign was mounted by Henry's advisors, led by Cardinal Thomas Wolsey, to prove that the marriage had never been valid in the eyes of God. Not surprisingly, the emperor Charles V took his aunt's part and Pope Clement VII, who found himself in an extremely awkward position, showed himself unwilling to support wholeheartedly one side or the other. From almost the beginning, the strategy of Henry and his counsellors involved consultation of ancient manuscripts, but especially after the adjournment of the legatine trial at Blackfriars in 1529, which had been called to examine the case in England, there was a concerted effort to search out supporting documentary materials – i.e. historical precedents – contained in monastic houses, universities and colleges at home and abroad.

By the early 1530s, if not before, Henry's concerns moved beyond the legality of the marriage itself – that is, the question of the right of a pope to dispense in matters of divine law – and he began seriously to question the limits of papal jurisdiction in England. More and more books from monastic houses were transferred to his libraries and some were annotated at relevant passages. They were put to good use. In 1533 the Act in Restraint of Appeals alleged the authority of 'divers sundry old authentic histories and chronicles' to establish that 'such cases as have been used to be pursued to the see of Rome shall not be from henceforth had nor used but within this realm'.[5] By this means the marriage to Anne Boleyn was validated and the pope's authority undermined. England was, as the Act defined it, 'an empire, and so hath been accepted in the world, governed by one supreme head and king having the dignity and royal estate of the imperial crown of the same'. In the following year the Act for the Submission of the Clergy and Restraint of Appeals stated unequivocally that 'from the feast of Easter... 1534, no manner of appeals shall be had, provoked, or made out of this realm... to the bishop of Rome'. In the same year the Act Concerning Ecclesiastical Appointments and Absolute Restraint of Annates affirmed that 'no person nor persons hereafter shall be presented, nominated, or commended to the said bishop of Rome, otherwise called the Pope'. Likewise the Act Concerning Peter's Pence and Dispensations released Henry's subjects from the 'exactions' formerly paid to the See of Rome and placed dispensations within the jurisdiction of monarch and lords temporal and spiritual. Meanwhile, the First Act of Succession declared that the marriage to Catherine, deemed to be in violation of the laws of God, was 'utterly void and annulled', whereas the union to Anne Boleyn was 'undoubtful, true, sincere, and perfect ever hereafter'. It was to this oath that all adult males were required to swear and to which Sir Thomas More and John Fisher, bishop of Rochester, refused to subscribe. All of these lesser acts culminated in the Act of Supremacy of 3 November 1534, which declared Henry 'to be Supreme Head of the Church of England and to have authority to reform and redress all errors, heresies, and abuses in the same'.

For many – both religious and lay – who were unable in good conscience to subscribe to the Acts of Succession and Supremacy, 1534 presented a time of crisis and moral dilemma. Inevitably, a number fled to the Continent. In 1534, for example, the Dominican theologian William Peryn sought refuge in Louvain. Another Dominican, Richard Hargreave, left for Brussels. The prior of the Cambridge Dominicans, Robert Buckenham, went first to Scotland in 1534, but by 1535 he too was in Louvain. Later he moved to Rome, and in 1538–9 he was at the English hospice where Henry's renegade cousin Reginald Pole was superintendent. Books went with the friars, most spectacularly a cache of some two hundred medieval manuscripts from the houses of the Austin, Dominican, and Franciscan friars in Cambridge which later came into the possession of Cardinal Marcello Cervini, librarian of the Vatican library from 1548, and briefly Pope Marcellus II in 1555.[6]

Ever since her arrival in England Catherine of Aragon had felt a strong affinity with the Observant Franciscans who had first been established in England in 1482. She had married Henry in the church of the Greenwich convent and subsequently became a member of the third order. Many of the friars showed themselves loyal to the queen during her tribulations. In 1532 William Peto, the English provincial, preached a formidable sermon against the divorce in the presence of the king; briefly arrested he fled soon afterwards to Antwerp where he was accused of writing books against the king's second marriage. Peto was also instrumental in smuggling manuscripts out of England for publication abroad. The Observants of Canterbury, Greenwich, and Richmond were among those accused of conniving with Elizabeth Barton, the 'Holy Maid of Kent', who predicted disaster for Henry and England if the divorce went ahead. Two members of the order, Richard Risby, warden of the Canterbury convent, and Hugh Rich, warden of Richmond, were among those executed with Barton as traitors at Tyburn on 20 April 1534. As Richard Rex has astutely noted, the trial and execution of Barton and her 'accomplices' was 'planned and timed to encourage acquiescence in the oath to the succession' which was administered to the citizens of London on the very day the executions occurred.[7] Those of the Observants who remained in England after the deaths of their confrères were imprisoned or transferred to the Conventual Friars, and thus the English houses of the order disappeared altogether. Indeed, when Catherine of Aragon requested on her deathbed to be buried in one of their convents (she died on 7 January 1536), she had to be reminded that there was none left.[8]

Also rigorous in their religious observance, the Carthusians and Birgittines found themselves in conflict with Henry's policies after his repudiation of his first wife. In the spring of 1534, some of the Carthusians signed a conditional acceptance of the Act of Succession, but Henry was not satisfied, and in April of the following year new oaths were imposed. Three priors – John Houghton, O Carth, of the London house, Robert Lawrence, O Carth, of Beauvale, and Augustine Webster, O Carth, of Axholme – refused to sign. As a result they were interrogated, tried and convicted of treason. Along with these three, the learned Birgittine priest-brother Richard Reynolds and John Hale, a secular priest and vicar of Isleworth, were dragged from the Tower on 4 May 1535 to Tyburn, disemboweled, then quartered and beheaded. Presumably the regime had hoped to make an example of these men, but – as an eye-witness account confirmed – many who were present were stirred by the example of their fortitude; the preaching of Reynolds, the last to be executed, was deeply moving and it no doubt served as an inspiration for further resistance.[9]

In spite of notable exceptions, however, the majority of the religious did conform, even if reluctantly, in 1534. On 13 April the new provincial of the English Dominicans, John Hilsey (who would succeed John Fisher as bishop of Rochester in 1535), was commissioned with George Browne (just appointed provincial of the Augustinians) to visit all the friaries in England and urge acceptance of the succession. Hilsey wrote to Cromwell in June stating that he had not come across any individuals who refused outright to swear the oath, although some had sworn reluctantly and 'slenderly hathe taken an othe to be obedyent' (see *LP* 7. 869). In 1535 he admonished the remaining Carthusians to attend St Paul's Cross every week in order to prove their conformity. As Peter Marshall has pointed out, however, 'acquiescence need not signal acceptance, and resistance could take passive as well as active forms' (Marshall, *Religious Identities*, p. 212). Oaths, moreover, could be taken casuistically, and mental reservations, as well as equivocation, were possible. Indeed, one might interpret Mary's submission to her father in June 1536 in this light. Maurice Chauncy, a monk of the London Charterhouse, was one of those who swore conditionally to the Act of Succession. Later exiled to Beauvale, he was recalled to London in 1537 when some twenty Carthusians swore to the Supremacy – making a tacit reservation – believing that this gesture would save the house. Years later he stated 'in this we are not justified'.[10]

From 1533 onwards Catherine of Aragon was kept under virtual house arrest. Her situation became even more vulnerable after 23 March 1534 when Rome pronounced definitively in her favour. In May she refused to swear to the Oath of Succession, and in the same month she was removed from Buckden, a residence of the bishops of Lincoln in Huntingdonshire, to the more remote Kimbolton, also in Huntingdonshire. Shortly before her removal she wrote a long letter admonishing her beloved daughter Mary to hold firm: 'Answer with few words, obeying the King, your father, in everything, save only that you will not offend God and lose your own soul; and go no further with learning and disputation in the matter.' As a consolation in this time of testing she promised Mary 'two books in *Latin*; one shall be *De uita Christi* with a declaration of the Gospels, and the other the Epistles of St. Jerome that he did write to Paula and Eustochium, and in them I trust you shall see good things'.[11] The first of these books is Ludolphus of Saxony's *Vita Christi*, written in the mid-fourteenth century and one of the most popular works of devotion during the later Middle Ages and early modern period. During the fifteenth and sixteenth centuries it was translated into almost every European language. First printed in 1472, and frequently reprinted over the next century, it was an especially appropriate gift from Catherine to Mary, emphasizing the resources of the inner spiritual life in dealing with the perils of the secular world. As in so much, Catherine's learning stood her in good stead.

The *Vita Christi*, which drew heavily on the fourteenth-century Pseudo-Bonaventurian *Meditationes vitae Christi* (*Meditations on the Life of Christ*) (but more 'lengthy and learned'),[12] also featured prominently in *The myrrour or glasse of Christes passion* (*RSTC* 14553), a treatise translated by John Fewterer, the confessor-general of the Birgittine house (d. 1536), at the behest of Lord John Hussey.[13] In the preface to the *Myrrour*, Fewterer stated that the motivation for his 'labour' was to provide reading matter that would be 'moche profytable' and 'edefyeng' to the devout. He also observed that: 'For amonges all the exercyses that helpe the spirite to obteyne the loue of god...no thynge is thought always more frutful, than the continual medi-tacion of the passion of our lorde Iesus Christ, for the exercyses of all other spirituall meditacions may be reduced and brought vnto this' (*Myrrour*, sig. +ii). Indeed his interest in this work is evident throughout his translation in his incidental remarks. In the first five 'particles' of the treatise itself, Fewterer described meditation and its benefits. Then the narrative *per se* begins with the entry into Jerusalem; the second, and by far the longest, part deals with the Passion; and the third carries the account up to the Last Judgement. The text is carefully constructed and each narrative 'particle' concludes with a prayer. The prayer has a twofold purpose: it provides a summary of the 'particle', and is also intended 'to kindle the deuocion of the reders'. For this reason all the prayers are in the singular 'to the intent that we may applye them to our selfe' (*Myrrour*, f. 57). This description of recall and personal application anticipates the 'spiritual exercises' that were soon to have such a wide appeal to a Catholic readership throughout Europe, and *c.* 1535 the prayers were extracted and printed independently (although anonymously) as *Deuoute prayers in englysshe of thactes of our redemption* (*RSTC* 20193.5).

As Jan Rhodes has pointed out, Fewterer's *Myrrour* (albeit a translation) 'represented the *Summa* of Passion treatises in English' (Rhodes, 'Prayers of the Passion', p. 32), and the intellectually advanced nature of such English devotional writing, dealing with materials normally reserved for those who could read and understand Latin, has prompted scholars to observe that the lay public, eager for traditional works of contemplation just at the moment they were being rendered otiose in England by religious change, was no longer satisfied with the 'mylke of lyȝte doctrine' provided by Nicholas Love (in his translation of the *Meditationes*) for 'lewed men and wommen' in 1409 (Salter, 'Ludolphus of Saxony', p. 34). Fewterer was not alone in filling this need. Two other Syon authors wrote equally influential treatises: William Bonde (d. 1530), whose *Pylgrimage of perfection* (London, 1526, 1531; *RSTC* 3277–8), claiming that 'the ende of religion... be the lyfe contemplatyue' (*Pilgrymage*, fol. 72v, *passim*), marked a high point of 'late medieval teaching on the religious life';[14] and Richard Whitford, Syon's most prolific writer, whose *The Pype, or tonne, of the lyfe of perfection* (London, 1532; *RSTC* 25421), dealt with the vows of religion and defended them against 'newe fangle persones', i.e. Tyndale, Luther, and other detractors (ff. lxxir–lxxiiir). So comprehensive, indeed, were the writings of these Syon brethren that it appears, as Rhodes has suggested, that 'some kind of co-ordinated programme of publication existed' (Rhodes, 'Syon Abbey', p. 17). No doubt the impetus was in part the attacks on religious life, as well as the increasing circulation of Lutheran writings, both of which were becoming more and more prevalent during the years of Anne Boleyn's ascendency.

Bonde's work, like Fewterer's, aimed 'to shewe the waye to that ioye and iubilie of the soule'– i.e., the life of perfection that contains the possibility of achieving contemplation – in the clearest possible manner. As he emphasized, however, the experience itself is ineffable: 'But the swetenesse and ioye of this gyfte, whan it is perfyte though it may be feled and perceyued with the herte, yet it may in no wyse be expressed with tonge (*Pilgrymage*, f. 285r). His imaginative use of metaphor, and particularly his division of the long third part of the work into a journey of seven days, the first five dealing with the active life and the last two with the contemplative, helped make this work accessible to a broad readership beyond the 'prelates or hedes that hath other in cure' (f. 2r). Like Fewterer, Bonde believed that 'the meditacion of the passion of Chryst excelleth all other' (f. 247r), and he concluded the *Pylgrimage of perfection* with an account of the Passion and accompanying meditations divided, as was typical of late medieval devotional practice, into the seven canonical hours.

Aptly described as 'a conservative reformer', Richard Whitford provided through his numerous writings instruction for novices and others embarked on the religious life. He was also sympathetic to the challenges facing those in the secular world, and one of his most popular treatises, *A Werke for housholders* (RSTC 25421.8 &c), reprinted seven times between 1530 and 1537, showed an awareness – as Walter Hilton had done more than a century earlier in his *Epistle on the Mixed Life* – of the difficulties of leading a devout life in a large and open household and in the face of the demands of daily living. His *Pype, or tonne, of the lyfe of perfection*, a compelling defence of the cloistered world, written at the request of a 'good deuout religious doughter', investigated contemporary abuses and provided remedies.[15] Whitford's ultimate aim was to uphold the primacy of the religious life, and he maintained that this 'vessel', so deeply under threat by 1532, was 'moste apte and moste conuenient to preserue this precious wyne of the lyfe or state of perfection' (*Pype*, f. ccxxxvr).

Criticism of the monastic life and concern about the need for reform was not new in the 1530s, and it was not unique to the evangelicals – apart from Whitford, Erasmus is an obvious example among the orthodox – but the transfer of powers to Henry as supreme head of the English church in 1534 necessitated some sort of major reassessment of the role of the monasteries within Henry's kingdom. On 25 January 1535 Thomas Cromwell was appointed royal vicegerent in spirituals and, following this appointment, he commissioned general visitations. The first commission pertained to finance and resulted in a detailed valuation of all church property, the *Valor Ecclesiasticus*, produced later in the year. The second was more wide ranging. Since members of the clergy owed their ultimate allegiance to the pope, the commissioners, not unexpectedly, set about testing conflicting loyalties by asserting the Supremacy and absolving the religious from oaths previously sworn to Rome. They also examined the internal conduct of the monasteries, and the records suggest that this visitation was primarily a means for gathering damaging evidence. This same evidence was used to good effect in the final session of the Reformation Parliament, which assembled in February 1536, and by 18 March both Commons and Lords had passed a bill for the dissolution of houses with an annual income of less than £200, the Act for the Suppression of the Lesser Monasteries. Cromwell next established the Court of Augmentations, which came formally into being on 24 April 1536 and, on the same day, commissions for dissolution were issued.

The injunctions resulting from the 1535 visitations undermined the very raison d'être of the monasteries, since the Word of God had now been

made central to religious life and the value of monastic observances, ceremonies, relics, and pilgrimages had been thrown into doubt. Contemplative
life held no place in this brave new world in which 'silence, fasting, uprising
in the night, singing, and such other kind of ceremonies' were rejected.[16]
Although Henry and his advisors may not have been fully aware of what
they were setting in motion, 'reform along such lines', as George Bernard has
observed, 'implicitly denied much that was central in monasticism [includ-
ing meditation] . . . in practice change on these lines would be very difficult,
if not impossible' (p. 255). In reaction to the abortive attempt to save the
monasteries by Robert Aske and the other Northern rebels in late 1536 and
1537, the Pilgrimage of Grace, Henry's attitude hardened, and his earlier
doubts about the value of monastic life turned to anger.[17] Voluntary surrenders followed the failure of the Pilgrimage and in 1539 a second Act was
passed declaring that the earlier surrenders were legal. The actual process
of dissolution was undertaken by commissioners, and by April 1540 every
monastery had surrendered. In some instances, as at Reading, Colchester,
and Glastonbury there were executions on the grounds of treason, but in
most cases the monks were pensioned off, significant numbers taking books
and other moveable goods with them.

As in 1534, many of those who chose to stay in England and accept their
pensions appear to have salved their consciences through silent resistance.[18]
Richard Whitford is a representative example. Although he had shown himself obstinate to Cromwell's agent Thomas Bedyll who came to secure the
submission of the Syon brethren in 1534,[19] he remained at the monastery
until its final suppression in 1539, during which time his *A dayly exercyse
and experyence of dethe* (London, 1537; *RSTC* 25414) was printed (probably there was a now lost earlier print [*RSTC* 25413.7]). He had, as he
explained, first composed the treatise more than twenty years earlier at the
behest of the abbess Elizabeth Gybbs (d. 1518), but subsequently had had
many requests for other copies: 'nowe *of late* [our emphasis] I haue ben com-
pelled (by the charytable instance and request of dyuers deuout persones) to
wryte it agayne & agayne. And bycause that wrytynge vnto me is very tedy-
ouse, I thought better to put it in print' (sig. A.iv). No doubt these requests
would have become more urgent by the mid-1530s when some had decided
to submit to exile and martyrdom rather than conform and abandon the life
of prayer and contemplation to which they had pledged themselves. Whitford himself, however, did not choose this lot even after 1539: he accepted a
pension of £8 a year and lived on in the London household of Charles Blount,
fifth baron Mountjoy, possibly as a tutor to his children, until his death, in
1542/3. During these last years, he continued his publishing campaign in an
attempt *inter alia* to bring solace to his dispossessed colleagues.

Fewterer's case was more complex, since he was both called upon to shepherd his own community through the twisting paths of the oaths of succession and supremacy, and he was also required to persuade others to submit. In fact, the letter of January 1536, sent to London Carthusians under Fewterer's endorsement was actually written by John Copynger, who by this time had been 'convinced' by the bishop of London to comply, and his colleague, Richard Leche (or Lache), who, having undergone imprisonment in the Tower, had decided to follow suit. Fewterer's postscript to the letter, 'Good brethren, yf I ware in good helthe I wolde wryte my full mynde vnto youe',[20] is a telling one. Given the strength of affective devotion and complete orthodoxy he revealed in the *Myrrour*, it seems to suggest that his ailment was a tactical illness, another example of the forms passive resistance could take.

Although Cromwell would choose the next confessor-general – i.e Copynger – and although Richard Reynolds had been lost to martyrdom, the community, both nuns and brothers, was still intact when Fewterer died on 26 September 1536. It carried on until 25 November 1539, when the religious were 'putt out',[21] albeit with handsome pensions. The community then divided into eight groups: the main one was led by the abbess, Agnes Jordan, who rented a house at Denham in Buckinghamshire for continuance of their accustomed monastic regime; six other groups went to family homes elsewhere in England; and the eighth, led by the young, but enterprising, Catherine Palmer, travelled abroad to Spanish Flanders where they were taken in by Augustinian canonesses in Antwerp.

After the fall of Thomas Cromwell in 1540 there was a return to a more conservative religious policy, which was articulated most forcefully in *A necessary doctrine and erudition for any christen man* (the King's Book) of 1543 (*RSTC* 5168). Nevertheless, monasticism itself continued to be dismissed in the King's Book as superstitious and there was no softening of attitude on pilgrimage and purgatory. In the same year as the King's Book appeared William Peryn returned from exile, supplicating for a B.Th. in May. His *Thre Godly and Notable Sermons* on the Sacrament, based in large part on John Fisher's *De ueritate corporis et sanguinis Christi in eucharistia* (*The Truth of the Body and Blood of Christ in the Eucharist*), were printed in 1546 (*RSTC* 19786). In these he pointedly observed that the 'malignity' of the times was a spur for the true Christian 'to bende and force hym selfe in the defence of the fayth catholycke' (sig. * iir). Claiming that his own sermons had been requested by 'certayne Catholyque parsons, my frendes', he singled out the disillusioned ex-Carmelite and polemicist John Bale for censure, a man whose pernicious influence – even in exile – was attracting so many 'busy readers'. He concluded the book with the observation 'Hec est fides Catholica.' Early in 1547 Peryn preached in favour of images, but on 19 June, following the accession of Edward VI, he recanted; later in the year he prudently withdrew to Louvain. He came back to England yet again in Mary's reign and was appointed superior of the refounded Dominican priory. His *Spirituall exercyses and goostly meditacions, and a neare waye to come to perfection and lyfe contemplatyve* (London, 1557; RSTC 19784), based on the *Exercitia theologiae mysticae* (*The Exercise of Mystical Theology*) of the contemporary Flemish theologian Nicolaus van Esch, itself deriving from Ignatius Loyola's *Spiritual Exercises*, was dedicated 'unto the deuoute and very religious Suster Katherin Palmer of the order of Saincte Brigit in Dermount and Suster Dorothe Clement of the order of Sainct Clare in Louaine', who had earnestly requested it.[22] Peryn died a matter of months before the ailing queen in 1558, and was buried in St Bartholomew's Smithfield on 22 August at the high altar. He was succeeded as superior by Richard Hargreave.

Mary herself was deeply pious and, as we have seen, her mother presented her with a copy of Ludolphus of Saxony's *Vita Christi* (which had become a major influence on Loyola) *c.* 1534. Her copy of the 1534 Paris edition was bound for her by the King Edward and Queen Mary Binder after she came to the throne.[23] The copy of the first edition of Bonde's *Pylgrimage of perfection*, now in the Pierpont Morgan Library in New York, was given to Edward Seymour, the future duke of Somerset, by Henry VIII and it has both Henry's and Seymour's signatures in it. Later it passed to Mary, who has written 'Marye the quene / Ave Maria' on the table to Book III. No doubt it is a book that had resonance for her, even if the 'lyfe contemplatyve' so strongly evoked by Bonde was not to be her lot.

Two copies of Rolle's writings can be associated with Mary's circle. At some point after the birth of her brother Edward in 1537, Henry Parker, eighth baron Morley (*c.* 1481–1556), presented her with a fifteenth-century copy of Rolle's commentary on the Latin Psalter.[24] In his prefatory letter Morley apologized for offering 'suche an olde boke', but explained that the contents combined with Mary's perspicacity redeemed it: 'thoughe percase sum that knowythe not what a precious thyng ys hyde in thys so rude a letter ... yet that hyghe and exellent wytt of yours wyll in the redynge of thys exposition of thys Psalter deme all other wyse'.[25]

A kinsman to the Observant friar John Forest martyred in 1538, William Forrest, author of 'A True and Most Notable History of the Right, Noble and Famous Lady, produced in Spain, entitled the Second Gresyld' (i.e. Catherine of Aragon), completed in 1558, was one of Mary's chaplains. He owned a fifteenth-century manuscript, now Trinity College Cambridge, MS B.I.18

(17), which contains a copy of Peter of Blois's *Epistolae*, Rolle's *Emendatio uitae* (*The Amending of Life*), Hugh of Saint-Victor's *Soliloquium de arra animae* (*The Soliloquy of the Soul's Pledge*), and other works. At the end he has added verses:

> Who liste be fedde withe foode spirituall
> Of sweete internall contemplation
> Heere maye be spedde in sorte most speciall
> Thorowe Goddes dyvine inspiration
> Thoughe layde aparte in sundrye nation.
> In readinge heere of Hampole and of Hughe
> It maye, to some, geve goode occasion
> This worldes vayne pleasures the lesse to ensue.

Unlike Leland, who had seen the *Emendatio uitae* at York Minster, Forrest has put Rolle squarely within the contemplative tradition and, like Morley, has recognized the importance of books from the monastic past for passing on the tradition.[26]

Although there were difficulties concerning the possible restoration of church property, something which was opposed even by the most conservatively Catholic among the gentry and nobility, during Mary's five years on the throne houses were refounded by at least six orders: the Benedictines at Westminster, the Birgittines at Isleworth, the Carthusians at Sheen, the Dominicans at St Bartholomew's, the Dominican nuns at Dartford, the Observant Franciscans at Greenwich and Southampton. On 21 June 1555 Pope Paul IV's bull *Praeclare charissimi* pronounced the old monasteries dead in order to make way for new foundations: Cardinal Pole envisaged these as reformed houses based on the Italian models with which he had become familiar during his long exile. Earlier that year sixteen former Benedictine monks, led by John Feckenham, ex-monk of Evesham, who had been imprisoned during Edward's reign, made a dramatic appearance at court and announced their intention to re-enter monastic life. Westminster Abbey was chosen as a feasible location for this undertaking, and it was here that Feckenham's group, which included former monks from Glastonbury, Evesham, Westminster, St Albans, and elsewhere, set up a monastic routine, based on the Cassinese model.

Under the leadership of Maurice Chauncy, who had returned from exile at the Charterhouse in Bruges, a group of surviving Carthusians renewed their vows and took up residence at Sheen in November 1555. 'With Christ to lead and guide us', Chauncy later wrote, 'we made a happy beginning by singing the divine office and observing all the duties that fall to men of our

Order and religion.' Books of contemplation – including the copy of *The Cloud of Unknowing* made by the Carthusian martyr William Exmew and later owned by Chauncy – came with them.[27]

Some of the houses were occupied primarily by former exiles, but there were also groups of dispossessed religious who had carried on in clandestine cells in England itself.[28] After the dissolution a group of former monks from the Cluniac (later Benedictine) house at Monk Bretton lived together at Worsborough under the leadership of the last prior, William Browne, and they held a large collection of books from their monastery. When Browne died in 1557 he passed them on to his colleagues, stipulating, however, that if the monastery were re-established the books and other goods be 'restored to the sayd monastre of Monke Bretton and brethren there without any delay' (our emphasis).[29] In 1557 this did not seem an unlikely possibility.

The religious revival was, however, a shortlived one; Mary died on 17 November 1558, the same day as her kinsman Cardinal Pole. Preaching at her funeral Feckenham took his text from Ecclesiastes and observed that the dead are happier than either the living or those as yet unborn. A statute of June 1559 having enacted the dissolution of Mary's religious foundations, the retiring Spanish ambassador, Dom Gomez Suarez de Figueroa, duke of Feria, obtained permission for the displaced religious to travel to the Continent: the Carthusians, Birgittines, and Dominican nuns departed in early July 1559; they were followed by the Observants on the 12th, and then the Dominicans on the 14th. Chauncy became the first prior of Sheen Anglorum in 1568 and died in the Paris Charterhouse in 1581. Safely abroad, Chauncy lamented that 'Whatever good thing sprang up and had increase while Mary guided and governed, has come utterly to an end under Elizabeth' (Curtis *et al.* (eds.), *The Passion and Martyrdom*, pp. 154–5). Feckenham stayed at Westminster until May 1560 when he was sent to the Tower for his opposition to the religious settlement of 1559. After various periods of limited freedom he died in prison at Wisbeach Castle in 1584. Like many others, whose wills bear testimony to their hopes that the old houses might once again rise, phoenix-like, William Forrest remained in England and adapted.[30] Although he continued to write verses on catholic themes, and in particular on the life of the Virgin Mary, he retained the living which he had been granted in 1556; he blamed the papacy for the schism in England; and he addressed Elizabeth as our noble queen. Until the arrival of the Jesuit mission in 1580, the execution of Mary, Queen of Scots, in 1587, the threat of the Armada in 1588, and the increased persecution of Catholics in the last years of Elizabeth's reign, this sort of accommodation was possible for those who were willing to compromise.

From his analysis of monastic manuscripts, N. R. Ker concluded that 'the kinds of books which had on the whole the best chance of surviving [the Dissolution] were historical, patristic, and biblical, and mainly of the twelfth and thirteenth centuries'.[31] There are also a goodly number of contemplative works and almost all of these date to the fifteenth century. A large proportion were formerly owned by the London and Sheen Charterhouses or the Birgittine monastery at Syon.[32] No doubt these were carried off by departing religious and they indicate the sorts of material that these individuals considered worthy of preservation. Some were later taken abroad, such as the fifteenth-century copy of Richard Rolle's writings formerly owned by Dom. John London of the Sheen Charterhouse, now Douai, Bibliothèque municipale, MS 396.[33] The survival, in England and elsewhere, of a number of devotional works bearing the names of individual Birgittines, mainly nuns of the sixteenth century, indicates that the contemplative tradition remained strong in the post-Dissolution community. Walter Hilton's *The Scale of Perfection*, in particular, seems to have been read by every nun. In 1546, Catherine Palmer gave her copy of the 1494 print by Wynkyn de Worde (now Cambridge, University Library, Inc.3.J.1.2.3534) to Anthony Bolney. Since this was the year in which Agnes Jordan, the last pre-Dissolution abbess, died and Palmer returned briefly to England to collect those who had been at Denham, the book is likely to have recognized generosity on the part of Bolney.[34] Palmer's name can also be found in de Worde's 1493 edition of *The Chastising of God's Children* (now Cambridge, Sidney Sussex College, Bb.2.14), and in a Latin edition (Cologne, 1548) of the works of the German contemplative, John Tauler (1290–1361).

Others, besides the Birgittines, valued the teachings of Walter Hilton. For example, the *Scale* was praised as 'a golden booke and sufficient to shape a saynte' in a recusant household in Fulham in 1580.[35] A printed copy, now in the Pierpont Morgan Library, bears the name 'Sister Dorothe Clement'. This is probably the Franciscan nun Dorothy, daughter of John Clement, physician to Thomas More, and Margaret Giggs, More's adopted daughter, who had moved to Louvain with her family after Edward VI came to the throne.[36] Abraham Ellis, a converse brother at Sheen Anglorum made a copy, probably from a printed text, in 1608. Robert Hare (c. 1530–1611) later owned the copy presented by James Grenehalgh, O Carth, to Joanna Sewell, a nun of Syon, as well as two other books – one containing Birgittine legislations and the other a Birgittine Psalter – from Syon.[37] Like others, he considered himself to be holding books in trust for possible refoundations, and in the copy of Thomas Elmham's *Historia abbatiae S. Augustini Cantuariensis* (*The History of the Abbey of St Augustine's Canterbury*), which he later gave to Trinity Hall Cambridge, there is a note that it should be returned to St Augustine's Canterbury 'if hereafter, by God's favour, the monastery should happen to be rebuilt'.

Less well known among recusant collectors is Queen Elizabeth's kinsman, Sir Thomas Copley (1532–84) of Gatton, Surrey, a Catholic convert who fled to the Continent in 1570.[38] After his departure, his erstwhile neighbour, Lord William Howard of Effingham, oversaw the confiscation of his goods. In 1604 Howard's son, Charles Howard, earl of Nottingham (1536–1624), presented a group of manuscripts and printed books to Sir Thomas Bodley, fifty-two titles in all, and four contain Copley's signature. Writing after 1604, Copley's granddaughters Mary and Helen, who were nuns at the Augustinian House of St Monica's in Louvain, claimed that among the treasures confiscated by Howard was: 'so fair a library of books that [Howard] pleasured therewith the universities of England'.[39] They must have been referring to Nottingham's gift, of which large parts can thus be assumed to have come from Copley, perhaps including three late-medieval devotional works in English. The first is the uniquely surviving copy of the Rule for Enclosed Minoresses, a fifteenth-century manuscript from the Franciscan Nuns of London, Aldgate, now Oxford, Bodleian Library, MS Bodl. 585, ff. 48–104.[40] MS Bodl. 505 contains two other titles from the Nottingham list, both fifteenth-century manuscripts deriving from the London Charterhouse: the first is the Middle English translation of *The Mirror of Simple Souls*, and the second *The Chastising of God's Children*. Where Copley obtained them (assuming that it was he) is not clear – Seton posited incorrectly that the Rule had been sequestered to Henry VIII's collection after the Dissolution – but they were almost certainly preserved as an act of pietas.

In 1549 John Bale observed that:

Yet this would I haue wyshed (and I scarsely vtter it wythout teares) that the profytable corne had not so vnaduysedly and vngodly peryshed wyth the vnprofytable chaffe, nor the wholsome herbes with the vnwholsome wedes, I meane the worthy workes of men godly mynded, and lyuelye memoryalles of our nacyon, wyth those laysy lubbers and popyshe bellygoddes.

(*Laboryouse Iourney*, sig. A.viiv–viiir)

With the final triumph of the reformed church in Elizabeth's reign and the lack of obvious recipients in the next generation for those books retained by the ex-religious, it is surprising that so much of what Bale considered to be chaff did survive, some, such as the unique manuscript of *The Book of Margery Kempe*, surfacing only in the twentieth century.

On 25 September 1534 Pope Clement VII died, some six months after the papal tribunal had finally pronounced the marriage of Catherine and Henry to be unquestionably valid. After a brief and unsuccessful attempt at reconciliation with Henry, Clement's successor, Paul III, took a harder line and, in a provocative gesture, made the imprisoned John Fisher a cardinal on 20 May 1535, just over a month before Fisher's execution on 22 June. In 1536 Reginald Pole was elevated to the College of Cardinals in defiance of Henry, and in 1537 he was sent to Flanders to try to implement Clement's 1533 bull of excommunication. In 1538 Paul himself excommunicated the king, ostensibly in response to the desecration of Thomas Becket's shrine. This led to a new round of attainders and executions, sparked off by the so-called Exeter Conspiracy, and a whole barrage of propaganda attacking the Roman church was produced as a result of fears of invasion. Even Morley, conservative as he was in religion, was implicated and his antipapal invective *The exposition and declaration of the psalme, Deus ultionum dominus* (*RSTC* 19211) was printed in 1539.

Basing himself on the Council of Constance the author of the *A glasse of the truthe* (London [1532]; *RSTC* 11918) had stated that in matters of faith the pope was subject to a general council.[41] Later tracts took the same position. Nevertheless, when in 1536 Paul III called for a council to be held at Mantua in 1537 Henry reacted with 'dread' and expressed himself in print. The *Illustrissimi ac potentissimi regis, senatus, populique Angliae, sententia, et de eo concilio, quod Paulus episcopus Romae Mantuae futurum simulauit* was printed in 1537 (*RSTC* 13081.7) (*A protestation made for the most mighty and moste redoubted kynge of Englande* in English [*RSTC* 13090]), and *An epistle ... wrytten to the emperours maiestie ... touchinge the councille at Mantua* appeared in 1538 (*RSTC* 13081). In both, Henry argued that any council summoned by the pope rather than by the authority of Christian princes was invalid. The council at Mantua was, as it turns out, a failure and in 1539 it was indefinitely prorogued. Finally, after many delays, the first formal session of the new council was held at Trent late in 1545. Although Pole was appointed one of the three legates to open the council, the English did not take part – they rejected its authority – and Pole himself soon relinquished his legateship.

The council, called to clarify the doctrines of the Church in the face of the Lutheran and other heresies, and to reform the Church by ridding it of the numerous abuses that had been partly responsible for their rise, soon became bogged down in procedural wrangling. It was not until the fourth session in April of 1546 that its real work began, and the one of the first subjects of discussion was the Scriptures as the source of Divine revelation. Although some of the most learned minds of Europe were present, nothing was decided in regard to the translation of the Bible into the vernaculars, and the Vulgate, with the possibility of textual emendations, was declared the authentic text for sermons and disputations. It was a retrograde decision.

Things might have gone differently if Pole had remained at the council. Slightly later, in his endeavour to establish a renewed Catholicism in England, Pole called together a legatine synod for the entire kingdom, and the legislation it enacted included measures which anticipated those undertaken throughout the entire Roman Catholic world after the Council of Trent ended in December 1563.[42] Indeed, the developing profile of Marian Catholicism, as Diarmaid MacCulloch has observed, was in some measure influenced by the Protestant Reformation. Although lectern Bibles were removed from churches, the medieval total prohibition on the Bible in English was not restored, and in his own provincial assembly, the Convocation of Canterbury, Pole made plans to commission a new reliable English translation of the New Testament. Attention was paid to teaching and popular instruction, and this resulted in the production of a catechism and collection of homilies by the bishop of London, Edmund Bonner (to whom Peryn had dedicated his *Thre Godly & Notable Sermons*). In addition, Pole commissioned a new catechism from Bartolomé Carranza, a Spanish Dominican who had accompanied Philip to England in 1554, and this work became the basis for the official catechism published in the aftermath of Trent. Although the death of Mary and Pole late in 1558 put an end to England's own 'counter-reformation', this English accomplishment did influence Trent which in turn provided the formulations on doctrine and worship which led to the reshaping of the medieval Catholic church as the modern Roman Catholic church.[43]

Conclusion

In 1529 Thomas More published his *A Dyaloge* (RSTC 18084) and in 1531 the exiled reformer and Bible translator, William Tyndale, responded with *An answere vnto sir Thomas Mores dialoge* (RSTC 24437). The first part of More's *The confutacyon of Tyndales answere* (RSTC 18079) appeared the next year. In the preface to *The confutacyon* More argued that good Christians, especially 'people unlerned', should avoid heretical books being written by individuals like Luther and Tyndale, and should rather 'occupye themselfe besyde theyr other busynesse in prayour, good medytacyon and redynge of suche englyshe bookes as moste may norysche and encrease deuocyon. Of whyche kynde is Bonauenture of the lyfe of Cryste, Gerson of the folowynge of Chryste and the deuoute contemplatyue booke of Scala perfectionis with suche other lyke.'[44]

Although both More and Tyndale died for their respective faiths soon after these acrimonious exchanges, it might seem that Tyndale's view that direct access to the Bible should replace the reading of traditional devotional writings triumphed in the following years. After all, his Biblical translations formed the basis of the Matthew Bible of 1537 and this was revised as the Great Bible of 1539 which was, by Cromwell's injunction, to be set up in every parish church. As Eamon Duffy has shown, however, the transition was not as sudden as most scholarship has had it and the old religious practices continued in many parts of the country long after they were officially banned.[45] Likewise in Mary's reign there seems to have been an enthusiastic return in many quarters to orthodox Catholicism, even if the earlier attacks on purgatory and the authority of the pope had a continuing influence with the result that this aspect of things was downplayed. Morley is, nevertheless, representative. In 1538/9 he could argue that Henry's 'Empire mooste triumphant, hath ben wrongfully kept, as tributarie unto the Babylonicalll seate of the Romyshe byshop' and that the king had brought it 'from thraldome to freedome'.[46] By 1556, however, he was lamenting that in Mary's father's reign 'first they denyed the head of the Church, the popes holynes, next wolde have no saintes honored but threwe vile matter at the crucifyx, and adding mischeife to myscheife, denyed the sevyn sacramentes of the Church... they not only expulsed the name of the precyous Mary, mother to Christ, out of ther common prayers but therunto wolde not the Ave Maria to be sayde'.[47] This was not, however, simply a matter of time serving, since Morley's original attack, as Richard Rex has observed, was not on doctrinal grounds, and he couched his arguments in terms of medieval political history, thus 'leaving the possibility of the sort of reconciliation which had *always* resolved such confrontations in the past' (our emphasis).[48] In Mary's reign, like so many others, he rejoiced that reconciliation had been achieved, that traditional religion, including the contemplative life of so many religious orders, had been restored and that 'you alone above all other Cristen quenes are worthy to have that honorable name to be the Defendoresse of the Faythe'.[49] For much of Elizabeth's reign, too, many individuals, exreligious and secular, held firm to the belief that there would eventually be a return to Catholicism; the Birgittines, for example, in 1580 were still prophesying that 'that their order shoulde be erected againe in the northe partes of Englande, whosoeuer shoulde live to see it'.[50] After a dark period towards the end of the century, the hope for some sort of reconciliation, or at least toleration, intensified when James, son of a Catholic martyr, first came to the throne in 1603.[51] But after the aborted Guy Fawkes plot of 1605 that exile became virtually permanent for the English religious communities, and for most lasted until the nineteenth century.

NOTES

Tom Betteridge, Cliff Davies, Tom Freeman, Diarmaid MacCulloch, and Peter Marshall have read this article in draft and have made many helpful suggestions. For specific points we are also grateful to Jonathan Smith, archivist at Trinity College, Cambridge.

1 This quotation is taken from Leland's letter to King Henry VIII; it was printed with commentary by John Bale as *The laboryouse Iourney & serche of Iohan Leylande, for Englandes Antiquitees, geuen of hym as a newe yeares gyfte to kynge Henry the viij. in the xxxvij. yeare of his Reygne, with declaracyons enlarged by Iohan Bale* (London, 1549) (*RSTC* 15445), sig. B.viiir.

2 See R. Sharpe *et al.* (eds.), *English Benedictine Libraries. The Shorter Catalogues* (London: British Library, 1996), B121.7–15.

3 See Agnes Ormsby (ed. and trans.), Nicholas Udall, and John Leland, *Verses and ditties made at the coronation of quene Anne*, in *Court and Culture in the Reign of Queen Elizabeth I: A New Edition of John Nichols's Progresses*, 4 vols. (Oxford: Oxford University Press, forthcoming).

4 On the use of the (highly-loaded) term Catholic by differing factions, see Peter Marshall, 'Is the Pope a Catholic', in *Religious Identities in Henry VIII's England* (Aldershot: Ashgate, 2006), pp. 169–97.

5 For text of this and the following acts, see G. R. Elton (ed.), *The Tudor Constitution: Documents and Commentary*, 2nd edn (Cambridge: Cambridge University Press, 1982).

6 On these manuscripts, see James P. Carley, 'John Leland and the Contents of English Pre-Dissolution Libraries: the Cambridge Friars', *Transactions of the Cambridge Bibliographical Society* 9 (1986–90), 90–100 (93), and the references cited therein.

7 Richard Rex, 'The Execution of the Holy Maid of Kent', *Historical Research* 64 (1991), 216–20 (218–19). See also Ethan H. Shagan, *Popular Politics and the English Reformation* (Cambridge: Cambridge University Press, 2003), pp. 61–88; also James Simpson, pp. 249–50 below. Wisely, Catherine distanced herself from Barton and her circle.

8 Henry was as hostile to the Observants as his first wife was sympathetic. After their brief reoccupation of the house at Newcastle during the Pilgrimage of Grace, he described them as 'disciples of the bishop of Rome and sowers of sedicion among the people', and ordered their arrest: see Marshall, *Religious Identities*, p. 237.

9 See David Knowles, *The Religious Orders in England*, 3 vols. (Cambridge: Cambridge University Press, 1950–9), III, 216–18; also *Letters and Papers, Foreign and Domestic of the Reign of Henry VIII*, vols. 1–4, ed. J. S. Brewer, vols. 5–13, ed. J. Gairdner, vols. 14–21 ed. J. Gairdner and R. H. Brodie (vols. 1–11 pub., London: Longmans, 1862–88; vol. 12, part 1, pub. London: H.M.S.O., 1890–), 8.661 (hereafter *LP*).

10 Quoted from L. E. Whatmore, *The Carthusians Under King Henry the Eighth*, *Analecta Cartusiana* 109 (Salzburg: Institut für Anglistik und Amerikanistik, 1983), p. 180.

11 Quoted from Garrett Mattingly, *Catherine of Aragon* (London: Cape, 1950), p. 292. Mattingly dated the letter to April 1534, as do the authors of the entry

on Catherine in the *ODNB*, but there is some dispute about this: see, in particular, David Loades, *Mary Tudor. A Life* (Oxford: Blackwell, 1989), p. 78, n. 5.

12 See Elizabeth Salter, 'Ludolphus of Saxony and His English Translators', *Medium Ævum* 33 (1964), 26–35 (26). For a recent discussion of the *Meditationes*, see M. G. Sargent (ed.), *Nicholas Love. The Mirror of the Blessed Life of Jesus Christ. A Reading Text* (Exeter: University of Exeter Press, 2005), pp. 7–23.

13 There is some uncertainty about whether the *Myrrour* was printed in 1533 or 1534. Although assumed to have been a translation compiled by Fewterer from a variety of sources, the *Myrrour* has recently been shown by Alexandra da Costa to be a direct translation of Ulrich Pinder's *Speculum passionis domini nostri*, written in the late fifteenth or early sixteenth century and printed on his own Nuremberg press in 1507 and 1519. (See 'John Fewterer's *Myrrour or Glasse of Christ's Passion* and Ulrich Pinder's *Speculum passionis domini nostri*', *Notes and Queries*, 56.1 (2009), 27–29.) For a full analysis of the sources of this work, see J. T. Rhodes, 'Prayers of the Passion: From Jordanus of Quedlinburg to John Fewterer of Syon', *The Durham University Journal* 85 (1993), 27–38; also id. '*Deuoute Prayers in Englysshe of Thactes of Our Redemption*', *The Library* 5th ser. 28 (1973), 149–51. A more recent discussion can be found in Roger Ellis, 'Further Thoughts on the Spirituality of Syon Abbey,' in W. F. Pollard and R. Boenig (eds.), *Mysticism and Spirituality in Medieval England* (Woodbridge: Boydell and Brewer, 1997), pp. 219–43, esp. 235–8.

14 See J. T. Rhodes, 'Syon Abbey and its Religious Publications in the Sixteenth Century', *JEH* 44 (1993), 11–25 (22).

15 In his chapter on 'Unto whome obedience is due', Whitford observed that 'Unto this I say that . . . no temporall lawe maye bynde any spirituall persone excepte it be graunted or ratified by a decre of the Pope and his Cardinalles or by a generall counsell. And therfore these heretikes done delude and decyue vtterly all them that doth gyue any credence vnto them' (f. lxxiiiir). These sentiments would have a deep resonance after the acts of 1534. The Bodleian copy of the *Pype* (40 W.2.Th.Seld), which has been corrected throughout in a contemporary hand, likely that of Whitford himself, was owned by the Syon nun Eleanor Fetiplace: her signature is found on the last page. This copy is reproduced by James Hogg in Richard Whytford's *The Pype or Tonne of the Lyfe of Perfection*, 5 vols. (Salzburg: Institut für Anglistik und Amerikanistik, 1979).

16 Quoted in G. W. Bernard, *The King's Reformation: Henry VIII and the Remaking of the English Church* (New Haven and London: Yale University Press, 2005), p. 253.

17 See for example his letter to the duke of Norfolk on 22 February 1537 in which he blamed the monks and canons for 'these troubles': *LP* 12/1.479.

18 There were, of course, some who welcomed the new dispensation, but they are not as numerous as one might have expected: see F. Donald Logan, *Runaway Religious in Medieval England c. 1240–1540* (Cambridge: Cambridge University Press, 1996), pp. 156–77.

19 Bedyll, who tried to frame Whitford with false charges, described him as having 'a brasyn forehed, whiche shameth at nothing': see Thomas Wright (ed.), *Three Chapters of Letters Relating to the Suppression of Monasteries*, Camden Society 26 (1843), p. 49.

20 *LP*.8.78, where the letter is wrongly dated to 1535.The letter is quoted in full in George James Aungier, *The History and Antiquities of Syon Monastery, the Parish of Isleworth, and the Chapelry of Hounslow* (London, 1840), pp. 430–3.
21 See W. D. Hamilton (ed.), Charles Wriothesley, *A Chronicle of England during the Reigns of the Tudors 1485–1559*, 2 vols. Camden Soc. 1 (1875–7), p. 109.
22 On these two women see below, p. 238. Catherine Palmer who had moved to the Flemish Birgittine house in Termonde or Dendermonde with an enlarged community after 1546, returned to England with her group of nuns between November 1556 and March 1557: see Ann M. Hutchison, 'Transplanting the Vineyard: Syon Abbey 1539–1861', in Wilhelm Liebhart (ed.), *Der Birgittenorden in der Frühen Neuzeit. The Birgittine Order in Early Modern Europe* (Frankfurt: Lang, 1998), pp. 79–107 (p. 85). In *The Theology and Spirituality of Mary Tudor's Church* (Aldershot, 2006), p. 33, William Wizeman has argued that the Spirituall exercyses form 'a link between the spirituality of the Marian church and that of Catholicism in Europe'. For a full discussion of this text see *ibid.*, pp. 209–17.
23 See James P. Carley, *The Books of King Henry VIII and his Wives* (London: British Library, 2004), p. 110.
24 British Library, MS Royal 2. D.xxviii: see James P. Carley, 'The Writings of Henry Parker, Lord Morley: A Bibliographical Survey', in Marie Axton and James P. Carley (eds.), *'Triumphs of English'. Henry Parker, Lord Morley: Translator to the Tudor Court* (London: British Library, 2000), p. 35.
25 Quoted in Herbert G. Wright (ed.), *Forty-six Lives Translated from Boccaccio's De Claris Mulieribus by Henry Parker, Lord Morley*, EETS OS 214 (1943 [for 1940]), p. 168. Lord John Hussey, Mary's chamberlain, to whom Fewterer dedicated his *Myrrour*, gave her an early fifteenth-century copy of Augustine's *Soliloquia*, now Cambridge, Queens' College, MS 13.
26 The York copy of Rolle's works was later owned by Henry Savile of Banke (d. 1617), whose family had strong catholic sympathies: see Andrew G. Watson, *The Manuscripts of Henry Savile of Banke* (London: Bibliographical Society, 1969); repr. in his *Medieval Manuscripts in Post-Medieval England* (Aldershot: Ashgatge, 2004), IX, no. 56.
27 Maurice Chauncy, in G. W. S. Curtis *et al.* (eds.), *The Passion and Martyrdom of the Holy English Carthusian Fathers: The Short Narration* (London, 1935), pp. 146–7. See M. G. Sargent, 'William Exmewe, Maurice Chauncy and *The cloud of unknowing*', in J. Hogg (ed.), *Spiritualität heute und gestern*, Analecta Cartusiana 35.4; (Salzburg: Institut für Anglistik und Amerikanistik, 1983), pp. 17–20. Exmew's book is now at Parkminster Charterhouse in Sussex. In the eighteenth century Anthony Wood noticed Chauncy's signature in it and ascribed the authorship of the text to him: his error was followed by subsequent writers. The Dartford nun, Elizabeth Exmew, who died at a Dominican convent near Bruges in 1585, may have been his sister.
28 Marshall has pointed out that: 'The monastic revival of Mary's reign, such as it was, depended heavily on exile leadership and manpower, the Venetian ambassador reporting in March 1555 that the queen had "sent for many English friars of the orders of St. Dominick and St. Francis, who to escape the past persecutions,

withdrew beyond the sea, and lived in poverty in Flanders"'(*Religious Identities*, pp. 259–60). In the case of the Birgittines, however, the first to re-inhabit Isleworth were those who had remained in England.

29 See James P. Carley, 'The Dispersal of the Monastic Libraries and the Salvaging of the Spoils', in Elisabeth Leedham-Green and Teresa Webber (eds.), *The Cambridge History of Libraries in Britain and Ireland* I (Cambridge: Cambridge University Press, 2006), pp. 265–91 (p. 284).

30 The most detailed analysis of wills of the ex-religious is found in Claire Cross and Noreen Vickers, *Monks, Friars and Nuns in Sixteenth Century Yorkshire* (Leeds: Yorkshire Archaeological Society, 1995). Their work is limited to Yorkshire, but similar patterns are emerging elsewhere.

31 'The Migration of Manuscripts from the English Medieval Libraries', *The Library*, 4th ser. 23 (1942–3), 1–11; repr. in his *Books, Collectors and Libraries; Studies in the Medieval Heritage*, ed. Andrew G. Watson (London: Hambledon, 1985) pp. 459–70 (p. 464).

32 See Michael G. Sargent, 'Walter Hilton's *Scale of Perfection*: The London Manuscript Group Reconsidered' *Medium Ævum* 52 (1983), 189–216 (p. 189); also Simpson, pp. 255–8 below.

33 See N. R. Ker, *Medieval Libraries of Great Britain*, 2nd edn (London: Royal Historical Society, 1964), p. 305. On the contents, see Hope Emily Allen, *Writings Ascribed to Richard Rolle Hermit of Hampole* (New York: MLA and London: Oxford University Press, 1927), pp. 37–9. The English College at Douai was founded in 1568 by William Allen (1532–94); by the 1580s it saw itself as the first Tridentine seminary and a base for missionary activity to England. (A copy of Henry VIII's *Assertio septem sacramentorum* in its original binding and signed by Henry, given to the English College by Allen, survives in the Royal Library at Windsor Castle RCIN 1006836.)

34 For a fuller discussion of the survival of Syon Books, see Christopher de Hamel, *Syon Abbey: The Library of the Bridgettine Nuns and Their Peregrinations after the Reformation* (The Roxburghe Club 1991; Otley, 1993); David N. Bell, *What Nuns Read: Books and Libraries in Medieval English Nunneries* (Kalamazoo, MI: Cistercian Publications, 1995); Ann M. Hutchison, 'What the Nuns Read: Literary Evidence from the English Bridgettine House, Syon Abbey', *Mediaeval Studies* 57 (1995), 205–22.

35 See Ann M. Hutchison (ed.), 'The Life and Good End of Sister Marie', *Birgittiana* 13 (2002), p. 50 and n. 57.

36 Her parents returned to England in Mary's reign but went back into exile after Elizabeth's accession. Margaret [Giggs] Clement had administered to the Carthusians in Newgate prison in 1537. Concerning Dorothy's move from the Poor Clares to St Ursula's, see Mary C. Erler, *Women, Reading, and Piety in Late Medieval England* (Cambridge: Cambridge University Press, 2002), p. 190, n. 21.

37 See Sargent, 'Walter Hilton's *Scale*', p. 189. See Andrew G. Watson, 'Robert Hare's Books', in A. S. G. Edwards, Vincent Gillespie, and Ralph Hanna (eds.), *The English Medieval Book: Studies in Memory of Jeremy Griffiths* (London: The British Library, 2000), pp. 209–32; repr. in his *Medieval Manuscripts in Post-Medieval England*, VI, nos. 119, 37 and 50. Hare also had a copy of *The Myrroure of Oure Lady* (London, 1530), now at Lambeth Palace (no. 104).

38 See James P. Carley, 'Sir Thomas Bodley's Library and its Acquisitions: An Edition of the Nottingham Benefaction of 1604', in James P. Carley and Colin G. C. Tite (eds.), *Books and Collectors 1200–1700* (London: British Library, 1997), pp. 357–86.

39 Quoted from *The Chronicle of St. Monica's* by Richard Copley Christie in his edition of the *Letters of Sir Thomas Copley* (London: Chiswick Press, 1897), p. xxvii.

40 R. W. Chambers (ed.), *A Fifteenth-Century Courtesy Book*, Walter Seaton (ed.). *Two Fifteenth-Century Franciscan Rules*, EETS OS 148 (1914; repr. 1962), pp. 81–116.

41 On the dating of this text, see Richard Rex, 'Redating Henry VIII's *A Glasse of the Truthe*', *The Library* 7th ser. 4 (2003), 16–27.

42 See Diarmaid MacCulloch, *Reformation: Europe's House Divided 1490–1700* (London and New York: Penguin, 2003), pp. 283–4.

43 MacCulloch, *Reformation*, p. 318. See also William Wizeman, 'The Pope, the Saints, and the Dead: Uniformity of Doctrine in Carranza's *Catechismo* and the Printed Works of the Marian Theologians', in John Edwards and R. W. Truman (eds.), *Reforming Catholicism in the England of Mary Tudor: the Achievement of Friar Bartolomé Carranza* (Aldershot and Burlington, VA: Ashgate, 2005), pp. 115–37, who concludes that 'by comparing the works of Marian authors with Carranza's *Catechism*, as well as with the canons, decrees, and Catechism of Trent and the sermons of [François] Le Picart, we see that Mary Tudor's Church had found, and sometimes foreshadowed, the spirit of the Counter-Reformation' (p. 137).

44 In a postscript to *The Pype*, likewise printed in 1532, Whitford distinguished between the active and contemplative lives at the request of his readers, observing that the latter, whose attainment the works More was recommending promoted: 'is a diligent beholdyng or inward lokyng with a desyre of hert. And this beholdynge or lokynge … doth apperteyne and belong rather unto þe soule or mynde than unto any bodely syght' (f. ccxxviir). He also pointed out that 'bycause this thynge maye be done by diuerse maners, and diuerse degrees of feruour and desyre diuerse doctoures and contemplatyfe persones haue set forth in wrytyng theyr myndes therin, some in englysshe and mo in latyne, and (I doute nat) in al other tonges, or langages' (f. ccxxviiv).

45 *The Stripping of the Altars: Traditional Religion in England c. 1400–c. 1558* (New Haven and London: Yale University Press, 1992), part II. In *Popular Politics and the English Reformation*, however, Shagan has argued that the process is more 'muddled' than conservative or triumphalist historians have maintained.

46 Quoted from *The Exposition and Declaration of the Psalme, Deus Ultionum Dominus* (London, 1539), in Axton and Carley (eds.), *'Triumphs of English'*, p. 232.

47 Quoted from Morley's 'Account of the Miracles of the Sacrament', in Axton and Carley (eds.), *'Triumphs of English'*, p. 254.

48 See 'Morley and the Papacy: Rome, Regime, and Religion', in Axton and Carley (eds.), *'Triumphs of English'*, 87–105 (p. 93). In his account of *The Fall of Religious Houses*, completed in 1591, the Yorkshire vicar Michael Sherbrook pointed out that 'whereas the subjects did take oaths at diuerse times against the

Pope; now they did swear on his side again, so that oaths were made as a noose of wax, fit for either way' (London, British Library, MS Additional 5813, f. 28r; A. G. Dickens (ed.) *Tudor Treatises* (Yorkshire Archaeological Society; Record Ser. 125 [1959], p. 141).

49 Quoted from Morley's 'Account of the Miracles of the Sacrament', in Axton and Carley (eds.), *'Triumphs of English'*, p. 253.

50 See Hutchison (ed.), 'The Life and Good End', p. 57.

51 A manuscript copy of an abbreviated version of Fewterer's *Myrrour*, now St Paul's Cathedral, MS 52.b.22, (s.xvi2) has a contemporary binding with the arms of the recusant Towneley family and the date 1603.

11

JAMES SIMPSON

1534–1550s: texts

Post-Reformation recusant institutions produced exceptionally important witnesses to the pre-Reformation English mystical tradition. Those same offshore institutions also produced some new contemplative texts of their own, as did some very isolated figures still in England. Despite this preservation and production, however, the mystical tradition was under immense cultural and political pressure in post-Reformation English culture. Already in the pre-Reformation period there are powerful signs of new devotional traditions that eschew the resources of mystical writing. Post-Reformation, the mystical tradition becomes a tenuous stream, barely surviving in a largely hostile environment.

The execution of Elizabeth Barton (known as 'The Holy Maid of Kent'), on 20 April 1534, might serve to mark the new and hostile climate with which English 'mystical' writings were obliged to contend. Elizabeth Barton (born *c.* 1506) was almost certainly illiterate, but in 1525 experienced visions; these were taken seriously enough by Archbishop Warham that Barton was admitted to the Benedictine priory of St Sepulchre, Canterbury. By 1527 she had taken her vows. Warham sent an account of her revelations to Henry VIII, and in the late 1520s she was the object of sympathetic interest by the king and his closest advisors. In 1530, however, she prophesied disaster for the king should he divorce Katherine of Aragon. Barton was convicted of high treason in 1534, and subsequently hanged and beheaded, along with others involved in her case; John Fisher, bishop of Rochester, was also implicated, and imprisoned at the king's pleasure. The authorities managed to destroy all copies (seven hundred, by one contemporary estimate) of a book of her revelations.

Action was taken against Barton clearly because her prophecies had become politically unacceptable to the king. Archbishop Cranmer (d. 1556) reports sceptically concerning the affair, in a letter written in December 1533, that Barton had 'in her trances many strange visions and revelations, as of heaven, hell, and purgatory, and of the state of certain souls departed'; she 'feigned' that her knowledge was from God, and sent letters designed to make people 'believe that those letters were written in heaven'. Having interrogated her, Cranmer reports that the truth is out: 'she never had a vision in all her life, but all that she said was feigned of her own imagination'.[1]

Cranmer's scepticism is driven most immediately by political alarm. But evangelical writing surrounding her execution also reveals a more theoretical hostility to the very idea of visionary writings and phenomena. If the Word of God was the sufficient and single path unto salvation, then supplements of any kind were to be rejected. Already in 1528 William Tyndale had described Barton's visions as 'done of the devil'; he says that they were designed to test whether or not we 'will cleave fast to God's word'.[2] Cranmer himself later returned to attack Barton in a more theoretical text, *The Confutation of Unwritten Verities* (1556).[3] Here he sets all visionary words in a wider category of unscriptural material. The *Confutation* begins by citing Deuteronomy 4:2: 'Ye shall put nothing to the word which I command to you.' Cranmer's is a culture of the revealed Word alone, to which nothing is to be added or subtracted. Successive chapters demolish all other, non-Scriptural forms of especially verbal authority: the 'writings of the old fathers, without the written Word of God'; the pronouncements of the General Councils; the oracles of angels; the apparitions of the dead; miracles; and custom: all are wholly without foundation. Attacking oracles, he dismisses 'miracles, dreams and revelations' (p. 41). The tract ends with an assault on various Catholic impostures and frauds, including Elizabeth Barton, who 'passed all others in devlish devices' (p. 65). In this text Barton serves as evidence not so much of treasonous activity, as of feigned claims to authority that have no scriptural foundation.

One of those feigned claims to authority is, clearly enough, the entire tradition of visionary writing. To be sure, the issue of discretion of spirits (and especially with regard to women's spirituality) was already acute in late medieval Europe. Jean Gerson, for example, tried to reverse the canonization of Birgitta of Sweden at the Council of Constance in 1415; he also wrote treatises about how to distinguish true visions from false. In, for example, his *On Distinguishing True from False Revelations* (1402), Gerson seems to be citing the case of Margaret Porete, burned as a heretic in 1310. She fell into error in her visions, since, of the soul's passions, love

is the one that penetrates deepest and alienates us from ourselves. And if love is true, chaste and holy, it helps us inconceivably much in coming to know heavenly things. But if it is vain, in error, and lustful, it will fashion for itself different illusions, so that a person thinks he sees or understands matters of which he is wholly ignorant.[4]

If Porete had applied her vision differently, she 'could hardly have expressed anything more sublime', but intellectual pride caused her to err (p. 357). Gerson's argument here is revealingly different from that of Cranmer in his attack on Elizabeth Barton: Gerson acknowledges the possibility of true visions, but is at the ready to spot the false; Cranmer, by contrast, denies the authority of visions altogether. In his *Catalogue* of British writers (1557), John Bale would seem to dismiss the entire late medieval feminine visionary tradition, in saying this about those churchmen who took the visions of St Birgitta (whom Bale confuses with St Bridget of Ireland) seriously:

> Eminent scholars of the time made learned commentaries, in both the schools of Oxford and in public places of teaching, on the murky dreams, or, as they call them, Revelations, of this Diana, in about 1370, in order that these sophists might obscure, with such ravings of little women, a truth clearer by the sun of God.[5]

In dismissing feminine vision so completely, Bale and Cranmer both express the deepest persuasion of sixteenth-century evangelical culture, of all stripes: that only Scriptural words have authority and credibility. In 1525 Luther himself had begun his attack on the 'enthusiasts' of Zwickau (who were claiming direct prophetic inspiration) by asserting that Christians should first pray to God for a 'right understanding of his holy, pure Word'.[6] Much later, in 1537, referring to the charismatic Münzer (d. 1525), Luther theorized the inherent insufficiency of non-Scriptural inspiration:

> In these things, which concern the spoken, external word, it is certain to maintain this: God gives no one his Spirit or grace apart from the external word which goes before. We are thus protected from the enthusiasts, that is, the spirits, who boast that they have the Spirit apart from and before contact with the word.[7]

However much Luther was writing against specific forms of prophetic inspiration that threatened his own programme of renovation, his uncompromising emphasis on Scriptural words and only Scriptural words has direct implications for all visionary, prophetic, and mystical writings. Not only that, but Lutheran emphasis on *sola scriptura* threatened a vast undergrowth of devotional practice that nourished the higher reaches of mystical vision. English evangelical writers clearly pitched Bible reading against conventional devotional practice. In his Preface to Numbers, for example, Tyndale contrasts Catholic and evangelical devotion: 'Devotion', he says, 'is a fervent love unto God's commandments, and a desire to be with God and with his everlasting promises.' He contrasts the riches produced by this verbal devotion to the Word of God with the unsatisfying devotions to saints.[8] In the attack on images made in his answers to the rebels of Devon (who opposed the imposition of the 1549 English Book of Common Prayer), Cranmer dismissed the whole culture of affective devotion as an expression of 'all manner of superstition and idolatry'; its corrupt tendency to worship creatures is found especially in 'fond women, which commonly follow superstition rather than true religion'.[9]

In short, the events of 1534 establish the conditions for a very different spiritual world from that of pre-Reformation spirituality that could, even if with profound reservations, countenance a variety of spiritual sustenance. In his *Epistle on the Mixed Life* (?mid-1380s), Walter Hilton says that the fire of love for God in each soul needs to be nourished, but it can be fed with wood of diverse kinds:

> And so it is good that eche man in his degree, after that he is disposed, that he gete him stikkes of o thing other of another – either of preieres, or of good meditaciouns, or reding in hooli writte, or good bodili worchynge – for to nourische the fier of love in his soule.[10]

Whereas pre-Reformation visionary culture had often been motivated in part by a need to short-circuit the textual protocols of a learned, literate culture, the new evangelical culture of the sixteenth century, with its rigid adherence to written verities and only written verities, prohibited that short-circuit of textuality; it insisted instead on a single path through the written, and through Scripture. In his *Dialogue Concerning Heresies* (1529), Thomas More grounds the Church in the ongoing tradition of unwritten verities: with regard to the Holy Spirit, More says that it was

> ... not promised by our Sauyour Cryst that he [the Holy Spirit] sholde onely tell his chyrch agayn his [i.e. Christ's] wordes but sayd further, 'I haue', quod he, 'besides all this, many thynges to say to you.'[11]

This Morean position was wholly out of step with an ascendant, evangelical culture committed to exclusively written verities.

The year 1534 saw, then, not only the Act of Supremacy, but also the execution of the visionary Elizabeth Barton. The second event, in the context of the first, marks a powerful break in the English visionary tradition, a break provoked not only by specific political needs but also by much more profound ideological persuasions.

That there was some interest in contemplative writing right up to 1534 is attested by the response of England's early printers to the possibilities of that market. Although Caxton himself did not print contemplative works, his followers, and especially Wynkyn de Worde, had modestly exploited interest in vernacular and Latin contemplative texts, of both English and

Continental origin.[12] Some of these works were clearly abridgements for a wider, print public, while others were substantial books, in some cases prepared specifically for religious houses. Thus in 1494 de Worde printed a complete text of Hilton's *Scale of Perfection*, which was reprinted in 1507, 1525, and 1533 (*RSTC* 14042–5). Hilton's *Epistle on the Mixed Life* was published by Richard Pynson in 1516 (*RSTC* 4602). The brief *Golden Epistle* was also printed by Thomas Godfray in 1531 and again in 1535 (*RSTC* 1915 and 1915.5),[13] along with a selection of four *Revelations* of Saint Birgitta concerning the contemplative life (*RSTC* 1915.5). The *Contemplations of the Dread and Love of God*, addressed to secular readers but including discussion of the contemplative life, was printed (in editions that attributed the work to Rolle) in 1506 and 1519 (*RSTC* 21259 and 21260). A short extract of Rolle's *Form of Living* was published as *The Remedy ayenst the Troubles of Temptacyons* in 1508 and 1519. All four of the last mentioned printings came from the shop of Wynkyn de Worde, who had also produced a radically abbreviated, seven-page edition of *The Book of Margery Kempe* in 1501.[14] Latin works by Richard Rolle, the *Lectiones super Iob* (*Readings on the Book of Job*) and *Speculum spiritualium* (*The Spiritual Mirror*), had been printed in, respectively, Oxford in 1483 and Paris in 1510 (*RSTC* 21261 and *RSTC* 23030.7).

Printers also capitalized on an interest in continental visionaries, who are in fact more substantially represented in print than English authors, Hilton aside. Birgitta of Sweden is represented by the *Lyfe of Seynt Birgette*,[15] and, as we have seen in the previous paragraph, by a selection of four texts from her *Revelations*.[16] The *Mirrour of Oure Ladye*, a Middle English translation of and commentary on the Birgittine office, was produced for the nuns of Syon Abbey in 1530. Catherine of Siena's *Lyf*, as well as the Middle English translation of her *Dialogo*, the *Orcherd of Syon* (originally also written for the nuns of Syon), were both printed by de Worde in, respectively, 1492 (reprinted in 1500) and 1519 (*RSTC* 24766, 24766.3, and 4815). Grisé reports that selections of Elizabeth of Hungary were printed in 1492 with the *Lyf* of Catherine of Siena.[17]

This printing activity comes to an abrupt halt in 1534. Before, however, we accept this crystal clear date as a marker of a new, anti-contemplative spirituality of the Word, we might pause to note that pre-Reformation, late medieval spirituality was already moving towards chastened, non-visual forms of spiritual experience. A passage from Thomas More's *Confutation of Tyndale's Answer* (1532) underlines the deeper changes that were underway behind the more spectacular jurisdictional disputes of the 1530s.

In the *Confutation*, More hankers after an age of innocence, in which English lay readers were unbothered either by the works of 'heretics' (e.g.

Tyndale) or of their respondents (e.g. More himself).[18] Instead, he advises them to read what he takes to be classics of the devotional tradition in English, which are also in conformity with 'the catholike faithe of thys 1500 yere'. The unlearned should be reading 'suche englishe bookes as moste may noryshe and encreace devocion. Of which kind is Bonaventure of the lyfe of Christe, Gerson of the folowyng of Christ and the devoute contemplative booke of Scala perfectionis'.[19] The works to which More refers here are, respectively: Love's translation (*c.* 1410) of the *Meditationes vitae Christi*, the original of which was once ascribed to the thirteenth-century Parisian theologian Bonaventure (*c.* 1217–74), but which was in fact written *c.* 1350–80; the *Imitation of Christ*, often ascribed to the Parisian theologian Jean Gerson (1363–1429), and now ascribed to the Netherlandish canon regular Thomas à Kempis (1379–1471); and the *Scale of Perfection* by Walter Hilton (d. 1396), canon of the Augustinian Priory of Thurgarton in Nottinghamshire.

More's account of that vernacular tradition as of long-standing is misleading in one respect. Certainly Love's work had been printed by Caxton in 1484 and 1490, and had been taken up by both Pynson and de Worde, the last of whom isssued it four times between 1494 and 1525 (*RSTC* 3259–66). As we have seen, de Worde also printed *The Scale* in 1494, and the work was reissued three more times before 1533.

The *Imitation of Christ*, however, had had a very restricted circulation before its first printing in 1504 (*RSTC* 23954.7). Until that date, 'The *Imitatio* had remained virtually inaccessible to those English readers who could not read Latin'; the number of manuscripts is small (four), and the evidence for readership prior to 1504 points to 'a small, conservative, intellectual and spiritual elite'.[20] After its first printing, however, the *Imitatio* became hugely popular: it was translated no fewer than six times, and went through fifty-one imprints up to 1639, being produced by both insular and recusant presses (*RSTC* 23954–93). Why was this so, and why did the *Imitation*, alone among pre-Reformation vernacular works and translations, vigorously survive the 1530s in both Protestant and more traditionalist cultures?

From the late fourteenth century at least some clerical vernacular writers expressed a deep distrust of the imaginative affectivity of vernacular visionary and devotional writing. The author of the late fourteenth-century *Cloud of Unknowing*, for example, attacks as no less than heretical those false contemplatives who are 'enflaumid with an unkyndely hete of compleccion', which must be a critique of the kind of bodily and intensely affective spirituality shaped by Richard Rolle (d. 1349).[21] The *Cloud*-author's spirituality places an utterly transcendent God at its centre; that immaterial transcendence subjects the world of created things and language to deconstructive pressure. The only certainty offered by language and images is that they must fail to gain access to God, and so should be used, if at all, only to be broken in recognition of their inadequacy.[22] The *Cloud*-author's hostility to images is epistemological rather than theological, but it amounts to a kind of interior iconoclasm, since the true contemplative is to undo the very processes of both imagination and thought in the psyche, by way of approaching purest being. The radically philosophical, a-historical nature of the *Cloud*-author's God produces a correlatively elitist text, which is directed to a 'privy' audience of single persons, who must read the work, in order, from beginning to end.

The *Cloud* survives in seventeen manuscripts, some of which were connected to Carthusian houses in both Yorkshire and London. Carthusian environments probably also produced the first translation into English of the *Imitation of Christ* in the mid-fifteenth century; a second translation was printed by Pynson in 1504, and a third translation, possibly by Richard Whitford, a Birgittine monk of Syon Abbey, was printed in 1531.[23] The first translation circulated in a very small group of readers within the Birgittines and the Carthusians. The heroic resistance of Birgittine and Carthusian monks from Syon Abbey and Sheen to Henry VIII's claim to the headship of the Church of England is well known. That resistance is not without its historical ironies: the religious houses from which these men came were founded by Henry V by way of harnessing powerful monastic foundations to royal interests; furthermore, the very spirituality of these houses, austere, and imageless as it was, was not out of keeping with aspects of evangelical spirituality, despite the fact (a further irony) that Syon was dedicated to a visionary female saint.[24] The *Imitation* was popular from its printing of 1504, of which eight reprints were made up to 1528, but its popularity remained undiminished across the 1530s and well beyond: Whitford's own translation was reprinted twelve times up to 1585, and competed with other translations throughout the sixteenth century (*RSTC* 23954.7–23993).

More's statement that the *Imitatio* was a classic of vernacular spirituality is, then, incorrect: unlike the other two books mentioned by More, the *Imitatio* expresses a chaste, austere, and largely imageless spirituality; the *devotio moderna* enjoyed no popularity in England until the sixteenth century, and it can be described as a classic in England only *after* the Reformation. This chaste spirituality, with its generally chaste prose, is also found in More's own *Dialogue of Comfort* written in the Tower in 1535 as More awaited execution.

Paradoxically, More's own chaste and Carthusian spirituality itself converges, in some respects, with its evangelical enemy. Certainly by the mid-sixteenth century evangelical authors were deploying the works of Erasmus, More's friend and exponent of 'Christian humanism', on the side of an imageless spirituality.[25] For More, as for his ostensible enemy, John Ryckes, the author of the *Ymage of Love* (1525) (*RSTC* 21471–2), the truest account of God is imageless.

Rather, then, than offering us a picture of a venerable pre-Reformation devotional or contemplative tradition, or both, about to come to a brutal halt, More instead delineates both a pre-Reformation and a post-Reformation tradition: Love and Hilton represent the past, while the *Imitation of Christ* points rather to the future. One can see the bridge across pre- and post-Reformation culture represented by the *Imitatio* through the lens of its treatment by two royal women. On the one hand, Lady Margaret Beaufort (mother to Henry VII) translated Book 4 of the *Imitatio*, from the French (a text printed by Pynson in 1504) (*RSTC* 23954.7); on the other, the Protestant queen Katherine Parr drew upon Book 3 of the *Imitatio* in her *Prayers or Meditacions* (1545).[26] Interestingly, however, whereas Book 3 of the *Imitatio* is a dialogue between the plangent soul and Christ, the Parr translation omits the (obviously unscriptural) voice of Christ, and leaves the importunate voice of the soul unanswered by non-Scriptural words.[27]

Changes in late medieval devotional practice, then, and in particular the introduction of the *devotio moderna*, were already, as it were, 'preparing' late medieval readers for chastened, non-visionary forms of spirituality, which were more rooted in the scriptural text. One last example will suffice, also from the writings of Katharine Parr. In his Good Friday sermon (?1531–4),[28] John Fisher used an unusual metaphor, as he called the crucifix a 'book'; the metaphor seems to be a new one, since Fisher registers the possible surprise of his listeners: 'But you marvell peradventure why I call the crucifix a book', he exclaims, before going on to elaborate the conceit.[29] Fisher's metaphor is designed to heighten devotion to the suffering body of Christ: just as a book has two 'boardes', so too 'the two boardes of this booke is the two partes of the crosse, for which the book is open and spread, the leaves be cowched vpon the boardes. And so the blessed body of Christ was spred vpon the crosse' (sig. E8r). Perhaps Fisher is himself wresting the terms of increasingly bookish culture back into the purview of a visual and potentially visionary devotional culture. If so, Katherine Parr wrests it back for books. In her moving, para-Psalmic text, *The Lamentation of a Sinner*,[30] she also deploys the metaphor: 'this crucifix is the boke, wherin god hath included all thynges, and hath moste compendiouslye written therin, al truthe, profitable and necessary for our saluation' (sig. C4r). Parr's elaboration of the 'book of the crucifix' moves in exactly the opposite direction from Fisher's: whereas Fisher's eye moves to the visible body, Parr's mind moves to (evangelical) theology: 'Christ hath shewed that in goddess sight, the righteousnes of the world is wickednesse: and he hathe yelded witness, that the workes of menne, not regenerated by him in faith, are evyl.'[31]

Where, then, did the English contemplative tradition go after 1534, when its room for development was under severe pressure of various kinds, both acute and chronic? The obvious answer is offshore, into recusant communities based in Flanders and Northern France. Many factors subtend mystical writing: such textual practice depends not only on a pre-existent devotional culture, but it often also depends on institutions that permit the practice of contemplative meditation. Not only did the Reformation in England produce theory hostile to visionary writing, but in the later 1530s it also proscribed the institutions of the regular religious life.

The writings of one Robert Parkyn (d. 1569) reveal the fragility, both cultural and institutional, of post-Reformation contemplative practice in England. By 1541 Parkyn was in orders and not long after this became curate at Adwick-le-Street in the West Riding, where he remained until his death.[32] Oxford, Bodleian Library, MS Lat. theol. d.15 contains copies by Parkyn of prose works by Richard Rolle (who had lived in Parkyn's own parish), poems by John Lydgate, and prayers in verse and prose by Thomas More. Parkyn had profoundly Catholic sympathies, as his transcribed texts demonstrate; he seems also to have composed works himself, preserved in Aberdeen, University Library, MS 185. Many of these texts seem to have been composed by 1551 (i.e. before the reign of Queen Mary in 1553–8), but the two works devoted to the contemplative life (the *Brief Rule* and its summary, the *13 preceptes necessarie for him that entendithe to lyve a contemplative lyffe*) seem to have been written between 1557–9. In his *Brief Rule* he directs that those who wish to come 'unto perfection' must in the first place 'detest and abhorre all heresies and scismes, strongly stickynge and humbly submittinge him selffe unto the Catholique chirche, for who so ever goethe frome the catholike churche, yea, thowghe they seyme to lyffe never so virtuusly, yet ar thay parttide and devidyde from god and the company of sanctis' (pp. 67–8). Given its circumstances, this apparently anodyne address has a certain piquancy, written as it is by a person of Catholic persuasion who knows that anodyne professions of faith to the 'Catholic Church' had become, and could very soon again become, anything but anodyne. That address to a virtual institution is implicit in his little tract on *The Highest Learning*, in which he says that anyone who wants to 'usse thacttes of contemplatyve lyffinge' must 'in no wysse to intromytt nor medle with worldlye besynes' (p. 61).

Certainly Parkyn can imagine the contemplative life, and the joys of union
with God; once brought to perfection, then

> is the luffynge sowlle drownyde in gostlie love, and ther is suche a counion of
> love bytwix god and the sowle, that god is in such a lovynge sowlle, and syche
> a lovinge sowlle is in god. Than burnithe the sowlle in love... the mynde is
> rapt from all terrestriall thinges in to god. Than whatt joye and cumfurthe,
> whatt gladness and spirituall myrthe the sowlle and bodie, the hertt and mynde
> doth fealle in god, no hertt can thinke, nor townge can tell. (p. 62)

This eloquent imagining is premised, however, on the possibility of with-
drawing from all 'worldlye besynes', when the obvious institutional bases of
that withdrawal have now all but disappeared from England. While refur-
bishment and instruction at parish level were much more urgent needs in
the reign of Mary (1553–8), the reign did nevertheless witness a modest
restoration of some monastic institutions. That modest restoration, reversed
after 1558, was, however, an exiguous basis for the contemplative practice
imagined by Parkyn.

If the institutional grounding for the practice of the contemplative life was
no longer available in England, such institutions were, however, founded on
the Continent, which is where we must look both for the preservation of the
English medieval contemplative tradition, and for texts newly produced in
aid of those wishing to pursue the contemplative life. Parkyn's *Brief Rule* is
in part dependent on William Peryn's *Spirituall exercises and goostly meditacions and a neare way to come to perfection and lyfe contemplatyue* (1557)
(*RSTC* 19784). That one of the addressees of this text is 'Sister Dorothy
Clement, of the Order of St Clare in Louvain' points to the geographical
change of location for English contemplative writing (p. 1). After the death
of Queen Mary and the 1559 statute dissolving Mary's religious foundations, the regular religious of those foundations dispersed to the continent,
the Carthusians of Sheen and the Birgittines of Syon to Bruges and finally
Nieuport; and a small community of Dominicans to Seland near Antwerp;
and the nuns of Syon eventually for a long period were based in Lisbon.
Benedictine monastic foundations for women were established in the following centres, from the late sixteenth-century: Brussels (1596), Cambrai
(1623), Ghent (1624), Paris (1651), Boulogne (1652), Dunkirk (1662), and
Ypres (1665).[33] Benedictine priories for men were founded at Douai (1606),
Dieulouard (1608), St Malo (1611), and Paris (1615).[34] I present such evidence as there is for the preservation of a pre-Reformation contemplative
tradition in these centres, before, very briefly, pointing to the major ways in
which that tradition was developed.

Two of the five manuscripts containing a full text of Julian of Norwich's *Revelations* derive from the period 1650–*c.* 1670, and were copied in English Benedictine nunneries in both Cambrai and Paris. One manuscript seems to have been copied by Mother Clementina Cary (d. 1671). [35] A fourth witness, the Serenus Cressy print of 1670,[36] also seems to derive from one of these copies, now Paris, Bibliothèque Nationale, Fonds Anglais, MS 40 (a text that attempts to reproduce the handwriting and *mise-en-page* of a medieval manuscript, though itself written *c.* 1650).[37]

Julian's was not the only text reproduced and read in recusant nunneries. In 1629 the Benedictine Augustine Baker (1575–1641), spiritual director for the Cambrai nuns between 1624 and 1633, wrote to Sir Robert Cotton asking for more pre-Reformation books fit for the nuns of Cambrai:

> Their lives being contemplative the common bookes of the world are not for their purpose, and little or nothing is in thes daies printed in English that is proper for them. There were manie English bookes in olde time whereof thoughe they have some, yet they want manie... Hampooles workes are proper for them. I wishe I had Hilltons *Scala perfectionis* in latein; it would helpe the vnderstanding of the English; and some of them vnderstande latein.[38]

Clearly other texts did make their way to recusant communities, since at least five manuscript copies of either the *Cloud of Unknowing* or the *Epistle of Privy Counsel* or both survive in copies made in Cambrai. Augustine Baker also made a curious commentary on the *Cloud*, known as *Secretum sive Mysticum, containing an exposition of the book called The Cloud.*[39] In about 1632 Baker made a complete and modernized version of the *Scale of Perfection.*[40] Serenus Cressy (who was responsible for the printing of Julian's *Revelations* in 1670 and had been chaplain to the English nuns at Paris in 1651–2), also had the *Scale of Perfection* printed in 1659, while he was at Douai.

These texts from an earlier contemplative tradition were clearly admired and actively read: Dame Margaret Gascoigne, for example, who was professed at Cambrai in 1629 and died in 1637, cites and meditates on Julian's *Revelations* in an independent work:

> Thou hast saide, O Lorde, to a deere child of thine, 'Let me alone, my deare worthy childe, intende (or attende) to me, I am inough to thee; rejoice in thy Saviour and Salvation' (this was spoken to Julian the Ankress of Norwich, as appeareth by the booke of her revelations.) This o Lorde I reade and thinke on with great joie, and cannot but take it as spoken allso to me.[41]

Extracts from Julian were also made in the Upholland Anthology, copied at Cambrai.[42]

English works from the pre-Reformation tradition were, however, clearly not the only material available for those practising the contemplative life. Benedict Canfield's *The Rule of Perfection* (first published 1609) was to have a long shelf-life in many languages; it was certainly designed to promote specifically mystical experience:

> This will, pleasure and contentment of God, is so delitious a thing and so pleasant to the sowlle, when so she tasteth it perfectly, that it draweth, illu-minateth, dilateth, extendeth, exalteth, ravisheth, and inebriateth her in such sort that she feeleth no more any will, affection or inclination of her owne, but wholly des[poyled] of herself, but all self-wil, interest and commoditie, is plunged into the bottomlesse gulfe of this will and the abyssal pleasure therof, and so is become one and the same spirit with God.[43]

And the newly developed, Ignatian devotional programme of spiritual exercises was also available to English monastic houses. In fact pre-Reformation English contemplative materials seem to have provided an alternative axis to the newer, 'activist' Ignatian spirituality, and to have been deployed in a larger cleavage between English Jesuits and Benedictines. Baker, for example, regarded Ignatian devotional exercise with condescension: 'All those directions given by those Fathers are but, as it were, the ABC of the spiritual life'; 'the experimentall knowledge of mystick matters doth not properly belong to the Fathers of the Society'.[44] Baker himself is a central figure in the preservation and reuse of the pre-Reformation contemplative tradition. As we have seen, the anthology of pre-Reformation spiritual texts prepared by Baker contains selections from Julian's *Revelations* and he also wrote a 'commentary' on the *Cloud of Unknowing* (more an occasion for a spiritual autobiography) that twice appears with the text of the *Cloud* itself.[45]

This is not the place for a conspectus of Baker's own spiritual writings. He wrote voluminously, without either stylistic or structural economy of any kind.[46] He excuses his style by referring to the intellectual simplicity of women, 'who haue good and pious wills, though no deep vnderstandinge'. If any 'learned reader' finds verbal superfluity, 'if thou reflect for whom it was written, the persons being religious women (who generallie are illiter-ate), the largenesse of [my] expressions may be excused'.[47] However much Baker seems to have had a low estimation of the capacities of recusant women, some testimonies suggest otherwise. From Cambrai, the remark-able Gertrude More's (1606–33) surviving series of meditations (*Confes-siones Amantis* (*The Confessions of a Lover*), 1625–33) attests a subtle, passionate spiritual culture grounded in Augustine's *Confessions*.[48] And, although outside the contemplative frame of the present volume, one should recognize the visionary power of Mary Ward (1585–1645), who, in the face of official persecution, founded what is now known as the Institute of the Blessed Virgin Mary.[49]

NOTES

I warmly acknowledge the counsel of my colleague Nicholas Watson in the writing of this article.

1 John E. Cox (ed.), Thomas Cranmer, *Miscellaneous Writings and Letters of Thomas Cranmer*, Parker Society (Cambridge: Cambridge University Press, 1846), pp. 272–4.

2 David Daniell (ed.), William Tyndale, *The Obedience of a Christian Man* (London: Penguin, 2000), p. 177.

3 Cox (ed.), Cranmer, *Miscellaneous Writings*, pp. 19–67.

4 Brian Patrick McGuire (trans.), *Jean Gerson: Early Works* (New York: Paulist Press, 1998), p. 357.

5 John Bale, *Scriptorum illustrium maioris brytannie, quam nunc angliam et scotiam uocant, catalogus* (John Oporinus, 1559). (Both the 1557 and the 1559 volumes are printed in this book; repr. in facsimile, 2 vols. (Farnsworth: Gregg International, 1971), II, 188.)

6 Conrad Bergendorff (ed.), Martin Luther, *Against the Heavenly Prophets in the Matter of Images and Sacraments*, in Helmut T. Lehmann (ed.), *Luther's Works* (Philadelphia: Muhlenberg Press, 1958), vol. XL, pp. 79–223 (p. 80).

7 Martin Luther, *Schmalkald Articles*, in William R. Russell, *Luther's Theological Testament: The Schmalkald Articles* (Minneapolis, MN: Fortress Press, 1995), Appendix A, p. 145.

8 David Daniell (ed.), *Tyndale's Old Testament* (New Haven: Yale University Press, 1992), p. 196.

9 'Answers to the Fifteen Articles of the Rebels, Devon, Anno 1549', in Cox (ed.), Cranmer, *Miscellaneous Writings*, pp. 163–87 (p. 179).

10 Barry Windeatt (ed.), Walter Hilton, *Epistle on the Mixed Life*, in *English Mystics of the Middle Ages* (Cambridge: Cambridge University Press, 1994), pp. 110–36 (p. 121).

11 T. M. C. Lawler, Germain Marc'hadour, and Richard Marius (eds.), Thomas More, *A Dialogue Concerning Heresies*, 2 parts, in *The Complete Works of St Thomas More*, 6 (New Haven: Yale University Press, 1981), I.178.

12 For Caxton's complaint that young gentlewomen 'occupye theym and studye ouermoche in bokes of contemplacion', see Jennifer Summit, 'William Caxton, Margaret Beaufort and the Romance of Female Patronage', in Lesley Smith and Jane H. Taylor (eds.), *Women, the Book and the Worldly: Selected Proceedings of the St Hilda's Conference*, ed. 2 vols. (Woodbridge: D. S. Brewer, 1995), II, 151–65 (p. 152). For an account of the printing of English mystical texts, see George R. Keiser, 'The Mystics and Early English Printers: The Economics of Devotionalism', in *MMTE IV*, pp. 9–26.

13 For editions of Richard Whitford's translation of the *Golden Epistle*, published between 1531 and 1535, see *RSTC* 25412, 23964, and 23964.7.

14 *RSTC* 14924. The Kempe selection was further published by Henry Pepwell in 1521 (*RSTC* 20972). For a differing view of the way in which de Worde and Pepwell abbreviated the text, see Sue Ellen Holbrook, 'Margery Kempe and Wynkyn de Worde', in *MMTE IV*, pp. 27–46, and Jennifer Summit, *Lost Property: The Woman Writer and English Literary History, 1380–1589* (Chicago: University of Chicago Press, 2000), pp. 126–38.

15 Appended to *The Kalendre of the Newe Legende of Englande*, which, as mentioned above, also includes Hilton's *Mixed Life*. For discussion of this edition, see Ann M. Hutchison, 'Reflections on Aspects of the Spiritual Impact of St Birgitta, the *Revelations* and the Bridgittine Order in Late Medieval England', in *MMTE VII*, pp. 69–82 (pp. 69–71).

16 These texts were also included in the first edition of Richard Whytford's *Werke for Housholders* in 1531 (*RSTC* 25412).

17 C. Annette Grisé, 'Holy Women in Print: Continental Female Mystics and the English Mystical Tradition', in *MMTE VII*, pp. 83–96 (p. 86).

18 The following six paragraphs are drawn from James Simpson, *Reform and Cultural Revolution* (Oxford: Oxford University Press, 2002), pp. 450–53.

19 Louis A. Schuster *et al.* (eds.), Thomas More, *The Confutation of Tyndale's Answer*, in *The Complete Works of St Thomas More*, 8 (New Haven: Yale University Press, 1973), 2 parts, Preface, I.37.

20 For the narrow circulation of the *Imitation of Christ* in the fifteenth century, see Roger Lovatt, 'The *Imitation of Christ* in Late Medieval England', *TRHS*, 5th ser. 18 (1968), 97–121 (100, 114). See also Michael G. Sargent, 'Minor Devotional Writings', in A. S. G. Edwards (ed.), *Middle English Prose: A Critical Guide to Major Authors and Genres* (New Brunswick, NJ: Rutgers University Press, 1984), pp. 147–63.

21 Phyllis Hodgson (ed.), *The Cloud of Unknowing and the Book of Privy Counselling*, EETS OS 218 (1944; repr. 1981), p. 86.

22 For an example of the *Cloud*-author's aggression towards the imagination, see Hodgson, *Cloud*, pp. 22–3.

23 For the first translation, see B. J. H. Biggs (ed.), *The Imitation of Christ*, EETS OS 309 (1997). See *RSTC* 23954.7 for Pynson's edition of 1503, and *RSTC* 23961 for the first printing of Whitford's translation.

24 For the Birgittines as neither producers of visionary texts, and yet founded on a commitment to belief in the truth of a visionary record, see Vincent Gillespie, 'Dial M for Mystic: Mystical Texts in the Library of Syon Abbey and the Spirituality of the Syon Bretheren', *MMTE VI*, pp. 241–68 (p. 262). For a nuanced account of late medieval Carthusian response to images, see Jessica Brantley, *Reading in the Wilderness: Private Devotion and Public Performance in Late Medieval England* (Chicago: University of Chicago Press, 2007).

25 See, for example, *A dialogue . . . of two persones . . . intituled the pilgremage of pure devotyon* (*RSTC* 10454).

26 *RSTC* 4818.5. The text is available in facsimile in *The Early Modern Englishwoman: A Facsimile Library of Essential Works*, part 1: *Printed Writings, 1500–1640*, selected and introduced by Janel Mueller, vol. III, *Katherine Parr* (Aldershot: Scolar Press, 1996).

27 Compare, for example, Parr, *Prayers or Meditacions*, Biir–Biiir, with Biggs (ed.), *The Imitation of Christ*, 3.30–3.32 (pp. 99–101). Parr's literary output is

discussed by Jonathan Gibson, 'Katherine Parr, Princess Elizabeth and the Crucified Christ', in Victoria Burke and Jonathan Gibson (eds.), *Early Modern Women's Manuscript Writing: Selected Papers from the Trinity/Trent Colloquium*, (Aldershot: Ashgate, 2004), 33–49.

28 For connections between the texts of Parr and Fisher, see Janel Mueller, 'Complications of Intertextuality: John Fisher, Katherine Parr and "The Book of the Crucifix" ', in Cedric C. Brown and Arthur F. Marotti (eds.), *Texts and Cultural Change in Early Modern England* (London: Macmillan, 1997), 15–36. Mueller's suppositions about the date of the sermon can be found on p. 20.

29 'A Sermon verie fruitefull ... Preached vpon a good Friday' (London, ?1578), *RSTC* 10899, included as part of another text by Fisher. For Fisher's usage, see Richard Rex, *The Theology of John Fisher* (Cambridge: Cambridge University Press, 1991), p. 46. For the larger tradition of using the body of Christ as a book, see Jeffrey Hamburger, 'Body Versus Book: The Trope of Visibility in Images of Christian-Jewish Polemic', in David Gantz and Thomas Lentes (eds.), *Ästhetik des Unsichtbaren: Bildtheorie und Bildgebrauch in der Vormoderne* (Berlin: Reimer, 2004), pp. 113–45.

30 *RSTC* 4827. Facsimile available in *The Early Modern Englishwoman*, selected by Janel Mueller, vol. 3, *Katherine Parr*.

31 Parr, *Lamentation of a Sinner*, sig. D2v. See Gibson, 'Katherine Parr, Princess Elizabeth and the Crucified Christ', for a further, evangelical use of the metaphor in *The Institution of a Christian Man* (1538) (p. 37).

32 For a brief biography of Parkyn, and further references, see *ODNB*. See also A. G. Dickens, 'Tudor Treatises', *Yorkshire Archaeological Society*, Record Series 125 (1959), 17–88. For a full list of the contents, see A. G. Dickens, 'Robert Parkyn's Narrative of the Reformation', *EHR* 62 (1947), 58–83 (58–60).

33 See David Lunn, *The English Benedictines, 1540–1688: From Reformation to Revolution* (London: Burns and Oates, 1980), p. 198.

34 See David Knowles, *The Religious Orders in England*, 3 vols. (Cambridge: Cambridge University Press, 1950–1959), III, 453.

35 See Edmund Colledge and James Walsh (eds.), *A Book of Showings to the Anchoress Julian of Norwich*, 2 vols. (Toronto: Pontifical Institute of Mediaeval Studies, 1978), pp. 6–18.

36 Wing (2nd edn), C6902A.

37 Images of folios from this manuscript can be seen in Nicholas Watson and Jacqueline Jenkins (eds.), *The Writings of Julian of Norwich: A Vision Showed to a Devout Woman and A Revelation of Love* (University Park, PA: Penn State Press, 2006), pp. 51–2.

38 Cited from Placid Spearritt, 'The Survival of Medieval Spirituality Among the Exiled English Black Monks', in Michael Woodward (ed.), *That Mysterious Man: Essays on Augustine Baker, Analecta Cartusiana*, 119.15 (Abergavenny: Three Peaks Press, 2001), p. 22.

39 John Clark (ed.), Augustine Baker, *Secretum, Analecta Cartusiana* 119.7 (Salzburg: Institut für Anglistik und Amerikanistik, 1997).

40 See Hywel Wyn Owen, 'Another Augustine Baker Manuscript', in Albert Ampe (ed.), *Dr L. Reypens-Album* (Antwerp: Ruusbroec-Genootschap, 1964), pp. 269–80 (p. 274).

41 Cited from Margaret Gascoigne, 'A Treatise... composed by a Religious Virgin of the holy order of St. Benet', reproduced in Watson and Jenkins (eds.), *Julian of Norwich*, pp. 443–4. The citation is to ch. 36 of the *Revelations*.

42 These extracts are also reproduced in Watson and Jenkins (eds.), *Julian of Norwich*, 446–8.

43 *The rule of perfection contayning a breif and perspicuous abridgement of all the vvholle spirituall life reduced to this only point of the (vvill of God.)*, 2nd edn (Rouen, 1635) (*RSTC* 10928.6), Ee2r. For Canfield's biography and works, see *ODNB*. For the sources of Canfield's mystical theology, see Kent Emery, *Renaissance Dialectic and Renaissance Piety: Benet Canfield's 'Rule of Perfection'* (Binghamton, NY: Medieval Renaissance Texts and Studies, 1987), pp. 60–85.

44 Cited from Lunn, *The English Benedictines*, p. 206. For the disputes between Baker and those proposing an activist, Ignatian spiritual practice, see Lunn, *The English Benedictines*, pp. 206–8 and Spearritt, 'The Survival of Medieval Spirituality'.

45 For discussion of which, see John P. H. Clark, 'Father Augustine Baker's *Secretum*: Sources and Affinities', in Woodward (ed.), *That Mysterious Man*, pp. 123–35.

46 The volume and repetitiveness have provoked heroic responses, first in the seventeenth-century abridgement by Serenus Cressy, *Sancta Sophia, or, Directions for the prayer of contemplation &c. extracted out of more then (sic) XL treatises / written by the late Ven. Father F. Augustin Baker* (Douai, 1657) (Wing, B480), and secondly in the editorial labours principally of John Clark, who has edited the corpus; see *Analecta Cartusiana*, 119.7–21.

47 John Clark (ed.), Augustine Baker, *Directions for Contemplation, Book D*, *Analecta Cartusiana*, 119.11 (Salzburg: Institut für Anglistik und Amerikanistik, 1999), pp. 4 and 7 respectively.

48 *The holy practises of a devine lover, or, The sainctly [sic] Ideots Deuotions the contents of the booke are contained in the ensuinge page* (Paris, 1657) (Wing, M2631A). The second edition (Paris, 1658) (Wing, M2632) has the title *Confessiones amantis*. For More's biography, see 'Helen [name in religion Gertrude] More', in *ODNB*. For an excellent account of More, see Marion Norman, 'Dame Gertrude More and the English Mystical Tradition', *Recusant History* 13 (1976), 196–211. For both Gascoigne and More, see Heather Wolfe, 'Reading Bells and Loose Papers: Reading and Writing Practices of the English Benedictine Nuns of Cambrai', in Burke and Gibson (eds.), *Early Modern Women's Manuscript Writing*, pp. 135–56.

49 For her remarkable life, see *ODNB*. For the ways in which Ward's life and writings might initiate new forms of British literary history, see the profound article by David Wallace, 'Periodizing Women: Mary Ward (1585–1645) and the Premodern Canon', *Journal of Medieval and Early Modern Studies* 36 (2006), 397–453.

GUIDE TO FURTHER READING

Preface

Vincent Gillespie

For a recent account of modern approaches, see Louise Nelstrop, *Christian Mysticism: An Introduction to Contemporary Theoretical Approaches* (Farnham: Ashgate, 2009).

For general histories of mystical and contemplative writing, see:

Jean Leclercq, François Vandenbroucke, and Louis Bouyer, *The Spirituality of the Middle Ages* (London: Burns and Oates, 1968).

Bernard McGinn, *The Presence of God: A History of Western Christian Mysticism* (London: SCM, 1991–).

Bernard McGinn, John Meyendorff, and Jean Leclercq (eds.), *Christian Spirituality: Origins to the Twelfth Century* (London: Routledge and Kegan Paul, 1986).

Jill Raitt, Bernard McGinn, and John Meyendorff (eds.), *Christian Spirituality: High Middle Ages and Reformation* (London: Routledge and Kegan Paul, 1987).

For a ruminative account of contemplative writing about God, full of helpful references and useful citations, see:

Charles Andre Bernard, *Le Dieu des Mystiques*, 3 vols. (Paris: CERF, 1994–2000)
————, *Theologie mystique* (Paris: CERF, 2005).

On kenosis and issues surrounding the ineffability of God, see:

C. Stephen Evans, *Exploring Kenotic Christology: The Self-emptying of God* (Oxford: Oxford University Press, 2006).

William Franke, *On What Cannot be Said: Apophatic Discourses in Philosophy, Religion, Literature, and the Arts*, 2 vols. (Notre Dame, IN: University of Notre Dame Press, 2007).

Michael Kessler and Christian Sheppard (eds.), *Mystics: Presence and Aporia* (Chicago, IL: University of Chicago Press, 2003).

Michael A. Sells, *Mystical Languages of Unsaying* (Chicago, IL: University of Chicago Press, 1994).

Chapter 1

Introduction

Nicholas Watson

For further reading on the issues raised in this chapter, see:

Giorgio Agamben, *Stanzas: Word and Phantasm in Western Culture*, trans. Ronald L. Martinez, Theory and History of Literature 69 (Minneapolis, MN: University of Minnesota Press, 1993).

David William Bebbington, *Evangelicalism in Modern Britain: A History from the 1730s to the 1980s* (London: Unwin Hyman, 1989).

Pierre Bourdieu, 'The Scholastic Point of View', *Cultural Anthropology* 5 (1990), 380–91.

_____, *Outline of A Theory of Practice*, trans. Richard Nice (Cambridge: Cambridge University Press, 1977).

Eric Colledge (later Edmund Colledge), *The Medieval Mystics of England* (New York: Scribner's, 1961).

Elizabeth A. Dreyer and Mark S. Burrows (eds.), *Minding the Spirit: The Study of Christian Spirituality* (Baltimore, MD: Johns Hopkins University Press, 2005).

Michel Foucault, *Care of the Self*, trans. Robert Hurley (London: Allen Lane, 1986).

Friedrich von Hügel, *The Mystical Element of Religion as Studied in Saint Catherine of Genoa and Her Friends*, 2 vols. (London: Clarke and Dent, 1961).

William James, *The Varieties of Religious Experience: A Study in Human Nature* (New York: Modern Library, 1929).

Stephen Katz (ed.), *Mysticism and Philosophical Analysis* (London: Sheldon, 1978).

David Knowles, *The English Mystics* (London: Burns and Oates, 1927).

Ronald Knox, *Enthusiasm: A Chapter in the History of Religion, With Special Reference to the XVII and XVIII Centuries* (Oxford: Clarendon Press, 1950).

Jean Leclercq, Françoise Vandenbroucke, and Louis Bouyer, *The Spirituality of the Middle Ages*, trans. the Benedictine of Holme Abbey (Tunbridge Wells: Burns and Oates, 1968).

Ursula Peters, *Religiose Erfahrung als literarisches Faktum: Zur Vorgeschichte und Genese frauenmystischer Texte des 13. und 14. Jahrhunderts* (Tübingen: M. Niemeyer, 1988).

Wolfgang Riehle, *The Middle English Mystics*, trans. Bernard Standring (London: Routledge and Kegan Paul, 1981).

Geoffrey Rowell, Kenneth Stevenson, Rowan Williams (eds.), *Love's Redeeming Work: The Anglican Quest for Holiness* (Oxford: Oxford University Press, 2001).

Spiritus: a journal of spirituality.

Brian Vickers (ed.), *Arbeit, Musse, Meditatio: Studies in the Vita activa and Vita contemplativa* (Zurich: Verlag der Fachvereine; Stuttgart: Teubner, 1991).

Nicholas Watson, 'The Middle English Mystics', in David Wallace (ed.), *The Cambridge History of Medieval English Literature* (Cambridge: Cambridge University Press, 1999), pp. 539–65.

On the history of mystical theology and spirituality studies, see:

Michel de Certeau, *The Mystic Fable*, trans. Michael B. Smith (Chicago, IL: Chicago University Press, 1992).

Bernard McGinn, *The Foundations of Mysticism*, vol. 1 of *The Presence of God: A History of Western Christian Mysticism* (New York: Crossroad, 1992–), pp. 263–343: Appendix: 'Theoretical Foundations: The Modern Study of Mysticism'.

Denys Turner, *The Darkness of God: Negativity in Christian Mysticism* (Cambridge: Cambridge University Press, 1995).

On *otium* as an ancient philosophical and cultural category, see:

Jean-Marie André, *L'Otium dans la vie morale et intellectuelle romaine, des origines à l'époque augustéenne* (Paris: Presses universitaires de France, 1966).

For a more general study, see:

Brian Vickers (ed.), *Arbeit, Musse, Meditation: Studies in the* Vita activa *and* Vita contemplativa (Zurich: Verlag der Fachvereine; Stuttgart: Teubner, 1991).

Peter Brown makes much of the impact of various versions of *otium* on Augustine's spiritual development in *Augustine of Hippo: A Biography* (Berkeley: University of California Press, 2000).

On the therapeutic mode, see:

Michel Foucault, *Care of the Self*, trans. Robert Hurley (London: Allen Lane, 1986).

On *otium* and the modern academy, see:

Pierre Bourdieu, 'The Scholastic Point of View', *Cultural Anthropology* 5 (1990), 380–91.

Fundamental to bibliographic work on contemplative writing is:

A. I. Doyle, 'A Survey of the Origins and Circulation of Theological Writings in English in the 14th, 15th and Early 16th Centuries with Special Consideration of the part of the Clergy Therein' (PhD thesis, University of Cambridge, 1954).

See also, e.g., Jeremy Griffiths and Derek Pearsall, *Book Production and Publishing in Britain 1375–1475* (Cambridge: Cambridge University Press, 1989), especially Vincent Gillespie: 'Vernacular Books of Religion', 317–44.

Ralph Hanna, *Pursuing History: Middle English Manuscripts and Their Texts* (Stanford: Stanford University Press, 1996).

Albert E. Hartung (ed.), *A Manual of Writings in Middle English, 1050–1500* (New Haven, CN: Connecticut Academy of Arts and Sciences, 1967–): Robert Raymo, 'Works of Religious and Philosophical Instruction' (vol. 7, 1986), chs. 20 and 23.

Valerie Lagorio and Michael G. Sargent, 'English Mystical Writings' (vol. 9, 1993).

For a recent study of the Spanish Carmelite mystics, see:

Edward Howells, *John of the Cross and Teresa of Avila: Mystical Knowing and Selfhood* (New York: Crossroad, 2002).

For an early exegesis from the viewpoint of mystical theology, see, e.g.:

Fray José de Jesus Maria, *L'apologie mystique de Quiroga: Saint Jean de la Croix et la mystique chrétienne*, trans. Jean Krynen (Toulouse: France–Iberie Recherche, 1990).

For the early twentieth-century phenomenological interest in 'mysticism', see:

Friedrich von Hügel, *The Mystical Element of Religion as Studied in Saint Catherine of Genoa and Her Friends*, 2 vols. (London: Clarke and Dent, 1961).

William James, *The Varieties of Religious Experience: A Study in Human Nature* (New York: Modern Library, 1929).

Evelyn Underhill, *Mysticism: A Study in the Nature and Development of Man's Spiritual Consciousness* (New York: Dutton, 1961).

On the assimilation of Eastern and Western meditative and contemplative traditions, see:

Thomas Merton's Paradise Journey: Writings On Contemplation, ed. William H. Shannon (Tunbridge Wells: Burns and Oates, 2000).

D. T. Suzuki, *Mysticism, Christian and Buddhist* (London: Routledge, 2002).

See also Robert Sharf, 'The Zen of Japanese Nationalism', *History of Religions* 33 (1993), 1–43.

On virginity literature, see:

Jocelyn Wogan-Browne, *Saints' Lives and Women's Literary Culture c. 1150–1300: Virginity and Its Authorizations* (Oxford: Clarendon Press, 2001).

Sarah Salih, *Versions of Virginity in Late Medieval England* (Cambridge: D. S. Brewer, 2001).

Chapter 2

c. 1080–1215: culture and history

Brian Patrick McGuire

For a broader perception of the period, see:

Charles Homer Haskins, *The Renaissance of the Twelfth Century* (Cambridge, MA: Harvard University Press, 1927).

Christopher Brooke, *The Twelfth Century Renaissance* (London: Thames and Hudson, 1969).

Robert L. Benson and Giles Constable, with Carol D. Lanham (eds.), *Renaissance and Renewal in the Twelfth Century* (Oxford: Clarendon Press, 1982).

Richard Southern, *Medieval Humanism and Other Studies* (Oxford: Blackwell, 1970), p. 140.

Colin Morris, *The Discovery of the Individual*, repr. the Medieval Academy of America in 1987, 1991, and 1995 in its series with Toronto University Press, Medieval Academy Reprints for Teaching.

On medieval monastic culture, the classic study is still:

Jean Leclercq, *The Love of Learning and the Desire for God: A Study of Monastic Culture*, trans. Catherine Misrashi (New York: Fordham University Press, 1961).
See Brian McGuire, 'Love of Learning: Remembering Jean Leclercq', *The American Benedictine Review* 57 (2006).

The former Benedictine monk and Cambridge scholar David Knowles had great insight into English monastic figures especially of the twelfth century. His work may in some respects be out of date, but his understanding of outstanding spiritual figures remains an inspiration:

David Knowles, *The Monastic Order in England: A History of its Development from the times of Saint Dunstan to the Fourth Lateran Council, 940–1216*, 2nd edn (Cambridge, 1963).
More recent is Janet Burton, *Monastic and Religious Orders in Britain 1000–1300* (Cambridge: Cambridge University Press, 1995).

For nuns, see:

Sally Thompson, *Women Religious: The Founding of English Nunneries after the Norman Conquest* (Oxford: Clarendon Press, 1991).
For the contribution of women to the spiritual life of the twelfth century in England C. H. Talbot's edition of *The Life of Christina of Markyate* is central (Oxford: Clarendon Press, 1987), now revised by Samuel Fanous and Henrietta Leyser (Oxford: Oxford University Press, 2008).
See also Samuel Fanous and Henrietta Leyser (ed.), *Christina of Markyate: A Twelfth-century Holy Woman* (London and New York: Routledge, 2005).

For Anselm of Canterbury, see:

R. W. Southern: *Saint Anselm and his Biographer: A Study of Monastic Life and Thought 1059–c. 1130* (Cambridge: Cambridge University Press, 1966) and *Saint Anselm: A Portrait in a Landscape* (Cambridge: Cambridge University Press, 1990).

For the Cistercians in general, see:

Pauline Matarasso (trans.), *The Cistercian World* (London, 1993).

For Aelred of Rievaulx, the question of his sexual orientation has bedevilled scholarship since the 1980s but can be left aside in considering his contribution to the spiritual environment of Cistercian England. See:

Brian Patrick McGuire, *Brother and Lover: Aelred of Rievaulx* (New York: Crossroad, 1994).

Also, Maurice Powicke's superb introduction to Walter Daniel's biography of Aelred is still worth reading:

The Life of Ailred of Rievaulx by Walter Daniel (Oxford: Oxford University Press, 1978).

Many of the Continental mystical theologians who may have had an effect on England have been translated in the useful series Classics of Western Spirituality, such as:

Grover A. Zinn (trans.), Richard of Saint Victor, *The Mystical Ark* (New York: Paulist, 1979).

It is noticeable that England in this period seems to have been home to a rich new visionary literature, as can be seen in the visions of the Monk of Evesham and of Thurkill. I will not examine this literature here, for it is problematic to what extent its existence reflects the contemplative spirituality. For an overview, see:

Eileen Gardiner (ed.), *Visions of Heaven and Hell before Dante* (New York: Italica Press, 1989).

For Jean of Fécamp:

Jean Leclercq, and Jean-Paul Bonnes, *Un maître de la vie spirituelle au onzième siècle: Jean de Fécamp*. Etudes de théologie et d'histoire de la spiritualité 9 (Paris: Vrin, 1946).

Chapter 3

c. 1080–1215: texts

Henrietta Leyser

On the historical context, see:

Robert Bartlett, *England under the Norman and Angevin Kings*, 1075–1225 (Oxford: Oxford University Press, 2000).

On the literary environment of this period, see:

Christopher Cannon, *The Grounds of English Literature* (Oxford: Oxford University Press, 2004).

On the devotional and theological contexts, see:

M. D. Chenu, *La théologie au douzième siècle*, in English as Jerome Taylor and Lester K. Little (eds. and trans.), *Nature, Man and Society in the Twelfth Century* (Chicago: University of Chicago Press, 1968).
Bernard McGinn, *A History of Christian Mysticism*, vol. 2 (London: SCM, 1995).
Jean Leclercq, *The Love of Learning and the Desire for God: A Study of Monastic Culture*, trans. Catherine Misrashi (NY: Fordham University Press, 1961).
Aelred Squire, *Aelred of Rievaulx: a Study* (London: SPCK, 1969).
Ann W. Astell, *The Song of Songs in the Middle Ages* (Ithaca: Cornell University Press, 1990).
Robert Boenig and William F. Pollard (eds.), *Mysticism and Spirituality in Medieval England* (Woodbridge: D. S. Brewer, 1997).
Rachel Fulton, *From Judgement to Passion: Devotion to Christ and the Virgin Mary 800–1200* (NY: Columbia University Press, 2002).

On women's spirituality and monasticism, see:

Jocelyn Wogan-Browne, *Saints' Lives and Women's Literary Culture: Virginity and its Authorisations* (Oxford: Oxford University Press, 2001).

Elizabeth Robertson, *Early English Devotional Prose and the Female Audience* (Knoxville, TN: University of Tennessee Press, 1990).

Stephanie Hollis (ed.) with W. R. Barnes, *Writing the Wilton Women: Goscelin's Legend of Edith and Liber confortatorius* (Turnhout: Brepols, 2004).

For Gilbert of Hoyland and John of Forde, see:

the entries in *ODNB*.

C. J. Holdsworth, 'John of Ford and English Cistercian Writing, 1167–1214', *TRHS* 5th ser. 2 (1961): 17–136.

H. Costello and C. Holdsworth (eds.), *A Gathering of Friends: The Learning and Spirituality of John of Forde* (Kalamazoo, MI: Cistercian Publications, 1996).

For Honorius of Autun, see:

Valerie Flint, 'The Commentaries of Honorius Augustodunensis on the *Song of Songs*', *Revue Bénédictine* 84 (1974), 196–211.

More generally on the Song, see:

Ann W. Astell, *The Song of Songs in the Middle Ages* (Ithaca, NY and London: Cornell University Press, 1990).

E. Ann Matter, *The Voice of My Beloved: The Song of Songs in Western Medieval Christianity* (Philadelphia, PN: University of Pennsylvania Press, 1990).

For a recent collection of essays on Christina of Markyate, see:

Samuel Fanous and Henrietta Leyser (eds.), *The Life of Christina of Markyate: A Twelfth-Century Holy Woman* (London: Routledge, 2005).

Chapter 4

1215–1349: culture and history

Alastair Minnis

For Innocent's life and works, see:

Jane Sayers, *Innocent III: Leader of Europe, 1198–1216* (London and New York: Longman, 1994).

James M. Powell, *Innocent III: Vicar of Christ or Lord of the World*, 2nd edn (Washington, DC: Catholic University of America Press, 1994).

On English ecclesial reform movements after Lateran 4, see:

Marion Gibbs and Jane Lang, *Bishops and Reform 1215–1272, with special reference to the Lateran Council of 1215* (London: Oxford University Press, 1934), p. 113.

W. A. Pantin, *The English Church in the Fourteenth Century* (Cambridge: Cambridge University Press, 1955), pp. 189–243.

On the development of new religious orders, see:

William A. Hinnebusch, *The History of the Dominican Order*, vol. I: *Origins and Growth to 1500* (Staten Island, NY: Alba House, 1966), pp. 93–5, 220–2, 312–17, 331.

John R. H. Moorman, *A History of the Franciscan Order from its Origins to the Year 1517* (Oxford: Clarendon Press, 1978), pp. 123–39.

Francis X. Roth, *The English Austin Friars, 1249–1538*, vol. I: *History* (New York: Augustinian Historical Institute, 1966), pp. 13–64.

Glyn Coppack and Mick Aston, *Christ's Poor Men: The Carthusians in Britain* (Stroud: Tempus, 2002).

Richard Copsey, 'The Carmelites in England 1242–1540: Surviving Writings', *Carmelus* 43 (1996), 175–224.

Bruce P. Flood, Jr., 'The Carmelite Friars in Medieval English Universities and Society, 1299–1430', *Recherches de Théologie ancienne et médiévale* 55 (1988), 154–83.

On developments in university curricula, see:

J. I. Catto (ed.), *History of the University of Oxford*, vol. I, *The Early Schools* (Oxford: Clarendon Press, 1992).

James A. Brundage, 'The Cambridge Faculty of Canon Law and the Ecclesiastical Courts of Ely', in Patrick Zutshi (ed.), *Medieval Cambridge: Essays on the Pre-Reformation University* (Woodbridge: Boydell, 1993), pp. 21–45.

On the early Franciscan *studia*, see:

Bert Roest, *A History of Franciscan Education (c. 1210–1517)* (Leiden: Brill, 2000), pp. 1–117.

On developments in contemporary theology, see:

M.-D. Chenu, *La théologie comme science au XIIIe siècle*, 3rd edn, Bibliothèque thomiste, 33 (Paris: J. Vrin, 1957).

Ulrich Köpf, *Die Anfänge der theologischen Wissenschaftstheorie im 13. Jahrhundert*, Beiträge zur historischen Theologie, 49 (Tubingen: Mohr, 1974).

On affective theology, see especially the seminal study:

Etienne Gilson, *The Mystical Theology of Saint Bernard*, trans. A. H. C. Downes (London: Sheed and Ward, 1940).

On the *artes praedicandi* see especially:

Th.-M. Charland, *Artes praedicandi: Contribution à l'histoire de la rhétorique au moyen âge* (Paris: J. Vrin, 1936).

For recent discussion of pardoners and pardoning, see:

Alastair Minnis, 'Reclaiming the Pardoners', *Journal of Medieval and Early Modern Studies* 33 (2003), 311–34.

———, 'Purchasing Pardon: Material and Spiritual Economies on the Canterbury Pilgrimage', in Lawrence Besserman (ed.), *Sacred and Secular in Medieval and Early Modern Cultures* (Houndmills: Palgrave Macmillan, 2006), pp. 63–82.

An excellent means of comparing the relevant scholarship of Thomas Gallus and Robert Grosseteste has been provided by the following editions and translations:

James McEvoy, *Mystical Theology: The Glosses by Thomas Gallus and the Commentary of Robert Grosseteste on De Mystica Theologia: Edition, Translation and Introduction*, Dallas Medieval Texts and Translations 3 (Paris: Peeters, 2003).

On Richard Fishacre, see especially:

R. James Long and Maura O'Carroll, *The Life and Works of Richard Fishacre OP*: Prolegomena to the Edition of his Commentary on the Sentences (Munich: Bayerischen Akademie der Wissenschaften, 1999).

On Thomas Bradwardine, see especially:

Edith Dolnikowski, *Thomas Bradwardine: A View of Time and a Vision of Eternity in Fourteenth-Century Thought* (Leiden: Brill, 1995).
H. A. Oberman, *Archbishop Thomas Bradwardine: A Fourteenth-Century Augustinian* (Utrecht: Kemink and Zoon, 1957).

On Trevet and the later 'classicizing friars', see:

Beryl Smalley, *English Friars and Antiquity in the Early Fourteenth Century* (Oxford: Blackwell, 1960).

For Trevet's knowledge of the Anglo-Saxon Boethius, see:

Brian Donaghey, 'Nicholas Trevet's Use of King Alfred's Translation of Boethius, and the Dating of his Commentary', in Alastair Minnis (ed.), *The Medieval Boethius: Studies in the Vernacular translations of De Consolatione Philosophiae* (Woodbridge: D. S. Brewer, 1987), pp. 1–31.

Chapter 5

1215–1349: texts

Denis Renevey

On *Ancrene Wisse* and its context, see:

Bella Millett: '*Ancrene Wisse* and the Book of Hours', in Denis Renevey and Christiania Whitehead (eds.), *Writing Religious Women: Female Spiritual and Textual Practices in Late Medieval England* (Cardiff: University of Wales Press, 2000), pp. 21–40.
———, 'The Origins of *Ancrene Wisse*: New Answers, New Questions', *Medium Ævum* 61 (1992), 206–28.
Cate Gunn, *Ancrene Wisse: From Pastoral Literature to Vernacular Spirituality*, Religion and Culture in the Middle Ages (Cardiff: University of Wales Press, 2008).
Bella Millett, '*Ancrene Wisse* and the Conditions of Confession', *English Studies* 80 (1999), 193–215.

See also:

Cate Gunn, 'Beyond the Tomb: *Ancrene Wisse* and Lay Piety', in Liz Herbert McAvoy and Mari Hughes-Edwards (eds.), *Anchorites, Wombs and Tombs: Intersections of Gender and Enclosure in the Middle Ages*, (Cardiff: University of Wales Press, 2005), pp. 161–71.

For a view which, like the one offered here, argues for a possible lay audience for *Ancrene Wisse* from the onset, see:

Robert Hasenfratz, '"Efter hire euene": Lay Audiences and the Variable Asceticism of *Ancrene Wisse*', *Anchorites, Wombs and Tombs*, pp. 145–60.

For a consideration of the manuscripts, see:

Yoko Wada, 'What is *Ancrene Wisse*', in Yoko Wada (ed.), *A Companion to* Ancrene Wisse (Woodbridge: Boydell and Brewer, 2003), pp. 1–28.

For generic complexity, see in the same volume:

Bella Millett, 'The Genre of *Ancrene Wisse*', pp. 29–44.

For a study of the influence of anchoritic texts, more particularly *Ancrene Wisse*, on the making of the Book of Hours for use of the laity, see:

Bella Millett, '*Ancrene Wisse* and the Book of Hours', in Denis Renevey and Christiania Whitehead (eds.), *Writing Religious Women: Female Spiritual and Textual Practices in Late Medieval England* (Cardiff: University of Wales Press, 2000), pp. 21–40.

For an historical discussion based on the patronage of anchorites, see:

Ann K. Warren, *Anchorites and their Patrons in Medieval England* (Berkeley, Los Angeles, and London: University of California Press, 1985).

On the physical and symbolic significance of enclosure, see:

Christopher Cannon, 'Enclosure', in Carolyn Dinshaw and David Wallace (eds.), *The Cambridge Companion to Medieval Women's Writing* (Cambridge: Cambridge University Press, 2003), pp. 109–23.
———,'The Form of the Self: *Ancrene Wisse* and Romance', *Medium Ævum* 70 (2001), 47–65.
Christopher Cannon, *The Grounds of English Literature* (Oxford: Oxford University Press, 2004), pp. 139–71.

For a view that, although not denying the importance of enclosure, nevertheless stresses the notion of community and exchange within the anchoritic culture, see:

Denis Renevey, 'Early Middle English Writings for Women: *Ancrene Wisse*', David F. Johnson and Elaine M. Treharne (eds.), *Readings in Medieval Texts: Interpreting Old and Middle English Literature* (Oxford: Oxford University Press, 2005), pp. 198–212.
Catherine Batt, Denis Renevey, and Christiania Whitehead, 'Domesticity and Medieval Devotional Literature', *Leeds Studies in English* 36 (2005), 195–250.

The AB language is the early Middle English dialect from the West Midland area as preserved in Cambridge, Corpus Christi College MS 402 (*Ancrene Wisse*) and Oxford, Bodleian Library, MS Bodley 34 ('Katherine Group'). For a recent discussion of this dialect, see:

Richard Dance, 'The AB Language: the Recluse, the Gossip and the Language Historian', in *A Companion to Ancrene Wisse*, pp. 57–82.

On the literary religious culture written for or by women in the Anglo-Norman language, see:

Jocelyn Wogan-Browne, *Saint's Lives and Women's Literary Culture c. 1150–1300* (Oxford: Oxford University Press, 2001).

On translation theory and practice in this period, and the trilingual cultural context, see:

Roger Ellis (ed.), *The Oxford History of Literary Translation in English*, Vol. I, *To 1550* (Oxford: Oxford University Press, 2008). See also Vincent Gillespie, 'Vernacular Theology', in Paul Strohm (ed.), *Middle English Oxford Twenty-First Century Approaches to Literature* (Oxford: Oxford University Press, 2007), pp. 401–20.

On virginity literature and the state of virginity in general, see:

Anke Bernau, Ruth Evans, and Sarah Salih (eds.), *Medieval Virginities* (Cardiff: University of Wales Press, 2003).

On the popularity of the virgin martyrs' legends among the laity in medieval Europe, see:

Sarah Salih, *Versions of Virginity in Late Medieval England* (Woodbridge: D. S. Brewer, 2001), pp. 46–50.

For a discussion of the feminization of Christ, see:

Caroline Walker Bynum, *Jesus as Mother: Studies in the Spirituality of the High Middle Ages* (Berkeley and Los Angeles: University of California Press, 1982).
_____, *Holy Feast and Holy Fast: The Religious Significance of Food to Medieval Women* (Berkeley and Los Angeles: University of California Press, 1987).
Barbara Newman, *From Virile Woman to Woman Christ* (Philadelphia: University of Pennsylvania Press, 1997).

For a detailed analysis of the Wooing Group, see:

Denis Renevey, 'Enclosed Desires: A Study of the Wooing Group', in W. F. Pollard and R. Boenig, *Mysticism and Spirituality in Medieval England* (Woodbridge: D. S. Brewer, 1997), pp. 39–62.
Susannah Mary Chewning, 'Mysticism and the Anchoritic Community: "A Time . . . of Veiled Infinity"', in Diane Watt (ed.), *Medieval Women and their Communities* (Cardiff: University of Wales Press, 1997), pp. 116–37.
_____, 'Gladly Alone, Gladly Silent: Isolation and Exile in the Anchoritic Mystical Experience', in *Anchorites, Wombs and Tombs*, pp. 103–15.
_____(ed.), *The Milieu and Context of the Wohunge Group* (Cardiff: University of Wales Press, forthcoming).

For a study of the accommodation of 'The Wooing Group' into *A Talkyng*, see:

Denis Renevey, 'The Choices of the Compiler: Vernacular Hermeneutics in *A Talkyng of þe Loue of God*', in R. Ellis, R. Tixier, and B. Weitemeier (eds.), *The Medieval Translator VI* (Turnhout: Brepols, 1998), pp. 232–53.

For discussions of later adaptations of *Ancrene Wisse* geared for a non-anchoritic audience, see:

Cate Gunn, 'Beyond the Tomb', pp. 165–7.

Nicholas Watson, '*Ancrene Wisse*, Religious Reform and the Late Middle Ages', in Yoko Wada (ed.), *A Companion to 'Ancrene Wisse'* (Woodbridge: D. S. Brewer, 2003), pp. 197–26.

Catherine Innes-Parker, 'The Legacy of *Ancrene Wisse*: Translations, Adaptations, Influences and Audience, with Special Attention to Women Readers', in Wada (ed.) *A Companion*, pp. 145–73.

On Rolle, the key recent monographs are:

Nicholas Watson, *Richard Rolle and the Invention of Authority* (Cambridge: Cambridge University Press, 1991).

Denis Renevey, *Language, Self and Love: Hermeneutics in the Writings of Richard Rolle and the Commentaries on the Song of Songs* (Cardiff: University of Wales Press, 2001).

Claire Elizabeth McIlroy, *The English Prose Treatises of Richard Rolle* (Woodbridge: D. S. Brewer, 2004).

For recent texts, see:

Ralph Hanna (ed.), *Richard Rolle: Uncollected Prose and Verse with Related Northern Texts*, EETS OS 329 (2007).

Chapter 6

1349–1412: culture and history

Jeremy Catto

Editions of the primary texts underlying this chapter are:

Epistolario di Santa Caterina da Siena, ed. E. Dupré Theseider (Rome, Fonti per la Storia d'Italia, 1940).

Phyllis Hodgson, *The Cloud of Unknowing and the Book of Privy Counselling*, EETS OS 218 (1944; repr. 1981).

P. H. Barnum (ed.), *Dives and Pauper*, 3 vols. EETS OS 275, 280, 323 (1976–2004).

J. P. H. Clark and Cheryl Taylor (eds.), *Walter Hilton's Latin Writings*, 2 vols., *Analecta Cartusiana* 104 (Salzburg 1987).

C. J. Ogilvie-Thomson (ed.), *Walter Hilton's Mixed Life* (Salzburg: Institut für Anglistik und Amerikanistik, 1986).

E. J. F. Arnould (ed.), Henry Duke of Lancaster, *Livre de seyntz médicines* (Oxford, Anglo-Norman Texts, 1940).

Edmund Colledge and James Walsh, *Showing to the Anchoress Julian of Norwich*, 2 vols. (Toronto: Pontifical Institute of Mediaeval Studies, 1978).

J. P. H. Clark (ed.), *Nubes Ignorandi*, *Analecta Cartusiana* 119 (Salzburg: Institut für Anglistik und Amerikanistik, 1989).

L. F. Sanders (ed.), *Omne Bonum*, 2 vols. (London: Harvey Miller, 1996).

R. Morris (ed.), *The Pricke of Conscience* (London: Philological Society, 1863).

R. O'Brien (ed.), William Rymington, *Meditationes sive Stimulus Peccatoris*, Cîteaux 16 (1965), 278–304.

F. D. Matthew (ed.), *The English Works of Wyclif hitherto Unprinted*, EETS OS 74 (1880).

Hope Emily Allen, *Writings Ascribed to Richard Rolle Hermit of Hampole* (New York: MLA and London: Oxford University Press, 1927).

On monastic meditative practice, see, for example:

D. H. Farmer, 'The Meditations of the Monk of Farne', *Analecta Monastica* 4 (1956), 141–245; D. H. Farmer, 'The *Meditatio devota* of Uthred of Boldon', *Analecta Monastica* 5 (1958), 187–206.

On Carthusian interest and possible circulation of contemplative texts, see:

M. G. Sargent, 'Transmission by the English Carthusians of some late medieval spiritual writings', *JEH* 27 (1977), 225–40.

M. G. Sargent, 'Contemporary criticism of Richard Rolle', *Analecta Cartusiana* 55 (Salzburg: Institut für Anglistik und Amerikanistik, 1981), 160–205.

A. I. Doyle, 'Carthusian participation in the movement of works of Richard Rolle between England and other parts of Europe in the 14th and 15th centuries', *Analecta Cartusiana* 55 (Salzburg: Institut für Anglistik und Amerikanistik, 1982), 109–20.

A. I. Doyle, 'Publication by members of the religious orders', in Jeremy Griffiths and Derek Pearsall, *Book Production and Publishing in Britain 1375–1475* (Cambridge: Cambridge University Press), pp. 109–23.

Vincent Gillespie, 'The *Cibus Anime* Book 3: a guide for contemplatives?', *Analecta Cartusiana* 35 (Salzburg: Institut für Anglistik und Amerikanistik, 1983), 90–119.

On Nicholas Love, see:

S. Ogura, R. Beadle and M. G. Sargent, *Nicholas Love at Waseda* (Woodbridge: D. S. Brewer, 1997); M. G. Sargent (ed.), *Nicholas Love's Mirror of the Blessed Life of Jesus Christ* (Exeter: Exeter University Press, 2005).

On the theory and practice of the pastoral care in the period, see:

L. E. Boyle, 'The *Oculus Sacerdotis* of William of Pagula', *TRHS* 5th ser. 5 (1955), 81–110.

Vincent Gillespie, 'The Evolution of the *Speculum Christiani*', in A. J. Minnis (ed.), *Latin and Vernacular: Studies in Late Mediaeval Texts and Manuscripts*, in (Woodbridge: Boydell, 1989), 39–62.

Jonathan Hughes, *Pastors and Visionaries* (Woodbridge: Boydell, 1988) offers a case study of the late fourteenth-century *familia* of Thomas Arundel while he was Archbishop of York, and explores their interest in contemplation and in pastoral care.

Two important unpublished studies on the period are:

Charles Everitt, 'Eloquence as Profession and Art', (D.Phil. thesis, University of Oxford), 1985.

Nicholas Heale, 'Religious and intellectual interests at St Edmund's Abbey at Bury and the nature of English Benedictinism, c. 1350–1450' (D.Phil. thesis, University of Oxford, 1994) esp. pp. 190–211.

Chapter 7

1349–1412: texts

Roger Ellis and Samuel Fanous

For recent discussion of writers covered in this chapter, see, for example:

Marion Glasscoe, *English Medieval Mystics: Games of Faith* (London: Longman, 1993).

Nicholas Watson, 'The Middle English Mystics', in David Wallace (ed.), *The Cambridge History of Medieval English Literature* (Cambridge: Cambridge University Press, 1999), pp. 539–65.

Helen Phillips (ed.), *Langland, the Mystics and the Medieval English Religious Tradition* (Woodbridge: D. S. Brewer, 1990).

William F. Pollard and Robert Boenig (eds.), *Mysticism and Spirituality in Medieval England* (Woodbridge: D. S. Brewer, 1997).

A. S. G. Edwards (ed.), *A Companion to Middle English Prose* (Turnhout: Brepols, 2000).

Dee Dyas, Valerie Edden, and Roger Ellis (eds.), *Approaching Medieval English Anchoritic and Mystical Texts* (Woodbridge: D. S. Brewer, 2005).

Older discussions (though still with much to commend them) include:

Edmund College (ed.), *The Medieval Mystics of England* (London: Murray, 1962).

Wolfgang Riehle, *The Middle English Mystics*, trans. Bernard Standring (London: Routledge and Kegan Paul, 1971).

On the apophatic tradition, see:

Denys Turner, *The Darkness of God: Negativity in Christian Mysticism* (Cambridge: Cambridge University Press, 1995).

On Lollardy, see:

Anne Hudson, *The Premature Reformation: Wycliffite Texts and Lollard History* (Oxford: Clarendon Press, 1988).

Secondary literature on Julian includes:

Brant Pelphrey, *Love Was His Meaning: The Theology and Mysticism of Julian of Norwich* (Salzburg: Institut für Anglistik und Amerikanistik, 1982).

Sandra J. McEntire (ed.), *Julian of Norwich: A Book of Essays* (New York, 1998).

Liz Herbert McAvoy (ed.), *A Companion to Julian of Norwich* (Woodbridge: Boydell, 2008).

Secondary literature on the *Cloud* includes:

Turner, *Darkness of God*, pp. 186–210.

Annie Sutherland, 'The Dating and Authorship of the *Cloud* Corpus: A Reassessment of the Evidence', *Medium Ævum* 71 (2002), 82–100.

On the *Scale* see:

Joseph E. Milosh, '*The Scale of Perfection' and the English Mystical Tradition* (Madison: University of Wisconsin Press, 1966).

A. J. Minnis, 'Affection and Imagination in *The Cloud of Unknowing* and Hilton's *Scale of Perfection*', *Traditio* 39 (1983), 326–66.

A convenient anthology of texts is found in:

Barry Windeatt (ed.), *English Mystics of the Middle Ages* (Cambridge: Cambridge University Press, 1994).

For the cultural context of this period, see:

Peter Brown (ed.), *A Companion to Medieval English Literature and Culture c. 1350–c. 1500* (Oxford: Blackwell, 2007).

Also very relevant is:

James Simpson, *Reform and Cultural Revolution*, The Oxford English Literary History Vol. II *1350–1547* (Oxford: Oxford University Press, 2002).

Generally, see:

Vincent Gillespie, 'Religious Writing', in Roger Ellis (ed.), *The Oxford History of Literary Translation in English*, Vol. I, *To 1500*, pp. 234–83 (Oxford: Oxford University Press, 2008), discusses the broad sweep of religious texts translated into or from English in the medieval period.

Michael G. Sargent (ed.), *De Cella in Seculum: Religious and Secular Life and Devotion in Late Medieval England* (Woodbridge: Boydell, 1988), which provides a good collection of essays on the increasingly permeable interface between lay, clerical and monastic lives.

On the lyrics generally, see:

Thomas G. Duncan (ed.), *A Companion to the Middle English Lyric* (Woodbridge: D.S. Brewer, 2005).

On the religious lyrics see:

Rosemary Woolf, *The English Religious Lyric in the Middle Ages* (Oxford: Clarendon Press, 1968).

Douglas Gray, *Themes and Images in the Medieval English Religious Lyric* (London: Routledge and Kegan Paul, 1972).

Chapter 8

1412–1534: culture and history

Vincent Gillespie

For recent assessments of the religious policies of Henry V and Henry VIII, see:

C. T. Allmand, *Henry V*, new edn (New Haven: Yale University Press, 1997).

Christopher Haigh, *English Reformations: Religion, Politics, and Society under the Tudors* (Oxford: Clarendon Press, 1993).

G. W. Bernard, *The King's Reformation: Henry VIII and the Remaking of the English Church* (New Haven: Yale University Press, 2005).

For a recent provocative and insightful overview of the ecclesiastical history of Europe in this period, see:

John Van Engen, 'Multiple Options: The World of the Fifteenth-Century Church', *Church History*, 77 (2008), 257–84.

For a highly flavoured account of late-medieval English religious life, see:

Eamon Duffy, *The Stripping of the Altars: Traditional Religion in England 1400–1580* (London: Yale University Press, 1992).
———, 'Religious Belief', in Rosemary Horrox and W. M. Ormrod (eds.), *A Social History of England 1200–1500* (Cambridge: Cambridge University Press, 2006), 293–339.
———, *Marking the Hours: English People and Their Prayers 1240–1570* (London: Yale University Press, 2006).

On the visionary writing provoked by the Schism, see:

Renate Blumenfeld-Kosinski, *Poets, Saints, and Visionaries of the Great Schism, 1378–1417* (University Park, PA: Pennsylvania State University Press, 2006).
Kathryn Kerby-Fulton, *Reformist Apocalypticism and Piers Plowman* (Cambridge: Cambridge University Press, 1990).
———, *Books under Suspicion: Censorship and Tolerance of Revelatory Writing in Late Medieval England* (Notre Dame, IN: University of Notre Dame Press, 2006).

For recent work on John Lydgate, see, for example:

James Simpson, *Reform and Cultural Revolution: The Oxford English Literary History*, vol. II: *1350–1547* (Oxford: Oxford University Press, 2002), pp. 34–67.
Maura Nolan, *John Lydgate and the Making of Public Culture* (Cambridge: Cambridge University Press, 2005).
Robert John Meyer-Lee, *Poets and Power from Chaucer to Wyatt* (Cambridge: Cambridge University Press, 2007).
Shannon Gayk, 'Images of Pity: The Regulatory Aesthetics of John Lydgate's Religious Lyrics', *Studies in the Age of Chaucer* 28 (2006), 175–203.

For a brief introduction to the Conciliar Movement, and a translated selection of key documents, see:

C. M. D. Crowder, *Unity, Heresy and Reform, 1378–1460: The Conciliar Response to the Great Schism* (London: Edward Arnold, 1977).
John Hine Mundy and Kennerly M. Woody (eds.), *The Council of Constance. The Unification of the Church*, trans. Louise Ropes Loomis (New York: Columbia University Press, 1961).

On the European reformist orthodoxy with which English bishops would have come into contact at the Councils, see, for example:

Brian Patrick McGuire, *Jean Gerson and the Last Medieval Reformation* (University Park, PA: Pennsylvania State University Press, 2005).
Brian Patrick McGuire (ed.), *A Companion to Jean Gerson* (Leiden: Brill, 2006).

For an outline of Chichele's biography and career (and that of many of the ecclesiasts mentioned here), see the relevant entries in *ODNB*.

E. F. Jacob, *Archbishop Henry Chichele* (London: Nelson, 1967) is still a useful introduction.

Chichele's church has tended to be overshadowed by an emphasis in recent scholarship on the 1409 decrees of Archbishop Thomas Arundel, in the wake of:

Nicholas Watson, 'Censorship and Cultural Change in Late-Medieval England: Vernacular Theology, the Oxford Translation Debate, and Arundel's Constitutions of 1409', *Speculum* 70 (1995), 822–64.

Many subsequent users of Watson's argument have failed to be as subtle and nuanced in their interpretations as he is. For a critique of this emphasis, see:

Vincent Gillespie, 'Vernacular Theology', in Paul Strohm (ed.), *Middle English* (Oxford: Oxford University Press, 2007), 401–20.

The best guide to much of this material is Jeremy Catto: see, for example:

'Religious Change under Henry V', in G. L. Harriss (ed.), *Henry V: The Practice of Kingship* (Oxford: Oxford University Press, 1985), pp. 97–115.
'Wyclif and Wycliffism at Oxford 1356–1430' and 'Theology after Wycliffism', both in *History of the University of Oxford*, vol. II, pp. 175–261 and pp. 263–80.
————, 'The Burden and Conscience of Government in the Fifteenth Century', *TRHS*, 6th ser. 17 (2007), 83–99.

On Lollardy and its continuing influence, see:

Fiona Somerset, Jill C. Havens, and Derrick G. Pitard (eds.), *Lollards and Their Influence in Late Medieval England* (Woodbridge: Boydell, 2003).
Robert Lutton and Elisabeth Salter (eds.), *Pieties in Transition: Religious Practices and Experiences, c.1400–1640* (Aldershot: Ashgate, 2007).
Robert Lutton, *Lollardy and Orthodox Religion in Pre-Reformation England: Reconstructing Piety* (Woodbridge: Boydell, 2006).

On developments in parish and institutional life, see:

Clive Burgess and Eamon Duffy (eds.), *The Parish in Late Medieval England: Proceedings of the 2002 Harlaxton Symposium* (Harlaxton Medieval Studies, 14, Donington: Shaun Tyas, 2006).
Clive Burgess and Martin Heale (eds.), *The Late Medieval English College and Its Context* (Woodbridge: York Medieval Press, 2008).

Important new work is being done on the religious life of London in this period. See, for example:

Caroline M. Barron, *London in the Later Middle Ages: Government and People, 1200–1500* (Oxford: Oxford University Press, 2004).
Caroline M. Barron and Anne F. Sutton (eds.), *Medieval London Widows, 1300–1500* (London: Hambledon, 1994).
Rosemary Horrox and W. M. Ormrod (eds.), *A Social History of England, 1200–1500* (Cambridge: Cambridge University Press, 2006).
Sheila Lindenbaum, 'London Texts and Literate Practice', in David Wallace (ed.), *The Cambridge History of Medieval English Literature* (Cambridge: Cambridge University Press, 1999), 284–309.

Matthew P. Davies and Andrew Prescott (eds.), *London and the Kingdom: Essays in Honour of Caroline M. Barron* (Harlaxton Medieval Studies 16, Donington: Shaun Tyas, 2008).

David R. M. Gaimster and Roberta Gilchrist (eds.), *The Archeology of Reformation 1480–1580: Papers Given at the Archeology of Reformation Conference, February 2001* (Leeds: Maney, 2003).

On new approaches to the religious writing of this period, see:

Vincent Gillespie and Kantik Ghosh (eds.), *After Arundel: Religious Writing in Fifteenth-Century England* (Turnhout: Brepols, forthcoming, 2011).

On the book history of the period, see:

Jeremy Griffiths and Derek Pearsall (eds.), *Book Production and Publishing in Britain, 1375–1475* (Cambridge: Cambridge University Press, 1989) is still a useful starting point.

More recently, see:

A. S. G. Edwards, Vincent Gillespie, and Ralph Hanna (eds.), *The English Medieval Book: Studies in Memory of Jeremy Griffiths* (London: The British Library, 2000).

Margaret Connolly and Linne R. Mooney (eds.), *Design and Distribution of Late Medieval Manuscripts in England* (York Medieval Press, Woodbridge: Boydell, 2008).

For recent work on Carthusian books and readers, see:

Jessica Brantley, *Reading in the Wilderness: Private Devotion and Public Performance in Late Medieval England* (Chicago: University of Chicago Press, 2007).

Julian M. Luxford (ed.), *Studies in Carthusian Monasticism in the Late Middle Ages* (Turnhout: Brepols, 2008).

For references to recent work, and some scepticism about the agency of the Carthusians, see:

Vincent Gillespie, 'Dial M for Mystic: Mystical Texts in the Library of Syon Abbey and the Spirituality of the Syon Brethren', in *MMTE VI*, pp. 241–68.

In addition to Michael Sargent's seminal article ('The Transmission by the English Carthusians of Some Late Medieval Spiritual Writings', *Journal of Ecclesiastical History* 27 (1976), 225–40), key discussions are:

A. I. Doyle, 'Carthusian Participation in the Movement of Works of Richard Rolle between England and Other Parts of Europe in the 14th and 15th Centuries'.

James Hogg (ed.), *Kartäusermystik und -Mystiker, Analecta Cartusiana* 55.2 (Salzburg: Institut für Anglistik und Amerikanistik, 1981), 109–20.

A. I. Doyle, 'Publication by Members of the Religious Orders', in Griffiths and Pearsall, *Book Production*, pp. 109–23.

A. I. Doyle, 'Book Production by the Monastic Orders in England (c. 1375–1530): Assessing the Evidence', in Linda L. Brownrigg (ed.), *Medieval Book Production: Assessing the Evidence* (Los Altos, CA: Anderson-Lovelace, 1990), 1–19.

James Hogg, 'The Contribution of the Brigittine Order to Late Medieval English Spirituality', *Kartäusermystic und -Mystiker, Analecta Cartusiana* 35.3 (Salzburg: Institut für Anglistik und Amerikanistik, 1981), 153–74.

See also:

Vincent Gillespie, '"Hid Divinite": The Spirituality of the English Syon Brethren', in *MMTE VII*, pp. 189–206.

On women's reading inside and outside convents, see:

David N. Bell, *What Nuns Read: Books and Libraries in Medieval English Nunneries* (Kalamazoo, MI: Cistercian, 1995).

Mary Erler, *Women, Reading, and Piety in Late Medieval England* (Cambridge: Cambridge University Press, 2002).

Rebecca Krug, *Reading Families: Women's Literate Practice in Late Medieval England* (Ithaca: Cornell University Press, 2002).

The standard account of the foundation of Syon is still:

George James Aungier, *The History and Antiquities of Syon Monastery, the Parish of Isleworth, and the Chapelry of Hounslow, Compiled from Public Records, Ancient Manuscripts, Etc* (London: J. B. Nichols, 1840).

See also Neil Beckett, 'St Bridget, Henry V and Syon Abbey', in James Hogg (ed.), *Studies in St. Birgitta and the Brigittine Order, Analecta Cartusiana* 35.19 (Salzburg: Institut für Anglistik und Amerikanistik, 1993), 125–50.

The standard discussion of early fifteenth-century English humanism has for many years been:

Roberto Weiss, *Humanism in England During the Fifteenth Century* (3rd edn; Oxford: Blackwell, 1967).

Exciting new work is now underway: see, for example:

James G. Clark, *A Monastic Renaissance at St. Albans: Thomas Walsingham and His Circle, C. 1350–1440* (Oxford: Clarendon Press, Oxford University Press, 2004).

Andrew Cole, 'Heresy and Humanism' in Paul Strohm (ed.), *Middle English* (Oxford: Oxford University Press, 2007), pp. 421–37.

Daniel Wakelin, *Humanism, Reading, and English Literature, 1430–1530* (Oxford: Oxford University Press, 2007).

On early printing, see the useful essays in Lotte Hellinga and J. B. Trapp (eds.), *The Cambridge History of the Book in Britain,* vol. III: *1440–1557* (Cambridge: Cambridge University Press, 1999).

Martin Davies (ed.), *Incunabula: Studies in Fifteenth-Century Books Presented to Lotte Hellinga*, The British Library Studies in the History of the Book (London: British Library, 1999).

Martha W. Driver, *The Image in Print: Book Illustration in Late Medieval England and Its Sources* (London: British Library, 2004).

On the sixteenth-century bishops and the new learning, see, for example:

Richard Rex, *The Theology of John Fisher* (Cambridge: Cambridge University Press, 1991).
Brendan Bradshaw and Eamon Duffy (eds.), *Humanism, Reform and the Reformation: The Career of Bishop John Fisher* (Cambridge: Cambridge University Press, 1989).

On saints' lives, see:

Oliver Pickering in A. S. G. Edwards, *A Companion to Middle English Prose* (Cambridge: D. S. Brewer, 2004), pp. 249–70.
Karen A. Winstead, 'Saintly Exemplarity', in Paul Strohm (ed.), *Middle English* (Oxford: Oxford University Press, 2007), 335–51, with excellent further reading.

Chapter 9

1412–1534: texts

Barry Windeatt

On devotional and meditative reading practice in the period, see:

Jessica Brantley, *Reading in the Wilderness: Private Devotion and Public Performance in Late Medieval England* (Chicago: University of Chicago Press, 2007).
Jennifer Bryan, *Looking Inward: Devotional Reading and the Private Self in Late Medieval England* (Philadelphia, 2008: University of Pennsylvania Press).

On women's spirituality, and the difficulties in its expression and valorisation, see:

J. Dor *et al.* (eds.), *New Trends in Feminine Spirituality: The Holy Women of Liège and Their Import* (Turnhout, 1998: Brepols).
Dyan Elliott, *Proving Woman: Female Spirituality and Inquisitional Culture in the Later Middle Ages* (Princeton: Princeton University Press, 2004).

On the (often gendered) suspicion and attempted institutional control of visionary and contemplative experiences, see:

Rosalynn Voaden, *God's Words, Women's Voices: The Discernment of Spirits in the Writing of Late-Medieval Women Visionaries* (Woodbridge: Boydell and Brewer, 1999).
Kathryn Kerby-Fulton, *Books under Suspicion: Censorship and Tolerance of Revelatory Writing in Late Medieval England* (Notre Dame, IN: University of Notre Dame Press, 2006).

On the reception of Margery Kempe, see:

Barry Windeatt, 'Reading and Re-Reading *The Book of Margery Kempe*', in John H. Arnold and Katherine J. Lewis (eds.), *A Companion to The Book of Margery Kempe* (Woodbridge: D. S. Brewer, 2004), pp. 1–16.
A. C. Spearing, '*The Book of Margery Kempe*; or, The Diary of a Nobody', *The Southern Review* 38 (2002), 625–35.

Barry Windeatt, '"I use but comownycacyon and good wordys": Teaching and *The Book of Margery Kempe*', in Dee Dyas, Valerie Edden, and Roger Ellis (eds.), *Approaching Medieval English Anchoritic and Mystical Texts* (Woodbridge: D. S. Brewer, 2005), pp. 115–28.

On Elizabeth Barton, see:

E. J. Devereux, 'Elizabeth Barton and Tudor Censorship', *Bulletin of the John Rylands Library* 49 (1966), 91–106; Richard Rex, 'The Execution of the Holy Maid of Kent', *Historical Research* 64 (1991), 216–220; Diane Watt, 'The Prophet at Home: Elizabeth Barton and the Influence of Bridget of Sweden and Catherine of Siena', in Rosalynn Voaden (ed.), *Prophets Abroad: The Reception of Continental Holy Women in Late Medieval England* (Cambridge: Cambridge University Press, 1996), pp. 161–76.

Diane Watt, *Secretaries of God: Women Prophets in Late Medieval and Early Modern England* (Woodbridge: D. S. Brewer, 1997), pp. 1–14, 51–80.

Sharon L. Jansen, *Dangerous Talk and Strange Behavior: Women and Popular Resistance to the Reforms of Henry VIII* (Basingstoke: St. Martin's Press, 1996).

Ethan H. Shagan, *Popular Politics and the English Reformation* (Cambridge: Cambridge University Press, 2003).

Dyan Elliott, *Proving Woman: Female Spirituality and Inquisitional Culture in the Later Middle Ages* (Princeton: Princeton University Press, 2004), pp. 264–96.

On Birgitta's career and achievement, see:

Claire L. Sahlin, *Birgitta of Sweden and the Voice of Prophecy* (Woodbridge: Boydell, 2001).

For textual networks and communities, and transferral of ownership of devotional books, including some contemplative texts, at less exalted social levels, see:

Mary C. Erler, *Women, Reading, and Piety in Late Medieval England* (Cambridge: Cambridge University Press, 2002).

―――, 'Devotional Literature' in Lotte Hellinga and J. B. Trapp (eds.), *The Book in Britain, Volume III 1400–1557* (Cambridge: Cambridge University Press, 1999), pp. 495–525.

Rice, Nicole R., *Lay Piety and Religious Discipline in Middle English Literature* (Cambridge: Cambridge University Press, 2008).

On aspects of the highly visual meditative and devotional culture of this period, see:

A. A. Macdonald, H. M. B. Ridderbos and R. M. Schluseman (eds.), *The Broken Body: Passion Devotion in Late-Medieval Culture* (Groningen, 1998: Egbert Forsten).

Ellen Ross, *The Grief of God: Images of the Suffering Jesus in Late Medieval England* (New York: Oxford University Press, 1997).

Sarah Stanbury, *The Visual Object of Desire in Late Medieval England* (Philadelphia, PA: University of Pennsylvania Press, 2008).

For a useful collection of less well-known texts from this period, see:

A. C Bartlett and T. H. Bestul (eds.), *Cultures of Piety: Medieval English Devotional Literature in Translation* (Ithaca, NY: University of Cornell Press, 1999).

Chapter 10

1534–1550s: culture and history

James P. Carley and Ann M. Hutchison

For a magisterial perspective on the European scene, see Diarmaid MacCulloch, *Reformation: Europe's House Divided 1490–1700* (London and New York: Penguin, 2003).

For recent overviews of the religious politics of the period, see:

Alistair Fox and John Guy (eds.), *Reassessing the Henrician Age. Humanism, Politics and Reform 1500–1550* (Oxford: Blackwell, 1986).
G. W. Bernard, *The King's Reformation: Henry VIII and the Remaking of the English Church* (New Haven and London: Yale University Press, 2005).
Peter Marshall, *Religious Identities in Henry VIII's England* (Aldershot: Ashgate, 2006).
Richard Rex, *Henry VIII and the English Reformation*, 2nd edn (Basingstoke: Palgrave, 2006).

On literary politics in the same period, see:

Tom Betteridge, *Literature and Politics in the English Reformation* (Manchester: Manchester University Press, 2004).
Greg Walker, *Writing Under Tyranny: English Literature and the Henrician Reformation* (Oxford: Oxford University Press, 2005).

On Elizabeth Barton, see the further reading for ch. 9.

On Cromwell and his use of propaganda in the religious upheavals of the 1530s, see:

G. R. Elton, *Policy and Police: The Enforcement of the Reformation in the Age of Thomas Cromwell* (Cambridge: Cambridge University Press, 1972).

For the continuing and evolving tradition of Bonaventuran meditation of the life of Christ, see:

M. I. Bodenstedt, *The Vita Christi of Ludolphus the Carthusian* (Washington, DC: Catholic University of America Press, 1944).
Michael G. Sargent (ed.), *Nicholas Love. The Mirror of the Blessed Life of Jesus Christ: a full critical edition* (Exeter: Exeter University Press, 2005).
Alexandra Da Costa, 'John Fewterer's *Myrrour or Glasse of Christes Passion* and Ulrich Pinder's *Speculum Passionis Domini Nostri*', *Notes and Queries* 56:1 (2009), 27–29.
W. F. Pollard and R. Boenig (eds.), *Mysticism and Spirituality in Medieval England* (Woodbridge: Boydell, 1997).

On Richard Whitford, see: *ODNB*.

James Hogg, 'Richard Whytford: A Forgotten Spiritual Guide', *Studies in Spirituality* 15 (2005), 129–42.
Ann M. Hutchinson, 'Richard Whitford's *The Pype or Tonne, of the Lyfe of Perfection*: Pastoral Care or Political Manifesto?', in Claes Gejrot, Sara Risberg and Mia Åkestam (eds.), *Saint Birgitta, Syon Abbey and Vadstena, Papers from a*

Symposium in Stockholm, 4–6 October 2007 (Stockholm: The Royal Swedish Academy of Letters, History and Antiquities, 2010), pp. 89–103.

M. B. Tait 'The Brigittine Monastery of Syon (Middlesex) with Special Reference to Its Monastic Usages' (D.Phil. thesis, University of Oxford, 1975), pp. 291–94. This thesis provides an invaluable archive of materials for those interested in Syon and its networks of affiliation and influence.

On the examination of the English religious houses, see:

James P. Carley, *The Libraries of King Henry VIII*, CBMLC VII (London: British Library, 2000), pp. xxx–xliii.

For the searches in Italy, see:

Jonathan Woolfson, 'A "remote and ineffectual Don"? Richard Croke in the Biblioteca Marciana', *Bulletin of the Society for Renaissance Studies* 17.2 (2000), 1–11.

On the dispersal of monastic libraries, see:

James P. Carley, *The Libraries of King Henry VIII*, CBMLC VII (London: British Library, 2000).

———, 'The Dispersal of the Monastic Libraries and the Salvaging of the Spoils', in *The Cambridge History of Libraries in Britain and Ireland* I, ed. Elisabeth Leedham-Green and Teresa Webber (Cambridge: Cambridge University Press, 2006), pp. 265–91.

James P. Carley with Caroline Brett (ed. and trans.), John Leland, *De uiris illustribus On Famous Men* (Toronto: Pontifical Institute of Mediaeval Studies; Oxford: Bodleian Library, 2010).

On the aftermath of the dissolution, see:

John Clark (ed.) with introduction by Peter Cunich, Maurice Chauncy, *The various versions of the Historia aliquot martyrum anglorum maxime octodeeim Cartusianorum sub rege Henrico Octavo ob fidei confessionem et summa pontificis jura vindicanda interemptorum by Dom Maurice Chauncy*, Analecta Cartusiana 86 (Salzburg: Institut für Anglistik und Amerikanistik, 2007).

Claire Cross and Noreen Vickers, *Monks, Friars and Nuns in Sixteenth Century Yorkshire* (Leeds: Yorkshire Archaeological Society, 1995).

Ann M. Hutchison, 'Transplanting the Vineyard: Syon Abbey 1539–1861', in Wilhelm Liebhart (ed.), *Der Birgittenorden in der frühen Neuzeit Beiträge der internationalen Tagung vom 27. Februar bis 2. März 1997 Altomünster* (Frankfurt: Lang, 1998), 79–107.

On the Marian restoration, see:

David Loades, *The Reign of Mary Tudor. Politics, Government and Religion in England 1553–58*, 2nd edn (London and New York: Longman, 1991).

John Edwards and Ronald Truman (eds.), *Reforming Catholicism in the England of Mary Tudor: the Achievement of Friar Bartolomé Carranza* (Aldershot: Ashgate, 2005).

William Wizeman, *The Theology and Spirituality of Mary Tudor's Church* (Aldershot: Ashgate, 2006).

Susan Doran and Thomas S. Freeman (eds.), *Mary Tudor, Old and New Perspectives* (Basingstoke: Palgrave Macmillan, 2009).

Eamon Duffy. *Fires of Faith: Catholic England under Mary Tudor* (New Haven: Yale University Press, 2009).

Scholarly opinion is still divided about monastic refoundations under Mary and Cardinal Pole.

In 'The English Church during the reign of Mary' in *Reforming Catholicism in the England of Mary Tudor* (see above), pp. 33–48 (p. 40)) David Loades has suggested that Mary 'seems to have had very little interest in the revival of the monastic *opus Dei*'.

On the other hand, Thomas F. Mayer has maintained that 'Pole had big plans for the restoration of the monasteries' at the beginning of the reign:

Reginald Pole: Prince and Prophet (Cambridge: Cambridge University Press, 2000), p. 283. See also pp. 288–89, on the various refoundations.

For other possible re-establishments, see:

Wizeman, *Theology and Spirituality of Mary Tudor's Church*, pp. 140–41.

For difficulties in regaining ecclesiastical land see:

Ethan Shagan, 'Confronting Compromise: the Schism and Its Legacy in Mid-Tudor England', in Ethan Shagan (ed.), *Catholics and the 'Protestant Nation'. Religious Politics and Identity in Early Modern England* (Manchester: Manchester University Press, 2005), pp. 61–5.

On the provisions in Mary's will for the refoundations see:

David Loades, 'The Personal Religion of Mary I', in Eamon Duffy and David Loades (eds.), *The Church of Mary Tudor* (Aldershot: Ashgate, 2006), pp. 1–29 (p. 24).

Concerning books taken abroad by Catholics in Elizabeth's reign, see:

Christian Coppens, *Reading in Exile* (Cambridge: LP Publications, 1993), p. 3, and the references cited therein.

Chapter 11

1534–1550s: texts

James Simpson

On Syon, early printing of contemplative texts, and the continuing influence of Birgitta of Sweden, see:

Vincent Gillespie, 'Dial M for Mystic: Mystical Texts in the Library of Syon Abbey and the Spirituality of the Syon Brethren', in *MMTE VI*, pp. 241–68.

Ann M. Hutchison, 'Reflections on Aspects of the Spiritual Impact of St Birgitta, the *Revelations* and the Bridgettine Order in Late Medieval England', in *MMTE VII*, pp. 69–82.

C. Annette Grisé, 'Holy Women in Print: Continental Female Mystics and the English Mystical Tradition', in *MMTE VII*, pp. 83–96.

Sue Ellen Holbrook, 'Margery Kempe and Wynkyn de Worde', in *MMTE IV*, pp. 27–46.

For a general discussion of the preservation of the medieval contemplative texts in this environment, see:

Placid Spearritt, 'The Survival of Medieval Spirituality Among the Exiled English Black Monks', in Michael Woodward (ed.), *That Mysterious Man: Essays on Augustine Baker, Analecta Cartusiana*, 119.15 (Abergavenny: Three Peaks Press, 2001), pp. 19–41.

On the dispute between Serenus Cressy and Bishop Edward Stillingfleet, see Nicholas Watson and Jacqueline Jenkins (eds.), The *Writings of Julian of Norwich: A Vision Showed to a Devout Woman and A Revelation of Love*, (University Park, PA: Penn State Press, 2006), pp. 448–55.

For the history of the relation between Scripture and the Church, see:

George H. Tavard, *Holy Writ or Holy Church?* (London: Burns and Oates, 1959). Tavard makes the important point that the doctrine of unwritten verities is a late medieval development; see Tavard, *Holy Writ or Holy Church?*, ch. 3.

On early modern women's reading communities, see:

Jennifer Summit, *Lost Property: The Woman Writer and English Literary History, 1380–1589* (Chicago: University of Chicago Press, 2000).

———, 'Active and Contemplative Lives', in Brian Cummings and James Simpson (eds.), *Cultural Reformations, From Lollardy to the Civil War* (Oxford: Oxford University Press, 2010), pp. 527–53.

David Wallace, 'Nuns', in Cummings and Simpson (eds.), *Cultural Reformations*, pp. 502–23.

———, 'Periodizing Women: Mary Ward (1585–1645) and the Premodern Canon', *Journal of Medieval and Early Modern Studies* 36 (2006).

Heather Wolfe, 'Reading Bells and Loose Papers: Reading and Writing Practices of the English Benedictine Nuns of Cambrai', in Victoria E. Burke and Jonathan Gibson (eds.), *Early Modern Women's Manuscript Writing. Selected Papers from the Trinity/Trent Colloquium* (Aldershot: Ashgate, 2004), pp. 135–56.

On Elizabeth Barton, see the further reading for ch. 9.

Paul Althaus, *The Theology of Martin Luther*, trans. Robert C. Schultz (Philadelphia, PA: Fortress Press, 1966; first published 1962), p. 36.

GLOSSARY OF THEOLOGICAL TERMS

Apophatic theology

A way of thinking and writing about God that works to signal the provisionality of all human attempts to talk about the deity using human language; respecting the Old Testament prohibitions against images, a way of thinking and writing about God that rejects representations and seeks to stress his radical incomprehensibility and ineffability. Sometimes called negative theology, it commonly expresses the view that all that can be said about God is what he is not. Influentially expressed in the writings of Pseudo-Denys the Areopagite, and reflected in works influenced by him, such as *The Cloud of Unknowing*, who comments that all that can be said about God is that he IS, and that he can be 'loved but not thought'. But the need finally to escape from human representations and explanations of God is common to much contemplative writing.

Cataphatic theology

Sometimes called affirmative theology, this branch of writing and representing God believes that there is some merit in using verbal and visual imagery when thinking and writing about God, even if that imagery needs ultimately to be effaced and discarded. Many contemplative and mystical texts use a mixture of cataphatic and apophatic techniques, using affirmative language to bring the contemplative or meditatory into an affective engagement with God before moving to discard its representational ambitions as too limiting for the unspeakable and incomprehensible truth of God.

Catechesis (-etic)

Relating to the Church's teaching of the rudiments of the Christian faith, codified in the thirteenth century as the basic prayers (Our Father, creed and in time the Hail Mary), the ten commandments, and the seven deadly sins. Lay people's knowledge of these basic tenets was to be examined in annual confession, and in England episcopal legislation usually required them to be reinforced by series of sermons or pulpit instructions preached four times a year.

Contemplation/Contemplative

A person or a state dedicated to a still and agenda-free receptiveness to whatever may be revealed in mystical experience. Often a monk, nun or other religious person who has taken vows to dedicate their life to seeking to discern and respond to the presence of God. But later in the Middle Ages, more widely available and practised among lay people as part of a repertoire of devotional postures. In its fullest forms, always likely to assume or require a radical disengagement from the world through solitude, retreat from business and the cares of life, and a single-minded attentiveness holding the mind, body and soul in readiness to behold whatever God may show.

Cura animarum

The 'care of souls', or the exercise of pastoral ministry by priests, usually in a parish context, focusing particularly on preaching, and on the administration of the Sacraments, especially Baptism, Penance, and the Eucharist. Given added impetus in 1215 by the decrees of the Fourth Lateran Council, which required all men and women to confess to their parish priests at least once a year. This stimulated an upsurge in pastoral theology, and an increasing concern for the training of men exercising parish ministry.

Discretio spirituum

From the early years of monastic theology, the 'discretion of spirits' or 'discretion of stirrings' was always an important part of the process by which contemplatives and their spiritual advisors learned how to discern the difference between true ('divine') and false ('diabolic') revelations, visions, voices, and other mystical 'experiences'. Later in the Middle Ages, this technique of discernment was further refined and codified, especially in relation to the increasing number of women claiming visionary experiences, and as a diagnostic tool for priests, with the pastoral responsibility for the care of souls, likely to encounter laymen and women in need of guidance. In her *Book*, for example, Margery Kempe obsessively tells 'the manner of her living' to priests she encounters, seeking their discernment and spiritual approval.

Eschatology

The study and the doctrine of the 'last things', that is the fate of the individual soul and of the whole of creation at the Last Judgement. In the Middle Ages, the Four Last Things (death, judgement, heaven, and hell) were often considered together.

Heterodoxy

Opinions, teachings, or doctrines at odds with the orthodox or officially sanctioned teachings of the church.

Immanence (-tist)

The omnipresence of God in the created universe, sometimes shading into a sort of pantheism. But in Christian thought always linked to a notion of Divine **transcendence** (i.e. that God exists entirely independently of the created Universe).

Ineffability

The ineffability of God is based on his transcendence above and beyond the created universe, and the impossibility of human understanding and human language (damaged and imperfect as a result of the Fall from Paradise) ever being able to comprehend or express his being or nature. Often linked to and articulated in **apophatic theology**.

Kenosis

A Greek term, derived from the so-called 'kenotic kymn' included by Paul in his Epistle to the Philippians, 2:7, and referring to Christ 'emptying himself' to become a humble and obedient man in the incarnation. Often therefore used in mystical and contemplative theology to talk about the reciprocal obedience, radical humility, and self-emptying of the concerns of the world necessary for the contemplative to focus their will and affections on the love of God, in the hope of becoming ready to receive and to 'behold' (as Julian of Norwich puts it) what God chooses to reveal of himself.

Magisterium

The teaching authority of the Church, and its ability to determine, define, and defend dogmas and core teachings. In Catholic tradition, divine revelation is not confined to the Scriptures: an important part of the Church's understanding of revelation is its accumulated tradition of teaching and authoritative and authentic interpretation of the Scriptures. The twin pillars of Scripture and Tradition support the teaching authority of the Church, which draws on its evolving understanding of revelation (usually seen as residing in the writings of the Fathers of the Church (or patristic texts), to articulate its teachings). This led to the view that there was no salvation outside of the Church, and to the energetic pursuit of heresy and heterodox thought.

Monophysite

A complex view found in some parts of the early Christian church which held that the incarnate Christ had only one nature, in contrast to the eventually orthodox view that in his earthly life Christ retained his Divine nature as well as taking on Human nature, the two remaining distinct. Some monophysites espoused a view that Christ's two natures blended into one.

Mystical

In medieval Latin, mystical strictly means 'hidden', and is usually applied to the ineffable and incomprehensible unattainability of God, as in negative or apophatic theology. As a description of alleged experiences of the transcendental other, it has little currency in medieval writing. In this book it is generally used to describe accounts of experiences and their attempted transcription into language, but generally contemplative is our preferred term.

Omnis utruisque sexus

The famous Canon 21 of the decrees of the Fourth Lateran Council of 1215, which commands every Christian who has reached the years of discretion to confess all his, or her, sins at least once a year to his, or her, own (i.e. parish) priest. This canon did no more than confirm earlier legislation and custom, but it served to stimulate the growth of pastoral theology, and the increase of vernacular catechetic handbooks and guides to assist priests in their pastoral responsibility. Such guides passed in time into lay hands and became the foundation of handbooks of spiritual self-guidance.

Otium

A state of calm disengagement, and freedom from the troubles of the world, considered conducive to the cultivation of a contemplative frame of mind.

Pastoralia

Materials to assist parish priests and eventually lay people in the exercise of their sacramental duties. These can range from catechetic handbooks, through pro-forma or model sermons, to embrace more ambitious and sophisticated spiritual handbooks and guides to godliness.

Patristic

Relating to the Fathers of the Church, those early teachers who formulated and codified the Church's doctrines, and who developed the rich exegetical resources that informed later theology. The four major doctors of the Latin church were Augustine, Gregory, Jerome, and Ambrose.

Pelagian (-ism)

The view, espoused by Pelagius, an ascetic British theologian of the late fourth and early fifth centuries, that man could begin the search for his own salvation by his own efforts. More conventional theology held that God's grace was always necessary for man, even for him to realize that such efforts to search for salvation were necessary. When Will asks in Piers Plowman 'How may I save my Soul?', the strictly orthodox answer is that he cannot without the grace of God. But the issue spasmodically resurfaced throughout the Middle Ages, and exploded into significance at the reformation with the competing doctrines of justification. In contemplative texts, the issue hovers round the notions of contemplative stillness and **otium**.

Phenomenology

'The science of phenomena': that is, a philosophical attempt to discover and analyse essential meanings, distinct from metaphysical (and theological) issues. Associated with German philosophers of the enlightenment, such as Kant, Hegel, and Husserl, and often revealing an underlying interest in

Platonic realism, from which its procedures and assumptions have gradually fed back into theological thinking and writing.

Probatio

The process of 'probatio spirituum', or the proving or testing of spirits, is linked to the techniques of *discretio*, and involved the discernment of apparent revelations and their recipients to see if they were of divine, diabolical or digestive origin.

Purgative, unitive, and illuminative ways

In scholastic and some monastic theology, three interlinked stages of contemplative development, culminating in a contemplative union with the Godhead (usually not considered achievable in this life). In vernacular contemplative writings, this terminology is less often used, though triadic structures to the contemplative life are quite common (as in Richard Rolle). This particular model achieves much more popularity and visibility in the sixteenth century, when the Spanish mystics try to codify the stages of contemplative experience. From them it has often been read back into and onto medieval texts, though often with little unity or illumination.

Syncretism

The attempt to combine and synthesize different philosophical or theological systems or doctrines. In mystical theology and philosophy, this has focused particularly on whether there is a common core to the various kinds of contemplative and mystical experiences reported from different cultures and different world religions, and whether, once language and thought systems are left behind in contemplation, it is the same essence or divine being that is being perceived or experienced.

Tridentine

Related to the reforming Council of Trent (1545–63), an ecumenical council of the Catholic church, called to address the crisis in Christianity caused by various reformation upheavals. The disciplined and fiercely enforced decrees of the Council enshrined the main features of the Catholic Counter-Reformation response to Protestantism with such vigour that they remained defining features of Catholicism until the second Vatican Council of the early

1960s. In some ways this Council marks an apotheosis of medieval Catholicism. In others, it marks the end of it, and a move to a more centralized and codified body of doctrine and ecclesiastical discipline.

Unio mystica

'Mystical union' is the end of contemplation: the union of the soul with God, where the soul is united ('oned' as Julian of Norwich says) with God, by process of refinement and purification linked to a lessening of self-awareness (Julian calls this 'noughting': if God is one, and we are to be oned with God, then mathematically that can only happen if we are noughted). Though mystical experiences are sometimes reported as giving a taste of this mysterious and inexpressible communion, the main strands of Christian thought believe that true union is only possible after death, following the idea that it is impossible to see the face of God and live.

INDEX

Cambridge Companions to...

AUTHORS